DREAM ROUTES OF
AUSTRALIA NEW ZEALAND
AND THE PACIFIC

Scenic drives to the most spectacular places

DREAM ROUTES OF AUSTRALIA NEW ZEALAND AND THE PACIFIC

Scenic drives to the most spectacular places

Page 2–3: North of the Western Australian city of Perth lies Nambung National Park with its bizarre limestone pillars, the Pinnacles. These were formed by sand accumulating and hardening on the remains of vegetation, followed by erosion.
Page 4–5: The 'X-ray' style is characteristic of many of the Aboriginal rock paintings in Kakadu National Park in the far north of Australia. The paintings depict the visible silhouette of the body as well as the skeletal frame and internal organs.
Page 6–7: The Great Barrier Reef stretches for more than 2,600 km (1,616 miles) along the east coast of Australia between 10 and 23 degrees latitude. Over millions of years, billions of corals have formed the world's largest system of coral reefs, often lying just a few metres below the surface of the water.
Page 8–9: The almost perfectly conical Mount Taranaki is situated on New Zealand's North Island and rises to a height of 2,518 m (8,261 ft).
Page 10–11: Okarito Lagoon to the north of the Franz Josef Glacier is the largest natural wetland in New Zealand, comprising some 3,000 ha (7,413 acres) of coastal waters and tidal pools.
Page 12–13: A tropical paradise on the palm beach of Octopus Bay on Waya in the Yasawa islands, one of the most beautiful groups in the Fiji Islands. Waya is situated to the north of the main island, Viti Levu.
Page 14–15 top: The Great Ocean Road to the west of Melbourne is one of the most spectacular coastal roads in the world. The steep coastline offers fantastic views of the 'Twelve Apostles' rock formations, rising up to 65 m (231 ft) out of the sea.
Page 14–15 bottom: The Opera House and Harbour Bridge are the icons of Sydney, Australia's largest and liveliest city.

The island of Bora-Bora in French Polynesia is the ultimate South Sea paradise. Beyond the turquoise waters of the famous lagoon towers Otemanu, the highest mountain on the island, in its usual veil of cloud.

CONTENTS

Route overview

Route 1

From Darwin through the wild north-west to Albany

Route 2

On the Stuart Highway through the 'Red Centre'

Route 3

Bruce Highway – from the Sunshine Coast to the Great Barrier Reef

Route 4

The Pacific Highway – from the Blue Mountains to the Gold Coast

Route 5

Crossing the continent: from west to east along the south

Route 6

New Zealand North Island: trademark volcanoes

Route 7

New Zealand South Island: glaciers, fiords and rainforests

Route 8

Fiji, Tonga and Samoa: island hopping in Western Polynesia

Route 9

From the Marquesas to the Cook Islands

Route 10

Hawaii: dream beaches, tropical flowers and volcanoes – from Big Island to Kauai

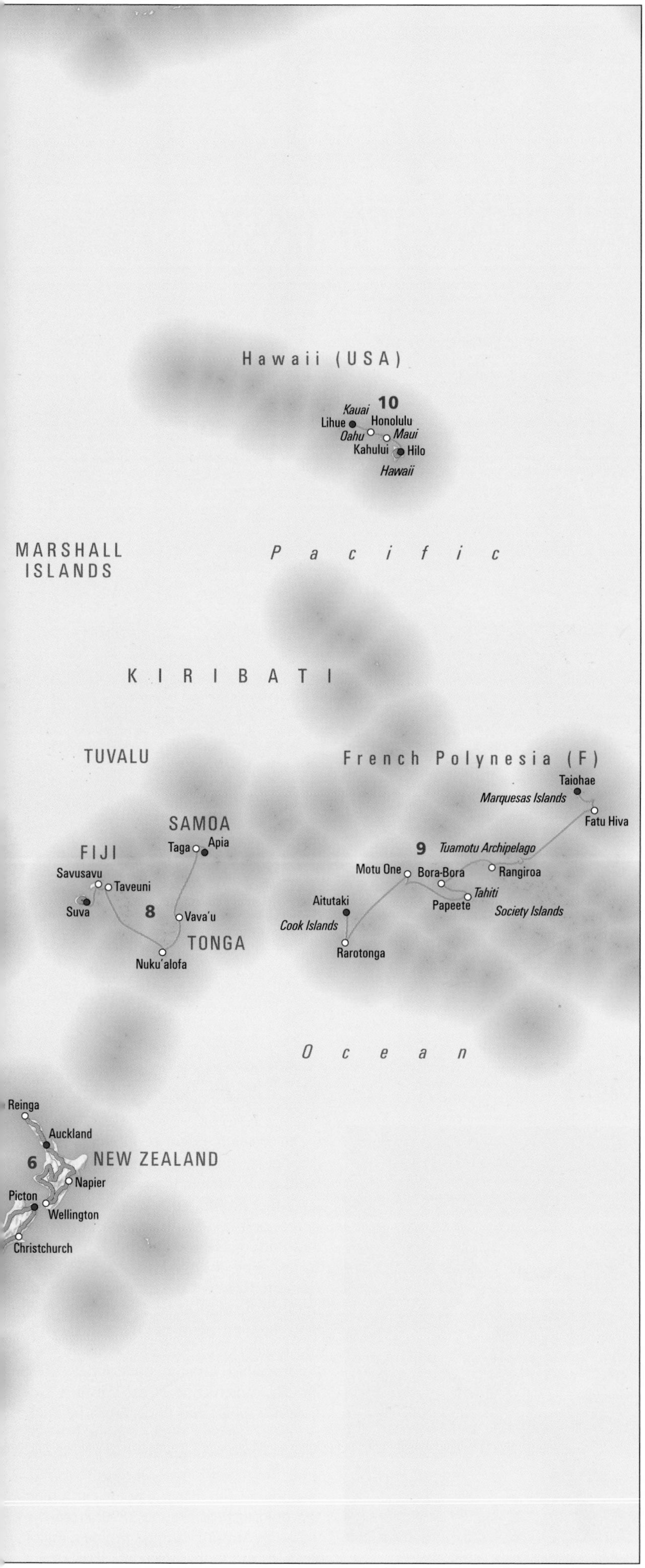

Introduction

Ten carefully researched tours cover the most fascinating destinations in Australia, New Zealand and Oceania, from magnificent natural landscapes, with both historical and cultural significance, to unique cultural monuments, from lively cities to remote, peaceful places. Our routes take in the coast of Western Australia, the legendary Stuart Highway through the heart of the Fifth Continent, Bruce Highway on the Sunshine Coast and the Pacific Highway on the Gold Coast, with round-trips through the beautiful scenery of New Zealand's North and South Islands and cruises through the Polynesian islands.

Route descriptions

An introductory text to each chapter outlines the journey's route and introduces the different countries and regions together with their significant natural, historical and cultural features. Places of interest and sights along the route are then described, illustrated with brilliant colour photographs and accompanied by details of the itinerary and travel directions. Each place described is given a number, which serves to locate it in the maps at the end of the relevant chapter. Each route has a Travel Information section, giving helpful information on the duration and length of the tour, national highway regulations, weather, the best time for travelling and some useful addresses. Side panels provide interesting information on culture and natural history, while coloured boxes at the margins suggest worthwhile detours (trips and excursions) along the way.

City street maps and maps of National Parks

Cities and National Parks along a given route are highlighted in special features, including a detailed map and comprehensive list of their attractions.

Tour maps

Specially drawn tour maps at the end of each chapter show the travel route and indicate major places and sights. The main route is always clearly marked and supplemented with a variety of suggestions for interesting trips along the way. The location and type of key sights en route are indicated by symbols, while colour photographs and captions around the edge of the map highlight outstanding places of interest. The key to the symbols is provided in the map section on page 213.

Atlas

The map section with its detailed alphabetical index is intended as an additional guide. Apart from geographical details, the maps also include the most important traffic routes and a wealth of tourist information.

Route 1

Australia

From Darwin through the wild north-west to Albany

The trip from Australia's Top End (as the second northernmost point is known) to its south-western tip gives an indication of the proportions and vastness of this country. The route passes through several climate and vegetation zones, from monsoon to a temperate Mediterranean climate. Travelling the route demands adaptability and a touch of pioneering spirit.

Most of this route, which covers a rough distance of 5,000 km (3,107 miles), passes through a single state – Western Australia. This alone is an indication of the sheer dimensions of WA, as the locals call it. Covering an area of 2.5 million km² (0.97 million square miles), this state represents one-third of Australia's total land mass. Yet this massive region is home to fewer than two million people, almost three-quarters of whom live in and around Perth. In other words, Western Australia is for the most part uninhabited pioneer country. Often the scattered settlements are made up of little more than a petrol station, bank, supermarket and a few houses. For Europeans, the distances involved in travelling to the next inhabited place can take some getting used to. A journey of several hundred kilometres or miles counts as a short trip – 'just down the track', as they say here.

Like the rest of Australia, Western Australia was inhabited by Aborigines long before Europeans arrived. All along our route you will find traces of their 30,000- to 40,000-year presence in the form of Aboriginal rock art. Several Aboriginal lands are located in the north but tourists are either prohibited from entering them or may only do so with a special entry permit. Portuguese and Dutch sailors began to arrive on the west coast of Australia from the 16th century, although it was not until the English arrived that 'New Holland' became permanently settled, with the founding in 1829 of the Swan River Colony, which became modern-day Perth. Initially, construction of the Western Australian colonies was undertaken by independent settlers; later thousands of convicts were enlisted for the job. Thereafter the region's mineral resources were responsible for many a boom, including the gold-rush of around 1890. From the mid-20th century mining became a major industry and today large quantities of ore

The unusual frilled-neck lizard.

Tropical storm clouds hang threateningly over Coconut Wells at the northern end of Cable Beach.

Koalas are native to south-eastern Australia and were once widespread in Western Australia too, but died out in this region in the Pleistocene era. If you want to see a koala in Western Australia today, you will have to visit one of the zoos or parks, such as Cohunu Koala Park in Perth. The leaves of the eucalyptus tree are koalas' favourite food.

(iron, nickel, tin), uranium, bauxite, gold, diamonds, crude oil and natural gas are extracted in Western Australia. Perth above all has profited from this development, becoming the only real metropolis in Western Australia and home to many international concerns.

The starting point for our tour is in the Northern Territory, in the capital Darwin. Just before Kununurra you cross the border into Western Australia and travel along the Kimberley Plateau. This savannah landscape of rocky plateaux and gorges is one of the most unexplored regions in Australia. In summer it is dominated by a tropical monsoon climate, with high humidity and a long rainy season. The adjoining Great Sandy Desert to the south meanwhile records the highest temperatures in Australia and in some parts suffers periods of drought lasting several years. In the northern Pilbara Region you leave the sandy coastal landscape for a trip inland to the Hamersley Range, a wild rock massif rising to 1,235 m (4,052 ft) with gorges and lakes, where mineral resources are often mined. The climate here is semi-arid, interspersed with tropical patches along the course of rivers. Further to the south in the direction of Perth, the climate becomes increasingly dry-Mediterranean, and your journey ends in the extreme south-west, a relatively densely populated region with mild, damp weather conditions.

In spite of the progress of civilization and tourism, a journey through WA still gives a hint of freedom and adventure. Here you can enjoy solitude and a sense of space and meet some interesting characters along the way. And where else can you experience such natural diversity?

Aborigine children near Derby decorated with white paint for the corroboree ceremony.

Salties and Freshies

The tropical north of Australia is home to the continent's only two species of crocodile. The saltwater crocodile (*Crocodylus porosus*), which is distinguished by two bumpy ridges on top of its long snout, is not only the largest living reptile but also shares a reputation with Africa's native Nile crocodile as the most aggressive and most feared crocodilian in the world. During the rainy season crocodiles venture far inland, so caution is necessary not only in coastal waters but also on rivers and at waterholes.

Until the 1980s these prehistoric reptiles were hunted rigorously; since then they have become a protected species and their numbers have increased substantially. They generally grow to a length of 5 m (16½ ft),

In water or on land, the saltwater crocodile will snap at anything that crosses its path.

occasionally 7 m (23 ft), and are real experts at starvation dieting: living off their own body fat, they can slow their metabolism down so much that their hearts beat just three times a minute. In this way the reptiles, known in Australia as 'salties', can survive for months without food but still remain strong enough to launch explosive attacks.

The freshwater crocodile (*Crocodylus johnstoni*), also called 'freshie' in Australia, is shorter than its close relative – it only grows to a length of up to 3 m (10 ft) – and has a long pointed snout. These reptiles are thought to be very timid, however, and attacks on humans are very rare.

Our route follows Highway 1, which from Broome runs close to the coast. The different sections of the highway go by the names of Stuart Highway, Victoria Highway, Great Northern Highway, North West Coastal Highway, Brand Highway and South Western Highway, in that order.

1 Darwin The capital of the Northern Territory, with its tropical climate, is closer to Indonesia than to Melbourne or Sydney – no wonder, then, that there is more than just a hint of Asia about the place. Here the old Australian pioneering spirit still dominates and has been responsible for the port on the Timor Sea getting back on its feet several times, for example in the wake of the devastating Cyclone Tracy, which almost wiped out the city in 1974. Today the city's flat-roofed bungalows spread over a wide area. Darwin is a good starting point for excursions to several of the National Parks. This is also where the Stuart Highway begins, connecting the north and south of Australia.

2 Litchfield National Park The park, which covers an area of 1,650 km² (637 square miles) lies 120 km (75 miles) to the south of Darwin and primarily consists of bush land, with some patches of tropical rainforest. The park also contains red termite mounds, some reaching a height of up to 2 m (6½ ft). The four waterfalls plunging from the sandstone plateau are particularly impressive, with the highest, Wangi Falls in the west, ending in a large waterhole. As there are no crocodiles anywhere in the park, it is safe to swim here. 'The Lost City' – bizarrely shaped sandstone pillars resembling a cityscape – is also worth a visit.

3 Katherine After Darwin, the second most important town in the Top End is Katherine, the traffic hub and support centre for many remote localities and cattle stations (farms on which only cattle are bred) in the region. With its hotels and campsites, Katherine is an ideal base for tours to nearby Nitmiluk National Park and Katherine Gorge or excursions into the outback. Attractive bathing spots like Edith Falls and the only

Travel information

Route profile
Length: approx. 5,000 km/ 3,107 miles (excluding detours)
Time needed: 6 weeks
Start: Darwin
End: Albany
Itinerary (main locations): Darwin, Katherine, Kununurra, Halls Creek, Broome, Port Hedland, Karratha, Tom Price, Exmouth, Carnarvon, Monkey Mia, Geraldton, Perth, Bunbury, Margaret River, Albany

Traffic information
Cars drive on the left in Australia. The maximum speed limit in built-up areas is 50 km/h (31 mph) and outside built-up areas is 100 km/h (62 mph). Many sights (National Parks, Kimberley) are off the beaten track and can only be reached in an off-road vehicle. This also applies to the Gibb River Road. During the rainy season (November to March) these stretches of road are often completely impassable.

Information
www.australia.com
Nitmiluk National Park:
www.nt.gov.au/nretalparks/find/nitmiluk.html
Western Australia:
Western Australian Visitor Centre, GPO Box W2081
Perth WA 6846
Tel: (0061) 894 83 11 11
www.westernaustralia.com

Weather information
www.bom.gov.au

accessible caves in the Northern Territory, the Cutta Cutta Caves, can also be reached from here. The Victoria Highway leading to Western Australia begins in Katherine.

❹ **Nitmiluk National Park** See page 24.

❺ **Gregory National Park** The park lies 285 km (177 miles) to the west of Katherine near Timber Creek and contains rock plateaux, gorges, savannah, the Victoria River and a large ford, used by early settlers to cross the river. The landscape is distinguished by part-tropical part semi-arid vegetation. The park is relatively undeveloped, and you will need a four-wheel drive to get around it. Popular routes for walkers are Joes Creek Walk featuring Aboriginal rock art and the Escarpment Walk for some spectacular views over gorges and cliffs.

❻ **Kununurra** This town, the first Western Australian stop on our tour, serves as the principal supply base for the region. It is also a starting point for tours to Lake Argyle and to Hidden Valley National Park, where visitors will find sandstone cliffs, Aboriginal rock art, eucalypt forests and a rich animal kingdom. Situated 70 km (43½ miles) to the south of Kununurra, Lake Argyle is the largest artificial water reservoir in Australia and is also used to irrigate the surrounding countryside. This is the place for anglers and water sports enthusiasts. Just behind Kununurra, the Great Northern Highway heads off to the south. A good 250 km (155 miles) down the road, you come to the turn-off to Purnululu National Park and the famous Bungle Bungles.

❼ **Purnululu National Park** See page 28.

❽ **Halls Creek** The next stop on the tour is Halls Creek, a *(continued p.30)*

1 This collection of termite hills near Darwin looks almost like a field full of tombstones.

2 Darwin on the Timor Sea is a popular sailing port. Here, yachts are moored at Cullen Bay Marina.

3 The strange shapes of the orange-and-black striped sandstone domes of the Bungle Bungle Range.

4 Tolmer Falls pour into a gorge from the Tabletop Range in Litchfield National Park.

Detour

Kakadu National Park

Kakadu National Park and its main town Jabiru are situated some 200 km (124 miles) to the east of Darwin and can be reached on the Arnhem Highway. Covering just under 20,000 km² (7,722 square miles) of land, the park, which is run jointly by the government and Aborigines, is Australia's largest nature reserve (one in which, regrettably, uranium has also been mined). In terms of its landforms, fauna and flora, this park is packed with superlatives.

The section of coast on Van Diemen Gulf is a tidal zone characterized by mangrove swamps. Further inland the contours of lakes and rivers are overrun during the monsoon to form a wide expanse of flood plain where sedge, aquatic flowers and marshlands flourish. In the eastern region of the park stretches the Arnhem Escarpment, a massively weather-beaten rock plateau with cliffs rising to 300 m (984 ft). Here and in the outliers (sections of rock that have become separated from the plateau by erosion) are thousands of Aboriginal rock paintings, such as those at Nourlangie.

Thanks to the tropical monsoon climate the park is home to many mammals, birds, reptiles, amphibians, fish and insects. Boat trips, bush walks or guided walks – to the Yellow Water Wetlands near Cooinda or on the East Alligator River – are the perfect way to see crocodiles, monitors and other lizards, cormorants and cranes.

Top: Waterlilies at Yellow Water. Bottom: Flood plains with eucalyptus trees.

Nitmiluk National Park

The main attraction of this National Park, located some 30 km (18½ miles) to the north-east of Katherine, is the series of gorges on the Katherine River, generally known as Katherine Gorge.

Over millions of years the Katherine River has carved its way deep into the Arnhem Plateau along a stretch of 12 km (7½ miles), creating thirteen gorges up to 100 m (328 ft) deep, some of which can be viewed by boat or canoe. During the rainy season the Katherine River turns into a raging torrent, which means that it is only accessible during the dry period (April to October). At this time the river is little more than a series of unconnected pools of water, and canoes have to be carried on foot over the dried-out rapids between the pools. If you are prepared to make this rather strenuous effort, you can explore a total of nine gorges and enjoy the wild beauty of the red rock face; the tourist boats stick to the first four gorges.

Viewing the 1,800 km² (695 square miles) of parkland from the water alone would mean missing a great deal, particularly the rich flora and fauna. The park is a real paradise for birds, boasting more than 160 species, including egrets, darters, grass finches and lorikeets. Freshwater crocodiles, monitor lizards and kangaroos are also found here. In more humid areas the park's vegetation consists primarily of paperbarks, screw trees and freshwater mangroves; on the drier Arnhem Plateau spinifex grass, sand palms and Woollybutt eucalyptus prevail. All this can best be observed on tracks such as the Lookout Walk, Biddlecombe Cascades Walk or Butterfly Gorge Walk, all of which set off from the park's visitor centre. There is also a campsite here and a group of several smaller waterfalls at Edith Falls that can be reached by a separate road from the Stuart Highway to the north of Katherine.

Keeping a watchful eye: the argus monitor.

in such a desert-like environment is thanks to the monsoon rainy season, which supplies the area with plenty of precipitation between the months of November and March. The orange bands around the domes are caused by iron and manganese staining.

Purnululu National Park

One of the most fascinating landscapes in Australia can be found in the east of Kimberley: the rock towers of the Bungle Bungle Range in Purnululu National Park.

Although the Range was first sighted by European Australians as early as 1879, it was not until 1982 that this unique rock massif was properly explored and became widely known. Rock paintings show that the area was used as a ceremonial site by Aborigine peoples from time immemorial. A mountain range of oddly shaped rock domes and cupolas extends over an area of 450 km² (174 square miles), rising up to 200–300 m (656–984 ft) above sea level. The weathered, beehive-like sandstone mounds with distinctive orange-and-black banding are characteristic features of the Bungle Bungles. The magnificence of this landscape is best viewed from the air – sightseeing flights are highly recommended and can be arranged in the park itself or from Kununurra.

Access to the park by road is on the pitched and pot-holed Spring Creek Track, which branches off the Great Northern Highway. En route to the Bungle Bungles you cross a savannah landscape of spinifex and spear grass enclosing the rocky mountain range and accounting for the larger part of the 2,100 km² (811 square miles) of National Park. The vegetation of the seemingly unviable Bungle Bungles (where temperatures reach up to 40°C/104°F) is amazingly diverse, thanks to the lengthy rainy season: eucalyptus trees, figs, palms, acacias and passionflowers thrive here. Even kangaroos, reptiles, fish and around 150 different types of birds manage to survive in this arid environment.

The conical beehive-shaped mounds of the Bungle Bungle Range.

The park is open only from April to December due to difficulty of access during the rainy season. There are few facilities in the park and there is no accommodation: campsites on the western edge of the Bungle Bungles are the only place for an overnight stay and are also the starting point for walks, such as to Echidna Chasm or Cathedral Gorge.

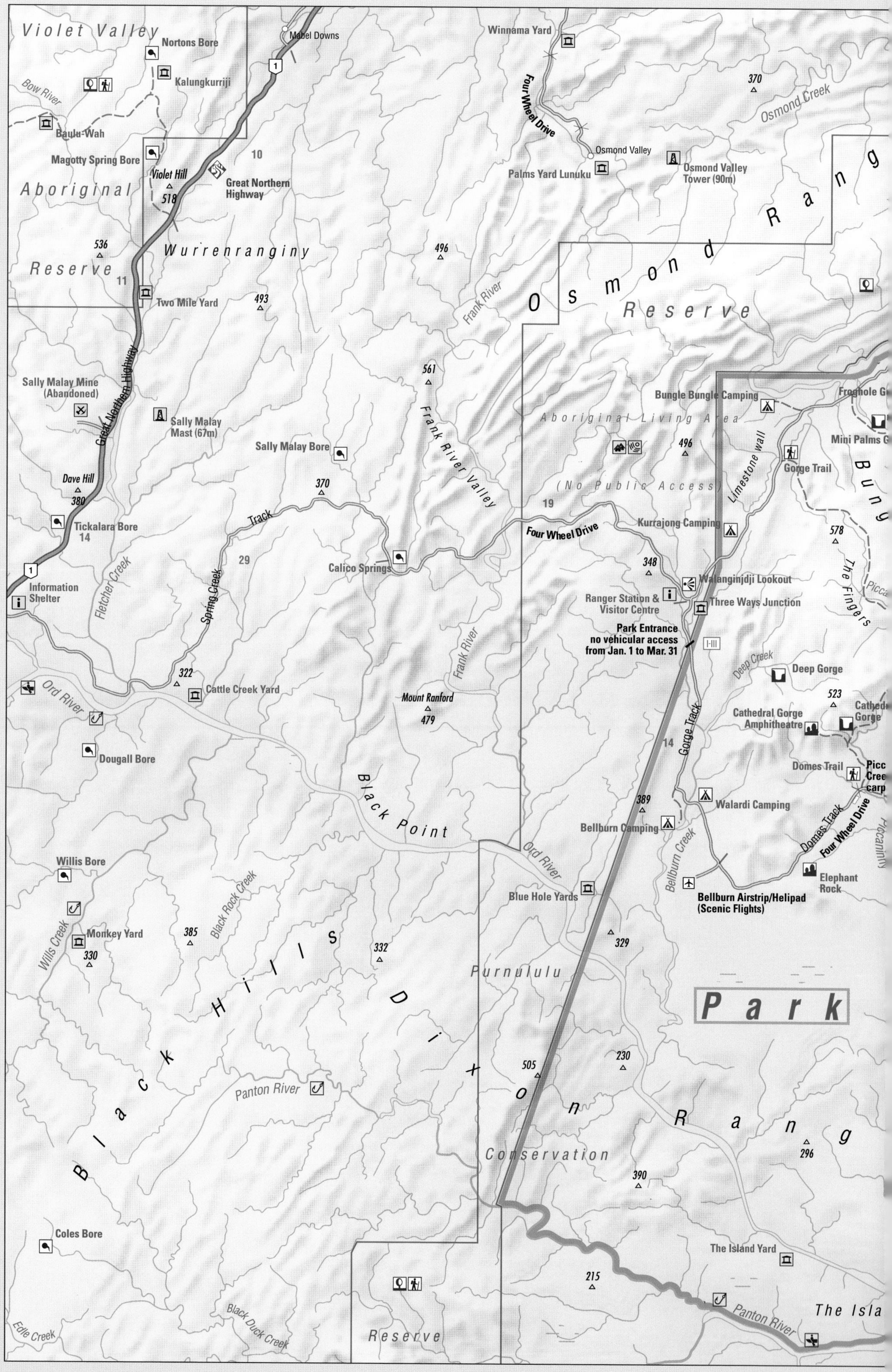

Violet Valley Aboriginal Reserve
Nortons Bore
Mabel Downs
Kalungkurriji
Bow River
Baulu-Wah
Magotty Spring Bore
Violet Hill 518
Great Northern Highway
Wurrenranginy
Two Mile Yard
Sally Malay Mine (Abandoned)
Sally Malay Mast (67m)
Sally Malay Bore
Dave Hill 380
Tickalara Bore
Information Shelter
Fletcher Creek
Spring Creek Track
Calico Springs
Cattle Creek Yard
Ord River
Dougall Bore
Mount Ranford 479
Black Point
Willis Bore
Wills Creek
Monkey Yard
Black Rock Creek
Black Hills
Panton River
Coles Bore
Edle Creek
Black Duck Creek
Reserve
Winnama Yard
Four Wheel Drive
Osmond Valley
Palms Yard Lunuku
Osmond Valley Tower (90m)
Osmond Creek
Osmond Range
Osmond Reserve
Frank River
Frank River Valley
Aboriginal Living Area
(No Public Access)
Bungle Bungle Camping
Froghole Gorge
Mini Palms Gorge
Limestone wall
Gorge Trail
Bungle Bungle
The Fingers
Kurrajong Camping
Walanginjdji Lookout
Ranger Station & Visitor Centre
Three Ways Junction
Park Entrance no vehicular access from Jan. 1 to Mar. 31
Deep Creek
Deep Gorge
Cathedral Gorge Amphitheatre
Cathedral Gorge
Gorge Track
Domes Trail
Piccaninny Creek carpark
Walardi Camping
Bellburn Camping
Bellburn Creek
Domes Track
Elephant Rock
Bellburn Airstrip/Helipad (Scenic Flights)
Blue Hole Yards
Purnululu Park
Dixon Range
Conservation
The Island Yard
The Island

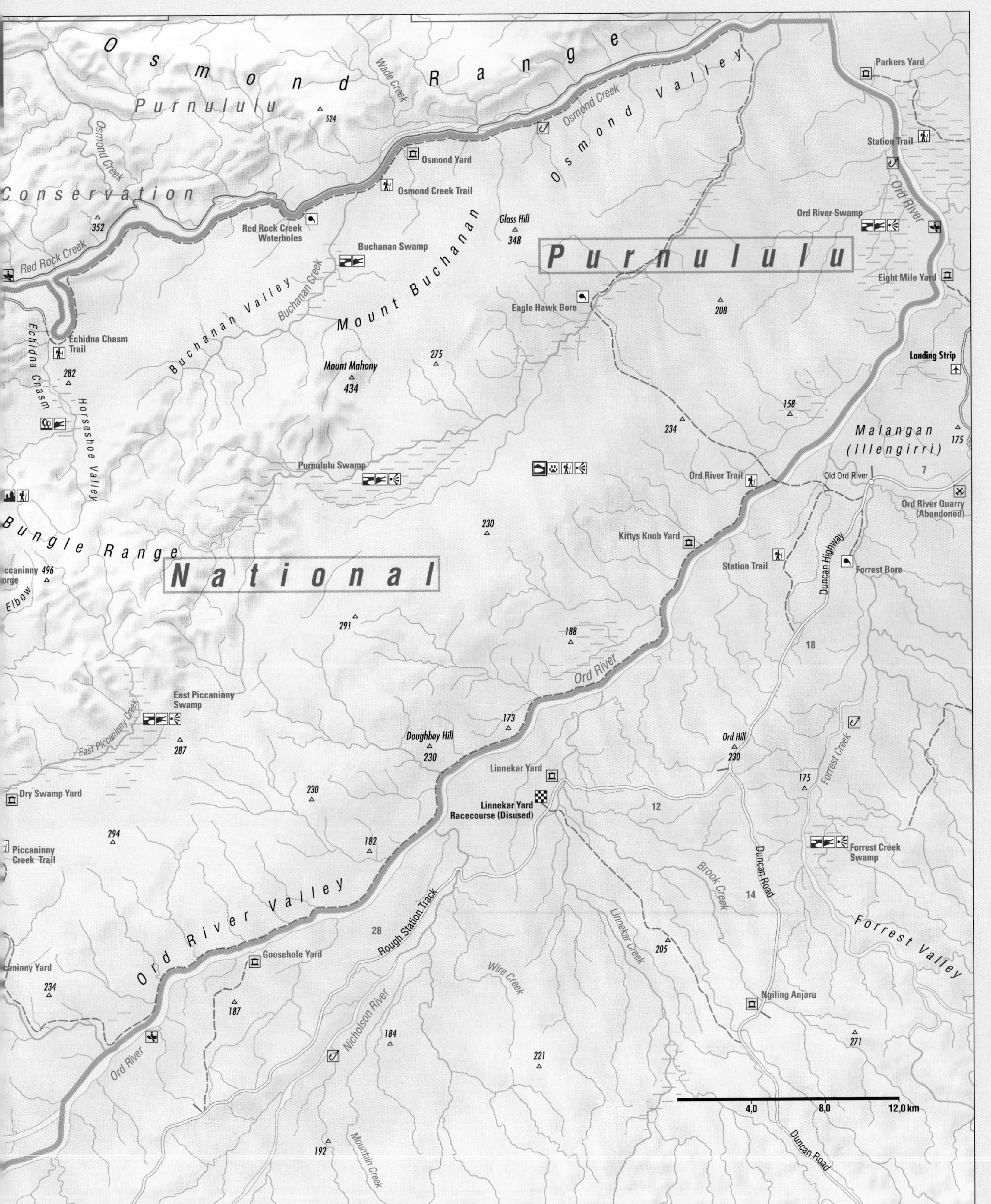
Osmond Range
Purnululu
Conservation
Purnululu
National
Osmond Valley
Osmond Creek
Wade Creek
Osmond Yard
Osmond Creek Trail
Red Rock Creek
Red Rock Creek Waterholes
Buchanan Swamp
Buchanan Valley
Buchanan Creek
Mount Buchanan
Glass Hill
348
524
352
Eagle Hawk Bore
Echidna Chasm Trail
Echidna Chasm
Horseshoe Valley
282
Mount Mahony
434
275
208
158
234
Purnululu Swamp
Bungle Range
Parkers Yard
Station Trail
Ord River
Ord River Swamp
Eight Mile Yard
Landing Strip
Malangan (Illengirri)
175
7
Old Ord River
Ord River Trail
Ord River Quarry (Abandoned)
230
Kittys Knob Yard
Station Trail
Duncan Highway
Forrest Bore
496
Elbow
291
188
18
East Piccaninny Swamp
East Piccaninny Creek
287
Doughboy Hill
230
173
Ord Hill
230
Linnekar Yard
Linnekar Yard Racecourse (Disused)
Dry Swamp Yard
230
12
175
Forrest Creek
294
Piccaninny Creek Trail
182
Forrest Creek Swamp
Duncan Road
Brook Creek
14
Ord River Valley
28
Rough Station Track
Linnekar Creek
Forrest Valley
Goosehole Yard
205
Wire Creek
234
187
Nicholson River
Ngiling Anjaru
184
271
221
4,0
8,0
12,0 km
192
Mountain Creek
Duncan Road

Detour

Wolfe Creek Meteorite Crater National Park

Some 300,000 years ago, a meteorite made of iron and nickel, measuring 10 m (33 ft) across and weighing about 50,000 tonnes, hit the earth on the north-eastern edge of the Great Sandy Desert at a speed of 15 km (9 miles) per second. The impact released energy equivalent to that of dozens of hydrogen bombs. The immense heat caused the meteorite to melt and vaporize, and the resultant explosion sent debris flying in every direction.
Evidence of meteor impact remains in the form of rusty balls of rock weighing up to 250 kg (551 lbs), containing the rare minerals reevesite, cassidyite and pecoraite in addition to other compounds such as iron-nickel and iron-phosphide. The impact crater itself measures just under 900 m (2,953 ft) in diameter, making Wolfe Creek

Wolfe Creek Meteorite Crater, at the edge of the Great Sandy Desert.

Meteorite Crater the second largest of its kind in the world. The rim of the crater rises 30 m (98½ ft) out of the surrounding countryside and it was originally 120 m (394 ft) deep; today it has filled up with sand and gypsum, and the height from the floor of the crater to the rim measures just 60 m (197 ft).
Wolfe Creek Meteorite Crater in the park of the same name is considered to be the most striking of the fifteen meteor craters in Australia. Access is easy from the Great Northern Highway around 100 km (62 miles) away, and helicopter trips are available from Halls Creek. An information point at the site of the crater gives relevant astronomical and geological information.

typically Australian outback town, comprising a petrol station, supermarket, shops and banks. To the south of the town heading towards the Great Sandy Desert is Old Halls Creek, where you can see some remnants of the 1885 gold-rush. Close by is the 'China Wall', which at first glance resembles a man-made wall but is actually a natural quartz rock formation. The various pools and springs here are also ideal for bathing: Palm Springs, Caroline Pool and Sawpit Gorge Pool. From Halls Creek you can take a detour to the south to visit Wolfe Creek Meteorite Crater National Park (see Detour, left).

9 Geikie Gorge National Park Heading onwards in the direction of Derby you arrive at Fitzroy Crossing, from where it is easy to reach Geikie Gorge National Park. Geikie Gorge, one of the most spectacular gorges in north-west Australia, is geologically very significant. Over time, the Fitzroy River has carved a channel in the sandstone. The rock face is a remnant of a coral reef, and the river provides a habitat not only to freshwater crocodiles but also to sawfish and stingrays, survivors from a primeval ocean that have become accustomed to fresh water. Over the years, various fossil strata and limestone formations have been exposed. A large portion of the gorge is a designated nature reserve, with just a narrow strip on the western bank open to visitors.

10 Windjana Gorge National Park Around 40 km (25 miles) after Fitzroy Crossing take a right turn to Windjana Gorge National Park. The park contains a 3.5-km (2-mile) gorge, which has been carved into the limestone rocks by the Lennard River. The steep limestone cliffs are a real treasure trove for fossil collectors. Caves such as Pigeons Cave and some impressive Aboriginal rock art were also discovered here. Windjana Gorge can be explored either in a canoe or on foot below the massive rock face. Freshwater crocodiles can be spotted lazing on the sandy banks and in the shallow water.
Gibb River Road takes you to Derby and from there back to the Great Northern Highway.

11 Broome This town on the Indian Ocean is 1,942 km (1,207 miles) from Darwin and 2,361 km (1,467 miles) from Perth, and was once the most famous pearling port in the world, accounting for a large proportion of the worldwide demand for mother-of-pearl. These riches attracted many Japanese and Chinese pearl divers and merchants, as the Japanese Cemetery and the exhibition in the Broome Historical Museum testify. Ever since, the town has had an Asiatic feel to it, with its own little Chinatown. The boom came to an end around 1950 with the advent of cultured pearls and plastic buttons and Broome reverted to being something of a sleepy backwater, until the old buildings in the Chinese quarter were restored around 1980. Today Broome is renowned for its relaxed and laid-back way of life and 'Have

(continued p.34)

1 The steep limestone walls of Windjana Gorge are reflected here in the still waters of the Lennard River.

2 The flood level of the Fitzroy River in the wet season is indicated by the colour of the rock face at Geikie Gorge.

Detour

Kimberley Coast

The Kimberley Coast between Joseph Bonaparte Gulf and Cape Leveque is probably the loneliest coast in Australia. Around three thousand islands run along this deeply indented coastline with its hundreds of bays. Over a stretch of 2,000 km (1,243 miles) there are no more than a few fishing villages and holiday camps. A fierce tidal range of up to 12 m (39½ ft) and regular cyclones make the land here extremely inhospitable. Large areas of the region are Aboriginal lands; thousands of rock drawings bear witness to the presence of indigenous peoples over many millennia.

Kimberley is one of the world's oldest geological formations (some 2½ billion years), consisting primarily of savannah and rock plateaux, the fossilized remnants of former coral reefs. In the monsoon season, the streams and rivers swell into raging torrents. Conversely, tidal waves from the ocean force massive volumes of water inland. As a result, Kimberley is constantly being reshaped by the forces of nature. In some areas, such as Talbot Bay, a phenomenon known as 'horizontal waterfalls' can be observed: when the tide turns, a type of maelstrom shoots through the gap between two cliffs, pushing a tidal wave metres high ahead of it.

There are just two dirt tracks to the coast (like all the roads in Kimberley they are impassable or only partly passable during the rainy season): from the legendary Gibb River Road, which crosses the Kimberley diagonally from Kununurra to Derby, Kalumburu Road branches off around 50 km (31 miles) before Gibb River. This road ends some 250 km (155 miles) later in Kalumburu, an Aborigine settlement and Mission at Honeymoon Bay. After about 150 km (93 miles), Mitchell Plateau Road turns off Kalumburu Road to the coastal locality of Port Warrender. Most travellers take this route only as far as the main attraction, Mitchell Falls, where the Mitchell River cascades spectacularly over four terraces from the Mitchell Plateau, a sandstone formation. The rock-pools make good (natural) bathing-places.

1 The strong tidal range produces a kind of 'horizontal waterfall' as seen here in the Buccaneer Archipelago.

2 One of the highest elevations in the region is Mount Trafalgar (385 m/ 1,263 ft) at St George Basin.

3 There are many waterfalls on the Kimberley Coast, including Camp Creek Falls.

4 The Mitchell Falls cascade down over four levels. The pools make an attractive place for a refreshing dip.

Australia is a land of cattle farmers. Some of Kimberley's cattle stations are the size of a small European country. Little wonder, then, that rodeos are big in Australia, the most famous ones in Western Australia being held in Broome, Katherine or Litchfield. At a rodeo, stockmen compete against one another

in several disciplines. In the timed competitions speed is crucial, while the rough stock disciplines – saddle bronco riding, bareback bronco riding, bull riding, a Broome time' is a common local expression. Over the last few decades there has been an influx of sailors and people seeking a more easygoing, relaxed lifestyle in Broome, not least because of the endless expanses of white beach, azure blue water and rocky red coastline. Cable Beach is a good 20 km (12 miles) long and everything a tropical beach should be. The pearl industry still continues to play a role and Broome is one of the world's largest producers of cultured pearls. The highlight of the year is 'Shinju Matsuri', the pearl festival, which attracts visitors from all over the world.

⓬ **Port Hedland** On the way from Broome to Port Hedland you pass the strip of coast named Eighty Mile Beach, one of Australia's most beautiful beaches. Port Hedland is situated on an island and connected by three causeways to the mainland, where satellite towns have emerged. The heat is intense here all year round, and everything is covered in a layer of red dust. Port Hedland owes its growth to salt production and the boom in iron ore. The largest ore carriers in the world dock at the local port. The local fishing trade also plays a significant role.

⓭ **Karratha** The fastest-growing town in the Pilbara Region is its administrative centre. For a long time it used to be known as 'Company Town', since it is home to many workers from the iron ore mines in Pilbara.
Just 20 km (12 miles) away is the port named after the explorer William Dampier. The town is dominated by the Dampier Salt Company and in spite of the hot dry climate a good irrigation system means that it is nevertheless a green town with lovely beaches. It is the starting point for a trip into Dampier Archipelago Nature Reserve, a group of forty-two uninhabited islands of rocks, cliffs and fantastic sandy beaches. This is an ideal location for diving, snorkelling, fishing and admiring Aboriginal rock art undisturbed.
From Dampier our route retraces its steps the short distance back to Karratha and then leaves the North West Coastal Highway between Roebourne and Whim Creek to head inland towards the Hamersley Range.

⓮ **Millstream-Chichester National Park** This park in the Pilbara steppe, home of the richest iron ore deposits in the world, has magnificent waterholes and oases such as Python Pool and Millstream Oasis. This area is the homeland of the Yinjibarndi Aborigines on the Fortescue River. Millstream palms, thought to have been planted by camel drivers from Afghanistan, also grow here. The park generally offers a rich variety of flora and fauna otherwise more likely to be found in the tropical north. From here there are plenty of opportunities for trekking into the bush and Millstream Homestead, the park's visitor centre, is worth visiting for its exhibitions about the Yinjibarndi Aborigines, early settlers and local flora and fauna.

⓯ **Karijini National Park** Travelling via Auski Roadhouse, where you rejoin the Great Northern Highway for a short distance, you come to Karijini National Park. It owes its name to the Banyjima Aborigines – 'Karijini' is the Aborigine name for the Hamersley Range, a weather-beaten rock massif extending over 320 km (199 miles) with heights of up to 1,200 m (3,937 ft). The numerous gorges with their shelves, steps and terraces carved into the red rock by rivers and streams are a spectacular and unforgettable sight. The landscape here is a kind of tropical semi-desert. After rainfall, the ground is covered in a delightful carpet of brightly coloured

Detour

Cape Leveque

A lighthouse, white sandy beaches, turquoise water, red sandstone cliffs – this is Cape Leveque at the tip of the Dampier Peninsula 220 km (137 miles) north of Broome. This stunning strip of land has been back

Sandstone cliffs at Cape Leveque.

under Aborigine ownership since 1986. The Aborigines lived here for over five thousand years before buccaneers and explorers like William Dampier or Nicolas Baudin began to arrive from the end of the 17th century. In Kooljaman – as the Aborigines call the Cape – there is a small, back-to-nature holiday resort where you can stay in simple huts and safari tents and go swimming and snorkelling. For a change of scene there are plenty of guided walks, which will give a good insight into Aboriginal culture, and excursions to Sunday Island, one of the islands in the Buccaneer Archipelago.

wild flowers. Make sure you have your camera ready!

⓰ **Tom Price** This mining town, at an altitude of 747 m (2,451 ft) at the foot of Mount Nameless (1,128 m/3,701 ft), is named after the American engineer Thomas Moore Price, who developed iron ore mining in the Pilbara region in the 1960s. Visitors to Tom Price can view the mine of the same name, and the town makes a good base camp for excursions into the Pilbara steppe and its National Parks. Highway 136 takes you back onto the North West Coastal Highway. Just before Winning, take a right turn in the direction of Exmouth.

⓱ **Exmouth and Cape Range National Park** Exmouth was established in 1964 as a supply centre for the nearby US Naval Communication Station, which left the region at the beginning of the 1990s. Today the base is used by the Australian naval service. From here it's easy to reach some of the wonderful, secluded beaches in the area.
To the south-west of Exmouth lies Cape Range National Park. With its fissured limestone and numerous gorges, this is good trekking country. One of the highlights is the red rock face of Yardie Creek Gorge reflected in the blue water of the river. The park's main attraction, however, lies underwater: the famous Ningaloo Reef in the south.

⓲ **Ningaloo Reef Marine Park and Coral Bay** Ningaloo Reef runs for a distance of over 250 km (155 miles) along the coast. It is, so to speak, the Great Barrier Reef of Western Australia. Although only one-eighth the size, Ningaloo Reef is just as colourful and has the same diversity of fish as its rival on the east coast, with some fantastic spots for snorkelling and diving. From March to May visitors are treated to a real spectacle when the whale sharks, the largest fish on earth, arrive.
Apart from Exmouth, another good starting place for tours to Ningaloo Reef is the small resort of Coral Bay. Here the reef begins just beyond the beach and is perfectly situated for snorkelling or exploring in a glass-bottomed boat.

⓳ **Carnarvon** Following the North West Coastal Highway for a further 130 km (81 miles) you arrive at the coastal town of Carnarvon. The town, which takes its name from a former British foreign minister, dates back to around 1880, as the Victorian architecture of a number of historic buildings in the town centre attests. Carnarvon lies at the mouth of the Gascoyne River, which flows underground for part of the year and irrigates a large section of the surrounding area, making the region a fertile oasis with many fruit plantations. Fishing is a further source of income in the town. The port of Carnarvon is very popular for sport fishing, and you can even swim at the picturesque Pelican Point. The jetty projects far out into the sea, and the Lighthouse Cottage Museum at the lighthouse is also worth a visit.

⓴ **Shark Bay and Monkey Mia** At Overlander Roadhouse turn off the North West Coastal Highway onto the track to Denham, the centre of the Peron peninsula, Shark Bay and the small Monkey Mia beach. Shark Bay has been a World Heritage

(continued p.38)

1 **Lifeguards with equipment on Cable Beach at Broome.**

2 **An unusual combination: riding a ship of the desert on Cable Beach.**

3 **Deep Reach Pool in Millstream-Chichester National Park.**

4 **Waterfalls at Hancock Gorge in Karijini National Park.**

5 **Eucalyptus trees and spinifex grass steppe in the Pilbara.**

6 **The red-and-white-striped rock formations of the Hamersley Range.**

With specimens up to 14 m (46 ft) long and weighing as much as 15 tonnes (16.5 tons), the whale shark is the largest fish on earth. Despite its size, the

plankton and small fish from the water flowing through its mouth. In Asia its fins are considered a delicacy, which explains why whale sharks have been hunted almost to extinction. The photo shows a specimen at Ningaloo Reef Marine Park, where schools of whale sharks congregate between March and July

Wildlife on the west coast of Australia

Like the rest of the country, Western Australia is home to a variety of unusual animal species. First up are the marsupials including, of course, kangaroos. Banded wallabies are found only on the islands of Bernier and Dorre off Shark Bay. The quokka (short-tailed kangaroo) likewise survives only on a single island, Rottnest Island off Perth. The eucalypt forests in the south-west are the territory of the numbat, the fauna emblem of Western Australia.
Reptiles are also plentiful in the west of the country. Monitor lizards such as the sand goanna or Gould's monitor give the Pilbara steppe a real primeval feel. Various snakes, including the woma python, make their home in the region's deserts and

Top: Horned shark in Shark Bay.
Bottom: Dugong, a type of sea cow.

marshlands, as well as numerous lizards, agamids and geckos.
The fluvial plains and marshlands are the preferred habitat of many birds, including oystercatchers, brolga cranes, cormorants and pelicans. Specifically Australian land birds on the west coast are emus, the blue-winged kookaburra, Australian magpies, wedge-tailed eagles and various types of cockatoo.
Finally, with its thousands of kilometres of coastline and many reefs, Western Australia offers plenty of opportunities for observing marine life. The real highlights here are the dolphins at Monkey Mia, the dugongs and sharks at Shark Bay and the whale sharks and humpback whales at Ningaloo Reef.

Site since 1992 on account of its natural flora and fauna. The shallow waters of Shark Bay Marine Park are home to an unusually rich array of marine life, including dugongs. However, the main attraction in the area is Monkey Mia Dolphin Resort. The dolphins have been visiting the beach for decades to play with the visitors, who feed them under ranger supervision. With a bit of luck, you might even spot some manatees here. François Peron National Park on the northern tip of the Peron peninsula is one of the most important nature reserves in Australia, a refuge for many rare and endangered species (thorny devils, monitor lizards or goannas, emus) and well worth a visit.

21 Kalbarri National Park From the North West Coastal Highway turn off at Ajana into Kalbarri National Park and the town of the same name at the mouth of the Murchison River. Here the river has carved deep, winding gorges, such as Loop Gorge, into the sandstone to create a breathtaking landscape extending over 80 km (50 miles). For the best views of the river, the 'Z-Bend' vantage point is a real must. If you want to go walking in the gorges you should do so in the early morning, as it can get very hot here. The park is also famous for the beauty and diversity of its wild flowers. Among its other attractions are the cliff coastline and beautifully clean, undisturbed beaches, excellent for swimming and fishing. Four km (2½ miles) to the south of Kalbarri, a Dutch sea captain marooned two mutineers on the Red Bluff cliffs in 1629; they had the distinction of being the first European settlers in Australia.

22 Geraldton Founded in 1849, the town first began to flourish at the end of the 19th century when gold was discovered in the Murchison Goldfields, for which Geraldton was the main port. Today Geraldton is a modern, up-and-coming city and administrative centre for the central coastal region of Western Australia. A warm sunny climate and beautiful sandy beaches make it a popular holiday destination for families from Perth.
The Houtman Abrolhos Islands lie 60 km (37 miles) off the coast. It was here that many vessels belonging to the Dutch East India Company once ran aground. Today the wrecks are on show in Geraldton Maritime Museum. The waters around the Houtman Abrolhos Islands are renowned for their rich diversity of fauna (especially seabirds) and are an important lobster-fishing ground.

23 Nambung National Park About halfway between Geraldton and Perth turn off at Badgingarra onto a track leading to the coastal town of Cervantes. From here Nambung National Park lies to the south. Its main attraction is the limestone pillars of the Pinnacles Desert, which Dutch discoverers first took to be the remains of a town. In fact they were formed many thousands of years ago, when sand and limestone accumulated on the roots of plants growing on the dunes. Later the plants died off and the dunes shifted, leaving behind them the bizarre limestone columns looking like a moonscape in the yellow sand. The Pinnacles are at their most impressive just before sunset, *(continued p.40)*

1 Shark Bay is renowned for its rich diversity of fauna. Here, a pelican is pictured on the beach at Monkey Mia.

2 The unusual and fascinating stromatolites at Monkey Mia are the product of calcium-secreting bacteria.

The Houtman Abrolhos Islands are a chain of islands situated some 60 km (37 miles) off the coast of Geraldton. Dutch seafarers ran aground here as early as the 17th century. The photo shows Pigeon Island and Little Pigeon Island. They are packed with fishing huts, set up for the booming lobster trade.

Detour

Wave Rock

One of the strangest rock formations in the world can be seen near Hyden, 350 km (217 miles) east of Perth. Here a wall of granite approximately 15 m (49 ft) high and 110 m

Wave Rock rises like a giant petrified wave.

(361 ft) long rises out of the ground like a massive wave frozen in time. Over billions of years, erosion has carved out a perfectly concave wall of rock with an overhanging crest. As water is washed down the rock, minerals are released, forming the characteristic pattern of red, ochre and grey-coloured bands in the rock. Just 20 km (12 miles) away, Bates Cave, containing Aboriginal rock painting and handprints, is worth a visit.

when the stone sculptures cast long shadows.

㉔ **Perth** See pages 42–43.

㉕ **Fremantle** From Perth it's just a few kilometres to the little port of Fremantle at the mouth of the Swan River. A settlement was established here by an English naval officer, Charles Fremantle, around 1840. Fremantle has managed to retain the charm of a 19th-century port to the present day and has one of the best-preserved historic centres in any developed town in Australia. The Prison Museum and the Maritime Museum are both worth a visit. Day trips to Rottnest Island can be made by boat to see the island's main attractions, coral reefs, rare seabirds and quokkas, a species of kangaroo found only on this island.

㉖ **Bunbury** This port is the commercial centre of the south west region of Western Australia. The Western Australian Gold Coast begins here, with its white, unpopulated beaches of fine sand. Humpback whales can be observed between September and November. In Bunbury, leave the South Western Highway and travel on Highway 10 along the coast to the holiday resort of Busselton. Here visitors will find one of the most beautiful beaches in Western Australia and the oldest stone church in the country, St Mary's Church (1845). Busselton is also a good starting point for a trip to Cape Naturaliste.

㉗ **Margaret River** A little further to the south, Margaret River is the centre of a renowned wine-growing region. This is a pretty little place with a spectacular rocky coastline where you can drink wine, visit the limestone caves, take a walk on the beach or go surfing. Margaret River is also the starting point for a trip to Leeuwin-Naturaliste National Park (see Detour, page 41) and to Australia's most south-westerly point, Cape Leeuwin near Augusta. From here follow Highway 10 and at Pemberton pass the Giant Karri Trees – huge eucalyptus trees which stand up to some 90 m (295 ft) tall.

28 Walpole This settlement at the mouth of the Franklin River has a mild climate and a picturesque coastal landscape and offers fishing, canoeing and sailing. It's within easy access of Walpole-Nornalup National Park, where you can bushwalk the Heritage Trail beneath gigantic eucalyptus trees.

29 Albany The final destination on our journey is attractively situated in the hills above Princess Royal Harbour, a natural harbour that broadens into King George Sound. Albany, which was first recorded in 1622, is the oldest white settlement in Western Australia; in 1826 it was already an outpost of the Sydney penal colony. Its many attractions include well-preserved streets and some very striking buildings that date back to the 19th century (church, post office), as well as Whale World, a whale and whaling museum that is situated on the site of a former whaling station.

1 The forest of rock pillars at the Pinnacles in Nambung National Park is an arresting and unusual sight.

2 Perth is the only large city in the whole of Western Australia.

3 Sailing is very popular in Perth. It's no coincidence that the America's Cup was held here in 1987.

Detour

Leeuwin-Naturaliste National Park

Leeuwin-Naturaliste National Park is a narrow strip of coastline that stretches 100 km (62 miles) to the west of Margaret River between Cape Naturaliste on Bunkers Bay and Cape Leeuwin, the most south-westerly point of the Australian mainland. It is a wildly rugged, wind-buffeted rocky coastline with excellent bathing beaches at Yallingup, Ingidup, Smiths Beach and Bunkers Bay. The section of coast between Bunkers Bay and Boranup Beach is a popular haunt for surfers and

Take a walk in the park to admire eucalyptus blossom (top, bottom) and 'black boys' (Australian grass trees, centre).

anglers. Close to Boranup is a forest of tall (around 90 m/295 ft) karri trees, a species of eucalyptus otherwise only found inland further to the east.

Dripstone caves are situated all along the park's coastline. Some of them, like Calgardup Cave and the Giants Cave, can be explored independently. If you have time and want to see more of the landscape's rugged beauty, you can explore the full length of coast along the 135 km (84 miles) Cape to Cape Walking Track.

Perth

Perth is often referred to as the most isolated city on earth. The distance to the next big city, Adelaide, is just under 3,000 km (1,864 miles) and Melbourne and Sydney are more than 3,500 km (2,175 miles) away.

It may be in the middle of nowhere, but Perth is an attractive city with some 1½ million inhabitants. Skyscrapers testify to the boom in raw materials and construction of recent years. Although historic buildings from the 19th century are few and far between, the city gives a relaxed and friendly impression. Its situation no doubt contributes to this feeling: Perth is located on the Swan River, which widens, before flowing into the Indian Ocean, to form a lake measuring 1 km (0.6 miles) across. Perth is very much a city on the water, where sailing and water sports are high priorities. Thanks to its expansive layout – Perth extends over some 5,000 km² (1,930 square miles) – and many parks, such as Kings Park on 4 km² (1½ square miles) of land, there is none of the usual stress of city life.

The city centre around St George Terrace is a manageable size and easy to get around on foot. This is the heart of the city, where its Business District, Hay Street Mall and London Court, a shopping arcade in mock-Tudor style, are situated. Buildings dating back to the 19th century include the Perth Mint,

Top: The Perth skyline.
Bottom: A Victorian house in Fremantle.

the Town Hall, The Cloisters (the former boys' school), Government House and the Old Courthouse. The Art Gallery of Western Australia, Perth Cultural Centre and Western Australia Museum offer a wide range of cultural events. Boats to Fremantle, Perth Harbour and Rottnest Island depart from Barrack Square on the Swan River.

HYDE PARK
HIGHGATE
FORREST PARK
SOCCER DORRIEN GARDENS
TEN ROBERTSON PARK
BIRDWOOD SQUARE
BRIGATTI GARDEN
JACK MARKS PARK
BANKS RESERVE
LOTON PARK
Perth Oval
EAST PERTH
Industrial Area
RUSSELL SQUARE
WELD SQUARE PARK
Graham Farmer Freeway
Graham Farmer Fwy.
Windan Bridge
Goongoonup Bridge
CLAISEBROOK
MCIVER
WELLINGTON SQUARE
VICTORIA GARDENS
PERTH JEWISH MEM. CEMETERY
EAST PERTH CEMETERY
PIONEER GARDENS
GLOUCESTER PARK
Trotting Stadium
QUEENS GARDENS
W.A.C.A. Oval Sportground
Trinity College
Small Oval Sportground
EAST PERTH PARKLAND
HEIRISSON ISLAND PARK
Heirisson Island
Causeway
Perth Railway Station
Perth Hospital
St. Mary's Cathedral
St. George's Cathedral
Concert Hall
Old Court House 1836
SUPREME COURT GARDENS
STIRLING GARDENS
ALF CURLEWIS GARDENS THE ESPLANADE
BARRACK SQUARE
Swan Bells
Bell Tower
Barrack Street Jetty & Old Perth Port
LANGLEY PARK
Riverside Drive
Kings Park & River Walk
Perth Water
Swan River
Victoria Park
MCCALLUM PARK
TAYLOR RESERVE
SIR JAMES MITCHELL PARK
South Perth
Canning Hwy.
Wellington Street
Murray Street
Hay Street
St. Georges Terrace
Adelaide Terrace
Newcastle Street
Lord Street
Beaufort Street
William Street
Barrack Street
East Parade
Plain Street
Bennett Street
250
500 m

Litchfield National Park The gigantic termite hills are an extraordinary sight. Their tombstone shape and precise layout ensure they get maximum exposure to the sun's rays.

Katherine Gorge in Nitmiluk National Park Katherine Gorge, the park's premier attraction, is made up of thirteen gorges in total. Most of them can be explored by boat along the Katherine River.

Mitchell Falls Not far from the Kimberley Coast, the Mitchell River cascades over four levels into the depths below.

Kakadu National Park Floodplains dominate the park's landscape during the monsoon season.

Cable Beach Where once the telegraph cable that ran from Broome to Java was laid, there are now 20 km (12 miles) of the finest beaches in Western Australia. They are well worth a visit.

Windjana Gorge The Lennard River has carved its way through the limestone rocks for 3.5 km (2 miles). During the dry season, all that remains of the river is a series of pools.

Purnululu National Park The rocky domes of the Bungle Bungles, a geological formation dating back over 350 million years, stand like giant beehives east of Kimberley.

Eighty Mile Beach It is worth taking a detour south of Broome to one of the longest sand beaches in Australia. Here it is still possible to experience real solitude on long beach walks.

Wolfe Creek Meteorite Crater A meteorite crashed to earth 300,000 years ago on the edge of the Great Sandy Desert, leaving a crater measuring some 900 m (2,953 ft) in diameter.

Halls Creek This small town roughly midway between Kununurra and Derby is a typical outback settlement with a petrol station, supermarket and a few shops. A number of sculptures and some remnants of Old Halls Creek, 15 km (9 miles) south of the present town, are a reminder of the 1885 gold-rush.

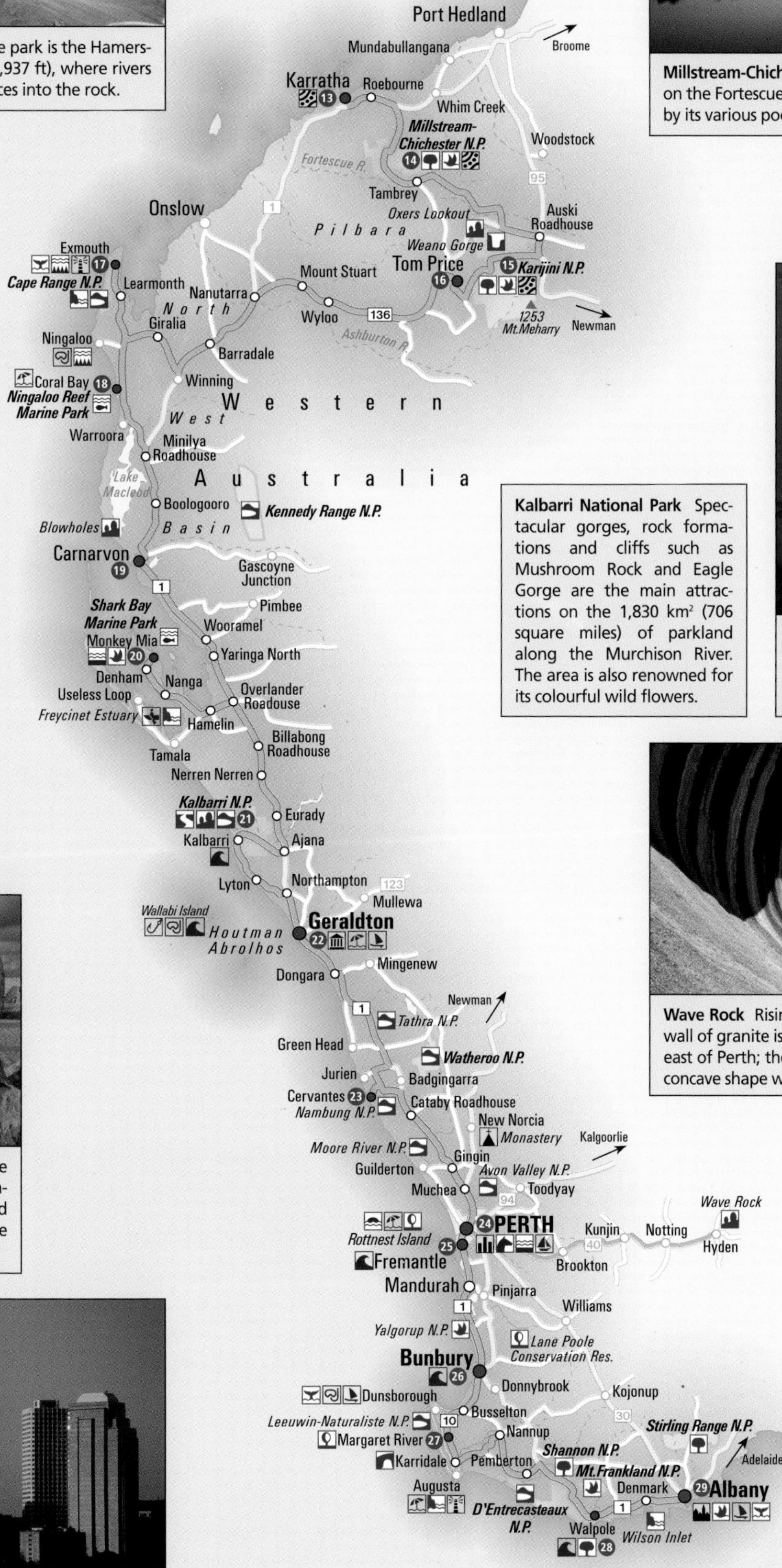

Karijini National Park The backbone of the park is the Hamersley Range, rising to a height of 1,200 m (3,937 ft), where rivers and streams have carved gorges and terraces into the rock.

Ningaloo Reef Each year between March and May, the 250-km (155-mile) reef attracts shoals of whale sharks, the largest fish in the world.

Shark Bay Marine Park This is where stromatolites, knobbly limestone formations dating back three billion years, can be found.

Pinnacles These bizarrely shaped limestone pillars rise out of the sandy desert in Nambung National Park. They were created through accretions of sand and limestone on vegetation, followed by erosion.

Perth The capital of Western Australia is one of the world's most isolated metropolitan areas. In recent decades many international mining companies have set up offices here.

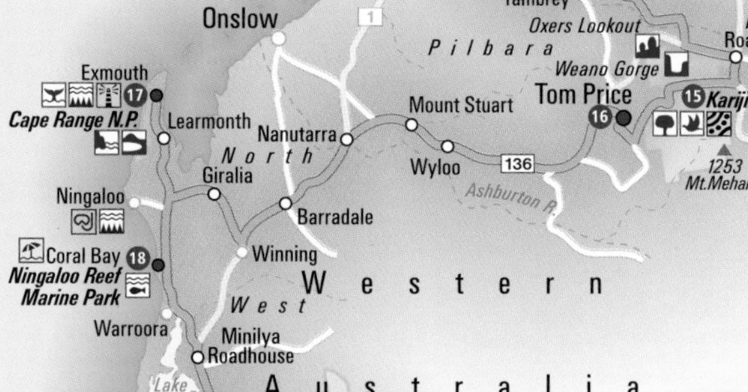

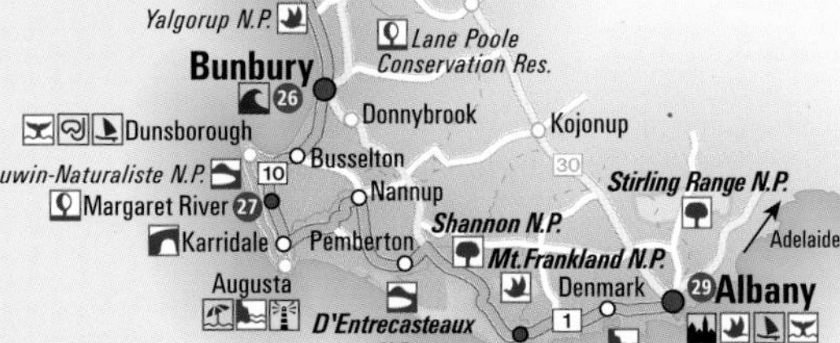

Kalbarri National Park Spectacular gorges, rock formations and cliffs such as Mushroom Rock and Eagle Gorge are the main attractions on the 1,830 km² (706 square miles) of parkland along the Murchison River. The area is also renowned for its colourful wild flowers.

Millstream-Chichester National Park Millstream Oasis, situated on the Fortescue River in the Chichester Range, is characterized by its various pools – here Deep Reach Pool.

Houtman Abrolhos Islands Pigeon Island is one of the 122 islands in this chain lying west of Geraldton. Lobster fishermen have built many little fishing huts here.

Wave Rock Rising like a wave to a height of 15 m (49 ft), this wall of granite is located near Hyden, 350 km (217 miles) to the east of Perth; the forces of erosion have carved out a perfectly concave shape with a characteristic banded pattern in the rock.

Leeuwin-Naturaliste National Park There are numerous dripstone caves along the park's coastline, including Easter Cave, shown here.

Kakadu National Park is characterized by broad lowlands and dry sandstone plateaux.

Route 2

Australia

On the Stuart Highway through the 'Red Centre'

The Stuart Highway stretches 3,200 km (1,987 miles) from Adelaide on the south coast all the way across the legendary outback, the 'Red Centre' of the continent, to Darwin in the north on the Timor Sea. Along this adventurous route you will pass some of Australia's most impressive natural sights. Indeed, long portions of the journey are devoid of any signs of life, much less human settlements, but it is precisely this emptiness and solitude that make this journey so fascinating.

The starting point for the adventure across the entire Australian continent is Adelaide, known as the 'greenest town' in the country. Today, tree-lined streets in this tidy city have replaced the rugged seaport where, in 1836, roughly 550 German settlers arrived bearing grape vines and a vision for the future. The heart of Australian wine production is now concentrated in a handful of picturesque regions including the Adelaide Hills, the Barossa Valley and the Clare Valley.

Port Augusta, 317 km (197 miles) further north, is the real starting point of the Stuart Highway. It is named after John McDouall Stuart, an explorer who in 1862 became the first white man to cross the continent from north to south. At one time known for being one of the country's most hazardous roads, the highway, which has been paved now since 1987, has become a fully developed traffic route. Parts of the road can become impassable after unusually heavy rainfall.

Aborigine with impressive body paint.

The first stretch of your route, from Port Augusta to Glendambo, is marked by dried-out salt lakes that are visible from the road. The first real town to the north after Port Augusta is Coober Pedy in the Stuart Range, a relatively inhospitable area where dramatic sandstorms are commonplace. It was here, in the 'opal capital of the world', that the first opal was discovered by chance during the gold-rush of 1915.

In general, between Port Augusta and Darwin, what may look like a town along the highway on the map is often nothing more than a roadhouse where you can buy fuel, spend the night and stock up on basic food supplies. One of these is the Kulgera Roadhouse, just 'across the border' in the Northern Territory. There are only 200,000 people living in this massive state (six times the size of Great Britain),

Kakadu National Park covers almost the entire catchment area of the South Alligator River, which crashes over the cliffs of Twin Falls and Jim Jim Falls.

The Stuart Highway leads hundreds of kilometres through the desert landscape of the 'Red Centre'.

and half of them live in Darwin. Coarse, rocky terrain and the endless spinifex grass steppe cover the land as far as the eye can see. The land is rusty red for hundreds of kilometres, with termite hills shimmering dark red in the hot sun. It is a unique symphony of shifting shades of red earth in which you will only rarely see anything other than natural landscapes. Roughly 80 km (50 miles) over the border at Erldunda, the Lasseter Highway turns off towards Uluru-Kata Tjuta National Park where two of Australia's most famous landmarks are located: Uluru (Ayers Rock) and Kata Tjuta (The Olgas). The most important city in the area is Alice Springs in the Macdonnell Ranges, a town that is also the geographical centre of the country and a comfortable starting point for trips to many well-known National Parks: Finke Gorge, Watarrka and the West Macdonnell Ranges. The next tourist highlight on the way to 'Top End' are the bizarre spheres of the Devils Marbles. Tennant Creek has been known as 'Gold Town' ever since the short gold-rush that took place there in 1932. At Renner Springs one finally leaves the inhospitable arid plains of the 'Red Centre' behind and the coastal savannah comes into view.

From the town of Katherine you can reach the Cutta Cutta Caves Nature Park as well as the Nitmiluk National Park with the spectacular canyons of Katherine Gorge. At Pine Creek, you have the choice between the road to Darwin or the drive through Kakadu National Park towards Jabiru.

Either way, after 3,200 km (1,987 miles) of hard going, you have finally reached the 'Top End'.

Giant red kangaroos measure up to 2 m (6½ ft) when standing on its hind legs.

Giant kangaroos

If you follow the Stuart Highway north towards Darwin you will regularly come across signs warning you of kangaroos crossing the road. These marsupials are the continent's national animal with an estimated population of about twenty-five million. Despite their cuddly popularity with tourists, these vegetarian creatures are viewed by local farmers as pests because they graze uncontrollably on valuable sheep pastures.

In Australia there are fifty-six kangaroo species, divided into two families: the 'real' kangaroos and the 'rat' kangaroos, a newer species. During your trip, you will mostly come across the 'real' kangaroos, the hopping kind with extremely short forearms and powerful legs and tails.

Giant red kangaroo.

Some are as small as large rabbits while others, like the giant red kangaroo, can reach 2 m (6½ ft) standing on their hind legs. Cape York is home to two species of tree kangaroo.

Kangaroo offspring are actually born during a late phase of embryonic development, the rest of which is completed from within the mother's pouch. Females have only one baby per year, which then feeds for seven to ten months in her pouch while she feeds another offspring with milk outside the pouch.

Kangaroos' long and powerful tails are used as counterweights for hopping and jumping, but their soft leathery feet do not damage the ground below them. In the open grasslands of the dry centre, you regularly come across giant red kangaroos which, like many kangaroos, live in herds.

1

Shortly after starting out from Adelaide, the Stuart Highway leads straight into the outback. Ayers Rock and Alice Springs lie at the halfway point of the route. The landscape turns into savannah in the far northern sections, and numerous National Parks give travellers an idea of the Northern Territory's flora and fauna.

1 Adelaide With more than a million inhabitants, Adelaide lies on the north and south banks of the Torrens River. The city's many parks, gardens, historical arcades and churches give it a European air. Yet despite all this, Adelaide is often considered a backwater by people from other Australian cities, in particular Sydney and Melbourne, although it does not deserve such a description.

Every two years one of the world's most important cultural festivals takes place here: the Festival of Arts, held in the Adelaide Festival Centre. This tolerant and multicultural city has several museums along the 'Cultural Mile', including the Art Gallery of South Australia, the Ayers House Historical Museum (one of the most attractive colonial buildings in Australia), the Migration Museum on the history of immigration, and the South Australia Museum, with a good collection of Aboriginal tools, weapons and everyday artifacts.

For a great view of the city climb Montefiori Hill. Then take a break in the enchanting Botanic Gardens. If you feel like a swim, take one of the nostalgic trams down to Glenelg or Henley Beach. A worthwhile day trip is the drive into the Adelaide Hills or to the Barossa Valley. The first vineyards were planted here in 1847 by a German immigrant, Johann Cramp. Today in the Barossa Valley, 40 km (25 miles) long and 10 km (6 miles) wide, there are more than four hundred vineyards producing wines that have slowly but surely gained recognition around the world. One of the year's cultural highlights is the Vintage Festival with music, sauerkraut, brown bread, apple strudel, and of course wine.

Another interesting detour takes you to Kangaroo Island, 113 km (70 miles) south-west of Adelaide, which can be reached via the Fleurieu peninsula with its inviting sandy beaches. Australia's third-largest island is 155 km (96 miles) long and 55 km (34 miles) wide. You will come face to face here with the kangaroos that gave the island its name.

In the Seal Bay Conservation Park, thousands of sea lions bask on rocks in the sun. In Flinders Chase National Park, koalas lounge in the eucalyptus trees.

2

Travel information

Route profile
Length: 3,200 km/1,987 miles (excluding detours)
Start: Adelaide
End: Darwin
Itinerary (main locations): Adelaide, Port Augusta, Coober Pedy, Alice Springs, Wauchope, Tennant Creek, Katherine, Pine Creek, Darwin.

Accommodation
Aside from signposted campsites, it's always possible to spend the night in a highway 'roadhouse'.

Traffic information
Cars drive on the left in Australia. The maximum speed limit in built-up areas is 50 km/h (31 mph) and outside built-up areas is 100 km/h (62 mph). International driving licences are required for some nations. The blood alcohol limit is 0.05 per cent and there are severe penalties if it is exceeded.
The Stuart Highway is completely sealed from Adelaide to Darwin. In general, the driving conditions on auxiliary roads east and west of the highway are good. If you want to explore the outback, a four-wheel drive vehicle is recommended. There are service stations and rest areas about every 200–300 km (124–186 miles) along the highway.

Information
www.australia.com
Australian Embassies:
www.dfat.gov.au
National Parks:
www.atn.com.au/parks

The real trip to the far north begins on Highway 1 from Adelaide. On the northern banks of Spencer Gulf is the industrial harbour town of Port Pirie, 250 km (155 miles) from Adelaide. Enormous grain silos bear witness to the extensive wheat farming in this region. Zinc and silver ore are processed here too, as is lead.
About 65 km (40 miles) further north, on the way to Port Augusta, it is worth taking the scenic detour into Mount Remarkable National Park at the south end of the Flinders Range. From the top of the 959 m (3,146 ft) Mount Remarkable you can get a fabulous panoramic view of the entire region.
After another 70 km (43½ miles) along Spencer Gulf, the industrial port town of Augusta awaits you and marks the actual starting point of the Stuart Highway (Highway 87).

2 Port Augusta This town is often called the 'Gateway to the outback'. In preparation for the trip, a visit to the Wadlata Outback Centre is highly recommended. A few historically important buildings including the Town Hall (1887), the Court House (1884) and St Augustine's Church, with lovely stained-glass windows, are worth seeing. The Australian Arid Lands Botanic Gardens to the north of town familiarizes you with the flora and fauna of the outback.
A detour to the nearby Flinders Ranges National Park is an absolute must.

3 Pimba This little town is right next to the enormous Woomera military base. Interestingly, the 'restricted area' on the base contains the largest uranium source in the world.
Australia's largest natural lakes can also be found around Pimba. These salt lakes are only periodically filled with water and are the remnants of what was once a huge inland sea. In dry seasons they transform into salt marshes or salt pans.
To the east of Stuart Highway is Lake Torrens, in the national park of the same name, which covers an area of 5,800 km² (2,240 square miles). Lake Frome and Lake Eyre are also in the park. Further west is Lake Gairdner, another salt lake that is part of a separate National Park.

4 Coober Pedy In 1915, fourteen-year-old Willie Hutchinson and his father discovered Australia's first opal completely by chance, about 270 km (168 miles) north of Pimba. The name Coober Pedy orginates from the Aborigine 'kupa piti' (white man in a hole). Since then it has been overrun with pits up to 30 m (98 ft) deep and giant slag heaps that, due to consistent demand for opals, are constantly expanding. In fact, seventy per cent of the world's opal mining takes place in the Coober Pedy area. The raging sandstorms and intense heat in the area have compelled nearly half of the 3,000 inhabitants to live in 'dugouts', underground homes built in decommissioned opal mines. These often well-furnished apartments maintain consistent temperatures between 23 and 25°C (73–77°F) and can be up to 400 m² (4,305 sq ft) in size. There is even an underground church in Coober Pedy, as well as underground bed and breakfast accommodation. Be sure to pay a visit to the lovingly restored Old Timers Mine while you are here.

(continued p.55)

1 Road signs along the route warn of kangaroos.

2 The night skyline of Adelaide reflected in the Torrens River.

3 At the base of the Stuart Range lies Coober Pedy, the 'Opal capital of the world'.

Detour

Flinders Ranges National Park

From Port Augusta take scenic Highway 47 through Quorn and Hawker to the mighty wall of Wilpena Pound. Gravel roads then lead to the most important sights of the 950 km² (370 square miles) Flinders National Park, one of the most beautiful in South Australia. It protects the 400-km-long (240-mile) Flinders Range, which extends like a wedge between the salt lakes of Lake Torrens, Lake Eyre and Lake Frome and continues far into the outback, providing life support to many of the animal and plant species in this arid region.

Flinders Ranges National Park is one of the earth's oldest geological formations.

The often bizarre rock formations come in red and violet hues, especially at sunrise and sunset. Bright, colourful flowers also grow in the valleys and gorges of the mountains in springtime. Giant red kangaroos live here, as do yellow-footed rock wallabies and other smaller species of rock wallabies. Bearded dragons (a type of monitor lizard) sun themselves on the hot rocks while broad-tailed eagles and brown falcons circle in the sky above.
The highlight of a trip into the National Park is the Wilpena Pound, one of Australia's greatest natural wonders: a 17-km (10½-mile) by 7-km (4½-mile) crater-like 'cauldron' that resembles a natural amphitheatre with its ring of high, pointed rocks. A small passage is the only way into the bowl, which is an Aboriginal sacred site. You will get the best view from the scenic outlook point.

Adelaide

The capital of South Australia may be home to around seventy per cent of the state's population, but it manages to retain an idyllic, English-style charm.

Adelaide was founded in 1836 and was the first city in Australia to be built by free settlers rather than convicts. It is laid out on an orderly grid of wide and narrow streets, following the model of the Sicilian town of Catania, and is surrounded by attractive park-land. The Torrens River flows through the centre of the city, and along its banks you will find the Botanic Garden, home to the largest glasshouse in the Southern hemisphere, and the futuristic Adelaide Festival Centre (1974).

On the imposing North Terrace, Adelaide's cultural boulevard, you will find a number of interesting museums, ranging in focus from Australian natural history and immigration to traditional Aboriginal art and culture. The street is also home to Parliament House, with its monumental granite-and-marble front and Corinthian pillars. Government House, the city's oldest public building and the residence of the Governor, the Queen's representative in South Australia, is located in impressive grounds. Holy Trinity (1838), the oldest Anglican church in southern Australia, looks small by comparison.

Top: An Adelaide house with its typical veranda.
Bottom: The South Australian Museum complex houses several museums and galleries.

Rundle Mall has fifteen arcades and 600 shops and was Australia's first pedestrian zone when opened in 1976. To the east is Rundle Street, a popular meeting place with shops, eateries and bars. Melbourne Street in North Adelaide is a chic, more upmarket area.

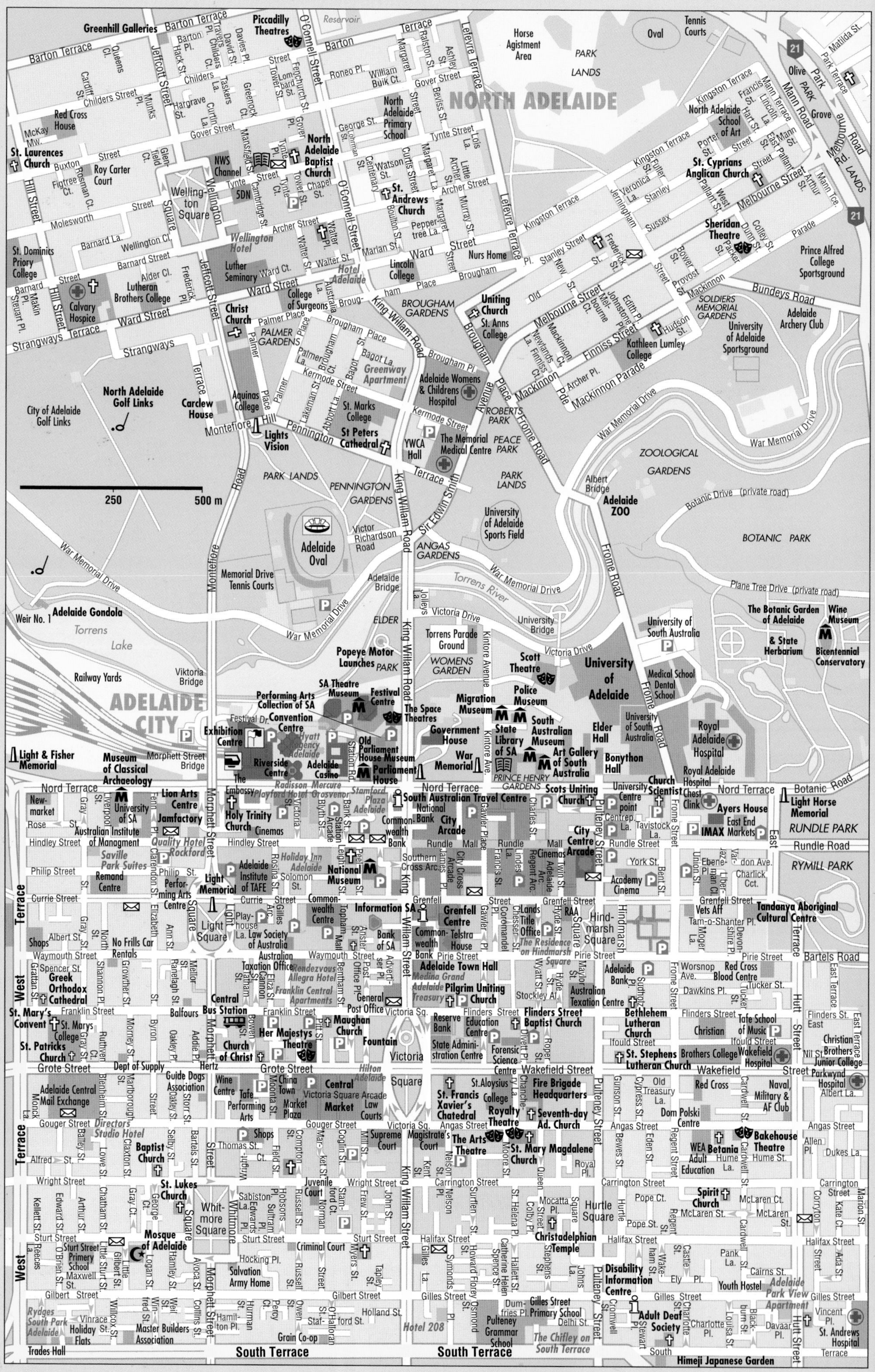

THE SCRIBE
healthsense

The large natural basin of Wilpena Pound lies at the heart of the northern Flinders Ranges and is the main attraction of the Flinders Ranges National Park. It covers about 80 km² (31 square miles) and can only be explored on foot. From the highest point, St Mary's Peak (1,170 m/3,837 ft), there is a magnificent

view over the huge natural amphitheatre. Wilpena means 'the place of bent fingers' in the local Aboriginal language because it looks like a cupped hand with frozen fingers.

Thousands of Aboriginal rock paintings dot the spectacular landscape of Kings Canyon in Watarrka National Park. A lush oasis has developed in the Garden of Eden

Eventually, the Lasseter Highway makes its way west at Erldunda towards the Yulara Resort and the Visitor Centre of the Uluru-Kata Tjuta National Park (1,325 km²/511 square miles).

If you are looking for outdoor adventure, turn right off the Stuart Highway onto a track towards Chambers Pillar, a 56-m (184-ft) sandstone monolith that early settlers used as a point of reference and in which many explorers have carved their names and dedications.

❺ **Ayers Rock** (see following pages). The Aborigines call this massive rock mountain Uluru (863 m/2,831 ft above sea level) and cherish it as a sacred site. For this reason, since the path to the top is one of sacred significance, they 'kindly ask' that people not climb it – although it is not forbidden. Instead, you are requested to admire it from below as you stroll along the 9.4-km (6-mile) 'base walk'. The rock itself measures 3.5 km (2¼ miles) by 2.4 km (1½ miles), and extends several kilometres down into the earth. It rises to 348 m (1,142 ft) above the steppe landscape like a whale stranded on a deserted beach. Due to its high iron content it changes colour with the movement of the sun: from crimson, rust, pink, brown and grey to a deep blue. After rainfall it even goes a silvery shade – a perpetually impressive show that will dazzle any visitor.

❻ **The Olgas** Known as Kata Tjuta by the Aborigines, The Olgas (1,066 m/ 3,497 ft above sea level) are a similarly spectacular site. Kata Tjuta, meaning 'many heads', is 32 km (20 miles) to the north-west of Uluru and comprises a group of 36 geologically similar, mainly dome-shaped monoliths that are spread out over an area of 35 km² (13½ square miles), the highest point peaking at 546 m (1,791 ft). It would appear that The Olgas were once a single mountain that eroded over time into individual hills. The Valley of Winds traverses a stark mountain range through which either seasonal icy winds blow or burning hot air turns each step into a torturous affair.

❼ **Henbury** Back on the Stuart Highway the journey continues to the north. Approximately 2,000–3,000 years ago a meteor impacted not far from Henbury, leaving twelve distinct craters. The largest has a diameter of 180 m (560 ft), the smallest just 6 m (20 ft).

At Henbury, the Ernest Giles Highway splits off towards Watarrka National Park. It is a dirt track until it joins the Luritja Road where it becomes a sealed road and eventually leads to the Kings Canyon Resort.

❽ **Watarrka National Park and Finke Gorge National Park** The centrepiece of the Watarrka National Park is Kings Canyon on the west end of the George Gill Range. With walls that rise to 200 m (656 ft), the canyon looks as if it were man-made.

A number of rock paintings and carvings by Aborigines adorn the rugged canyon façades. The nearby beehive-like eroded sandstone domes are aptly called the 'Lost City'. Kings Canyon is best visited on foot by taking the Kings Creek Walk.

From the resort, the Mereenie Loop (a dirt road) leads to the Aboriginal town of Hermannsburg. On this slightly daunting stretch of road you'll cross low sand dunes that lead up to the base of the Macdonnell Range. East of the old Hermannsburg Mission, Larapinta Drive turns south and for the last 16 km (10 miles) it runs through the dried-out Finke riverbed to Palm Valley. This last section is only really accessible with four-wheel

(continued p.62)

1 **Chambers Pillar rises 56 m (184 ft) over the Simpson Desert.**

2 **The Finke River eroded the steep ravine in Finke Gorge National Park.**

Roadtrains

The infamous Australian roadtrains are lorries that can measure up to 53 m (174 ft), have as many as fifteen axles

'Roadtrains' ensure the supply of provisions to isolated areas.

and sixty-two tyres and supply the outback with basic necessities. Without them, life on an isolated farm or an inland mine would be impossible. These monsters of the road have 400–500 horsepower and barrel down highways, gravel roads and sand tracks brushing aside any possible obstacles. The tractors are fitted with large grilles designed to protect the radiator from collisions with animals.

Roadtrains run mostly across the sparsely populated outback. They can carry up to 80 tonnes of freight and regularly travel 4,000 km (2,484 miles). Overtaking a roadtrain can be dangerous: airborne gravel can destroy a windscreen and they tend to swerve due to heavy winds and massive loads.

Every visitor to Uluru – known by some by its 'European' name, Ayers Rock – senses immediately why the place is sacred to Australia's Aborigines. Since 1985 the sacred mountain has been back in the hands of the indigenous people. Part of the price they paid, however, was to allow tourists to climb the

rock, as they did before the handover. The thirty-six monoliths of Kata Tjuta – named 'The Olgas' by Europeans – are also on Aboriginal sacred lands. Only two footpaths lead through the ochre gorges and ravines, the inspiring 2-km (1-mile) Kantju Gorge Walk and the spectacular 6.4-km (4-mile) Valley of the Winds Walk.

The rock domes of Kata Tjuta.

Uluru-Kata Tjuta National Park

The huge monolith in the middle of the Australian outback, Uluru (Ayers Rock) is one of the most popular tourist attractions in Australia. Just 30 km (18½ miles) from Uluru is another extraordinary natural monument: Kata Tjuta (The Olgas) with its cluster of thirty-six rounded domes.

The rock formations, at times ochre-brown, at times deep red, rounded by erosion, are the major tourist attraction in the Uluru – Kata Tjuta National Park, established in 1958. The first thing to do when you get to the park is explore the rocks, either independently or as part of a guided tour. You can find out all you need to know about the rocks and about Aboriginal culture at the Yulara Visitor Centre and Uluru Kata Tjuta Cultural Centre.

If you want to escape the crowds (a quarter of a million visitors come to the park every year), explore beyond the rocks and enjoy the flora and fauna of the outback. In this hot and arid terrain only the hardiest of plants can survive, including spinifex grass, acacias, desert casuarinas and poplars, river eucalyptus, rock figs and bush vegetation. The 1,325 km² (511 square miles) of park are also home to a wide range of wildlife, including red kangaroos, dingoes, thorny devils, giant goannas, and no fewer than 150 species of birds, among them cockatoos.

The Aborigines have regained ownership of Uluru-Kata Tjuta National Park. It is a place of deep spiritual significance for them. The Australian government has leased the area back for ninety-nine years, in order that tourists are able to visit.

Uluru and Kata Tjuta are sacred sites for the Aborigines. Uluru represents many of their traditional 'Dreamtime' stories, and rock drawings of people and animals adorn both. Some of the distinctive rocks are shaped like totem animals. There are also a number of ritual waterholes, filled with water throughout the year.

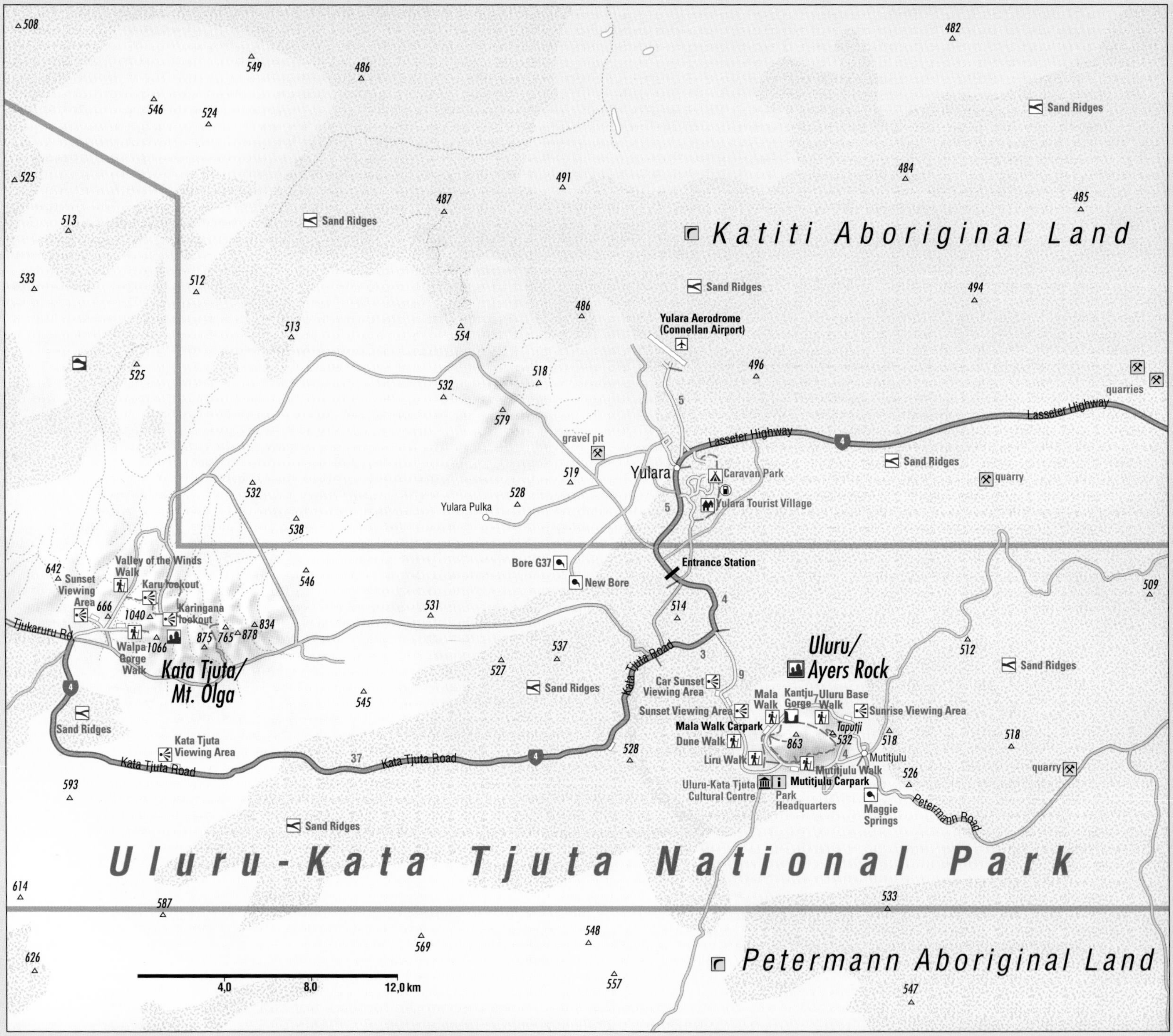

Katiti Aboriginal Land
Sand Ridges
Yulara Aerodrome (Connellan Airport)
Lasseter Highway
quarries
quarry
gravel pit
Yulara
Caravan Park
Yulara Tourist Village
Yulara Pulka
Bore G37
New Bore
Entrance Station
Valley of the Winds Walk
Karu lookout
Karingana lookout
Sunset Viewing Area
Tjukaruru Rd
Walpa Gorge Walk
Kata Tjuta/ Mt. Olga
Kata Tjuta Viewing Area
Kata Tjuta Road
Uluru/ Ayers Rock
Car Sunset Viewing Area
Sunset Viewing Area
Mala Walk
Kantju Gorge
Uluru Base Walk
Sunrise Viewing Area
Mala Walk Carpark
Dune Walk
Liru Walk
Taputji
Mutitjulu
Mutitjulu Walk
Mutitjulu Carpark
Uluru-Kata Tjuta Cultural Centre
Park Headquarters
Maggie Springs
Petermann Road
Uluru-Kata Tjuta National Park
Petermann Aboriginal Land
4,0 8,0 12,0 km

Watarrka (Kings Canyon) National Park

The Australian outback is full of wonderful surprises. At the western end of the George Gill Range, the Kings Creek River embedded itself in the desert-like terrain, carving out an impressive gorge, complete with an oasis, 2 km (1 mile) long and 200 m (656 feet) deep.

Kings Canyon is the main attraction of Watarrka National Park, some 350 km (217 miles) south-west of Alice Springs. There's a sheer drop from the crumbling pastel-coloured sandstone walls of the canyon to the gorge below. Although the riverbed is usually dry, there is sufficient water to sustain a remarkable diversity of flora and fauna. More than five hundred species of plants grow here, among them a palm fern that has survived from the time before the 'Red Centre' dried out. It now thrives in a few of the wetter areas. River eucalyptus and rock figs flourish at the waterholes, where kingfishers and other birds gather. The 'Garden of Eden' river oasis is perfect for a cooling swim. On the other side of the imposing ravine you will be able to make out the ghostly silhouette of the 'Lost City'. At first glance it looks like a ghost town, but closer inspection reveals a group of rock domes rounded by erosion. Desert casuarinas, desert poplars, ghost gums (a type of eucalyptus with a white trunk) and clumps of spinifex grass grow on the arid plateau.

You can explore Kings Canyon and the 'Lost City' on foot. There is the shorter Kings Creek Walk, and a longer Kings Canyon Rim Walk, a 6-km (3½-mile) loop with awesome views. It is best to head out very early in the morning or late in the afternoon, as the midday heat can be unbearable.

The cooler months (April to September) are the most pleasant. This scenic landscape of rugged ranges, rockholes and gorges, together with its many plants and animals, make the National Park an important conservation area and one of central Australia's most stunning sights.

The precipitous walls of Kings Canyon.

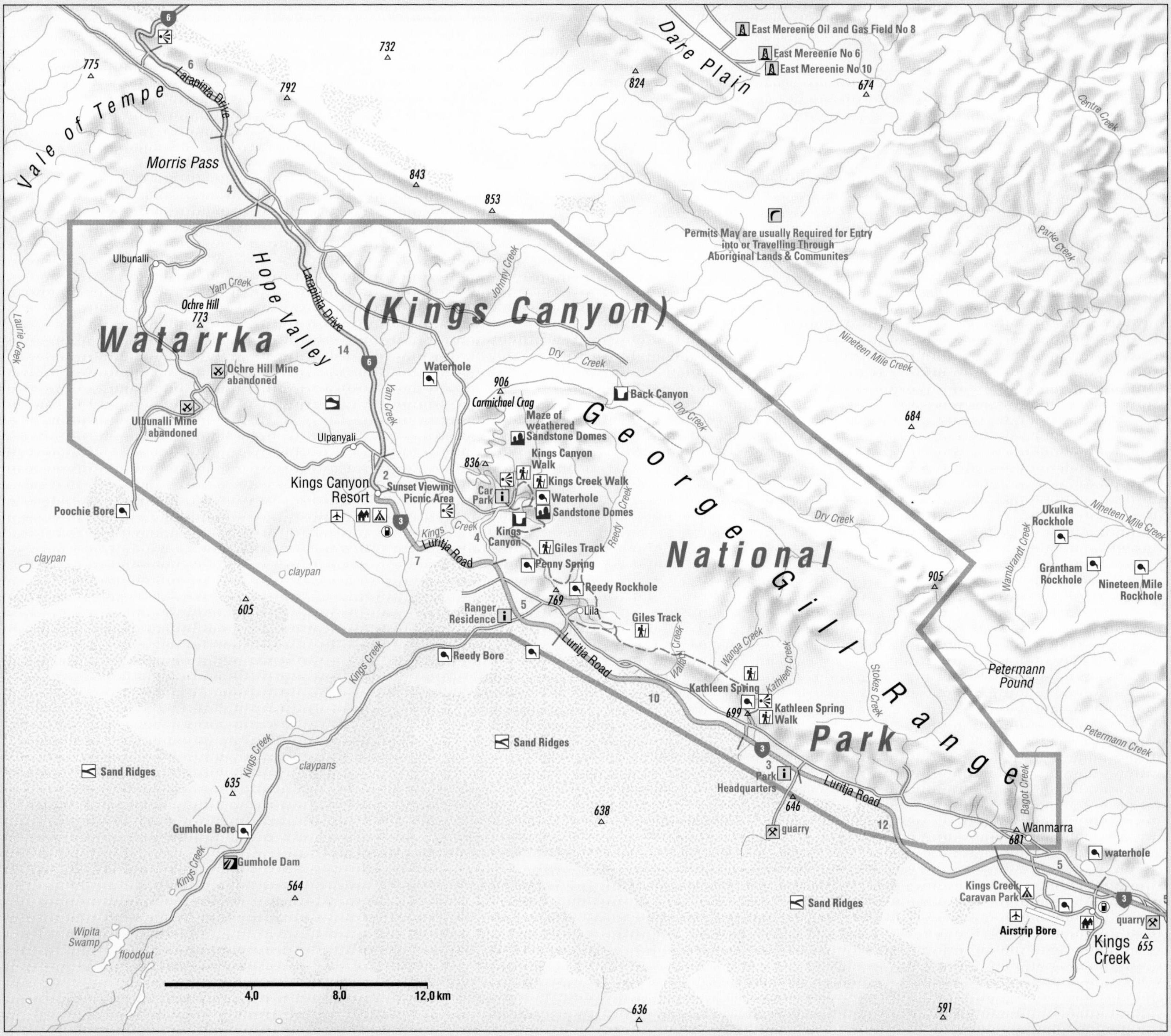

Watarrka (Kings Canyon) National Park
George Gill Range
Vale of Tempe
Hope Valley
Dare Plain
Morris Pass
Larapinta Drive
Luritja Road
East Mereenie Oil and Gas Field No 8
East Mereenie No 6
East Mereenie No 10
Permits May are usually Required for Entry into or Travelling Through Aboriginal Lands & Communites
Ulbunalli
Ochre Hill 773
Ochre Hill Mine abandoned
Ulbunalli Mine abandoned
Ulpanyali
Kings Canyon Resort
Sunset Viewing Picnic Area
Poochie Bore
Waterhole
Carmichael Crag
Back Canyon
Maze of weathered Sandstone Domes
Kings Canyon Walk
Kings Creek Walk
Car Park
Waterhole
Sandstone Domes
Kings Canyon
Giles Track
Penny Spring
Reedy Rockhole
Lila
Giles Track
Ranger Residence
Reedy Bore
Kathleen Spring
Kathleen Spring Walk
Sand Ridges
Park Headquarters
quarry
Wanmarra
waterhole
Kings Creek Caravan Park
Airstrip Bore
quarry
Kings Creek
Ukulka Rockhole
Grantham Rockhole
Nineteen Mile Rockhole
Petermann Pound
Gumhole Bore
Gumhole Dam
Wipita Swamp
floodout
claypan
claypans
Sand Ridges
Sand Ridges
4,0 8,0 12,0 km

Aborigines have been living on the Australian continent for around 50,000 years and over this long period they have adapted well to the harsh environment. They are great observers of nature and highly skilled trackers. Their culture is clan-based and does not value possessions. Central to their traditional beliefs is the

existence of spirit beings that lived on earth during the 'Dreamtime' or creation time. The numerous Aboriginal rock paintings and their styles of body painting are also related to 'Dreamtime' concepts.

drive vehicles. The main attraction of Finke Gorge National Park is Palm Valley, home to more than three thousand species of palm trees – all of them unique to this area – that line the picturesque watering holes.
The route then leads via Hermannsburg and Larapinta Drive to the turnoff for Namatjira Drive, which will take you further to the west.

9 West Macdonnell National Park The Tropic of Capricorn runs straight across these mountains to the west of Alice Springs, which rise to heights of 1,524 m (5,000 ft). The principal attractions of the park are the numerous gorges that lie on a fault line alongside Larapinta Drive and Namatjira Drive. The most spectacular one is near Alice Springs and is called Simpsons Gap. The Standley Chasm, with depths of up to 100 m (328 ft), only gets sunshine for twenty minutes in the middle of the day.
Ellery Creek Big Hole, Serpentine Gorge, Ormiston Gorge (giant blocks in Ormiston Pound) and Glen Helen Gorge are up to 133 km (83 miles) further down the road. The small lake at Serpentine Gorge is sacred to the Aborigines because the mythical giant water snake is meant to live there. The return route or continued drive to Alice Springs follows the same road.

10 Alice Springs The geographical centre of Australia is about 1,700 km (1,055 miles) north of Adelaide and 1,500 km (931 miles) south of Darwin.
Alice Springs was founded in 1872 and its main attractions are the carefully restored Old Telegraph Station (1872) and the Flying Doctors centre from which medical assistance has been organized to serve the outback since 1939. You can enjoy a magnificent view of the nearby Macdonnell Range from Anzac Hill. The famous Camel Cup takes place in July when up to fifteen dromedaries take part in a hard desert race. At the comical Henley-On-Todd regatta in springtime, 'oarsmen' race each other on foot in bottomless boats along the usually dry Todd River. North-east of the town is Trephina

Gorge National Park in the East Macdonnell Range. It can be reached via the paved Ross Highway. Eucalyptus trees grow alongside watering holes tucked between the steep walls of the gorge. A dirt track to the N'dhala Gorge Nature Park also branches off the Stuart Highway. Another track leads to Maryvale, the last outpost of civilization in the Simpson Desert. From there it is about 58 km (36 miles) to Chambers Pillar.
On the way to the Devils Marbles near Wauchope, the view to your right overlooks the Davenport Range, another (proposed) National Park. To the north of the West Macdonnell Range there are Aborigine reserves on both sides of Stuart Highway, for example the Pawu Aboriginal Land west of Barrow Creek. It was not until the 20th century that the lands were returned to the indigenous people.

11 Devils Marbles These eroded granite spheres look as if they

have been scattered across the rocky plateau with mathematical precision by a mightier power, and that the slightest breeze could blow them away. The Aborigines believe the spheres to be rainbow water snake eggs.

⓬ Tennant Creek When the last gold-rush began in Australia in 1932, Tennant Creek was known as 'Gold Town'. Within a few years, however, it became more of a ghost town. It was eventually reawakened by the discovery of silver and copper nearby. The Battery Hill Mining Centre recalls the short-lived gold bonanza. Some 11 km (7 miles) north-west of here are the Devils Pebbles, another scattering of granite boulders. A roadside memorial for John Flynn, the founder of the Flying Doctors, lies some 20 km (12 miles) in the same direction.

⓭ Renner Springs Further along the route towards Katherine, north of Helen Springs, the road takes you to Renner Springs. This small town marks both the climatic and geographical border between the outback of the 'Red Centre' and the savannah of the northern coastal areas.
Newcastle Waters to the north was once an important telegraph station and crossing point for livestock herds.

⓮ Daly Waters Still further north, it is definitely worth making a stop in Daly Waters, where the oldest pub in the Northern Territory has been wetting whistles since 1893. For decades, travellers have left various items here – from tickets for the legendary Ghan Express to autographed underwear. These are now all carefully arranged to decorate the walls of the pub. In this hot, dry environment, a cold beer here tastes even better than in other roadhouses along the highway.
The next stop is Larrimah with its historical train station. From there it's on to Mataranka where you should not miss out on a refreshing dip in Mataranka Pool in Elsey National Park roughly 9 km (5.5 miles) away. Accommodation is also available at the Mataranka Homestead Resort.
The thermal hotsprings are surrounded by paperbark trees, from which hang long strips of bark. The aborigines used this bark for thousands of years as wrapping for their food. From Mataranka it's now only 110 km (68 miles) to Katherine on the banks of the Katherine River, a river that never dries out.

⓯ Katherine This town offers limited attractions, but there is a nostalgic train station dating from 1926 and the first biplane *(continued p.66)*

1 As if the gods had tossed them: the Devils Marbles.

2 Bizarre rock formations in the West Macdonnell Range.

3 The desert lives, even on this red sand dune in the Northern Territory.

4 The most impressive way to view the cliffs of Katherine Gorge is on a boat trip down the Katherine River.

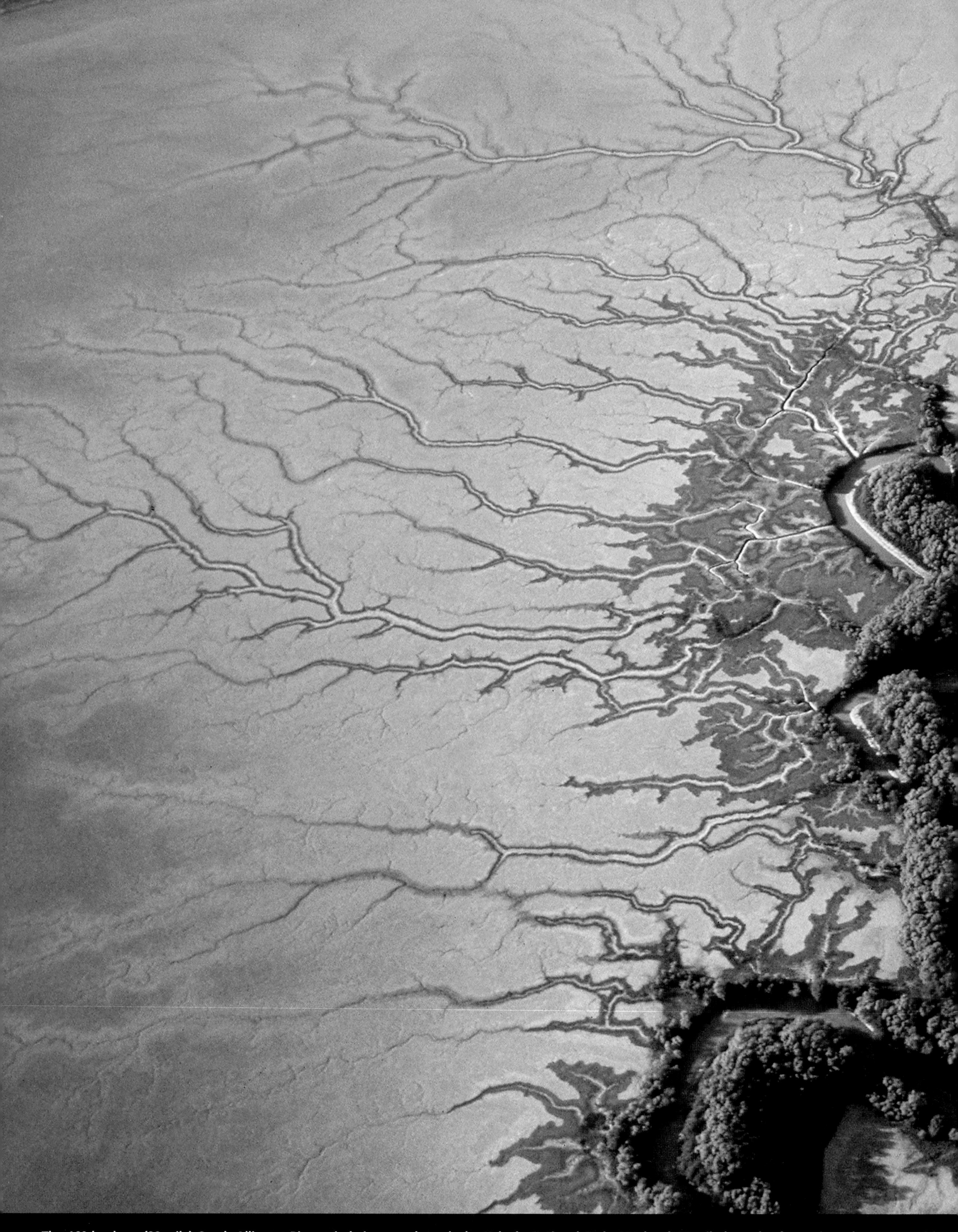

The 160-km-long (99-mile) South Alligator River winds its way through the Kakadu National Park, 250 km (155 miles) south of Darwin. It has an exquisite network of small adjoining streams and flows through rainforests, eucalypt forests, mangroves and swamps on its way to its estuary in the Timor Sea.

Saltwater crocodiles live in the river and often venture deep into the backcountry. Due to the unique nature of this wetland and the cultural heritage of the Aborigines who have lived here for 50,000 years, the park has been listed by UNESCO as a World Heritage Site.

Aborigines

When the European settlement of Australia began at the end of the 18th century, they saw the country as 'terra nullius' or unowned land, but at least 350,000 Aborigines (from the Latin 'ab origine', meaning from the origin or beginning) had lived on the continent for some 50,000 years. The Aborigines were organized in kinships, clans and tribes and roamed the continent as hunters and gatherers. They lived on the natural resources of the desert or the rainforest. Magic and totemism defined their belief system for thousands of years: mountains, cliffs, rivers, lakes and trees were – and still are – thought to possess a soul.

At the core of Aboriginal beliefs is the concept of 'Dreamtime', in which the past, present and future are all inextricably linked. In the beginning the world was a flat plate shrouded in darkness, until giant beings rose out of the barren earth to create light, water, clouds, rain and all life forms. When their work was done they transformed into mountains, rivers, lakes, trees and animals. The Aborigines believe that the entire natural world was given a soul by divine beings or spirits during Dreamtime, and this forms the basis of Aboriginal rites, customs and tradition, such as body-painting, songs and rock art. For more than fifty years, indigenous Australians have been fighting to regain ownership of their ancestral land and for social equality and acceptance.

One of the many X-ray-style rock drawings in Kakadu National Park.

1

2

3

used by the Flying Doctors is on exhibit here. Nature lovers in particular stop in Katherine because the Cutta Cutta Caves Nature Park is just 24 km (15 miles) away to the south-east. The stalactite and stalagmite formations in the caves are an important refuge for rare bats and tree snakes.

16 Nitmiluk National Park This impressive network of canyons formed over thousands of years by the Katherine River is one of the greatest natural wonders of Australia: Katherine Gorge. Red-brown limestone canyon walls rise up to 100 m (328 ft) above the river. The best way to view them is from a sightseeing boat that embarks in Katherine, or you can explore the river by canoe when it is not the rainy season. During the rainy season the otherwise calm river turns into a raging torrent and is not really navigable.

Biologists often marvel at Katherine Gorge for its unbelievable variety of wildlife: freshwater crocodiles live here along with more than 160 species of birds and numerous butterfly species. All in all, nine of the thirteen gorges in the park are open to visitors.

Edith Falls is a particularly spectacular natural phenomenon. You can reach the falls by either walking the rough 75-km (48-mile) track, or driving via the Stuart Highway. Smaller pools and waterfalls invite sun-weary visitors for a refreshing swim.

17 Pine Creek This town, 90 km (56 miles) north-west of Katherine, was once a hotspot for gold diggers. Today it's a supply station for those on their way to Darwin, or the starting point for excursions to Kakadu National Park to the east.

If you would like to visit that world-famous National Park, leave the Stuart Highway at Pine Creek and take the Kakadu Highway towards Jabiru. You'll find the park visitor centre there and can plan your trip.

18 Kakadu National Park Covering an area of 20,000 km^2 (7,800 square miles), this National Park in Arnhem Land is one of the largest and most attractive in Australia. The scenery shifts from the tidal zone at Van Diemen Gulf and the flood plains of the lowlands to the escarpment and the arid plateaux of Arnhem Land. The most impressive attraction is the escarpment, a craggy 500-km (310-mile) outcrop with spectacular waterfalls such as the Jim Jim Falls and Twin Falls, which are at their best towards the end of the rainy season. The name of the park comes from 'Gagudju', which is the name of an Aboriginal language originating in this flood plain region.

Biologists have counted 1,300 plant, 10,000 insect, 240 bird and 70 reptile species, including the feared saltwater crocodile. The rare mountain kangaroos, wallabies and one-third of the country's bird species are also native to this area. Due to its diversity, this impressive park has been made into a UNESCO World Heritage Site.

There are more than five thousand Aborigine rock paintings here, the most famous of which are on Nourlangie Rock, Ubirr Rock and at Nanguluwur. The

paintings, some of which date back as many as 18,000–23,000 years, not only demonstrate the area's climate change, but are also a striking portrayal of the culture of the Aborigines, who have allegedly lived on the continent here for 50,000 years. The best time of year to visit the park is in the dry season from May to November, as the roads may be otherwise impassable.

The Arnhem Highway leads back through Cooinda and Jabiru to the Stuart Highway. From Noonamah the road leads south before heading west through Batchelor into Litchfield National Park.

⓳ **Litchfield National Park** The main attractions of this park are immediately visible: the open eucalypt forests, the thick rainforest around the escarpment, and the massive, masterfully crafted gravestone-like mounds of the magnetic termites, which can reach heights of 2 m (6½ ft). Due to the extreme midday heat the termites have cleverly aligned the long side of their mounds with the north–south axis in order to warm their homes in the morning and evening sun while protecting them from the midday sun.
The Tabletop Range escarpment is a spectacular sight where waterfalls like Sandy Creek Falls, Florence Falls, Tolmer Falls and Wangi Falls cascade down the ridge even in the dry season. The unique environment around the falls has developed its own unique spectrum of monsoon rainforest wildlife.

⓴ **Darwin** Due to its proximity to the South-east Asian countries to the north of Australia, Darwin has developed into a culturally very diverse city, which is reflected in its numerous markets and restaurants. One of the specialities here is the slightly odd, daily Aquascene Fish Feeding at Doctor's Gully. At high tide various fish swim inland to be fed by hand from humans. Wonderful white sand beaches can be found on the shores of Beagle Gulf.
Since the destruction caused by Cyclone Tracy during Christmas of 1974, the city of Darwin has changed dramatically. After the storm, almost nothing was left of the historical 19th-century buildings apart from the Old Navy Headquarters, Fannie Bay Gaol, the Court House, Brown's Mart and the Government House with its seven gables. Your journey across the mighty outback ends here, on the coast at the doorstep to Asia.

1 The Arnhem Land Plateau escarpment located in Kakadu National Park.

2 Magnetic termite mounds, bizarre yet clever constructions in Litchfield National Park.

3 Wangi Falls are one of many waterfalls on the edge of the Tabletop Range plateau.

4 Kakadu National Park: The falls cascade into the depths along the 500-km (310-mile) edge of the escarpment.

The wildlife of Kakadu National Park

The National Park is home to a range of wildlife. Ornithologists have recorded no fewer than 250 species of birds, including storks, ibis, herons, kingfishers, darters, brolgas, cormorants, cockatoos and sea-eagles. Of the seventy species of reptile found here, the saltwater crocodile is the most distinctive. There are also around fifty species of mammal in the park, with kangaroos forming the largest group, including the antilopine wallaroo, the shy black wallaroo and the nabarlek.

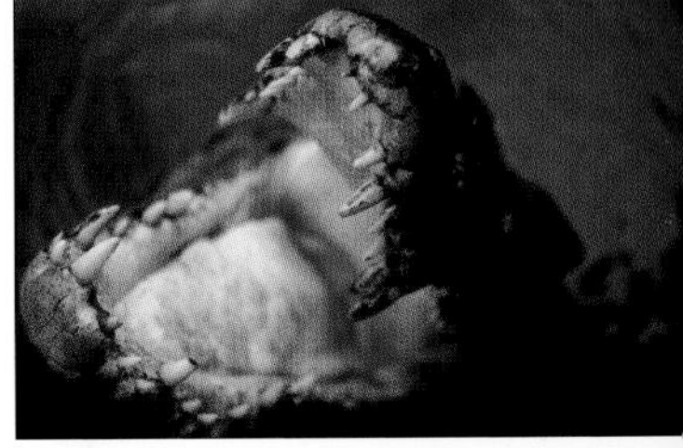

**Top: The sand goanna is a type of monitor lizard and is widespread in northern Australia.
Centre: 'Snappy' the saltwater crocodile once again living up to its name.
Bottom: The jaribu is the only stork native to Australia.**

5,0
10,0
15,0
20,0 km
Van Diemen Gulf
(Timor Sea)
Gardangarl
(Field Island)
Kakadu National Park
Gularri
(Point Farewell)
East Alligator River
Cooper Lagoon
Cooper Lagoon Landing Strip
Cairncurry Plain
Cunningham Channel
Waldak Irrmbal
(West Alligator Head)
Djidbordu
(Barron Island)
Midnight Point
White Lily Waterhole
Carrew Spring
White Lily Creek
Pococks Beach
Waldak Irrbal Camping
Point Stuart
Mary River National Park
Finke Bay
Swim Creek Plain
Gunburdel
Killuppa Spring
Yagada Yagada
(Flying Fox Island)
Mamurdi
Arndolk
Imagirrk
South Alligator River
Balayangardi
(Bellyungardy Spring)
Djidjidjidji
(Didygeegee Swamp)
Mayambanjdju
(Mount Hooper)
Culaly Plain
Ngardama Goyida
(Myaranjie Spring)
Cobabby Waterhole
Oenpelli Aerodrome
Manjdjalanjarrk
(Unawanllurk Billabong)
Cannon Hill
Manngarre Monsoon Trail
Ranger 49 Mine
(Uranium Mine)
Carmor Plain
Wildman River
Manassie Floodplain
Numerous Pools
Point Stuart Road
Love Creek
Thrings Creek
Rrimil
(Ramil Waterhole)
Marnanj Tower (115m)
Red Lily Lagoon
Ubirr Aboriginal Rock Art
Ubirr
Boat Ramp
Merl Camping
Kakadu Hostel
East Alligator Ranger Station
Ironstone Billabong
Palm Swamp
Coobanbora Spring
Marnanj
(Magela Plain)
Four Wheel Drive
Mary River National Park
Bukardi
Bardedjilidji Trail
One Horse Creek Swamp
Munmarlary Landing Strip
Jabiluka Mineral Lease
Balkanini Hill
Munmarlary
(Manmalarri)
Garden Springs
Burrud
(Barote Spring)
Kakadu
Galijigu Spring
Nanjbagu
(Boggy Plain)
North Ranger Mine
Kapalga Landing Strip
Four Mile Hole
Big Swamp
Coolaboo Waterhole
Waterholes
Uralugoorwa Waterhole
Mundginberri Landing Strip
Gurndurrk
(Corndorl Waterhole)
Gabarlga Ruin
Nembargoo Waterhole
Cubbarnby Spring
Twin Sisters Lagoons
Cole Spring
Biku Spring
Man Giririr
(Mungeno Waterhole)
Ranger 37 Mine
Hunters Camping
Jabiru East Airport
Coonjimba Billabong
South Alligator River Boat Ramp
Arnhem Highway
Aurora Kakadu Resort
Mamukala Wetlands
Observatory Building
Bowali Visitor Centre & Park Headquarters
Kakadu Lodge
Jabiru
Aurora Kakadu Camping
Ranger 13 Mine
Gagudju Crocodile Hotel
Ranger Uranium Mine
West Wildman River Waterholes
Two Mile Hole
Gungarre Trail
Jarrahwingkoombarngy Swamp
Jabiru Shopping Center
Jabiru Golf Course
Naramu Camp
Kakadu Ranger Station
(Emergency Information)
Fishless Billabong
Arnhem Highway Scenicroad
Tower (62m)
Chirracarwoo Lagoons
Malabanbanjdju Camping
Kakadu Highway Scenicroad
Mount Brockman
Baroalba Waterhole
Gulungul
(Radon Spring)
Nourlangie (Anlarrh) Landing Strip
Iligadjarr Trail
Burdulba Camping
Quarry Mine
Northern Entrance
Northern Park Entrance Station
Baroalba Landing Strip
Gubara Pools Trail
Ngarrababa
(Bucket Billabong)
Djunda (Red Lily Billabong)
Nourlangie Aboriginal Rock Art
Arnherm Highway Scenicroad
East Wildman River Waterholes
Gurdurunguranjdju
(Alligator Billabong)
Yellow Water Boat Ramp
Warradjan Aboriginal Cultural Center
Muirella Park
Landing Strip
Nourlangie Rock
Koongarra Mineral Lease
Cooinda Camping
Cooinda
Mount Cahill
Mirrai Lookout
Anbangbang Gallery
Mt. Bundey Landing Strip
Old Jim Jim Road
Cooinda Landing Strip
Gagudju Cooinda Lodge
Jim Jim Ranger Station
Sandy Billabong
Pinnacle
Nourlangie Creek Waterholes
Namarrgon Falls
Namarrgon Gorge
Mardugal Camping
Paradise Farm
Jim Jim Billabong
Spring Peak
Mount Bundey Training Area
(Prohibited Area)
due to seasonal flooding
Black Jungle Range
(Gunbumbuk)
Gunkumulu Waterholes
Jim Jim Road
Gulurruyu Waterholes
Mount Basedow
Nourlangie Creek Waterhole
Deaf Adder Outstation
Table Top
Kakadu Highway Scenicroad
Anbalawala Waterholes
Giyamungkurr
(Black Jungle Spring)
Giyamungkurr
(Black Jungle Camping)
Kunkamoula Billabong
(Gunkumulu)
Mundogie Hill
Required Waterhole
Deaf Adder Gorge
Mount Partridge
Deaf Adder Waterholes
Dird Djahdjom
Kaduke Waterhole
Djuwarr Falls
Mary River National Park
National
Goodparla Creek Waterholes
Barramundie Lagoon
Waterholes
Nourlangie Falls
Garnamarr Camping
Gonbolok
Graveside Waterholes
Numerous Rocky Outcrops
Buffalo Creek Waterholes
Long Billabong
Barramundie Waterhole
Jim Jim Falls Camping
Abandoned Iron Mine
Graveside Tower
Abandoned Tin Mine
Shovel Billabong
Jim Jim Falls
(Barrkmalam)
Jim Jim Waterholes
Gungurul Lookout
Maguk Camping
Graveside Gorge
Abandoned Tin Mine
Numerous Rocky Outcrops
Arnhem Land Plateau
Goodparla Landing Strip
South Alligator River Waterhole
Ankarrkarrkarrini
Maguk
(Barramundie Gorge)
(dry season only)
Gungkurdu
(Twin Falls)
(Access to Falls by boat shuttle only)
Djadjora
Inbarlin Hills
Mt. George
Abandoned Gold Mine
Gurrwirluk
Yinangankarrh
Numerous Rocky Outcrops
Park
Gunlom Falls
Numerous Rocky Outcrops
West Bekluk Creek Waterhole
East Bekluk Creek Waterholes
Mary River Waterholes
Kakadu Highway Scenicroad
Gunlom
(Waterfall Creek)
Jarrangbammi
(Koolpin Gorge)
Bekluk

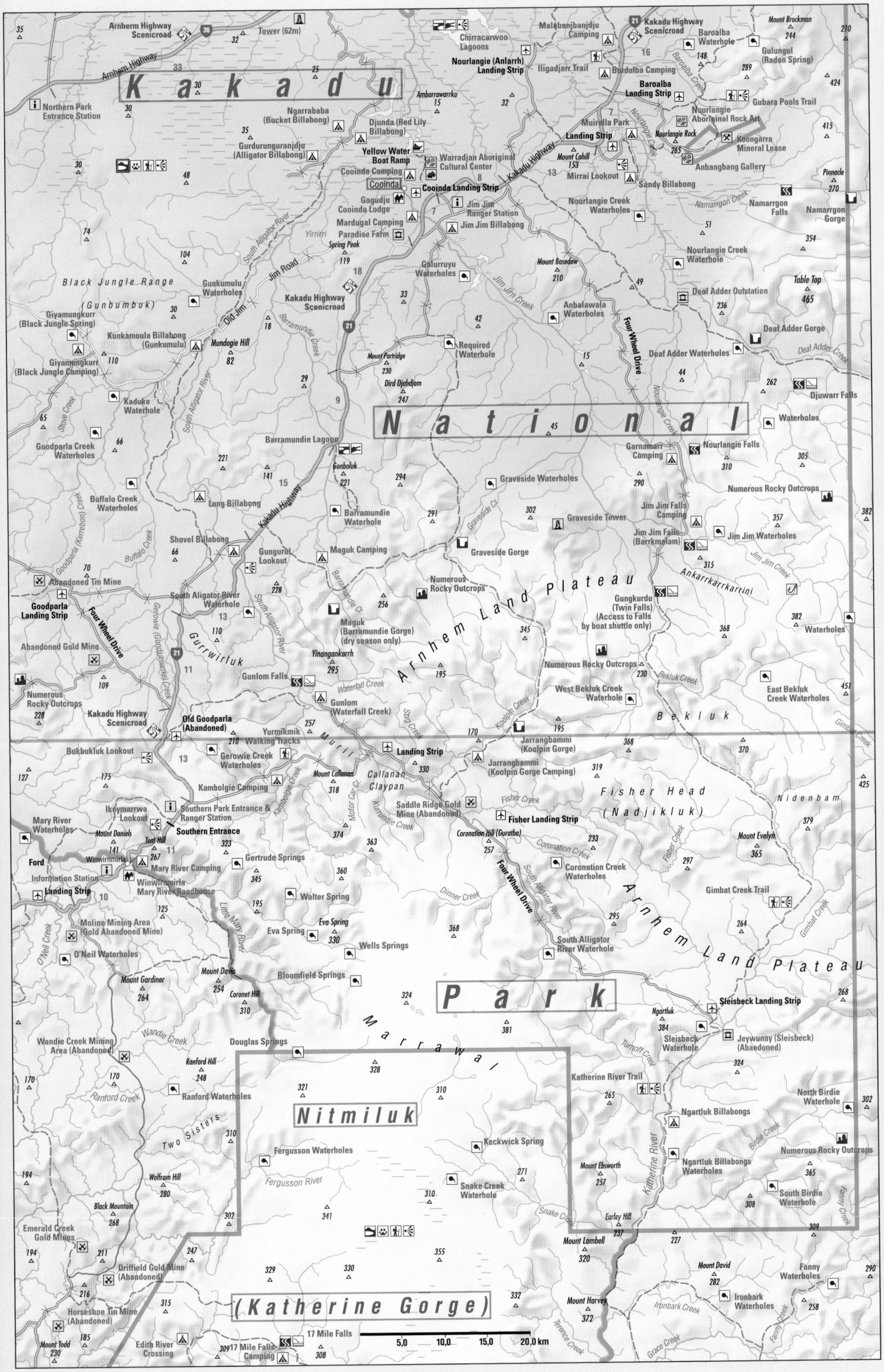

Kakadu National Park

Located 200 km (124 miles) south-east of Darwin, Kakadu National Park is a natural paradise. Most visitors head to the park for its diverse and spectacular wildlife, but the changing landscape, variety of habitats and important Aboriginal rock-art sites are also well worth a visit.

For a first taste of the local flora and fauna and Aboriginal culture, visit the Bowali Visitor Centre in Jabiru, the only sizeable settlement in the park, and the Warradjan Aboriginal Cultural Centre near Yellow Water. A boat trip in the Yellow Water Wetlands to spot crocodiles and various birds is a must.

The natural pathways offer an alternative way to explore the park. On the Yurmikmik or Bardedjilidji walks, and other bush trails, you can learn much about the wide range of local flora, including eucalyptus trees, paperbarks, screw palms, lotus plants, water lilies and spinifex. You will come across spectacular waterfalls and billabongs (pools), rock formations and caves. Other places worth a visit are the Gunlom Billabong with its own lovely waterfall and rock formations, the Maguk rainforest and waterfall, the Anbangbang Billabong or the Jim Jim Falls and Twin Falls.

You will see some wonderful X-ray-style Aboriginal rock art at Ubirr Rock and Nourlangie Rock. In fact, the park's name does not come from the bird (which has Malayan origins) but from a mispronunciation (as 'kakadu') of the word 'gagudju', a local Aboriginal language.

The Kakadu National Park is paradise for nature-lovers. It has everything from flood plains to rocky highlands.

Kings Canyon Aboriginal rock paintings line the steep walls of this spectacular canyon.

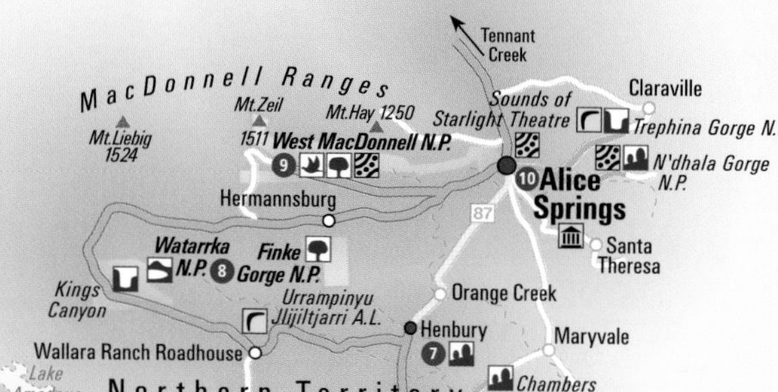

Finke Gorge National Park In this park, 12 km (7½ miles) south of Hermannsburg, you will find the beautiful Palm Valley. Thanks to the tropical climate, many rare palm trees grow here, some as high as 25 m (82 ft).

Kata Tjuta The name means 'many heads' in the Aboriginal language. This group of thirty-six rock monoliths in the middle of the steppe in central Australia is also known as The Olgas.

Chambers Pillar Various tracks lead to the 56 m (184 ft) high reddish-yellow sandstone rock south-east of Henbury. The pillars were used as an orientation point by early colonists who had gone astray in the desert.

Uluru Like a beached whale, the 348 m wide (1,142 ft) outcrop, called Ayers Rock by Europeans, emerges stoically from the red outback landscape. A mythical and sacred site for Aborigines, Uluru is an essential element in the divine acts of the ancestors who created life on earth.

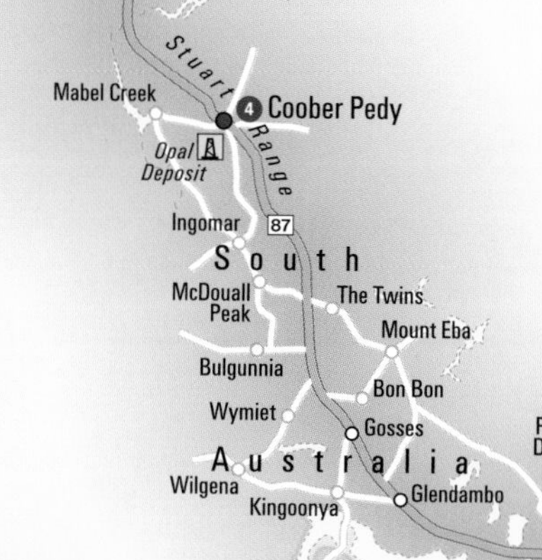

Flinders Ranges This 400-km (248-mile) range begins north of Clare Valley and passes between Lake Torrens and Lake Frome. The National Park extends deep into the outback and includes the famous Wilpena Pound.

Coober Pedy Opals have been mined at the foot of the Stuart Range since 1915. Nearly seventy per cent of the world's opals are mined here. Many people live in underground dwellings owing to temperatures above 50°C.

Dreamtrack For Aborigines, Australia's landscape is filled with traces of the creators. Songs and dances tell the complex stories of the creators and how the giants became the contours of the land.

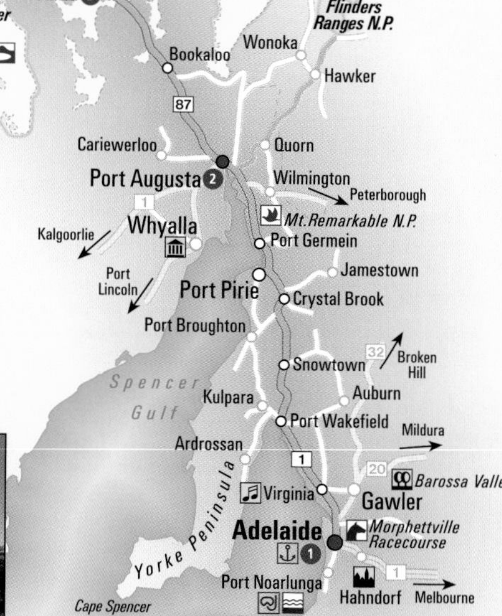

Adelaide The capital of South Australia was founded in 1836 between the beaches of Gulf St Vincent and the Mount Lofty Range. It was named after Queen Adelaide.

Barossa This is the collective name for Barossa Valley and Eden Valley, the best wine-growing region in Australia originally settled by Germans in the mid 19th century.

Fleurieu Peninsula This headland to the south of Adelaide boasts a series of beautiful beaches, bays and ports. Divers and snorkellers enjoy Port Noarlunga on the western coast, and surfers head for the high breakers on Waitpinga Beach on the southern side.

Darwin The port on the northern edge of the 'Top End' benefits from a subtropical climate. The few historical buildings include the Old Navy Headquarters, Fannie Bay Gaol and Brown's Mart.

Wangi Falls These waterfalls in Litchfield National Park crash spectacularly into the depths. It is safe to bathe in the pool.

Litchfield National Park This park is known for its magnetic termite mounds, which are cleverly designed to take advantage of the sunshine.

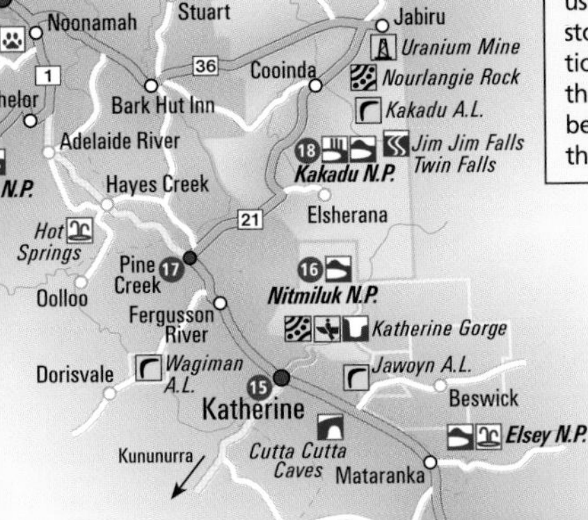

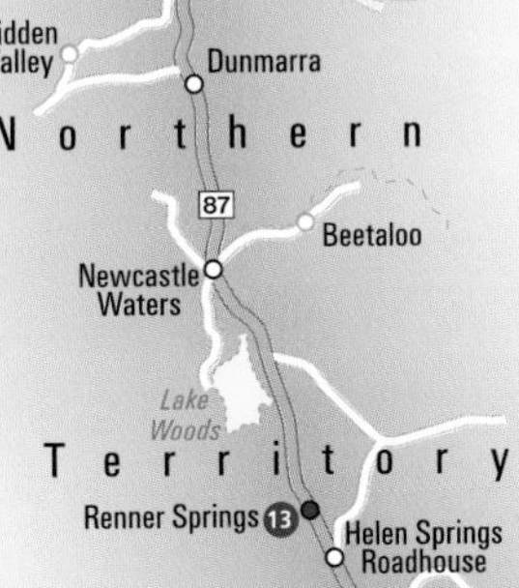

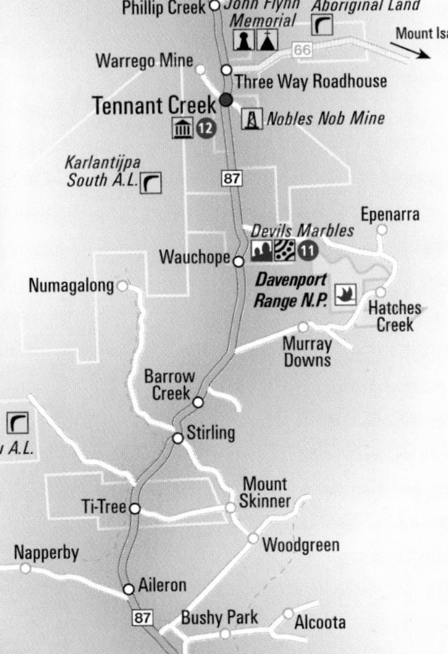

Aboriginal rock art Rock carvings, rock and cave paintings, drawings of animals, sand designs, totem poles, carvings and wickerwork are all part of traditional Aborigine culture. The designs that feature in their stone paintings were applied using ochre, charcoal and limestone and symbolize the relationship between humans and the environment, which are believed to mythically coexist in the 'Dreamtime'.

Nourlangie Rock The Aborigine rock paintings at Nourlangie Rock in the Kakadu National Park are examples of the so-called 'X-ray style'.

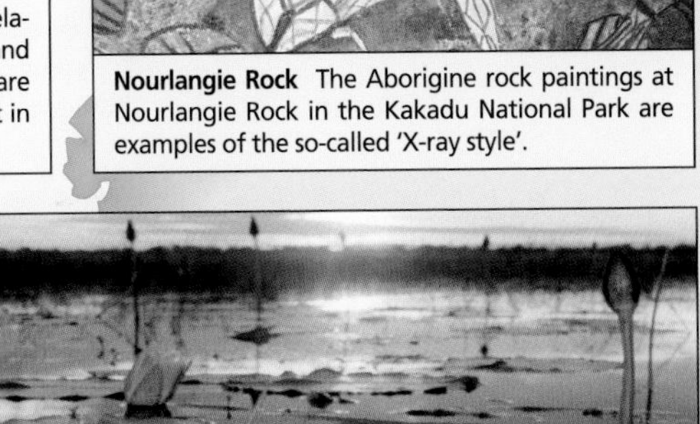

Kakadu National Park Stone plateaux, waterfalls, flood plains and the South Alligator River characterize this park's landscape, one of Australia's best-known attractions in the 'Top End'.

Cutta Cutta Caves Nature Park Rare bat species live alongside equally rare snakes in limestone caves 25 km (15 miles) south-east of Katherine, a jumping-off point for the park.

John Flynn Memorial This memorial, located 20 km (12 miles) north of Tennant Creek, is dedicated to John Flynn (1880–1951), founder of the Flying Doctors back in 1939. The service was the most effective way to provide medical assistance to people in the outback.

Nitmiluk National Park Some of the highlights of this park are the rivers and ravines of Katherine Gorge, which reach depths of 100 m (328 ft).

Tennant Creek The second-largest town on the Stuart Highway was once a telegraph post on the Overland Telegraph Line. In 1932 gold was found here.

Devils Marbles The red granite boulders near Wauchope are 170 million years old and were formed by a process of erosion and severe changes in temperature.

Pawu Aboriginal Land The 2,500 km² (975 square miles) around Mount Barkly, west of Barrow Creek and south of Willowra, was returned to the Aborigines in 1981, sixty-one years after they were driven off the land by European settlers.

Davenport Range National Park Waterfowl and giant red kangaroos have found refuge in the mountains and steppes of this park.

West Macdonnell Ranges The highest peak in this craggy mountain range to the east and west of Alice Springs is Mount Liebig, at 1,524 m (5,000 ft).

Alice Springs 'Alice' is the heart of the 'Red Centre', 1,700 km (1,055 miles) from Adelaide and 1,500 km (931 miles) from Darwin.

Trephina Gorge National Park This park in the East Macdonnell Range is famous for its quartz cliffs and the eucalyptus stands that box in the Trephina Gorge watering holes.

Route 3

Australia

Bruce Highway – from the Sunshine Coast to the Great Barrier Reef

The stunning Pacific coastline of Queensland, Australia's 'Sunshine State', offers some of the country's most splendid scenery. It has it all: endless sandy beaches for those who enjoy relaxing in the sun, the magnificent Great Barrier Reef, a paradise for water sports enthusiasts, and tropical rainforests rich in natural diversity and unspoiled wilderness. Brisbane and Cairns lie at the heart of the region, connected by the Bruce Highway.

More than half of all overseas visitors to Australia come to Queensland, the second largest Australian state boasting a coastline of almost 10,000 km (6,214 miles). The Great Barrier Reef lies offshore, embracing some 2,500 individual coral reefs and stretching for over 2,600 km (1,616 miles) along the east coast of Australia. This extraordinary, unbelievably colourful underwater paradise is hard to beat. The reef has been a designated UNESCO Natural World Heritage Site since 1981. More than 400 species of coral and 1,500 species of fish inhabit the reef, along with some 4,000 species of mollusc and 800 echinoderms, such as sea cucumbers. However, like so many other natural wonders, the Great Barrier Reef is under increasing threat from pollution and global change.

Queensland is on the boundary between the subtropics and the tropics. In the north of the state, the south-eastern trade winds bring rain to the slopes of the Great Dividing Range, which runs parallel to the

Coral rock on the Great Barrier Reef.

coastline. Giant trees reach heights of 50 m (164 ft) in this warm, humid climate. The tropical mountain and coastal rainforests provide a wonderful habitat for rare ancient palm ferns, such as the tree fern or Royal Fern, and some of the more unusual members of the animal kingdom, including the duck-billed platypus.

The subtropical rainforests of Queensland are among the oldest on earth, the relics of the primeval forests that covered the southern supercontinent Gondwana some 100 million years ago. Their isolated location made them a haven for animal and plant species that have survived for millennia and are unique to this spot. You won't find them anywhere else on earth.

The English explorer Captain James Cook also left his mark on the coast of Queensland. Several places bear his name, and a number of settlements are associated with

Whitehaven Beach, on the south-east coast of the Whitsunday Islands, boasts the longest sandy beach in the group.

The Great Barrier Reef is one of the greatest natural wonders of the world. Its marine ecosystem is home to the largest diversity of species on the planet and covers an area of approximately 350,000 km^2 (135,136 square miles). The photo shows the heart-shaped Green Island to the north-east of Cairns.

incidents from his travel journals. As in New South Wales, settlement in Queensland began with the deportation of British convicts. The spot where today you can admire Brisbane's modern skyline, set against a brilliant blue sky, marks the place where the first convicts came ashore in chains in 1824. A succession of settlers hungry for land and adventure soon followed and it was soon apparent that Queensland was a fertile area, rich in mineral resources. Gold-seekers poured into the unexplored 'Far North', venturing into the tropical wilderness of the interior, penetrating regions far beyond those accessed by Captain Cook in 1770 when his ship ran aground and he was forced ashore on the banks of the Endeavour River, not far from present-day Cooktown. Some of the buildings here still bear traces of the gold fever of pioneering days.

Most of Queensland's cities are located along the Pacific coastline but Cairns, the 'Boomtown' of the north, is the starting point for trips to the northern part of the reef and for one of the most exciting adventures in the area – a journey to the isolated Cape York Peninsula. However, Queensland's true heart still beats in the south, in the capital, Brisbane, the most populous city in the state.

With the western highlands and dramatic peaks of the Great Dividing Range on the one side and the Pacific coast on the other, the Bruce Highway is the main route through the coastal plains. It connects Brisbane and Cairns with the many little ports along the Pacific coast and takes you to some of the most stunning sections of coastline and to the National Parks, home to a vast range of plant and animal species.

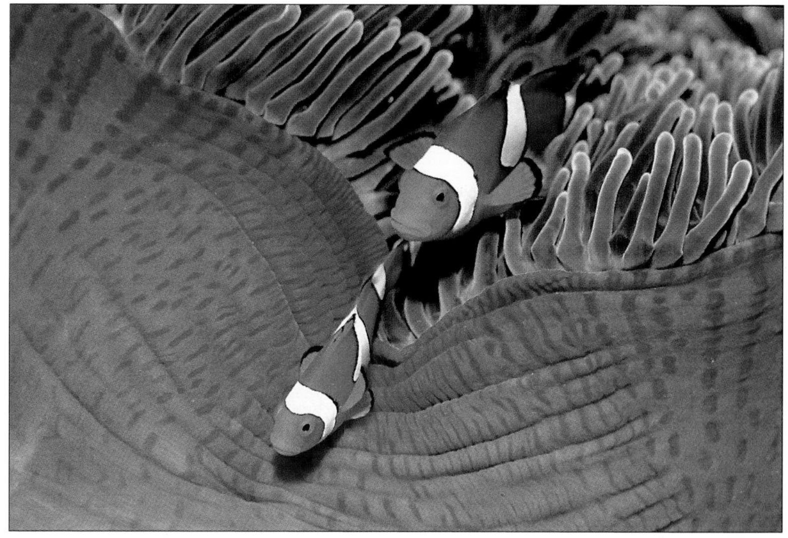

Anemone fish are among the species that inhabit the underwater world of the Great Barrier Reef.

Detour

Moreton Island

Ferries leave from Brisbane (Howard Smith Drive), Whyte Island and Scarborough for the best-known of the islands in Moreton Bay. In 1824, Moreton Island was the site of the first British penal colony in Queensland. The shell mounds ('middens') found here date back to the period when the island was inhabited by Aborigines, and are thought to indicate the location of sites of worship or sacrifice.
Large sections of Moreton Island are designated as a National Park – 17,000 ha (42,000 acres) in total – because of the wonderful diversity of plants and animals for which it provides a habitat. The island has fantastic sandy beaches with dunes,

Top: Moreton Island off the coast of Brisbane.
Bottom: The Australian pelican has a wingspan of up to 340 cm (134 in).

heath land and a huge variety of birdlife and is famous for its dolphins, which visitors can watch from the beach. Sea turtles come here from November to February to lay their eggs, and humpback whales pass the northern tip of the island. Mount Tempest is the highest sand dune on the island, rising to a mighty 285 m (935 ft) above sea level. The Blue Lagoon is the largest of the island's lakes. There are three small settlements on the sheltered western side, while the eastern side remains uninhabited. There are no proper roads on the island so it is advisable to use a four-wheel drive to get around. One of the island's landmarks is the Cape Moreton Lighthouse, situated at the north-easterly end of the island. Standing 23 m (75 ft) tall, it dates back to 1857.

1

The Bruce Highway is Queensland's main traffic artery, running parallel to the coast for most of its length. It is perfect for quick detours into the rainforests of the Great Dividing Range and the stunning beaches and offshore islands along the coast. It is not a dual carriageway for the entire route.

1 Brisbane (See also pages 76–77.) 'Brissie', as Queenslanders affectionately call their capital, is located on the Brisbane River and is home to 1½ million people. Atmospheric and stylish, it has a pleasant subtropical climate. It is Australia's third largest city and dates back to 1824, when a penal colony was established on the present site. The first non-convict settlers began to arrive in 1842, following the lead of farmers who had already established farms in the fertile hinterland. Today, the city's skyline is punctuated by glittering glass and chrome skyscrapers. You can enjoy the elegant shops of Queen Street Mall, dine in one of the many chic restaurants or absorb a spot of culture in some of the excellent museums and galleries.
Brisbane is Queensland's most important commercial hub and its gateway to the Sunshine Coast, just a short journey to the north on the Bruce Highway (Hwy. 1). South of Brisbane, the coastal section begins at Moreton Bay, whose three hundred islands, conveniently located on the city's doorstep, are popular destinations.

2 Glass House Mountains Just beyond the small town of Caboolture and to the west of the Bruce Highway are the extraordinary Glass House Mountains. A group of sixteen mighty volcanic columns of trachytic rock rises abruptly out of the sugar plantations that spread over the coastal plain. Eight of the mountains enjoy protected status in the National Park of the same name. In 1770, Captain James Cook spotted the dramatic rock formations from the sea and gave them the name they still bear today. The Forest Drive begins in Beerburrum and makes its way between mountains rising to 364–555 m (1,194–1,821 ft) over a distance of 22 km (14 miles).
Highway 1 continues to the north along the Sunshine Coast. Over the past thirty years, this stretch of coast between Caloundra and Noosa Heads has developed into a key tourist region. The bleached white silica sand beaches are much less busy than those of the Gold Coast to the south of Brisbane. From Noosa Heads it is just 150 km (93 miles) to Maryborough, known as 'Queensland's Heritage City' because of its impressive villas and typical 19th-century architecture. From Maryborough you can take the road to Hervey Bay.

3 Hervey Bay This is a wonderful place for a spot of whale-watching. Between August and

Travel information

Route profile
Length: approx. 2,100 km/ 1,305 miles (excluding detours)
Time needed: min. 2 weeks
Start: Brisbane
End: Cooktown
Itinerary (main locations): Brisbane, Hervey Bay, Rockhampton, Mackay, Whitsunday Islands, Great Barrier Reef Marine Park, Townsville, Cairns, Cooktown

Traffic information
Cars drive on the left in Australia. Traffic regulations may differ from state to state. The maximum speed limit in built-up areas is 50 km/h (31 mph) and outside built-up areas is 100 km/h (62 mph). A four-wheel drive vehicle suitable for off-road terrain is strongly recommended on this route. Some of the attractions are off the beaten track, and only four-wheel drives are allowed on the unmade roads on Fraser Island and the last section of the tour from Cape Tribulation to Cooktown.

Information
www.australia.com
Queensland:
www.queenslandholidays.com.au

Weather information
www.ourbrisbane.com

2

early November, humpback whales make a stopover in the waters of Hervey Bay on their annual migration to Antarctica. A Whale Festival officially opens the season in August. Boat trips depart from Urangan Harbour. Hervey Bay is also the perfect starting point for trips to Fraser Island, just a few minutes by boat from the coast.

4 Fraser Island The world's largest sand island measures some 120 km (75 miles) from north to south and up to 25 km (16 miles) across. The island is a paradise of lush, dense forest, bizarre sandstone formations, lakes and sand dunes, known locally as 'sandblows', that tower up to 250 m (820 ft) above sea level. The dunes were formed some 140,000 years ago, when rain washed rock debris from the Great Dividing Range into the ocean. Currents and winds caused the debris to accumulate on rocky outcrops, the drifted sand formed dunes, the wind and birds brought plant life, and gradually the dune system was stabilized by prolific plant *(continued p.80)*

1 A view across the Brisbane River of downtown Brisbane. The city centre sits on a bend in the river, which is spanned by a total of seven bridges.

2 Covering an area of 172,000 ha (425,021 acres), Fraser Island, with its impressive dunes, is the largest sand island in the world. Since 1993, it has been listed as a UNESCO Natural World Heritage Site.

The dingo

Dingoes were not originally native to Australia. These wild dogs came to the continent only around 8,000 years ago and now inhabit the sparse woodland and the areas between the eucalypt forests and grassland, avoiding open terrain as much as possible.

A dingo, Australia's wild dog.

They are active both day and night; most cattle farmers tolerate them because they hunt the cattle's main rivals for food (wild rabbits, goats and pigs). Sheep farmers, on the other hand, hate dingoes because they occasionally attack sheep. The longest fence in the world – the Dingo Fence – stretches from the coast of southern Australia to beyond northern Queensland and was erected in an attempt to protect flocks of sheep from Australia's largest predator.

The Brisbane River is the lifeline of Queensland's capital. Story Bridge (top) is one of the seven bridges that cross the river; built between 1934 and 1940, the steel bridge is 1.3 km (¾ mile) long. Above the river, towers of steel, concrete and glass define the city's imposing skyline.

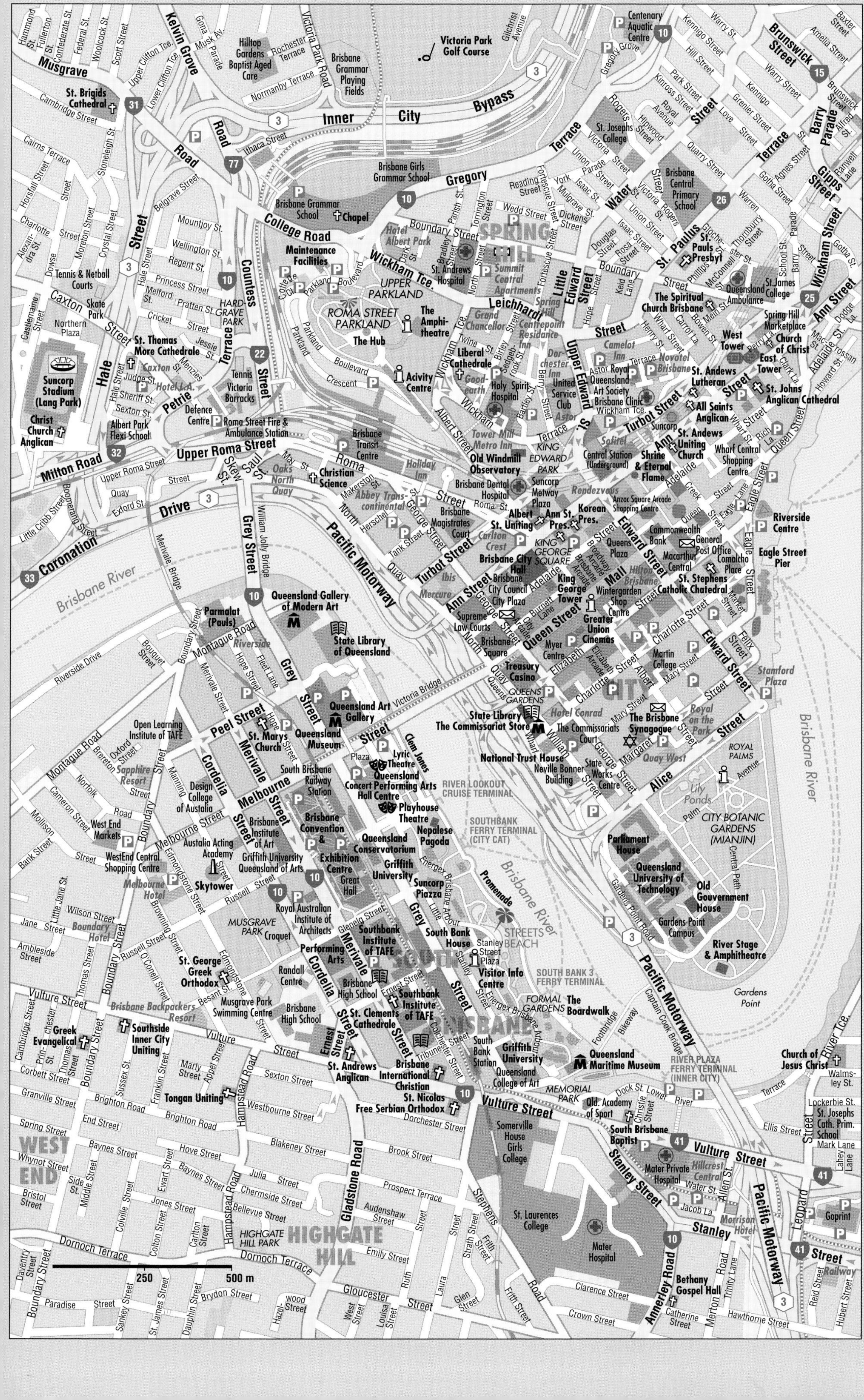

Brisbane

'Brissie' boasts an annual quota of 300 days of sunshine. 'Summer in the city' lasts almost all year in Brisbane, as the characteristically laid-back lifestyle of its 1½ million inhabitants certainly reflects.

Right in the centre of Queensland's capital city, Brisbanites can enjoy a relaxing swim in their local watery paradise and sunbathe on Streets Beach, along the banks of the Brisbane River. The open-air cafés and restaurants, large and small theatres, and the weekend market for local arts and crafts are just some of the attractions of the South Bank Parklands. At no distance at all down the road you can get your first taste of a tropical rainforest in the Gondwana Rainforest Sanctuary. Another absolute must on the South Bank is the Queensland Cultural Centre. The Art Gallery exhibits European and Australian art, while the Queensland Museum tells you all you need to know about the state's history and its flora and fauna.

On the opposite bank of the Brisbane River is the Botanic Garden, which dates back to 1828 and is the oldest public park in Queensland. Just a few minutes away is the shoppers' paradise, Queen Street Mall, complete with 200 shops, cafés, restaurants and the Myer Centre shopping arcade. The General Post Office is a Victorian gem dating back to 1871. The towering St Stephens Cathedral, built in 1874, is nearby. King George Square is dominated by City Hall, a building in neoclassical style offering excellent views of the city and river from its impressive tower, 91 m (299 ft) high. Brisbane's oldest surviving building, the Windmill, built in 1828, is located in nearby Wickham Park.

St Stephens Cathedral with a skyscraper in the background.

For a taste of politics in the city, head to the south-western edge of the Botanic Garden; here you will find the Old Government House, once the residence of the Governor of Queensland, and the Parliament House, dating back to 1868. In the Treasury, formerly the Finance Ministry, the one-armed bandits and gaming tables of the Conrad Treasury Casino have taken over from civil servants the task of emptying pockets.

A Gould's monitor lies in wait for its prey on a paperbark tree. The reptile grows up to 1.5 m (5 ft) long and eats insects, lizards, frogs, small mammals, birds and, occasionally, its own young. It is the second largest and most common species of mo[illegible]r in Australia, home to around twenty species of monitor, fifteen

of them endemic/native. Gould's monitors or sand goannas ('goanna' is the Australian common name for monitor lizards) are found in sandy regions almost

Detour

Atherton Tableland

The Atherton Tableland covers an area of some 150 km (93 miles) inland from the coast between Cairns and Innisfail. It rises to an altitude of more than 1,000 m (3,281 ft) in places, making it considerably cooler than the coast. Substantial rainfall keeps the landscape green, lush and dotted with waterfalls.
To view the plateau at its best, turn onto Highway 25 (Palmerston Highway) in Innisfail and head west over the highlands, making a detour via Atherton; then head back towards the coast to Gordonvale. This is a detour of around 200 km (124 miles) in all. Millaa Millaa is around 65 km (40 miles) west of Innisfail, and just a stone's throw

A scenic railway crosses the Atherton Tableland.

from here are the most spectacular waterfalls in the region – the Millaa Millaa Falls. A circular trail takes you to two further waterfalls, the Zillie and Ellinjaa Falls. The next stop on the road is Malanda. Just before you enter Malanda, a path to the left leads to the Malanda Falls, which cascade into a natural pool surrounded by rainforest.
The small town of Atherton is the midpoint of the highlands. The Heritage Village of Yungaburra is around 13 km (8 miles) east of Atherton on the Gillies Highway. A giant fig tree stands in the middle of the nearby rainforest; its aerial roots drop 15 m (49 ft) to the ground in dense, curtain-like rows from the overhanging branches. After the Lake Tinaroo reservoir, head for Gordonvale to rejoin the Bruce Highway.

growth. If you want to explore the island in your own vehicle (four-wheel drive only), you must obtain a permit before boarding the ferry.

5 Bundaberg Back on the Bruce Highway, just a few kilometres beyond the little town of Childers, a road branches off to Bundaberg, famous for distilling rum. Bundy Rum – 'the famous Aussie Spirit' – has put Bundaberg on the world map. The country town (population 45,000) sits among fields of sugar cane, 15 km (9 miles) from the coast. In the Bundaberg Rum Distillery visitors can see how rum is made from sugar-cane juice. On the journey north from Bundy, the entire length of the Bruce Highway runs just a few kilometres from the coast. Your next stop is Rockhampton, some 200 km (124 miles) up the road.

6 Rockhampton The city on the mighty Fitzroy River forms part of a region 'where the Outback meets the Reef'. Rockhampton's prosperity comes from cattle and it is the self-styled beef capital of Australia. Cattle breeders were the first people to settle here in the mid-19th century, and soon after, when gold was discovered in the north and south, Rockhampton made its fortune as a gold-trading centre.
'Rocky', as the 60,000 inhabitants affectionately call their city, has plenty to offer tourists, including many historic buildings dating back to the 19th century. If you want to experience living Aboriginal culture, the Dreamtime Cultural Centre 4 km (2½ miles) to the north of the city is definitely worth a visit. The next part of the journey passes through seemingly never-ending sugar-cane plantations. After 350 km (217 miles) you arrive in Mackay, the 'sugar capital' of Australia.

7 Mackay A third of all sugar produced in Australia comes from Mackay. The city is also an important coal-loading centre for shipments from the mines in central Queensland. Many of the original buildings from the early days of the city still exist, including the old town hall, the bank and the courthouse. The Botanic Gardens boast an orchid house, tropical trees, shrubs and flowers and are well worth a visit. From Mackay, minor roads via Marian, Mirani and Finch Hatton take you to Eungella National Park, 80 km (50 miles) to the north-west.

8 Eungella National Park Located on the boundary between the tropics and subtropics, this beautiful park is set in the craggy Clarke Range, which reaches heights of up to 1,280 m (4,200 ft), in stark but wonderful contrast to the sugar-cane fields of the coastal plain.

3

At higher altitudes, the subtropical rainforest is often veiled in cloud and wafts of mist – 'Eungella' is Aborigine for 'land of clouds'. Tropical rainforest dominates the lower-lying regions, with open eucalypt woodland towards the dry western margin of the park.
On the way back to the Bruce Highway, you can head off along the perimeter of the park at Mirani and proceed north towards Mount Ossa, rejoining the Bruce Highway from there. From Proserpine, around 80 km (50 miles) further on, take the road to Shute Harbour and take one of the many boat trips on offer to the Whitsunday Island archipelago.

9 Whitsunday Islands National Park (See also page 82.) Captain Cook named this group of islands after discovering this section of the coast on Whit Sunday, 1770. The Whitsundays comprise more than ninety islands lying within a radius of 50 km (31 miles) off Shute Harbour. In fact, these offshore islands are the tips of a former coastal mountain range that now juts out of the sea. The National Park is made up of thirty-one islands, and tourists can visit them only on guided boat trips or by plane. On a peninsula to the south of Shute Harbour lies Conway National Park, offering impressive views of the Whitsunday Passage and the islands beyond.
Our route takes us back to the Bruce Highway, which now skirts the coastline over a partly mountainous, partly flat terrain.

10 Bowling Green Bay National Park Just to the south of Townsville, a section of the park protects the bay of the same name as far as Cape Bowling Green. A track leads off the Bruce Highway, passable in wet weather only in a four-wheel drive vehicle, to the national parkland to the north of Cape Cleveland. A third section of the park lies to the west of the Bruce Highway around Mount Elliot, a remote, inaccessible mountain wilderness that reaches a height of 1,342 m (4,403 ft) and lies some 10 km (6 miles) to the north of the turnoff for Cape Cleveland. Here Australia's southernmost tropical rainforests have been afforded official protection.

11 Townsville Around 120,000 inhabitants make Townsville the largest city in the Australian Tropics. The Bruce Highway takes you *(continued p.92)*

1 **Whitsunday Island is a listed National Park.**

2 **Lindeman Island also has National Park status.**

3 **This building in Townsville is a reminder of past gold-digging days.**

Coastal habitats

Large sections of Queensland's coastline boast popular beaches and the opportunity to get close to nature. The shores are home to a variety of aquatic birds: herons, broad-billed sandpipers and pelicans, as well as the

The broad-billed sandpiper is a type of wader.

black swan, which is is found only in Australia. In winter hundreds of sea turtles crawl up the beaches to lay their eggs. The mangrove swamps of the northern sections of coastline and the muddy river estuaries also provide a haven for countless numbers of breeding aquatic birds.

Great Barrier Reef – Whitsunday Islands

Islands, sun, sandy beaches, blue sea – Australian for 'tropical holiday paradise'.

This group of around ninety islands, located to the north of Mackay, has it all. Right on their doorstep is the central section of the Great Barrier Reef, stretching some 2,000 km (1,616 miles) along the east coast, at between 10 and 23 degrees latitude. The most diverse marine ecosystem in the world is made up of 2,500 individual reefs and was given protected status as a Marine Park in 1983. Departing from Airlie Beach or Hamilton Island, you can make a short trip to the coral gardens of the continental shelf, including the heart-shaped island aptly named Heart Reef.

Many of the eucalyptus, araucaria and acacia-clad islands are uninhabited and listed as National Parks, as is the group's namesake, Whitsunday Island, which lures many visitors with the magnificent Whitehaven Beach, one of the finest beaches in Australia. Long Island, Hamilton Island, Lindeman Island, South Molle Island, Daydream Island, Hook Island and Hayman Island offer a wide choice of holiday resorts. You can enjoy swimming, snorkelling, diving, fishing, sailing, reef-walking or trekking. In September, sailing enthusiasts from all over the world come to

Top: Hook Island and Nara Inlet. Bottom: The Whitsunday Islands are a popular sailing destination.

Hamilton Island for the annual Race Week. If none of these activities appeals you can simply spend time watching the native seabirds and marine mammals or visit the Underwater Observatory on Hook Island. Between July and September whales pass by the islands and make a spectacular sight.

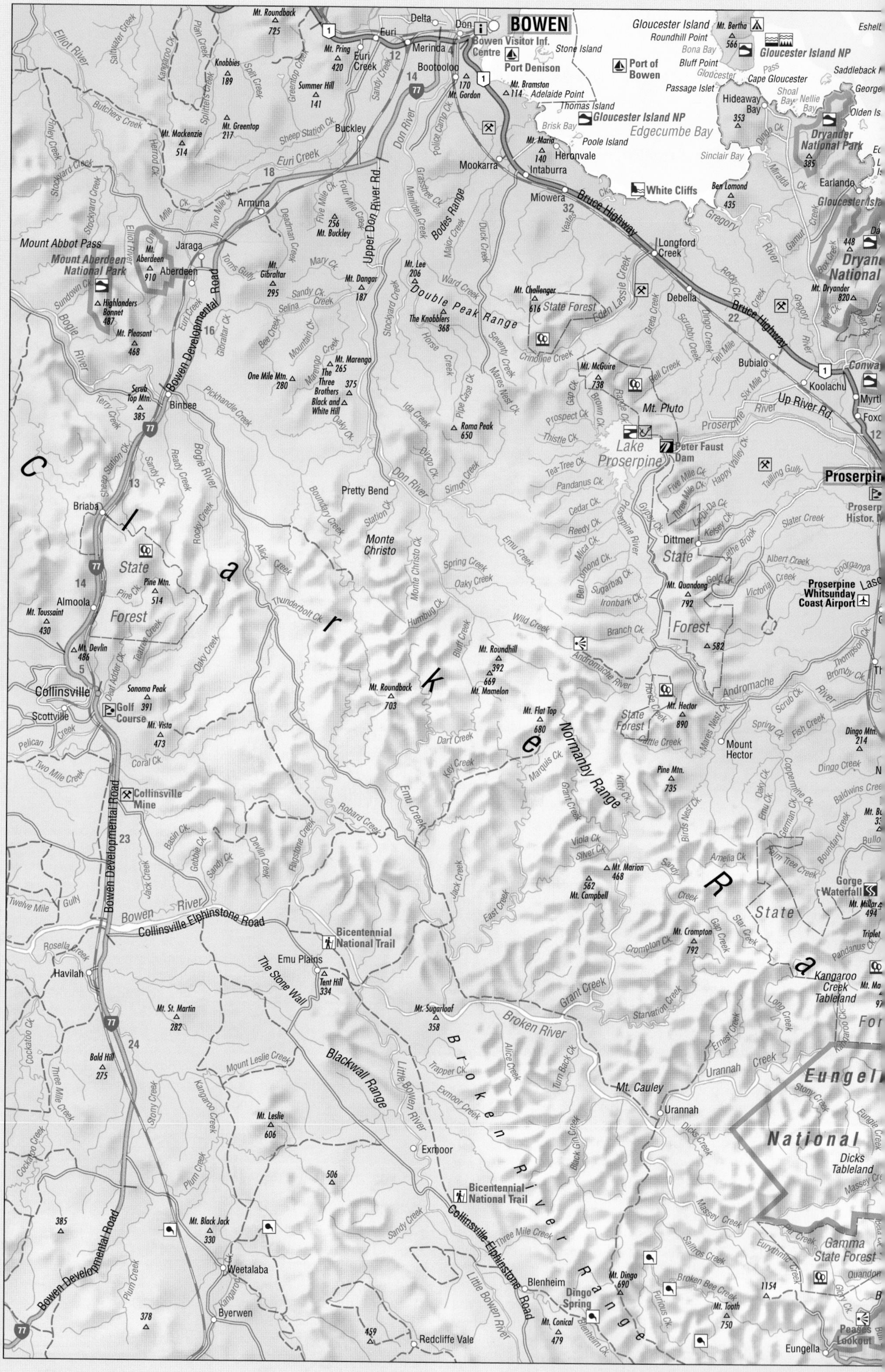

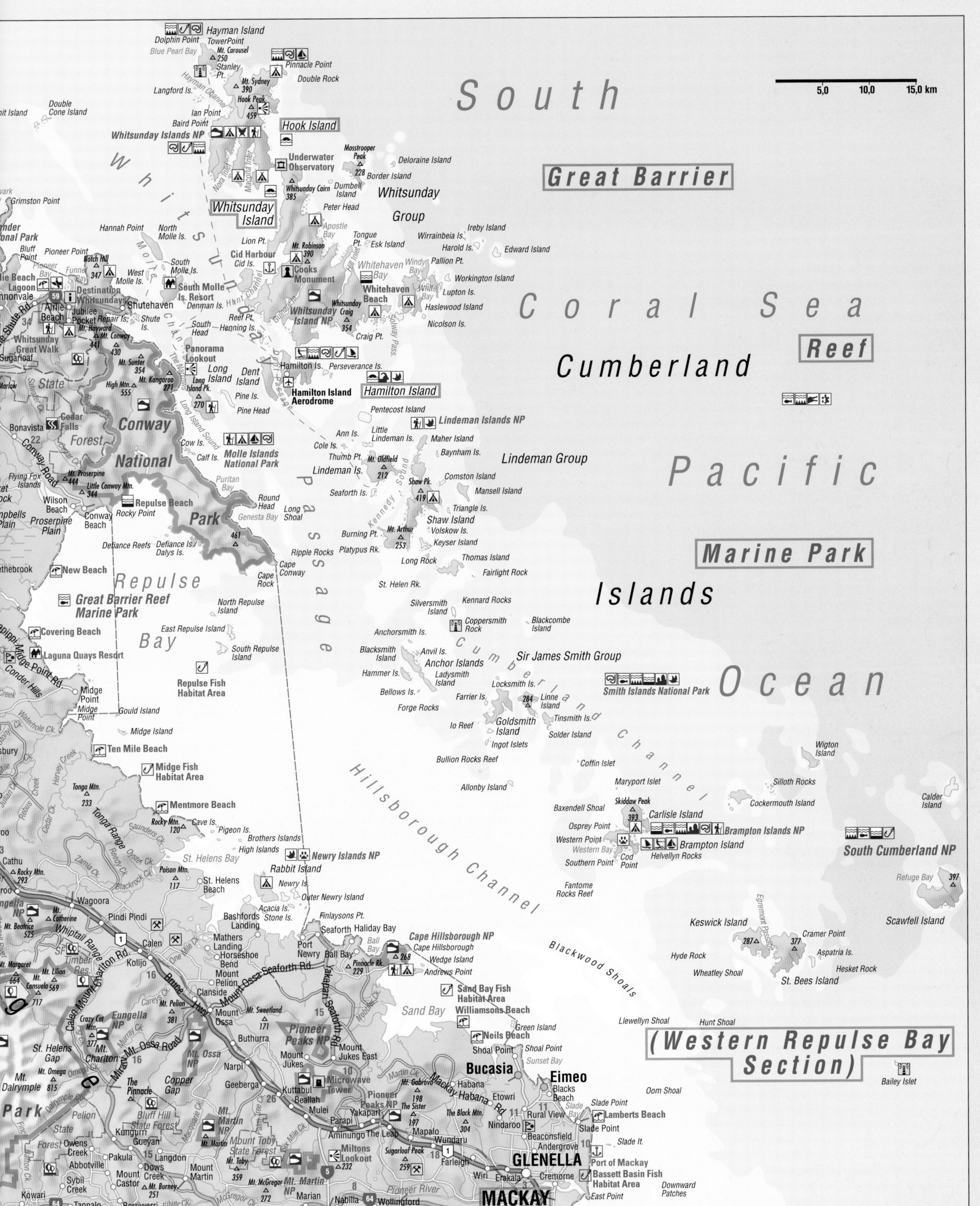
South
Coral Sea
Pacific
Ocean
Great Barrier
Reef
Marine Park
Cumberland
Islands
(Western Repulse Bay
Section)
5,0
10,0
15,0 km
Hayman Island
Hook Island
Whitsunday Island
Whitsunday Group
Whitsunday Islands NP
Hamilton Island
Hamilton Island Aerodrome
Lindeman Group
Lindeman Islands NP
Molle Islands National Park
Conway National Park
Repulse Bay
Great Barrier Reef Marine Park
Sir James Smith Group
Smith Islands National Park
Brampton Islands NP
South Cumberland NP
Newry Islands NP
Cape Hillsborough NP
Hillsborough Channel
Cumberland Channel
Whitsunday Passage
Shutehaven
Airlie Beach
Proserpine Plain
Bucasia
Eimeo
GLENELLA
MACKAY
Keswick Island
St. Bees Island
Scawfell Island
Carlisle Island
Brampton Island
Goldsmith Island
Shaw Island
Anchor Islands
Pioneer Peaks NP
Eungella NP
Blackwood Shoals

Great Barrier Reef – Hinchinbrook Island National Park

Australia's largest island National Park lies midway between Townsville and Cairns on the far side of the Hinchinbrook Channel.

Hinchinbrook Island belongs to the Central Section of the Great Barrier Reef Marine Park but has no coral reefs of its own. If you want to discover more about the truly magnificent world of coral, take a trip to the nearby Brook Islands. However, Hinchinbrook Island does have its own very special charms: a dense rainforest stretches along the coast, interspersed with dreamlike sandy beaches (e.g., Orchid Beach). Towards the centre of the island, the terrain grows steeper in places, and Mount Bowen, the highest mountain on the island, rises 1,120 m (3,675 ft) above sea level.

On the west coast of the island, the mangrove belt in the Hinchinbrook Channel is a particularly impressive sight. Other sections of the coast are lined with beds of seagrass. The island and coastal area are home to a large variety of seabirds, including herons, and oyster catchers, the dugong (a species of sea cow), green sea turtles, saltwater crocodiles and – unfortunately – a mass of insects including sand flies and mosquitoes.

Top: Zoe Bay overshadowed by the 1,120 m (3,675 ft) Mount Bowen. Bottom: Little Ramsay Bay.

The highlight for walkers is the Thorsborne Trail, running 32 km (20 miles) along the east coast from Ramsay Bay to George Point. There are no facilities along the trail, so you have to take everything you need with you. Only a limited number of visitors is allowed on the island. Early booking is essential – even for those just planning to walk.

5,0 10,0 15,0 km
Great Barrier Reef
Marine Park
(Central Section)
South Pacific
Coral Sea
Ocean
Great Barrier Reefs
Palm Passage
Magnetic Passage
The Slashers Reefs
Pith Reef
Britomart Reef
Walker Reef
Trunk Reef
Bramble Reef
Tread Shoal
Needle Reef
Urchin Shoal
Thimble Shoal
Roxburgh Reef
Arab Reef
Kelso Reef
Little Kelso Reef
Westmoreland Reef
Backnumbers Reef
Rib Reef
Fore And Aft Reef
French Reef
Braggs Reef
Hopkinson Reef
John Brewer Reef
Helix Reef
Lodestone Reef
Keeper Reef
Sandwich
Eva Island
Ramsay Bay
Agnes Island
Hinchinbrook Island
Zoe Bay
Hillcock Point
Mulligan Falls
Mulligan Bay
George Point
Dungeness
Lucinda
Halifax
Halifax Fish Habitat Area
Taylors Beach
Lady Elliot Reef
Forrest Beach
Cassady Beach
Palm Creek Fish Habitat Area
Bronte Beach
Cattle Creek Fish Habitat Area
Halifax Bay Wetlands NP
Halifax Bay
Pelorus Island/ North Palm Island Yanooa Island
Iris Point
Orpheus Island National Park
Orpheus/ Goolboddi Island
Little Pioner Bay
Hazard Bay
Orpheus Island Resort
Yanks Jetty
Harrier Point
Juno Bay
Curacoa Channel
Curaçoa Island/ Noogoo
Palm Islands
Sunballa Point
Elk Cliff
Great Palm Island
Fantome Is./ Eumilli
Challenger Bay/ Gowyarowa
North East/ Othoorakool Bay
Electra Head
Hayman Rock
Paluma Rock
South East Cape
Palm Island
Mt. Bentley 541
445
Falcon Island/ Carbooroo
Esk Island/ Soopun
Miranda Pt.
Eclipse Island/ Garoogubbee
Fawn Head
Barber Island/ Boodthean
White Rock / Albino Rock
Chilcott Rock
Dido Rock
Brisk Island/ Culgarool
Pandora Reef
Fly Island
Havannah Island
Acheron Island
Phillips Reef
Cordelia Rocks
Bramble Rock
Herald Island
Lorne Reef
Rattlesnake Island
Coolbie
Barrilgie
Mutarnee
Moongobulla
Bruce Highway
Balgal Beach
Crystal Bridge
Rollingstone State Forest
Rollingstone
Circle View Mtn. 831
Douglas Hill 48
Toomulla
Paluma Range National Park
Mt. Halifax 1068
Clemant State Forest
Toomulla Beach
Paluma Shoals
Halifax Bay
Paluma Range
Toolakea
Jalloonda
Bohle River Fish Habitat Area
Mount Low
Bluewater
Cobarra
Purono
Tailings ponds
Bushland Beach
Yabulu
Kulburn
Black River
Deeragun
Nightjar
Annaville
Cordelia Estate
State Forest
Mt. Black 409
Forest Field Training Area
Ponto Hut
Magnetic Island
Bay Rock Lighthouse
Five Beach Bay
White Rock
Horseshoe Bay
Radical Bay
Bungalow Bay YHA
Gowrie Bay
Liver Pt.
Florence Bay
Bay Rock
West Pt.
Magnetic Island National Park
Arcadia Bay
Bremner Point
Geoffrey Bay
Nelly Bay
Cockle Bay Reef
Picnic Bay
Hawkings Point
West Channel
Townsville Town Common Conserv. Park
Cape Pallarenda
Pallarenda
Virago Shoal
Townswille International Airport
Kising Pt.
TOWNSVILLE/ THURINGOWA
Garbutt
SOUTH TOWNSVILLE
Mus. of Tropical Queensland
Maritime Mus.
TOWNSVILLE WEST
Cleveland Bay
Cape Cleveland
Cape Cleveland Lightstation
Bowling Green Bay Conservation Park
Twenty Foot Rock
Red Rock Bay
Long Beach
Paradise Bay
Bray Islet
Mt. Cleveland 558
Cape Woora
Cape Ferguson
Australian Institute of Marine Science
Chunda Bay
Bowling Green Bay

Top: Daintree National Park north of Cairns has one of the last virtually unaltered tropical rainforests in Australia. The Mossman Gorge Section offers a nature trail for exploring the rainforest, while the Cape Tribulation Section in the north can also be explored by boat, for example along the Daintree River.

Bottom: Millaa Millaa Falls on the Atherton Tableland are situated some 30 km (18½ miles) east of Ravenshoe. The waterfalls, close to the small, sleepy town of the

Great Barrier Reef, Cairns Section Daintree National Park

The Cairns Section of the Great Barrier Reef marks the point 'where the rainforest meets the reef', stretching from Innisfail south of Cairns up to Cooktown.

Here the coral reefs are only a few metres below the surface and relatively close to the coast, making access from Cairns and Port Douglas particularly easy. But there is more to come: the Wet Tropics World Heritage Area is yet another highlight. The hot and humid climate enjoyed by the coastal slopes for millions of years has helped to preserve one of the oldest rainforests on earth, teeming with plant and animal species.

One-third of the area is protected by National Park status. Daintree National Park is situated north of Port Douglas and is made up of two separate sections: the Mossman Gorge section to the west of Mossman and, to the north, the Cape Tribulation section between Daintree River and Bloomfield River. The main attraction in the Mossman Gorge section is the gorge of the same name, where the Mossman River waterfalls plunge over blocks of granite. At Cape Tribulation the rainforest sweeps all the way down to the magnificent beaches.

Coral reefs attract bass (top) and moray eels.

Visitors can choose to take rainforest walks, boat trips on the Daintree River for a spot of crocodile-watching, swimming, diving, excursions to the reefs, or simply relaxing.

Snorkelling on the Great Barrier Reef: even with just a mask and flippers, exploring the underwater paradise is a spectacular experience.

Coral Sea
Great Barrier Reef
South Pacific Ocean
Great Barrier Reef Marine Park (Cairns Section)
5,0
10,0
15,0 km
Cairns Reef
West Hope Island
Papuan Passage
Andersen Reef
Rachel Carson Reef
Endeavour Reef
Escape Reef
Pickersgill Reef
Evening Reef
Lake Reef
Bonner Rock
Morning Reef
Agincourt Reefs
Agincourt Reef No.4
Agincourt Reefs No.3
Agincourt Reefs No.2
Agincourt Reef D
Agincourt Reef No.1
Spitfire Reefs
Mackay Reef
St. Crispin Reef
Undine Reef A
Undine Reef B
Pratt Rock
Chinamen Reef
Opal Reef
Rudder Reef
Togue Reef
Trinity Opening
Spur Reef
Norman Reef
Onyx Reef
Saxon Reef
Batt Reef
Satellite Reef
Hastings Reef
Jorgensen Patch
Pixie Reef
Michaelmas Reef
Michaelmas and Upolu Cays National Park
Pretty Patches
Oyster Reef
Middle Cay Reef
Vlasoff Cay
Upolu Cay
Arlington Reef
Green Island
Green Island National Park
Green Island Reef
Trinity Bay
Rossville
Home Rule Falls
Home Rule Rainforest Lodge
Lorna Doone
Mt. Hartley 797
Obree Point
Cedar Bay National Park
Cedar Bay
Bicentennial National Trail
Mt. Sampson 790
The Little Forks
Mt. Finnigan 1148
586 Mt. Finlay
Rattlesnake Point/ North Head
583
Normanby Mine
Grass Tree Pocket
Mt. McMillan 785
Mt. Misery 867
Mt. Romeo 791
Wyalla Plain
Weary Bay
Bonnie Glen
Monkhouse Timber Reserve
Yorkey Range
Mt. Boolbun North 921
Mt. Boolbun South 1008
Ayton
Wujal Wujal
The Horse Crossing
The Jump Up
Bloomfield Falls
Degarra
Bloomfield Track
Cowie Point
Zig Zag
Dawnvale
Roaring Meg Falls
Round Mtn. 444
Mt. Donovan
Donovan Point
Duncans Flat
China Camp
Daintree National Park
Mt. Pieter Botte
Cape Tribulation
Myall Beach
McDowall Range
Lemon Tree Lookout Mine
Thornton Range
Noah Head
Noah Beach
Thornton Peak 1314
Creb Track
Cooper Creek Wilderness Lodge
Struck Island
Thornton Beach
Alexandra Bay
Bailey Point
Cow Bay
410
Allanton Hill 211
Daintree
River Cruises
Daintree River
Black Rock
Long White Beach
Cape Kimberley
Penguin Channel
Snapper Island
Snapper Island National Park
Halls Point
Mossman Daintree Rd.
Dagmar Range
Cairns Marine Park
Pinnacle 337
1288
Main Coast Range
Daintree National Park
Wonga Beach
Trinity Bay
Low Island
Low Isles Lighthouse
Low Isles Reef
Woody Island
Low Isles
Dayman Point
Rocky Point
Trinity Inlet/Marlin Coast Marine Park
Palm Beach
Mialo
Black Mtn. 1337
Mount Spurgeon Forest Reserve
1378
Mt. Somerset 221
Roots Mt. 1331
Devils Thumb 1330
Mt. Spurgeon 1322
Mount Carbine Tableland
Mossman Gorge
Newell
Cooya
Morey Reef
Mossman
South Mossman
Port Douglas
Four Mile Beach
Port Douglas Beach
Spurgeon Falls
Shannonvale Tropical Winery
390
Burton Ridge
Mount Lewis Forest Reserve
Mount Carbine Mine
Round Mtn. 1009
Lyons Lookout
Craiglie
Wentworth Reef
Egmont Reef
Cairns Marine Park
Mt. Carbine Village & Caravan Park
Mount Carbine
Riflemead Forest Reserve
Alexandra Reefs
Korea Reef
Yule Point
Yule Reef
Captain Cook Hwy.
Rex Range Road
Leichhardt Creek Mine
Mowbray National Park
Cassowary Range
Pebbly Beach
White Cliffs Hang Gliding
Garioch Reef
Oak Beach
Pretty Beach
Mt. Lewis 1224
Rumula
Maryfarms
Mulligan Highway
Riflemead Forest Reserve
Julatten
Black Mountain Road
Mt. Charlie 583
Turtle Creek Beach
Slip Cliff Point
Rex Lookout
Unity Reef
Mount Holmes Mine
Kanbrae
Black Mtn. 1066
Timber Reserve
Wangetti
Mt. Holmes
Wetherby
Kuranda State Forest
Hartleys Creek Crocodile Farm
Red Cliff Point
Faulty Towers
Captain Cook Hwy.
Southedge Lakes Road
Macalister Range Reserve
Bakers Blue Mtn.
Rifle Glen
Mount Molloy
871
Simpson Point
Ellis Beach
Double Island
Haycock Island
Buchan Point
Buchan
Mount Molloy Mine
Mona Mona
Palm Cove
Palm Cove Camping Ground
Palm Beach
Font Hills 1124
Salty Range
Spring Valley
Clifton Beach
Taylor Point
Trinity Beach
Yalkula
Mt. Consider
Fairchance Mine
Cairns Tropical Zoo
Yorkeys Point
Yorkeys Knob
Dora Creek
Fairyland
761
Oak Forest
Kowrowa
Mybola
Smithfield Heights
Koah
Scenic Railway
Kuranda
San Remo Beach
Holloway Beach
Machans Beach
Hann Tableland National Park
Barron Falls
Barron Gorge NP
Southedge
Lake Mitchell
592
Bilwon
Formartine State Forest
Freedom County
Caravonica
Cairns Airport
Ellie Point
Port of Cairns
Cairns Harbour
False Cape
Mission Bay
Rocky Is.
Gribble Point
Cape Grafton
372
Turtle Bay
Little Turtle Bay
Fitzroy Island
Fitzroy Island Lighthouse
Bicentennial National Trail
572
Goose Swamp Waterhole
Bilwon State Forest
Mareeba Wild Animal Farm
Speewah
Redlynch
Mount Whitfield Conservation Park
632
Timber Reserve
Yarrabah Aboriginal Reserve
Yarrabah
399
King Beach
Wide Bay
Fitzroy Island Resort
Fitzroy Island National Park
Golden Pride Winery
Biboohra
Forest
Reids Pocket
Chujeba Peak 1060
CAIRNS
Centre of Contemporary Arts
Flecker Botanic Gardens

Members of the Tjapukai Aboriginal Cultural Park ensemble in Caravonica near Cairns perform with traditional equipment and painted bodies. The Park was an initiative of the Aborigines from Kuranda. In 1987, they founded a Dance Theatre to showcase indigenous Australian culture and tradition through theatre

and entertainment. The initiative was a success and the Cultural Park has become a successful enterprise that now embraces theatres, museums, spectacles and

Wildlife in the Wet Tropics

The term Wet Tropics refers to 900,000 ha (2,223,948 acres) of tropical rainforest along a 450-km (298-mile) stretch of coast between Cooktown and Townsville. Queensland's rainforests are among the oldest on earth. They are the last relics of the primeval forests that once covered the supercontinent of Gondwana some 100 million years ago.

Top: The nocturnal common spotted cuscus is a tree-climbing marsupial. Bottom: Brushtail possums also feel at home in the branches of eucalyptus trees.

Geographical isolation helped preserve unique ancient species of flora and fauna in this region. Curiosities of the animal world include the musky rat-kangaroo, two species of tree-kangaroo and the flightless southern cassowary, one of the largest birds on the planet. The rainforests teem with different species of mammal, birds, bats, frogs and reptiles.

through the centre, where Flinders Mall may tempt those in desperate need of a spot of retail therapy.

From the top of Castle Hill, at a height of some 300 m (984 ft), you can take in a stunning view of Magnetic Island, which lies off the coast and was given its name by Captain Cook, who mistakenly thought that the island's granite cliffs had interfered with his compass.

One of the most interesting attractions in Townsville is the Great Barrier Reef Wonderland. This aquarium is home to a living coral reef and is one of the largest of its kind. From the safety of a glass tunnel, visitors get a splendid view of the underwater world of the Great Barrier Reef: morays, manta rays, sharks and shoals of colourful fish swim above your head, making a trip round the aquarium the next best thing to diving.

On the way to Cairns, it is worth making a detour from Cardwell to Hinchinbrook Island, a listed National Park (see page 84).

⓬ **Cairns** This energetic, booming northern city, with a population of over 100,000, had a very modest start in life: a suitcase and a tent pole were all that marked the beginnings of the first outpost. When gold was first discovered in 1873, prospectors flocked to Cairns. Their ships docked in the small harbour, which was named after Sir William Cairns, the governor of Queensland at the time. Since then, tourism has turned the capital of the Tropical Far North into a lively city, with Cairns serving as the gateway to both the Great Barrier Reef and the Cape York Peninsula. To the north, not far from the city, you will find attractive beaches bordered by dense rainforest. The Mediterranean-style architecture along the beach at Palm Cove makes it one of the most charming spots in the area.

The Flecker Botanical Gardens in the suburb of Edge Hill are one of Cairns' most impressive attractions. Dating back to 1886, the gardens display a wide variety of tropical plants and over a hundred species of palm. Paths through the gardens lead to the Mount Whitfield rainforests, offering spectacular views of the city and the coast. Edge Hill also has a visitor centre for the Royal Flying Doctor Service, offering an excellent insight into its work.

⓭ **Kuranda** The road winds its way around hairpin bends to the small town of Kuranda at the northern tip of the Atherton Tableland. Small villages are dotted among lush meadows in this fertile, hilly landscape. The air up here is pleasantly fresh and invigorating after the tropical humidity on the coast. An added bonus is that you can also visit Kuranda without a car: Skyrail is a gondola cableway, 7.5 km (4½ miles) long, connecting Cairns and Kuranda in just 25 minutes. Enjoy a unique bird's-eye view of the tops of the rainforest. Instead of, or even in combination with, the cableway you can experience the delights of the Kuranda Scenic Railway, which winds from Cairns to Kuranda. The track was built between 1882 and 1891 to transport tin and other metal to the port of Cairns. Today it transports only tourists and the spectacular stretch of railway, 34 km (21 miles) long, climbs to a height of 300 m (984 ft), passing through fifteen tunnels, crossing forty bridges and negotiating no fewer than ninety-eight bends.

⓮ **Tjapukai Aboriginal Cultural Park** Visitors to Tjapukai Aboriginal Cultural Park in Caravonica, near Kuranda, can learn more about, and interact with, the culture and origins of the indigenous rainforest people. The impressive and educational programme includes everything from boomerang-throwing and didgeridoo-playing to authentic performances of dance and legends from 'Dreamtime'. The Tjapukai Dance Theatre puts on displays of celebration dances, survival skills and corroborees.

From Highway 1, Highway 44 heads north to the attractive fishing port and resort town of Port Douglas. This charming resort, located 75 km (46½ miles) to the north of Cairns, has become a popular alternative to its larger neighbour and offers another starting point for trips to the reef.

From Port Douglas, it is just a few kilometres to Mossman, the centre of the most northerly sugar-growing region of Queensland. Most tourists pass through this quiet town on the way to the picturesque Mossman Gorge in the

southern section of the Daintree National Park.

⑮ Daintree National Park, Mossman Gorge Section (See also previous pages.) Located some 5 km (3 miles) to the west of Mossman, the southern section of Daintree National Park encompasses an area of 565 km^2 (218 square miles), some of which you can explore on a 3-km (2-mile) trail. Most of the park remains undeveloped. If you want to venture deeper into the parkland, the Kuku Yalanji Aborigines from the lowland rainforests to the north of Port Douglas offer guided tours leaving from Mossman. The 'Dreamtime Walks' give a real insight into the world of the Aborigines. Daintree is 35 km (22 miles) north of Mossman, and boat trips take you into the northern section of the park. The ferry across the Daintree River – the only link to the Cape Tribulation Section – also runs from Mossman.

⑯ Daintree National Park, Cape Tribulation Section (See also previous pages.) The National Park is a UNESCO World Heritage Site and beats the forests of Europe and North America hands down in terms of biodiversity. An extraordinary number of plant, mammal, butterfly and fern species live in the coastal rainforests. Dwarf kangaroos, brightly coloured cockatoos, parakeets and parrots, quicksilver possums and the rare green tree python inhabit the dense rainforest around Cape Tribulation, which sweeps down to the shore. Its microclimate provides a habitat for ancient ferns, flowering plants and insects, some of which originated as much as 120 million years ago. The climate in this part of Queensland has remained unchanged for millions of years and the region is home to no fewer than seventy native animal and 700 native plant species. During the dry period, the Bloomfield Track (passable in a four-wheel drive) leads to Cooktown, 150 km (93 miles) away. A longer, alternative route heads inland from Mossman via Mount Molloy and Lakeland to Cooktown. The 250-km (155-mile) track is often closed between November and May.

⑰ Cooktown This is the site of the first – albeit temporary – European settlement on the east coast of Australia. In 1770, Captain Cook was forced to beach his vessel, the *Endeavour*, here after it ran aground on a coral reef. Later, in 1872, gold was discovered on the Palmer River and Cooktown quickly became the centre for the surrounding gold fields. However, by 1900 the gold deposits had been exhausted and Cooktown sank into virtual oblivion, isolated as it was on the Cape York Peninsula.

Today, the growing popularity of Queensland's Far North has put Cooktown back on the map. Tourist accommodation is available and the settlement, with its 1,400-strong population, is easy to reach by the new sealed all-weather Mulligan Highway. Cooktown's attractions include the James Cook Historical Museum, housed in an imposing, ornamented brick building that dates back to 1888. The Cape York Peninsula is also worth a trip.

1 **The National Parks in the Wet Tropics of Queensland have been under the protection of UNESCO since 1988.**

2 **At low tide, the upper parts of the coral are exposed briefly to the air.**

The Great Barrier Reef is one of the most biodiverse regions in the world. It is home to the brightest-coloured corals and fish you are ever likely to see. Visibility in the crystal clear water reaches to a depth of around 60 m (197 ft), making it ideal for snorkelling and diving. Diving on the reef is like swimming in a gigantic

aquarium. The fish are amazingly friendly and the sheer diversity is overwhelming. The most amazing annual event on the reef is the coral-spawning in November. If you prefer to experience this underwater wonderland without getting wet, choose from one of the many glass-bottomed boat trips on offer.

1

Detour

Great Barrier Reef Marine Park

In reality, the Great Barrier Reef, the planet's largest reef system, is a network of over 2,500 separate coral reefs that stretches roughly between 10 and 23 degrees latitude south, off the north coast of Queensland. The reef starts level with Mackay on the Southern Tropic and runs all the way up to Papua New Guinea. The Outer Reef, built on the Australian continental shelf, is around 250 km (155 miles) off the mainland to the south (on a level with Mackay) and approximately 30 km (18½ miles) offshore from the York Peninsula. A distinction is generally made between reefs on the coasts and islands and the actual barrier reef along the edge of the continental shelf, which reaches depths of 40 m (131 ft) in places.

The reef system is made up of coral polyps. When they die off, they leave behind a hard skeleton of lime shell that accommodates a new polyp. This is how the vast reef network gradually developed over millions of years – the oldest parts of the reef are up to 18 million years old. They provide a habitat for around four hundred species of coral that vary not only in size, shape and colour but also in the speed at which they grow. Most species grow between 1 and 10 cm (⅔–4 inches) a year.

2

The underwater splendour of the reef relies entirely on the living corals, which are some of the most sensitive life forms found in nature. They need three things to flourish: sunlight, a good supply of plankton, and water at the correct temperature, with a strong current. The clarity of the water determines the amount of sunlight that reaches the polyps. Sunlight is essential for their growth. Corals are formed only at depths of around 40 m (131 ft); any deeper and there is not enough sunlight to sustain life and growth. The temperature at the surface of the water must not fall below 20°C (68°F).

The Great Barrier Reef boasts an extraordinary biodiversity: apart from the corals, over 1,500 species of tropical fish and more than 4,000 species of sponge have been identified. The only creatures potentially dangerous to humans are poisonous stonefish, a few types of mussel and venomous sea snakes. Between November and March, box jellyfish – tiny, ultra-venomous cube-shaped creatures with long tentacles – move into the coastal waters and pose a real threat to people; swimming is strictly prohibited during this period.

In the past, mankind has not been particularly kind to the Great Barrier Reef. A number of islands on the reef were seriously damaged by overgrazing (goats were kept on some islands to provide food for stranded shipwreck survivors). The cultivation of sea cucumbers flourished in the 19th century, and some islands were recklessly mined for guano at the turn of the 20th century. Around 1970, environmental initiatives put a stop to plans for large-scale exploitation of limestone and exploratory drilling for petroleum in the reef.

Regrettably, the coral system of the Great Barrier Reef remains under threat, with its greatest enemies being such dangers as water pollution and global warming of the sea and atmosphere, El Niño, coral disease and voracious starfish.

The Australian Institute of Marine Science and other organizations have taken on the task of preserving and revitalizing the Great Barrier Reef. They monitor the reef, annually documenting its condition and the natural processes of change on over a hundred individual reefs. Special reef organisms known as 'key species' play an important role: the state of their health helps the scientists to draw conclusions about the current conditions over the entire reef and predict future developments.

1 The brilliant coral gardens enchant divers and snorkellers alike.

2 The Great Barrier Reef includes 600 continental islands and 350 coral islands.

Cooktown Captain Cook landed here in 1770. Gold was discovered in 1872, and the town was founded in the following year. At its peak, its population was 35,000.

Daintree National Park Long boat trips and 'Dreamtime Walks' guided by Aborigines are the perfect way to experience the tropical rainforest.

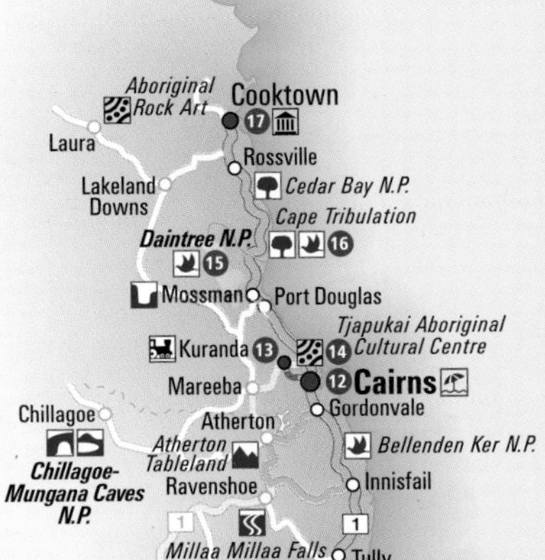

Cape Tribulation 'Cape Trib' is a UNESCO Natural World Heritage Site and home to one of the rare coastal rainforests, teeming with hundreds of plant species.

Great Barrier Reef The largest reef system on earth extends for 2,600 km (1,616 miles). There are many ways to enjoy this underwater paradise: you can snorkel, dive or take a trip on a glass-bottomed boat.

Whitsunday Islands National Park Magnificent sandy beaches, fabulous dive sites, relaxing walks and an amazing variety of flora and fauna make this an idyllic retreat.

Millaa Millaa Falls Visitors to the Millaa Millaa Falls on the Atherton Tableland are tempted to take a dip in the heart of the rainforest.

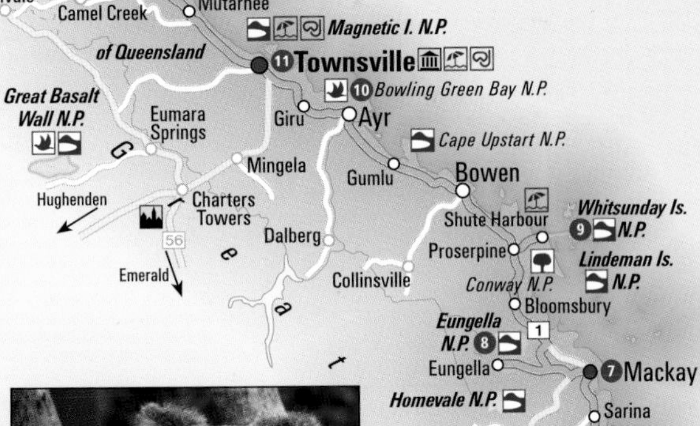

Conway National Park Beautiful ferns and stunning orchids flourish in this natural paradise.

Wet Tropics The north of Queensland enjoys a tropical climate, with heavy rain and high temperatures. A key feature of the vegetation in the tropical rainforest is a wide range of fern species.

Magnetic Island National Park Visitors here can watch a large population of koala bears at home in their natural habitat.

Sunshine Coast Pure-white sandy beaches and emerald-green water make this coast a paradise for holidaymakers and surfers.

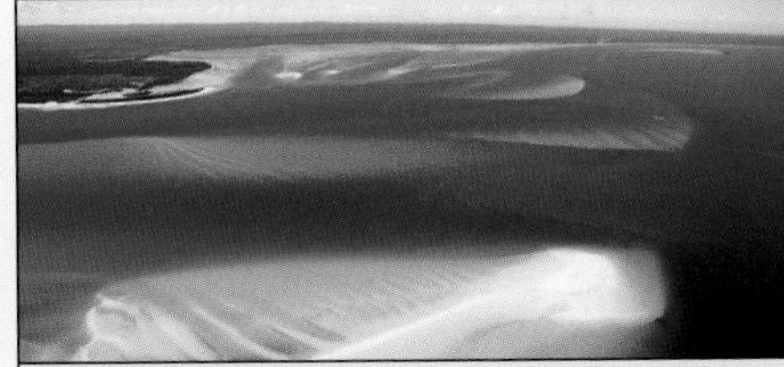

Fraser Island The largest sand island in the world is home to imposing sand dunes towering to heights of 250 m (820 ft), lush green forests and lakes.

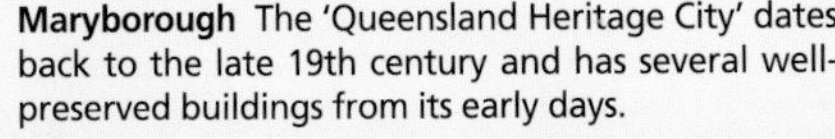

Maryborough The 'Queensland Heritage City' dates back to the late 19th century and has several well-preserved buildings from its early days.

Moreton Island The island has magnificent sandy beaches with dunes and is home to a variety of bird species. Dolphin-feeding takes place every evening.

Brisbane Today, 'Brissie', the capital of Queensland, is a sun-drenched, subtropical city, in marked contrast to its much darker past. Glittering skyscrapers have replaced the Edenglassie penal colony, which was founded in 1824.

Glass House Mountains Many vantage points offer excellent views of the massive volcanic plugs that jut out of the flat landscape. Thousands of years of erosion have worn away the actual volcanoes.

Route 4

Australia

The Pacific Highway – from the Blue Mountains to the Gold Coast

As you travel along Australia's colourful Pacific coastline, you will soon appreciate why Australians call their homeland 'the lucky country'. The National Parks transport visitors into a magical, largely unspoilt, subtropical wonderland. The stunning and romantic ranges in the Blue Mountains, formed on a sandstone plateau, reach altitudes over 1,000 m (3,281 ft) and alternate with magnificent primeval rainforests dating back millions of years. The coast is dotted with interesting towns and impossibly long beaches.

New South Wales, proudly named the 'Premier State', offers one of the most attractive sections of the country's Pacific coast. Not only the oldest of the Australian states, it is also its most populous and the most densely populated. New South Wales also boasts the strongest economy of all the states. It is thought that the explorer Captain Cook gave it this name in 1770 as the coastline reminded him of Wales, back in his own homeland.

With its heavily populated areas and developed landscape, New South Wales forms a stark contrast to the vast, deserted expanses of the Australian continent.
It would be hard to beat the variety and views offered by the coastline that links Sydney and Brisbane. The steep slopes and deep wooded gorges of the Blue Mountains, cloaked in a romantic, bluish haze, are among the most impressive landscapes in Australia. This magical, dramatic land-

Border Ranges National Park is home to tall palm ferns and strangler figs.

Sydney Harbour Bridge is a magnificent construction. The city's iconic building is the striking Opera House, opened in 1973 and declared a UNESCO World Heritage site in 2007.

With its vast coastline, Australia competes with Hawaii as a surfing paradise.

scape of bizarre rock formations lies not far from the lush subtropical rainforests that flourish on the coastal plains, home to a huge variety of plant and animal life. Lamington and Border Ranges National Parks on the border with Queensland contain gigantic, primeval trees swathed in vines, strangler figs and tree ferns. The string of National Parks along the coast is a UNESCO World Natural Heritage Site, designated as East Coast Temperate and Subtropical Rainforest.

The Eastern Highlands run parallel to the coast, falling away dramatically to the east where the Great Dividing Range gives way to a fertile coastal plain. The plain opens and widens to the north, traversed by estuaries that have formed countless pretty bays and attractive sandy beaches. The major towns and cities are concentrated in this region. The Gold Coast, in the south of Queensland, has developed into a very popular holiday area for both locals and tourists. Favourable wind conditions and endless sandy beaches make this a paradise for surfers in particular, but beach fans are in heaven here, too.

Nestling in the romantic valleys at the edge of the highlands are Australia's oldest vineyards, including the Lower Hunter Valley to the west of Newcastle. Of the cities along the Pacific coast, Sydney holds the number one slot. It boasts many examples of impressive modern engineering and architecture and offers a huge variety of cultural attractions.

You can access the south-east coast of Australia via the multi-lane Pacific Highway. This route connects the Bruce Highway, which itself starts in Brisbane, with the Princes Highway heading south from Sydney.

Eastern Australia's coastal waters are home to many shark species.

Detour

Kanangra-Boyd National Park

Kanangra-Boyd National Park, south-west of the southern section of the Blue Mountains National Park, covers just under 700 km^2 (271 square miles) of land and forms part of this designated UNESCO site. The park lies 180 km (112 miles) west of Sydney and is easily reached on the Great Western Highway, via Katoomba and the famous Jenolan Caves. From here, a track leads into the park.

The Jenolan Caves are among the largest, and most magnificent, limestone caverns on the continent. You can visit nine of the extraordinary caves, all of them mysterious and spectacularly lit. They were discovered in 1867 but part of the cave system still remains uncharted and you can explore only a small section of the forest of stalagmites and stalactites unaccompanied. Try to avoid visiting the popular caverns during the day, when they can be extremely busy, and join a guided evening tour instead. Make sure you arrive as early as possible during holiday periods.

The overhanging rocks of the Kanangra Walls.

The landscape of the National Park is full of variety and contrasts, with deep valleys alternating with almost flat limestone plateaux that suddenly fall away to reveal spectacular views over the Blue Mountains. The tall overhanging cliffs of the Kanangra Walls are particularly impressive, and a paradise for adventurous rock climbers. The valleys are covered in dense forests of eucalyptus trees, but in contrast, growth on the plateaux is limited to chest-high bushes.

The Pacific Highway connects Sydney with Brisbane. The Highway mainly runs parallel to the coast, and roads off it lead to the most famous sights and attractions along the Australian east coast. These include the mountains of the Great Dividing Range, idyllic vineyards in the Hunter Valley, coastal rainforests and the holiday paradise of the Gold Coast.

1 Sydney (See also page 105.) Sydney lies in the centre of Australia's south-east coast. The 2000 Olympic Games are now a thing of the past, but the city still has something for everyone. You're unlikely to be bored in Sydney, unless none of the following grabs your interest: fabulous restaurants, huge shopping centres, a spectacular variety of cultural attractions and events, a fascinating past charted in various museums and buildings, stunning beaches close to the city, and a range of National Parks on the doorstep.

2 Ku-Ring-Gai Chase National Park The park is sited on a sandstone plateau, crossed by rivers. Its northern border is formed by Broken Bay, an estuary of the Hawkesbury River. It encompasses a classic Sydney landscape of beaches, bushland, eucalypt forests and heath land, and boasts a huge network of waterways to keep canoeists and anglers happy.

Preserved rock paintings and engravings by the Gurringai Aborigines, who once lived here and gave the park its name, are well worth seeing.

Travel information

Route profile
Length: approx. 1,100 km/ 684 miles (excluding detours)
Time needed: min. 1 week
Start: Sydney
End: Brisbane
Itinerary (main locations): Sydney, Blue Mountains National Park, Port Macquarie, Yuraygir National Park, Byron Bay, Gold Coast, Brisbane

Traffic information
For general traffic information see page 22. The Pacific Highway connects the two largest cities on the east coast and serves the major holiday regions in Queensland. Be prepared for a high volume of traffic in the densely populated coastal areas at weekends and during the holidays.

Information
Australian Tourist Commission: *www.australia.com*
New South Wales: *www.visitnsw.com.au*
Queensland: *www.queenslandholidays.com.au*
Sydney: *www.sydney.com.au*

Weather information
www.bom.gov.au
www.ourbrisbane.com

Follow the route inland, via Sydney, along the Great Western Highway (Hwy. 32) to the Blue Mountains.

3 Blue Mountains National Park (See also page 106.) For many years the Blue Mountains, part of the Great Dividing Range, formed an insurmountable barrier for people living along the coast. The first successful crossing of the mountain range was not made until 1813, finally allowing access to much-needed pastures in the west. Sydneysiders flock to the Blue Mountains and their magnificent cliffs, gorges and caverns. The Three Sisters rock formation and the Jenolan Caves, the latter located in the World Heritage Site, are just two of the many attractions that lure city dwellers to the mountains. Putty Road, between the small gold-rush towns of Windsor and Singleton, passes through the northern Blue Mountains and along the eastern boundary of Wollemi National Park.

4 Wollemi National Park This is the largest park of its kind in New South Wales, a huge forested wilderness covering 5000 km² (1,930 square miles), largely unspoilt and very isolated in parts. The park features deep sandstone gorges and wonderful untouched landscapes along the Colo River and Wollemi River. Basalt outcrops reach heights of over 1,200 m (3,937 ft), and rainforests thrive on the mountains and in the valleys. Visitors can choose from a variety of activities: bushwalking or hiking in the mountains, climbing or canoeing. In 1994, Wollemi Pines were discovered in the park; until then, these 150-million-year-old trees were thought to be extinct. At Singleton, in an industrial

(continued p.110)

1 The fine blue haze that gives the Blue Mountains their name is formed by an oily mist released by the eucalyptus trees.

2 The magnificent 'Three Sisters' rock formation south-east of Katoomba is a landmark in the World Heritage-listed Blue Mountains Area.

Wildlife in south-east Australia

South-east Australia is home to many of the country's best-known animals. At the top of the list are various kangaroo species, common to most parts of Australia. These marsupials of the macropod family have long, powerful hind legs, which are responsible for their highly effective and energy-efficient means of locomotion – hopping. As they hop, the tendons in their hind legs act as springs, while the powerful tail helps the animals keep their balance. All kangaroos have an open pouch on their front. South-east Australia's eucalypt forests are the perfect place to look for koala bears, high up in the trees. The koala's diet has become extremely specialized and they feed on just a few kinds of Australian eucalyptus, of which there are more than five hundred species. The nutrients in the leaves differ according to type, season and region, and koalas sometimes go in search of alternatives. Koalas have an in-built 'fermentation plant' to help them digest

The superb lyrebird, a ground-dwelling songbird of the south-east Australian forests.

their cellulose-rich diet: a koala's caecum (part of the gut) is 2 m (6½ ft) long (while the animal itself grows to a maximum of 80 cm/2½ ft) and contains micro-organisms that help break down food. Koalas are frequently prone to various diseases, including colds, pneumonia and eye infections, but they are also hard-hit by bushfires every year and the ongoing clearing of their habitats. There are two bird species of particular interest in the region: the highly distinctive and stunning lyrebird and the kookaburra. The pheasant-sized lyrebird can mimic sounds perfectly, while the laughing kookaburra is renowned for its loud echoing, cackling call. The latter is around 45 cm (17½ in) high, with a strong beak measuring almost 7 cm (2½ in) long and is one of the best-known Australian birds.

Top: The roofs of the Sydney Opera House look like upturned seashells or billowing sails, and are an iconic feature of the city's harbour. In the shadow of the Harbour Bridge, Dawes Point offers a magnificent [illegible]

Bottom: Sydney Harbour Bridge is the city's second great icon: opened to traffic in 1932, the bridge was built during the Great Depression.
… finally paid off in 1988. The distinctive arch has a span of 503 m (1,650 ft).

MORT BAY PARK
Yeend St. Wharf
Simmons Point
Goat Island
Walsh Bay
DAWES POINT
Sydney Harbour Bridge
Pylon Lookout
Neutral Bay, Mosman Bay
Taronga Zoo
Bennelong Point
Balmain (Thames St.) Wharf
Mort Bay
SIMMONS POINT RES.
McMahons Point, Circular Quay
Millers Point
Sydney Dance Theatre Company
Wharf Theatre
Pier One
Theatre for Young People
Hickson Road
Bradfield Highway
THE ROCKS
Sydney Harbour Tunnel
Tug Berths
THE ZIG ZAG
School
Moores Wharf
Sydney Ports Marine Services
CLYNE RES.
Park Hyatt
Sydney Showboats
Campbells Cove
Sydney Opera House
Man O'War Jetty
ORIGLASS PARK
THORNTON PARK
Balmain East (Darling Street) Wharf
Harbour Control Tower
Colonial House Museum
Santa's Cottage
The Rocks Market
Sailor's Home
Old Sydney Holiday Inn
Sydney Cove
BALMAIN EAST
Anglican Church
Balmain Watch House
Tug Berths
ILLOURA
MUNN RES.
Hero of Waterloo
Garrison Church
Foundation Park
Visitors Centre
Overseas Passenger Terminal
Cadman's Cottage
Writer's Walk
Opera House Car Park
Government House
Water Police
EWENTON PARK
Cameron's Cove
MILLERS POINT
OBSERVATORY PARK
Sydney Observatory & Observatory Hill
Orient Hotel
Museum of Contemporary Art
Opera Quays
Quay Grand Suites
WHITE BAY PARK
Grafton St.
Peacock Point
Toll Plaza
The Observatory
Susannah Place
FIRST FLEET PK.
Ferry Wharves
Circular Quay
Gate
BIRRUNG PARK
Conaust Container Terminals
National Trust Centre & SH Ervin Gallery
Shangri-La
Cahill Expressway
Northern Depot
Darling Harbour
Quay West
Four Seasons Hotel
CIRCULAR QUAY
Sir Stamford at Circular Quay
Johnstons Bay
Observatory Tower
Customs House
AMP Plaza
Justice & Police Museum
Sydney Ports Central Maintenance Depot
St. Patricks
Grosvenor Place
Sydney Harbour Marriott
Sydney Conservatorium of Music
White Bay
PYRMONT POINT PARK
Jones Bay
Darling Island
Stamford Plaza
Maritime Trade Towers
Grosvenor St.
Museum of Sydney
ROSE GARDEN
Glebe Island
GIBA PARK
COMMUNITY PARK
Pyrmont Bay
St. Philips
Western Distributor
Bridge St.
HERB GARDEN
ROYAL BOTANIC GARDENS
Elizabeth (MacArthur) Bay
Darling Harbour Passenger Terminal & Function centre
Scots Church
Rydges Jamison
Australia Square
Sofitel Wentworth
Cahill Tunnel
Sydney Tropical Centre
Palm House
ROZELLE
JAMES WATKINSON RES.
The Elizabeth Piazza
CADI PARK
Gate
The Menzies
WYNYARD
George Street
Radisson Plaza
Kindersley Hse.
Chifley Plaza & Tower
Main Depot & Nursery
Grain Elevator
Conaost Car Terminal
Police
Light Rail
COMMUNITY PARK
Marina
King Street Wharf
The Promenade
Endeavour Fountain
State Library of N.S.W.
Cahill Expressway
Refinery Sq.
Star City
Maritime Heritage Centre
Pyrmont Bay Wharf
Erskine Street
Angel Pl.
Cenotaph
Parliament House
Park Restaurant & Kiosk
Old Glebe Island
JOHN STREET SQUARE
PYRMONT BAY PARK
Wharf 7 Plaza
Medina Grand Harbourside
G.P.O.
The Westin
Martin Pl.
MARTIN PL.
Sydney Hospital
Sydney Eye Hospital
THE DOMAIN
Art Gallery of New South Wales
Pyrmont
Incinerator
Sydney Harbour Casino
PYRMONT
ANZAC Bridge
Australian National Maritime Museum
Sydney Wildlife World
Sydney Aquarium
King Street
Theatre Royal
MLC Centre
Supreme Court
St. James
The Mint
Hyde Park Barracks
DOMAIN
Citywest Office Park
TEN Channel 10 TV Studios
FISH MARKET
Maybanke Courts
HARBOURSIDE
Aquarium Wharf
Four Points by Sheraton
Clarence
York
Strand Arcade
Imperial Arcade
Sydney Tower
Land Titles Office
Domain Car Park (underground)
BLACKWATTLE BAY PARK
Blackwattle Bay
Grand Mercure
Ibis Hotel
Darling Harbour
Harbourside
Pyrmont Bridge (footbridge)
Market Street
Queen Victoria Bldg.
State Th.
City Centre
Sheraton on the Park
Archibald Fountain
St. Marys Cathedral
Eye Hospital
GLEBE POINT
Western Distributor
Cockle Bay Wharf
D.H. Marina
Gavala Aboriginal Cultural Centre
Novotel Darling Harbour
Genesian Theatre
Sydney Hilton
GALERIES VICTORIA
HYDE PARK
Cook & Phillip Park
Sydney University Women's Rowing Club
Sydney Fish Market
Harris
CONVENTION
Motor Museum
Sydney Convention Centre
Cockle Bay
Amphitheatre
IMAX Theatre
Crowne Plaza Darling Harbour
Druitt St.
The Galeries Victoria
Town Hall
Park
Pilgrim Theatre
Great Synagogue
SANDRINGHAM GARDENS
Council Depot
Allen Street
Oaks Goldsborough Apts.
St. Andrews Cathedral
Park Regis
201 Elizabeth St.
St. Georges
Australian Museum
William Street
Cross City Tunnel
The Sydney Boulevard
Sydney Sec. College
Blackwattle Bay Campus
WENTWORTH PARK
Pyrmont Bridge Rd.
Distributor
DARLING HARBOUR
Darling Walk
TUMBALONG PARK
Regent Th.
Flying Angel House
Judges House
Hoyts Village Cplx.
Telstra House
MUSEUM
Sydney Grammar School
St. Paul
Court House
Bridge Road
WENTWORTH
Fig Street
The Sydney Art Gallery
Sydney Exhibition Centre
CHINESE GARDENS
Harbour Street
Radisson Hotel & Suites
Metro Theatre
Police HQ
ANZAC War Memorial
Sydney Marriott
Oaks Hyde Park Plaza
Wattle Street
Sports House
Greyhound Track
Main Entrance
Exhibition Place
Novotel Century
World Tower
World Square
Downing Centre
Whitlam Square
Oxford Street
Saville Park Suites
GLEBE
Quarry
EXHIBITION CENTRE
Community Centre
Ultimo Public School
Powerhouse Museum
Sydney Entertainment Centre
CHINATOWN
Baptist Church
Sydney Plaza
Lutheran Church
Travelodge Wentworth
Community Health Centre
Valhalla Theatre
PARK
William Henry Street
ULTIMO
Harwood Bldg.
Hay Street
Capitol Theatre
Southern Cross
EA Substation
Oxford Square
St. Vincents Caritas Centre
St. James Prim. School
Bridge Road
DR.H.J. FOLEY REST PARK
City of Sydney Depot
PADDY'S MARKETS
University of Technology Sydney
Paddys Markets
Market City
Reading Cinemas
Barclay Theatre
CAPITOL SQ.
Sydney Central
Central Square
Sydney Police Centre
Taylor Square
Sacred
Berman Hse.
HILLS RES.
Campbell Street
HAYMARKET
Pacific Int. Rawson St.
BELMORE PARK
Reservoir St.
Islamic Ctr.
Oriental Garment Hse.
Crown St. Public School
Institute of Technology Sydney
Australian Broadcasting Commission
Citigate Central
Crystal Palace
St. Laurence
Centennial Plaza (RTA)
Interstate & Country Coach Terminal
St. Francis
St. Margarets Hospital
St. Michael
GLEBE
Hoyts Broadway Cinema
Broadway Shopping Centre
BROADWAY
University of Technology Sydney
Inst. of Technology Sydney
Railway Square
The Marque Hotel
Medina Executive
Parcel Office
Central Station
CENTRAL
SURRY HILLS
Chinese Presbyterian
Youth Hostel
School
Catherine St.
Arundel St.
Broadway
Lee St.
Dental Hospital
Club
Devonshire Street Pedestrian Subway
News Limited
Foveaux St.
SHANNON RES.
Fitzroy Street
Bourke Street
State Coroners Court
Chapman Steps
(Great Western Highway)
Parramatta Rd.
Macleay Museum
Zoology
Tennis
Lake Northam
St. Benedict Blackfriars College
Carlton & United Breweries
Regent Street
Bus Parking
Readers Digest
Riley St. Peter
CSIRO
Ross St. Bldg.
Holme Footbridge Theatre
MAIN QUAD
Great Hall
Fisher Library
Nicholson Museum
VICTORIA PARK
Victoria Park Aquatic Centre
City Road
Abercrombie Street
Wallace Theatre
Institute of Education
Manning Bldg.
Stephan Roberts Theatre
CHIPPENDALE
Regent St. (Mortuary)
Tom Mann Theatre
Pavilion
STRAWBERRY HILLS
No. 2 Oval
Squash
Anderson Stuart Bldg.
Tennis
E. David Bldg.
S. Roberts Bldg.
Hockey Field
Geology
Chemistry
Carslaw Bldg.
International House
Seymour Theatre Centre
Cleveland Street
Coronation Playground
PRINCE ALFRED PARK
Presbyterian Church
College
Brett Whiteley Museum
WARD PARK
The Langton Clinic
No. 1 Oval
QE Research
Physics
Health
University of Sydney
Madsen Bldg.
Architecture
Aeronautical Eng.
Sydney South
St. Pauls Pl.
Cleveland St. Intensive English High School
Australian Opera
Belvoir St. Theatre

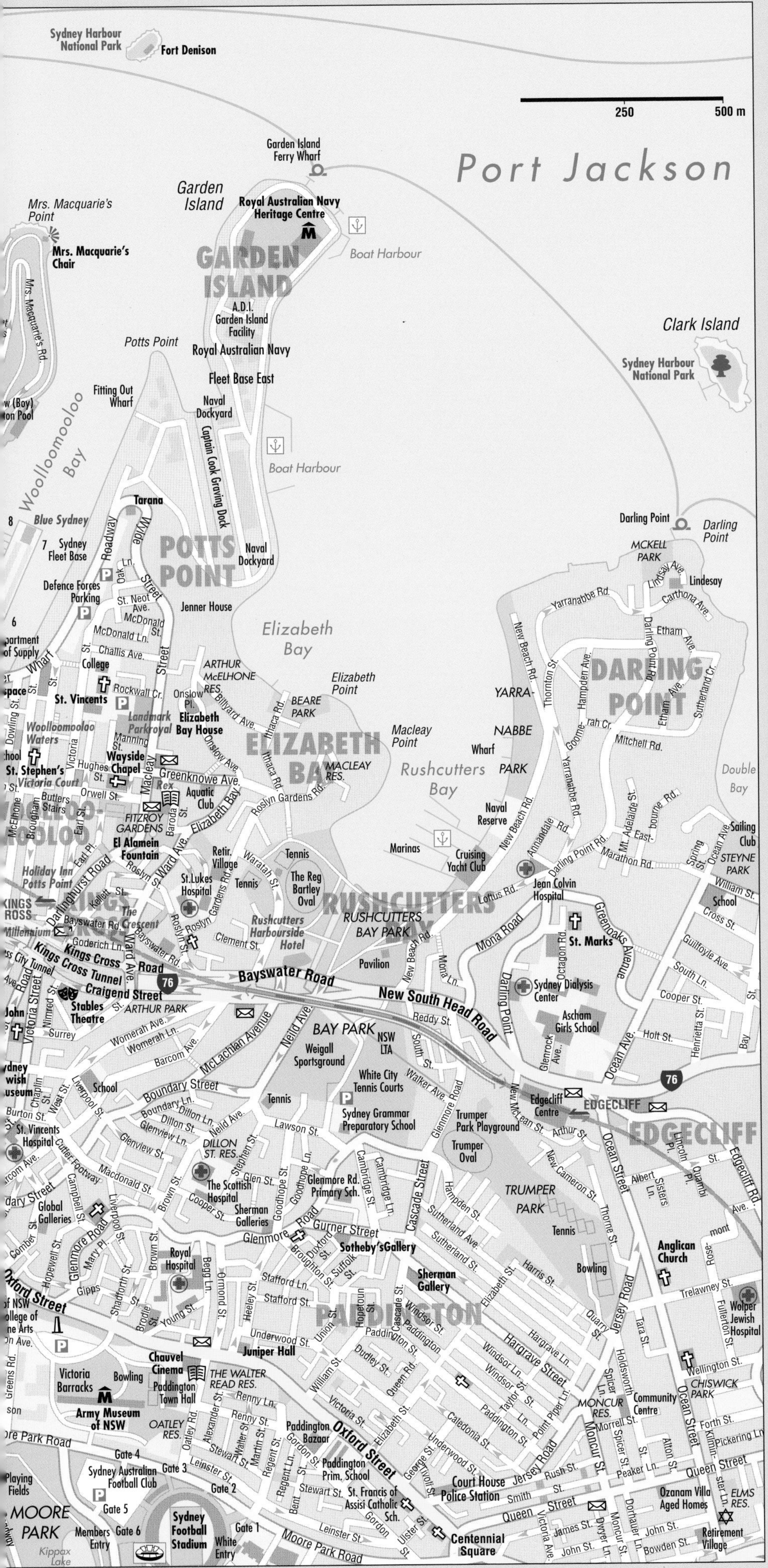

Sydney

The oldest and largest city on the Australian continent, with a population of over four million, Sydney is the capital of New South Wales and Australia's commercial and financial headquarters. Numerous universities, museums and galleries also make Sydney the cultural centre of the south-east coast.

When, in 1788, the first settlers – convicts and their guards – went ashore under the command of Captain Arthur Phillip, none of them could have imagined that Port Jackson would one day become one of the most beautiful cities in the world, under a different name. Admittedly, there was none of the laid-back, almost Mediterranean charm of present-day Sydney in those days: life for convicts and soldiers was tough and rough.

Things began to change towards the end of the 18th century with the first free settlers. Several gold-rushes followed, the first of them taking place in 1851.

Sydney's expansion began with the arrival first of European and then of Asian immigrants, explaining the city's multicultural atmosphere. Today, Sydney is a major economic hub, and for most visitors to Australia it marks the first stop on their tour of the fifth continent.

From the viewing platform 250 m (820 ft) up Sydney Tower (305 m/1,001 ft), enjoys a magnificent panoramic view of the skyline, the harbour, the smart residential suburbs, the Pacific coast and, further inland, the Blue Mountains, not to mention the city's second great landmark, Sydney Harbour Bridge. This amazing construction forms a graceful arc across the harbour at a height of 134 m (440 ft) and with an arch span of 503 m (1,650 ft).

The best place to begin your tour of the city is the harbour, with the Harbour Bridge and the Opera House within sight. Alternatively, spend some time people-watching from one of the many cafés, listen to the street musicians or take a boat trip around the harbour. The Rocks area is a must for shoppers and pub-goers. From the city centre, an elevated railway takes you to Darling Harbour and its many attractions. On the somewhat quieter side, the Botanic Gardens feature a representative cross-section of Australian flora in a tranquil and relaxing setting.

The south of the city is home to Chinatown. The Chinese quarter has its own unique charm and reflects the close links with, and proximity to, Asia. Cabramatta, an outlying district some 30 km (18½ miles) west of the city, is the Vietnamese equivalent of Chinatown. Other districts worth visiting include Victorian-style Paddington to the east of the city and the neighbouring nightclub district, Kings Cross.

Above: Sydney and its Harbour Bridge, one of the most stunning views in Australia.
Centre: Enjoy a walk along the largest natural harbour in the world.
Below: Sydney Tower rises between the roofs of the Sydney Opera House. The viewing platform is 250 m (820 ft) up.

Blue Mountains National Park

The Blue Mountains are situated 50 km (31 miles) west of Sydney on the western edge of the Cumberland Plain basin. It is an area of outstanding natural beauty, attracting over three million visitors every year.

In fact, the Blue Mountains range comprises a sandstone plateau that reaches a height of over 1,000 m (3,281 ft) in places. Over millions of years, its rivers have eroded and dug their way into the rock to depths of hundreds of metres. The signs of these geological processes are unmistakable: gigantic gorges, precipitous cliffs, raging waterfalls, along with a huge variety of flora and fauna, including over a hundred species of birds, eucalyptus trees, mosses, ferns and pretty wild flowers. The Blue Mountains take their name from the bluish haze that envelops them, caused by the release of essential oils from the eucalyptus trees.

Blue Mountains National Park covers an area of some 2,700 m² (1,043 square miles) and was established in 1959. The park has good facilities and is easy to get around: by car you can reach some spectacular vantage points on the Great Western Highway and Cliff Drive between Leura and Katoomba. Two tourist rail services, the Katoomba Scenic Railway and the Zig Zag Railway serve the park. However, the best way to explore it is still on foot. Choose from one of the many walks, among them the Federal Pass Walk, the Prince Henry Cliff Walk or the Grand Canyon Nature Track.

The park's top attractions include the Wentworth Falls, some 300 m (984 ft) high, the Giant Stairway complete with over one thousand steps at Echo Point and the Blue Gum Forest (blue gum is a type of eucalyptus) in Grose Valley. The ultimate, must-have photograph is of the 'Three Sisters', three giant rock formations towering high above the Jamison Valley. Try to avoid visiting these places at the weekend and you will have a greater chance of enjoying this wonderful natural landscape in peace.

The 'Three Sisters' tower high above the valley of the Jamison River.

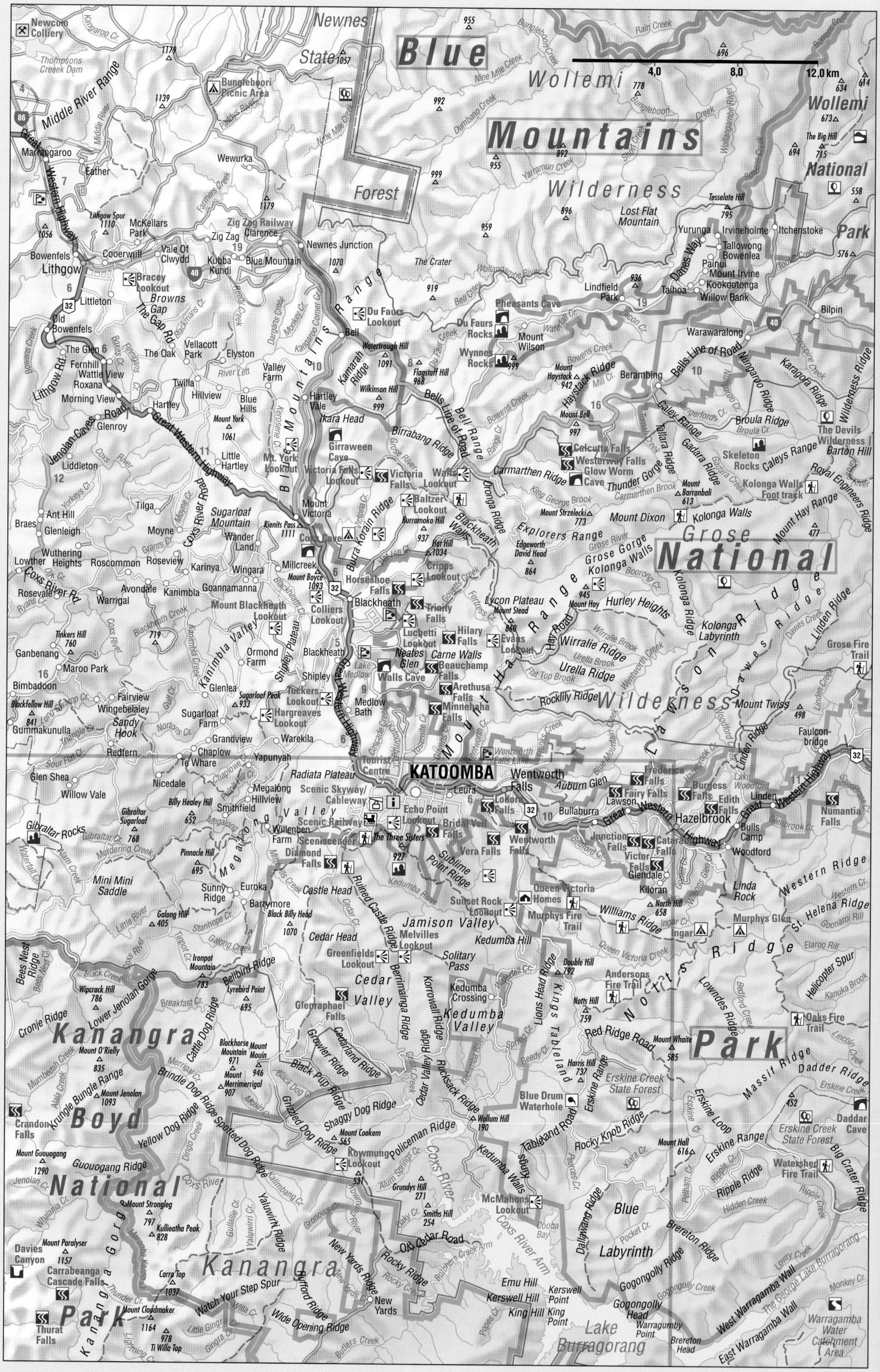

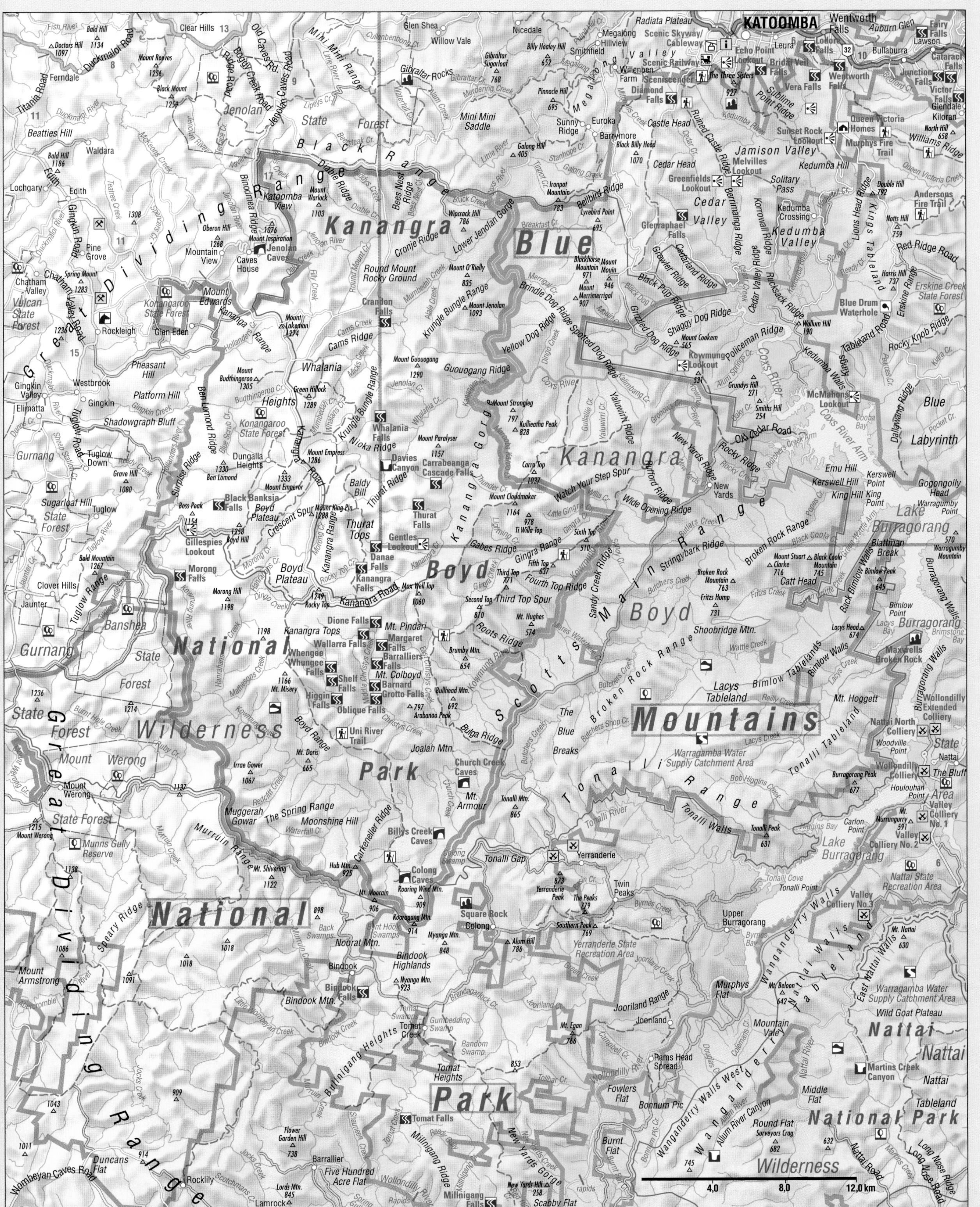
KATOOMBA
Wentworth Falls
Leura
Bullaburra
Radiata Plateau
Megalong
Hillview
Smithfield
Megalong Valley
Scenic Skyway/ Cableway
Echo Point Lookout
Scenic Railway
Scenicsender
The Three Sisters
Bridal Veil Falls
Wentworth Falls
Jamison Valley
Kedumba Valley
Cedar Valley
Kanangra
Blue
Boyd
Mountains
National
Wilderness
Park
National
Park
Great Dividing Range
Black Range
Jenolan Caves
Caves House
Jenolan State Forest
Kanangra Walls
Kanangra Road
Kowmung Lookout
Coxs River
Lake Burragorang
Burragorang
Yerranderie
Tonalli Range
Tonalli Walls
Lacys Tableland
Scotts Main Range
Kanangra Boyd
Nattai
National Park
Wilderness
Colong Caves
Church Creek Caves
Billys Creek Caves
Tuglow Caves
Oberon Hill
Mount Werong
Gurnang State Forest
Bindook Highlands
Tomat Falls
Milnigang Falls
Barrallier
Scabby Flat
Rocklily
Lamrock
Duncans Flat
Wombeyan Caves Road
Lake Burragorang
Warragamba Water Supply Catchment Area
Wanganderry Walls
4,0
8,0
12,0 km

Australian grass trees (*Xanthorroea fulva*), known to the Aborigines as 'black boys' because of their black trunks, are woody evergreens from the lily family found primarily in the dry regions of the country. The photo shows a handful of specimens growing on the rocks of Cape Byron. Captain Cook named the

headland after John Byron, grandfather of the poet Lord Byron and, like Cook, a navigator. Cape Byron marks the easternmost tip of the Australian mainland.

Detour

Dorrigo National Park

Picturesque Dorrigo is situated on a plateau bordering a steep escarpment covered in primeval subtropical and cool-temperate rainforest. The entrance to Dorrigo National Park is 4 km (2½ miles) south-east of the town. The forest adjoins the New England National Park and, like its neighbour, belongs to the East Coast Temperate and Subtropical Rainforest Parks.
The wilderness of the subtropical rainforest and wet eucalypt woodland is an impressive sight, teeming with an abundance of orchids, ferns and mosses. The animal world in the National Park is equally colourful and diverse, allowing visitors the opportunity to see and hear a variety of brightly plumed birds with their shrill birdsong. Guided tours at night shed careful light on the many nocturnal mammals that live in the park.
The steeply rising terrain attracts heavy rainfall in summer, making a visit to the waterfalls a memorable experience. The visitor centre at the entrance to the National Park provides much useful information on the native animal and plant life. Nearby is the Skywalk: this wooden walkway extends 70 m (230 ft) above the treetops and provides some breathtaking views over the rainforest canopy. A number of good tracks lead from the two picnic spots, The Glade (1 km/½ mile from the visitor centre) and Never Never, in the middle of the park, through areas of rainforest and to some of the waterfalls.
If you are interested in the didgeridoo, the Aboriginal musical instrument, the charming nearby hill town of Bellingen is the place to go. The distinctive wind instruments are made from tree trunks hollowed out by termites and fitted with a beeswax mouthpiece. They make a wonderful sound.

A jungle of ferns in Dorrigo National Park.

coal-mining area, join Highway 15 and head east through the Upper Hunter Valley, a region famous for its horse-breeding and wine-growing, to one of Australia's most famous wine regions, the Lower Hunter Valley.

5 Lower Hunter Valley Cessnock, the main town of this wine-producing area, lies at the heart of the valley. Farms and vineyards nestle among gently undulating hills, and to the west you can just make out the foothills of the Great Dividing Range. Vines have been cultivated in the fertile soil of this region since the 1830s. There are around 140 wineries in the valley, most of them open to visitors, and among the most famous are Lindemans, Tyrrell's Wines and Wyndham Estate. In stark contrast, the key industries of Newcastle, the second largest city in New South Wales, are steel, coal and its busy docks. Around 40 km (25 miles) north of Newcastle, it is worth making a stop in Port Stephens, known as the 'dolphin capital of Australia'.

6 Port Stephens Many tourists come to this port to enjoy a dolphin-watching boat trip. Around 150–200 dolphins make their home in Nelson Bay. Between May and July, and September and November, schools of whales swim past the coast, among them killer whales, minke whales and humpback whales. Port Stephens is also famous for Stockton Beach, some 33 km (21 miles) long, where you can even take your four-wheel drive for a spin. Myall Lakes National Park lies 60 km (37 miles) to the north and is the largest lake area in New South Wales.

7 Port Macquarie This is one of the oldest towns in the country, founded in 1821 as a penal colony. Built in the 19th century, the Port Macquarie Museum and Courthouse, St Thomas' Anglican Church and the Roto House still stand today. Since the 1970s, tourism has boosted the town's fortunes remarkably. It is popular with retired Australians, who enjoy the town's relaxed atmosphere, and there are plenty of swimming and surfing beaches together with a wide variety of water sports on offer.
Heading north along the Pacific Highway, you pass through

increasingly humid and damp regions, home to dense, heavily protected rainforests. The route leaves the coastal highway at Kempsey for a further detour into the impressive Great Dividing Range. You travel via Bellingen and Dorrigo en route to the New England National Park.

8 New England National Park Covering an area of 300 km^2 (116 square miles), the park is situated on the escarpment of the New England Plateau (1,400 m/4,593 ft high) and encompasses one of the largest areas of rainforest in New South Wales. Snow gum trees grow in the upper regions, temperate rainforest flourishes at medium altitudes, and a subtropical rainforest, full of tree-high ferns, is located at the foot of the plateau. Drive the 1,562 m (5,125 ft) up to Point Lookout to enjoy a wonderful view of the

tableland escarpment and the Bellinger Valley. On the return journey to the coast, it is certainly worth making a detour to Dorrigo National Park (see Detour, left). From Dorrigo, the Waterfall Way takes you back to the coast. Coffs Harbour boasts a series of attractive beaches and is one of the most popular holiday resorts in the state. Banana plantations have been the mainstay of the region's agriculture for more than a hundred years, reflecting the gradual change in climate from subtropical to tropical. Just a few kilometres north of Coffs Harbour, the Pacific Highway heads inland towards Grafton.

9 Grafton This country town, nestled on the banks of the Clarence River, is known as the 'Jacaranda capital of Australia', and, indeed, its wide and elegant streets are lined with beautifully fragrant jacaranda trees. The Jacaranda Festival takes place when the trees come into blossom in late October or early November. The settlement was founded by lumberjacks around 1830, with cattle farmers following later. When gold was discovered in the upper reaches of the Clarence River, the town developed rapidly and a busy river port flourished around 1880. Traces of the town's late 19th-century prosperity can be seen in a number of well-preserved buildings on the north side of the river. A track from Grafton leads to Wooli, the gateway to Yuraygir National Park, approximately 50 km (31 miles) away.

10 Yuraygir National Park This National Park encompasses the longest stretch of unspoilt coastline in New South Wales. It illustrates perfectly how the coast looked before it became so densely populated. This unspoiled landscape boasts isolated sandy beaches, heaths, swamps and lagoons. The National Park has some excellent walking trails and offers perfect conditions for both surfers and anglers.

11 Yamba This 19th-century fishing village is located 60 km (37 miles) further north, and is now an angler's paradise. Beautiful beaches, a huge choice of water sports and rewarding fishing spots – you can find them all on the Clarence River, the nearby coastal lakes and the ocean. Angourie Point, 5 km (3 miles) south of Yamba, is one of the top surfing beaches in the country. The Pacific Highway now heads north along the apparently endless coastline of pure-white beaches to Byron Bay, some 120 km (75 miles) away.

12 Byron Bay This holiday resort gets its name not from the famous poet but from his grandfather, John Byron, a renowned navigator in the 1760s. It has a mild and sunny climate, splendidly long beaches and perfect wind conditions, all of which

(continued p. 114)

1 The most powerful lighthouse in Australia is on the Cape Byron headland, 107 m (351 ft) above the ocean.

2 The Lower Hunter Valley has been home to the Lindemans Pokolbin winery since 1870.

Detour

Lamington National Park and Border Ranges National Park

Lamington National Park is a well-developed park first listed as a conservation area in 1915 and easy to reach on the Pacific Highway. In the middle of the park is the Lamington plateau, which reaches 900–1,200 m (2,952–3,937 ft), ending in steep cliffs and gorges to the south. The parkland contains more than five hundred waterfalls and a variety of woodland, ranging from tropical and subtropical rainforest to southern beech forest at higher altitudes. The park also boasts a rich diversity of animal life, including almost two hundred different species of birds.

Border Ranges National Park, lying between New South Wales and Queensland, contains the remains of an extinct shield volcano. The park's rainforests are home to gigantic strangler figs, pademelons (small kangaroos) and rare yellow-eared cockatoos.

Above: A waterfall in Lamington National Park.
Below: Subtropical plant life in Border Ranges National Park.

Surfing is a national sport in Australia. It originated in Hawaii, where Captain Cook first observed locals riding the waves on boards in 1778. Surfing became popular in Australia at the beginning of the 20th century – the metre-high breakers along its coastline offer perfect conditions for the keen surfer.

Around three-quarters of all Australians live no more than an hour from the coast. The photo shows surfers off Burleigh Heads against a backdrop of tourist hotels at Surfers Paradise on the Gold Coast.

have made this surfing paradise into one of the most popular holiday resorts on the north-east coast of New South Wales.
If you don't feel like exploring the beaches of the neighbouring Gold Coast to the north, take a detour into the hinterland instead. Some 50 km (31 miles) north of Byron Bay, in Murwillumbah, the Summerland Way turns off into Border Ranges National Park (see side panel, page 111).

13 Gold Coast There's nowhere else in Australia quite like it. The Gold Coast, and the city of the same name at its heart, is home to more luxury hotels, holiday complexes, motels, holiday apartments, guesthouses and youth hostels than anywhere else in the country. It offers an unrivalled variety of sporting and leisure activities and more opportunities for entertainment and shopping than you are likely to find anywhere else. This section of coastline begins on the border with New South Wales and stretches to Coomera, south of Brisbane. The subtropical climate, with temperatures ranging from 22°C to 28°C (71.6°F to 82.4°F) and an annual quota of 300 days of sunshine, attracts over three million visitors per year.

14 Surfers Paradise In 1923, the first holiday development opened in the Gold Coast's best-known resort. It was called 'Surfers Paradise Hotel' and just a few years later the whole area adopted the same name. The town flourished in the 1950s, mostly because of the triple-S factor: sun, surf and sand. Buildings sprang up, and today the entire length of lovely, sandy beach is lined with a strip of hotel and apartment complexes. With all the leisure and sporting activities, entertainment and a lively nightlife on offer, Surfers Paradise is as popular with tourists today as it ever was.

15 Coomera The northern end of the Gold Coast is now home to a string of leisure and theme parks. Located on the Pacific Highway, Dreamworld offers thrilling rides. Not far to the south is Movie World, a movie theme park. Wet'n'Wild offers aquatic fun, while Sea World, Australia's largest commercial marine park, entertains visitors with a variety of shows featuring dolphins and sealions, together with aqua ballet.
Before reaching Brisbane, it is worth making a quick detour into the hinterland to the south-east of the city. From Coomera a minor road takes you to Highway 15 (90 km/56 miles). Main Range National Park is 15 km (9 miles) to the south.

16 Main Range National Park This National Park covers an area of just under 200 km² (77 square miles) and features impressively

high mountains, steep escarpments and plateaux. It forms the western border of the Scenic Rim, a spectacular semi-circle of mountains that runs from here to Lamington National Park, south-west of Brisbane. It is protected by an almost uninterrupted chain of National Parks. The park features a range of types of vegetation: from rainforest in the humid, protected areas, eucalypt woodland at higher altitudes and on the dry slopes, and montane heath on the escarpments of the plateau and on the mountain peaks. The various zones provide a much-needed habitat for a range of animals endangered elsewhere by land clearing and bushfires. Leaving Main Range National Park and its many hiking trails through the forests and bushland, it is only another 120 km (75 miles) on Highway 15 to Brisbane and the end of the Pacific Highway.

17 Brisbane The capital of Queensland lies on the Brisbane River, a few kilometres west of the point at which the river flows into the Pacific. It is Australia's most sun-kissed city, with a population of 1½ million and a modern, expanding economy. In the 1980s, Brisbane enjoyed a boom, triggered by EXPO 88, the World Fair, which was sited on the Brisbane River. Today, Brisbane does not take part in national competitions for Australia's best city. It is confident that it would win hands down anyway. Tourism and agriculture have made Brisbane an affluent city. It boasts a variety of cultural institutions, including the Queensland Cultural Centre, and several exhibition halls, concert and theatre venues and parks. The relatively small inner city area is easy to explore on foot, but for added charm and speed, try the old-style tram.
The Sunshine Coast in the north and the Gold Coast in the south both epitomize the Brisbane lifestyle – sun, sand, surf.

1 Monuments to the tourist boom: high-rise hotels line the beach at Surfers Paradise on the Gold Coast.

2 Boats moored off the banks of the Brisbane River against the skyline of Queensland's capital.

Lamington National Park Five hundred waterfalls, subtropical rainforest and diverse birdlife make this the most popular park in Australia.

Border Ranges National Park The park contains the remnants of a one-time shield volcano. Its subtropical rainforests have UNESCO World Heritage listing.

Main Range National Park A unique wet forest with an impressive array of plant and animal life flourishes where the highlands descend into the coastal plain.

Surfers Paradise The array of leisure activities, sports and entertainment leaves no time for boredom in what is probably Australia's best-known seaside holiday resort.

Dorrigo National Park Various trails and the Skywalk take visitors through subtropical rainforest and eucalypt woodland filled with orchids, ferns and birdlife.

Byron Bay The lighthouse gives a magnificent panoramic view over land and sea.

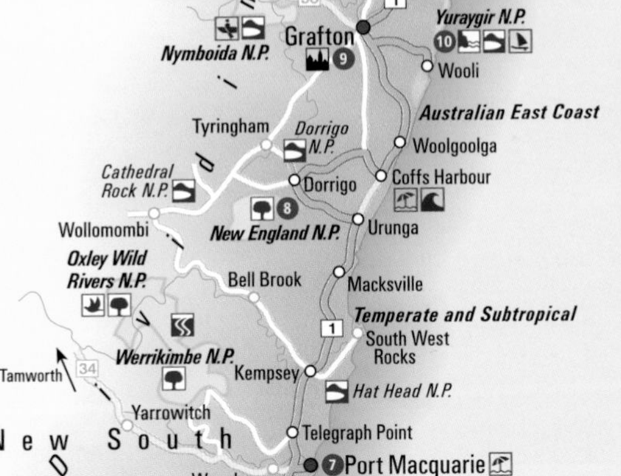

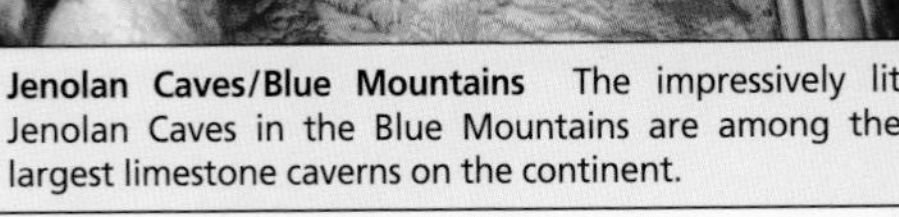

Jenolan Caves/Blue Mountains The impressively lit Jenolan Caves in the Blue Mountains are among the largest limestone caverns on the continent.

Surfers' coast Australia's coasts offer surfers the best possible conditions for their sport. In Australia, surfing means riding the waves in the traditional way; windsurfing is less popular here.

Port Macquarie This sun-blessed coastal resort, one of the oldest settlements in Australia, is popular with all ages and a paradise for water sports enthusiasts.

East Coast Temperate and Subtropical Rainforest Parks Wet eucalypt forests typify the vegetation in the temperate and subtropical latitudes of Australia's Pacific coast. Mosses and ferns also grow in these zones.

Port Stephens The port is famous for its dolphins. Take a boat out into the bay and in no time at all you'll be joined by a couple of these lively creatures; you can even swim with the dolphins in the safety of a drift net. It is a magical and unforgettable experience.

Kanangra Walls Walks along the clifftops and ledges next to the vertical drops afford some breathtaking views.

Hunter Valley Visitors to the vineyards located in Australia's oldest winegrowing region can sample some of the excellent local wines.

Sydney The oldest and largest city in Australia is one of the world's best-loved ports – even more so after the 2000 Olympic Games. In just 200 years, Sydney has grown from a miserable penal camp into the most important economic centre on the continent.

Perth is Australia's most isolated city but it is also a thriving economic centre.

Route 5

Australia

Crossing the continent: from west to east along the south

Bustling cities, deserted outback, desert, steppe and rainforest: a journey through Australia is like a journey around the world. No other continent of its size embraces so many extraordinary and contrasting landscapes, and the Australians themselves are open and friendly towards travellers in their characteristically laid-back way.

Australia is earth's smallest continent, covering just 7.7 million km^2 (3 million square miles) in land mass. It is 3,700 km (2,299 miles) from north to south and more than 4,000 km (2,485 miles) from west to east. Part of the way our route runs parallel to the 'Indian Pacific Express', traversing the Australian continent from the Indian Ocean in the west to the Pacific Ocean in the east. Between Kalgoorlie-Boulder and Woomera the route passes through the treeless, arid Nullarbor Plain and the red outback with its old mining villages. Via Port Augusta it continues through the Mount Lofty Ranges into historic Broken Hill, through the green Sun Belt and the spectacular Blue Mountains all the way to Sydney.

The koala is an Australian emblem.

The landscape and climate of the states en route – Western Australia, South Australia, Victoria and New South Wales – could not be more different. Western Australia, the largest state in Australia, is extreme territory: this mostly uninhabited region has less than 2 million inhabitants, almost all of whom live in and around the populous city of Perth on the south-west coast.

The relaxed lifestyle of those who enjoy the endless sandy beaches of Perth is in stark contrast to the rigours of the outback, the arid and virtually deserted interior of the country. Where the climate becomes more temperate and humid in the east and south-east, the continent's major cities have grown up along the Pacific coast. The fertile coastal areas are likewise Australia's main agricultural and wine-growing regions. Arriving at the Pacific, travellers find one of the most stunning cities in the world, both in appearance and position: Sydney. From this unique city, the Princes Highway runs parallel to the coast and along the Great Dividing Range to Victoria. The southern 'Garden State' is also called the 'State of Diversity', and not without good reason, since it has many dramatically different aspects: precipitous and bizarrely formed cliffs, historic gold-mining towns, snow-topped mountains and semi-deserts shimmering with heat, green and fertile plains, golden beaches and cascading waterfalls. And then there is Melbourne, a city whose influence extends well beyond the confines of this small state.

The 'Twelve Apostles' are some of the most impressive natural sculptures on the south coast of Australia. These limestone monoliths were separated from the mainland by erosion. Their colour changes according to the sun's position.

Devonport Lighthouse, one of the best-known historic monuments on the island, guides ships safely into Tasmania's busiest port.

The history of European settlement in Australia dates back to 1788, when a penal colony was established on the Pacific coast. In the ensuing decades, the east coast was colonized mainly by former convicts, while settlement in the south and west of Australia took a more planned approach.

When the penal colonies were dissolved towards the end of the 19th century, there was an influx of sheep breeders and farmers to Australia. In 1851, the discovery of gold triggered an enormous gold-rush, attracting at least half a million people to the country. The spread of land settled by the growing migrant population came at the expense of indigenous Australians, the Aborigines, whose population shrank dramatically. Today, many Aborigines still live in slums or reservations.

Ferry services run from Melbourne to Tasmania, the large island situated on the other side of the Bass Strait. An alpine landscape, one of the last rainforest regions in the temperate zone and a variety of indigenous animal and plant species make a visit to this island an unforgettable experience. Around a quarter of this unique island is listed as a UNESCO World Heritage Area.

'Down under', where average population density is only 2.5 people per square kilometre, visitors from more densely populated countries are fascinated most of all by the wildness and sheer expanse of space. This in itself is one of the reasons that a journey through 'terra australis incognita', the unknown land of the South as the first maps called it, makes a lasting impression.

These imposing dolerite cliffs rise out of the sea off the Tasman Peninsula.

Indian Pacific Express

The Indian Pacific Express is one of the world's most famous trains. Connecting Perth in the west with Sydney in the east, it traverses the entire continent. The train takes 65 hours to cover the 4,352 km (2,704 miles) of its journey and departs twice a week. In the Nullarbor Plain, the train travels a record 478 km (297 miles) in a straight line, without a single curve, bend or turn. To Australians, the Indian Pacific is just a regular means of transport – albeit a bit slower and more expensive than others. A trip on the Indian Pacific through the south of Australia does not come cheap: a second-class ticket from Perth to Adelaide in a two-berth cabin costs around $1,000 per person.
The first stop on the journey after nine hours' travelling time is the old gold town of Kalgoorlie, where gold-mining still continues today. The next morning, the train rolls through the South Australian outback. Not a single tree grows in the Nullarbor Plain; all you will see are a few kangaroos searching for shade in the bush. The Indian Pacific has been crossing this inhospitable territory since 1917. It took eleven years of dispute over the rail project and another five years of construction work to complete the line after engineer Henry Dean had surveyed this never-ending void. In the early days, passengers had to change trains frequently on account of the varying gauges used in different Australian colonies. The non-stop service from Perth to Sydney has been in operation only since 1970.
Impressive as the technical achievement may be, construction of the line also had some depressing consequences. Curious about the 'devil's snake', as they called the railway line, the Aborigines were drawn into the area around it. Once there, they caught diseases against which they had no natural defences or were killed by the settlers: entire tribes were virtually wiped out as a result – and with them their unique culture.

The Indian Pacific Express has connected Perth and Sydney since 1917.

1

This transcontinental journey, from Perth in the west to Sydney in the east and on through the south to Adelaide and the island of Tasmania, gives travellers a unique opportunity to experience and appreciate Australia in all its amazing diversity.

1 Perth The site on the gently rolling hills along the banks of the Swan River may be isolated, but Perth is one of the richest cities in the country. John S. Roe designed Perth, essentially as it is today, in 1829. In 1890, the gold-rush triggered an upturn in Perth's fortunes that continues to this day: there are more millionaires per square kilometre living in Perth than anywhere else in Australia. Following the discovery of huge reserves of natural resources at the end of the 20th century, the rambling St Georges Terrace quickly grew into a mile-long stretch of office buildings and banks, and Hay Street and Murray Street became busy pedestrian precincts.
The city is also the starting point of the Eyre Highway, connecting Perth with Adelaide in South Australia some 2,400 km (1,490 miles) away. Just a few kilometres east of Perth, the Highway heads into the mountains of the Darling Range.

2 Avon Valley National Park The Darling Range gets a certain amount of rainfall on account of its altitude, so it is not quite as dry in the mountains as on the coast or in the hinterland. The most scenic section of the Darling Range is the Avon Valley, listed as a National Park for its rich abundance of wild flowers. A dense network of trails leads to places of great natural beauty in the park, including Emu Falls and Bald Hill, a splendid vantage point for panoramic views of the surrounding countryside. After crossing through the Darling Range, the Eyre Highway enters the arid Australian hinterland: treeless savannahs and bush land slowly give way to the endless deserts of the outback.

3 Kalgoorlie-Boulder The barren stretches of land some 500–600 km (310–373 miles) east of Perth are prized as the continent's biggest goldfields, giving Western Australia its nickname 'The Golden State'.
This is where the gold-rush reached its peak, and the land around the twin towns of Kalgoorlie-Boulder still contains the largest gold deposits on earth: since 1893, over 1,000 tonnes (1,100 tons) of the precious metal have been extracted here. This 'golden age' is reflected in the magnificent and

2

Travel information

Route profile
Length: approx. 7,500 km/ 4,660 miles (excluding detours)
Time needed: 6–8 weeks
Start: Perth
End: Adelaide or Devonport/ Tasmania
Itinerary (main locations): Perth, Kalgoorlie, Port Augusta, Broken Hill, Sydney, Canberra, Melbourne, Warrnambool, Adelaide, Devonport/ Tasmania, Hobart, Cradle Mountain National Park

Traffic information
Cars drive on the left in Australia. Traffic regulations may differ from state to state. The maximum speed limit in built-up areas is 50 km/h (31 mph) and outside built-up areas is 100 km/h (62 mph). Some attractions are off the beaten track, so it is advisable to use an off-road vehicle.

Tourist information
Australian Tourist Commission: *www.australia.com*
Western Australia: *www.westernaustralia.com*
South Australia: *www.southaustralia.com*
Victoria: *www.about-australia.com/vic.htm*
Indian Pacific Express: *www.railaustralia.com.au/indian_pacific.htm*

Weather information
www.bom.gov.au

in some cases lovingly restored buildings of the era in both towns. Prospecting still continues in the gold mines today, and some large nuggets are on show at the Museum of the Goldfields. Visitors to the mines can join a guided tour to learn more about the trials and tribulations of the gold-miners, the various prospecting methods and how gold is made.
From Kalgoorlie the route continues on Eyre Highway, a road that has only had a continuously sealed surface since 1969, and runs parallel to the railway line all the way across the Nullarbor Plain.

4 Nullarbor National Park The name Nullarbor comes from Latin and describes the landscape here very astutely: there is 'not one tree' as far as the eye can see and flowers and grasses only spring up after plenty of rain in the winter. Geologically speaking, the endless-seeming barren saltbush plain is sediment from an ancient sea, which was uplifted and turned into hot, arid desert-like terrain. Tracks lead to some parts of the steep coast on the stormy Southern Ocean, with its limestone cliffs, sinkholes and overhanging ledges. From June to October, whales can be spotted off the coast on their annual migration.
The border with South Australia runs through Nullarbor National Park, just beyond the remains of the old telegraph station at Eucla. The landscape gradually starts to change: the first trees begin to appear and there is a scattering of grass and flowers. Shortly before Port Augusta, a minor road turns off to the north and passes through Hawker into the mountains of the Flinders Ranges.

5 Flinders Ranges National Park This chain of mountains stretches several hundreds of kilometres through the east of South Australia from north to south. The most attractive parts of this hikers' paradise are protected in a National Park. The park's valleys are home to abundant vegetation, with a sea of wild flowers blooming in spring. This contrasts dramatically with the extremely barren surrounding terrain. The colours and shapes of the mountains and deep ravines have inspired many a painter and writer. Many of the roads are passable by car, although it is advisable to use a four-wheel drive on the gravel tracks in the north. Alternatively, it is possible to explore the National Park on foot.

6 Port Augusta The port and industrial town experienced an enormous boost when the State Electricity Trust built its massive coal power-stations here. As depressing as the town may appear on the outskirts, its centre is in fact very pretty and has a whole host of historic buildings. These include the Town Hall, the Courthouse and St Augustine's Church in particular. The road linking the Stuart Highway with the Barrier Highway leads to Mount Remarkable National

(continued p.122)

1 Sand dunes and withered tufts of grass characterize the Nullarbor Plain.

2 Towering 249 m (817 ft) above the city, Central Park is the highest skyscraper in Perth.

3 The land around Kalgoorlie has the richest gold deposits in Australia.

4 The Nullarbor cliffs on the Great Australian Bight rise 80 m (262 ft) above sea level.

Detour

Nambung National Park

'White Hell' is what locals warily call the area around Nambung National Park. The park covers 175 km² (68 square miles) of land and is situated 200 km (124 miles) north of Perth. The best times to visit are at the end of the winter and in spring, when the wild flowers are in bloom and temperatures are pleasantly mild. There are no facilities for an overnight stay in the park itself, and you will need an off-road vehicle on the unsealed sandy tracks.
The best way to get to the park is via the little port of Cervantes in the north, which you reach on the North West Coastal Highway. The 17-km (10½-mile) track to the Pinnacles begins here. During summer, the sun heats the snowy-white sand dunes to high temperatures. The desert extends 20–30 km (12–18½ miles) inland and stretches over a distance of 50 km (31 miles) along the coast. It originated more than 20,000 years ago in the ice age, when the sea temporarily dropped many metres below its current level. Fine sediment was swept from the sea bed and settled on the strip of coast between Perth and Geraldton.
Right in the middle of this desert, limestone pillars rise 3–5 m (10–16½ ft) out of the yellow sand. The Pinnacles came into being between 15,000 and 80,000 years ago, when vegetation was completely covered with sand. Over thousands of years, the organic matter was transformed and petrified. Eventually the wind exposed the now weather-beaten and bizarrely shaped limestone pillars that still stand today. Some of the rocks look like human beings turned to stone. A 5-km (3-mile) circuit takes visitors through the forest of pillars and offers good vantage points for some dramatic photos.

Rock columns in Nambung National Park.

The Indian Pacific, one of the most famous trains in the world, crossing the Australian outback at dusk. A non-stop service over the 4,352 km (2,702 miles) between Perth and Sydney has been operating twice a week on

Tarcoola and Port Augusta. From there, the Indian Pacific makes a detour via Port Pirie and Crystal Brook to Adelaide on the coast and back before continuing

Mining in the outback

Broken Hill is a small town almost 1,200 km (745 miles) north-west of Sydney on the Barrier Highway (Hwy. 32), surrounded by the barren grass steppes of the Australian outback. The flat landscape and unstinting heat here make the town an inhospitable-looking place, although it has been called 'The Oasis of the West'. The town became prosperous towards the end of the 19th century when the discovery of rich deposits of silver, lead and zinc triggered a rapid upswing in its fortunes. The Post Office and clock tower, the Town Hall and the Catholic

Top: Broken Hill Town Hall (1891). Bottom: Winding towers and mining equipment from the 19th century.

cathedral are reminders of Broken Hill's past prosperity. White's Mineral Art Gallery and Mining Museum showcases the town's mining past. Delprat's Mine and the Day Dream Mine are open to the public.

Art buffs are also well catered-for in Broken Hill: since the 1970s, a number of famous outback artists have made the town their home and exhibit their work here. Broken Hill has also made a name for itself as a base for the Flying Doctor service.

1

Park. At Wilmington a road branches off to the south and into the park.

7 Mount Remarkable National Park The centre point of this mountainous park is Mount Remarkable; rising to a height of 959 m (3,146 ft), it is literally the biggest attraction in the southern part of the Flinders Ranges. Magnificent panoramas, wild ravines and diverse fauna (particularly birdlife) attract visitors to the park. From here the route takes you via Wilmington and Peterborough to the Barrier Highway. Some 280 km (168 miles) later, you come to the border with New South Wales.

8 Broken Hill This little oasis is the right place to experience the singular, raw charm of a mining town in the Australian interior (see side panel, this page). Despite its remote location and tough living conditions, 'Silver City' boasted a population of 35,000 in 1915. Mining is still a presence today, with mounds of coal slag dotted around the town.

9 Mutawintji National Park The National Park stretches some 130 km (80 miles) north of Broken Hill into the Byngnano Ranges, a semi-arid landscape of rugged sandstone rocks, valleys and gorges (access to the park is via Wilcannia and White Cliffs).

2

At Mutawintji Historical Site, which reverted to Aborigine ownership in 1998, visitors can admire a large number of Aboriginal rock drawings. Returning to Broken Hill, it is worth stopping off in the ghost town of Silverton, where silver was mined between 1883 and 1889. Kinchega National Park lies 100 km (62 miles) south-east of Broken Hill; the park features a number of lakes and a distinctive overflow system to control their water level. Continue on the Silver City Highway through barren landscapes to Mildura and from there take the track into Mungo National Park.

10 Mungo National Park Red canyons, sand dunes and a fascinating karst landscape are characteristic features of the 2,400 km^2 (1,104 square miles) of National Park. The park has been under UNESCO protection since 1981 as part of the Willandra Lakes World Heritage Area. Archaeologists found evidence here of human occupation dating as far back as 40,000 years ago and the remains of what has come to be known as 'Mungo Man'. These finds are among the oldest traces of *Homo sapiens* on earth.

Standing in the bleak semi-desert, it is hard to believe that the entire basin was once under water. After the last ice age and a period of rapid warming on the Australian continent, the flat chain of lakes quickly began to dry out. The 'Walls of China' is the name given to the shimmering white scarps of petrified dunes that have been moulded by the ceaseless west wind. Our journey continues on the Sturt Highway to Narrandera and the Newell Highway (up to Parkes) into the eastern section of New South Wales and to the foothills of the Great Dividing Range.

11 Orange At an altitude of 950 m (3,117 ft), the town on the foothills of the extinct Mount

Canobolas volcano was named after William of Orange. This agricultural centre flourished in the 1880s, as the splendid Town Hall reflects. The Botanic Gardens, full of indigenous and imported plants, are also worth visiting. Wine, including a number of prize-winning vintages, is made to the south-west of Orange and can be tasted at the local cellars. Around 50 km (31 miles) further east, Highway 32 arrives in the town of Lithgow in the Blue Mountains.

⓬ **Lithgow** This town on the north-western edge of the mountains is a favourite spot for train enthusiasts, who come from all over the world to see the Zig Zag Railway. This feat of engineering, dating from the second half of the 19th century, only operated along its winding route through tunnels and over imposing viaducts until 1910. Today, the old steam locomotives run on a short stretch of track purely for the entertainment of tourists. Lithgow and the Blue Mountains have been top destinations for Sydney-siders for over a hundred years.

⓭ **Blue Mountains** This low mountain range is part of the Great Dividing Range. At its highest points, the sandstone plateau rises to more than 1,000 m (3,281 ft) above sea level. The region's most iconic landmark is the 'Three Sisters', three needles of rock towering some 300 m (984 ft) above the Jamison Valley. The Blue Mountains take their name from the bluish haze that envelops them. It is caused by the dense eucalypt forests that release a fine mist of essential oil into the air. The Blue Mountains region contains seven National Parks in total and has been part of the UNESCO World Heritage Area since 2000. Sydney, Australia's best-known city, lies just 50 km (31 miles) to the east.

⓮ **Sydney** The oldest, biggest and most beautiful city in Australia sprawls over a large area. With no real reason to be economical with space, the four-million-plus inhabitants have spread themselves over an area of 12,000 km² (4,633 square miles). In just 200 years, Sydney has grown at a tremendous pace and transformed itself from a miserable penal camp into the largest commercial and service centre in Australia. The city's

1 **Bizarre formations: the 'Walls of China' are petrified dunes in Mungo National Park.**

2 **Deeply fissured sandstone cliffs in Mutawintji National Park.**

3 **Eucalyptus trees on Menindee Lake in Kinchega National Park are submerged in the rainy season.**

4 **Weeping Rock and Wentworth Falls located in the Blue Mountains National Park.**

5 **The 'Three Sisters', three sandstone formations in the Blue Mountains.**

Detour

Wilsons Promontory National Park

The conservation area usually referred to as 'Wilsons Prom' is one of the best-known National Parks in Australia. Magnificent beaches, rugged cliffs, beautiful trails suitable for all levels of walks and not least easy access to the park ensure high visitor numbers. The National Park encompasses the entire peninsula, which is also the southernmost point of the Australian mainland. The landscape on the southern tip of Australia on the

Visitors are attracted by the unspoilt nature of Wilsons Promontory National Park.

Bass Strait consists of ancient granite foothills with wooded slopes, valleys, heaths and sand dunes. Visitors get a taste of the diverse animal kingdom as soon as they enter the park on the well-constructed and robust access road, with herds of grazing emus, kangaroos and friendly wombats along the way. Different paths and short tracks turn off the road into parking areas and form the starting points for walks covering a total distance of 80 km (50 miles). Information brochures and detailed maps are available from the Tidal River Visitor Centre, 35 km (21½ miles) after the Yanakie Entrance. A branch of the road to Tidal River leads up to the car park below Mount Oberon; it takes around an hour to climb the 558 m (1,830 ft) to the top. From the peak, your efforts are rewarded with an amazing view over the National Park.

1

major landmarks and premier attractions are the Opera House, the striking Harbour Bridge, The Rocks historic quarter and Sydney Tower. The heart of the city is centred around its harbour that encompasses an area of 55 km² (21 square miles) on the estuary of the Parramatta River.

15 Morton National Park From Sydney, Highway 1 passes through densely populated residential areas and runs parallel to the coast heading south. Rising to an altitude of up to 700 m (2,297 ft), the Southern Highlands begin to the west of the town of Nowra and are home to Moreton National Park. One of the best trips to the park sets out from Nowra via Mount Cambewarra and into Kangaroo Valley, a fertile valley flanked by steep wooded hills. This is a good starting point for walks into the wilderness of the National Park with its sandstone cliffs, gorges, river valleys, waterfalls and rainforests. The main attraction is the Fitzroy Falls, which are located 17 km (11 miles) northwest of Kangaroo Valley and plunge 80 m (262 ft) into a ravine. Via Goulburn the motorway (Highway 31) leads to the Australian capital.

2

3

16 Canberra 'Kamberra' – meeting place – was the name Ngunnawal Aborigines gave to the area of the Monaro highlands where the capital of Australia, Canberra, now lies. Where the indigenous Australians once met for ceremonies, politicians and business people now come together from all over the globe. The city came off the drawing board in 1911 and is built around Lake Burley Griffin, named after the architect who designed the capital. The lake divides the city into the City Hill business district in the north and the Capital Hill government district in the south. The best panoramic views over the city and its surrounds are from the Telstra Tower, which stands 195 m (640 ft) tall on Black Mountain (812 m/2,664 ft) west

of the city centre. Highway 23 leaves the city from the south and crosses the Great Dividing Range towards the coast.

⑰ **Wadbilliga National Park** North-west of the little town of Bega, the park protects fissured mountain terrain and one of the largest undisturbed river catchment areas in Australia. The waterfalls and gorges of the Tuross River in the north-west of the park are particularly attractive, while tall eucalypt forests and wide expanses of heath land dominate in its western section. Bushwalks – for example from the Cascades car park to the Tuross Falls – and bush camping are possible along the Brogo and Wadbilliga rivers. From Bega our route once more follows the Princes Highway. The South East Forest National Park adjoins the Wadbilliga National Park to the south; access to the park is via a track.

⑱ **South East Forest National Park** The park is home to a unique eucalypt jungle. Ancient indigenous species of tree grow in forests that originated before the arrival of Europeans. Selective felling in the forests gave way to rigorous clearing in the 1970s, prompting protests from conservationists and ultimately leading to the establishment of a National Park here.

⑲ **Snowy River National Park** The Snowy Mountains between Canberra and Highway 1 are part of the Great Dividing Range. Many of the mountains are protected by the Snowy River National Park in the south and the adjoining Kosciuszko National Park to the north. The highest peaks on the fifth continent are found here, including Mount Kosciuszko at 2,228 m (7,310 ft). The National Parks through which the Snowy River flows are also Australia's largest snow region, making the Snowy Mountains a popular winter-sports destination. Known as the Australian Alps, the easily accessible mountains, partly alpine landscape with dense forests, meadows full of wild flowers, canyons, waterfalls and reservoirs also attract a lot of hikers in summer. The next stop on the route is Bairnsdale, some 200 km (124 miles) away.

⑳ **The Lakes National Park** Lakes Entrance is Victoria's top holiday destination on the south-east coast and gateway to the Gippsland Lakes. The Lakes National Park includes this lakeland region, woodlands and coastal heath land, Sperm Whale Head Peninsula and a number of islands. The interconnected lakes with their network of rivers and canals are separated from the sea by a narrow strip of dunes.
Krowathunkoolong Keeping Place, an Aboriginal cultural centre, is situated to the west of Bairnsdale. From here it is just another 300 km (186 miles) or so to the capital of Victoria.

㉑ **Melbourne** See page 129.

1 **Together with the Opera House, Sydney Harbour Bridge is one of Sydney's icons.**

2 **The centre of political power: the Parliament Building in Canberra.**

3 **The Melbourne skyline rises out of the Yarra River.**

4 **From Cape Conran south of Snowy River National Park, the view opens out over the Tasman Sea.**

Detour

Ballarat

'Balla Arat' (resting place) is the name the indigenous people gave to the area that is now the largest inland city in Victoria, home to 75,000 inhabitants. Any chance of it remaining a resting place came to an abrupt end in August 1851, when the first gold was discovered here and thousands of adventurers transformed the one-time settler camp on the Black Swamp into tent city. In just one year, the population swelled by an estimated 20,000. In 1858, one of the largest gold nuggets ever found in Australia was uncovered near Ballarat. 'Welcome', as it was named, was found 58 m (190 ft) down and weighed an impressive 62 kg (137 lbs).

A historic street in Ballarat.

One of the most distinctive buildings in Melbourne is Flinders Street Station on the corner of Swanston Street. The complex was completed in 1910 in Edwardian baroque style and even at that time housed an impressive array of luxurious restaurants and elegant facilities. Flinders Street Station is still

the central station for the local train network, and more than 100,000 people pass through it every day. The photograph shows the clock tower of the station building.

NORTH MELBOURNE
CARLTON
CARLTON GARDENS SOUTH
WEST MELBOURNE
FLAGSTAFF GARDENS
MELBOURNE
DOCKLANDS
Victoria Harbour
DOCKLANDS PARK
Yarra River
BATMAN PARK
SOUTHBANK
SOUTH MELBOURNE
QUEEN VICTORIA GARDENS
ALBERT PARK
LINCOLN SQUARE
ARGYLE SQUARE
Royal Exhibition Building
IMAX
Queen Victoria Market
Telstra Dome
Spencer Street Station
Flinders Street Station
Federation Square
Melbourne Aquarium
Crown Casino
Crown Towers
Crown Promenade
Melbourne Exhibition Centre
Melbourne Convention Centre
Melbourne Maritime Museum
Immigration Museum
Police Museum
National Gallery of Victoria
The Arts Centre
State Theatre
Victoria Barracks
Vietnam War Memorial
Port Melbourne Cricket Ground
Port Phillip Specialist School
Chinese Museum
Her Majesty's Theatre
Princess Theatre
Comedy Theatre
Regent Theatre
Forum Theatre
Melbourne Theatre Company
Royal Historical Society of Victoria
Former Royal Mint
City Mosque
St. James Anglican
St. Francis
Welsh Church
Old Melbourne Gaol
Trades Hall
State Library
Storey Hall
Shot Tower
Melbourne Central
Galleria Shopping Plaza
Banking Museum
Rialto Towers Observation Deck
Bethany International Church
Greek Orthodox
Church of Christ
South Melbourne Market
Town Hall
Court House
Westgate Freeway
Wurundjeri Way
Dynon Road
Footscray Road
Harbour Esplanade
Docklands Drive
Spencer Street
King Street
William Street
Queen Street
Elizabeth Street
Swanston Street
Russell Street
Exhibition Street
Peel Street
Victoria Street
La Trobe Street
Lonsdale Street
Bourke Street
Collins Street
Flinders Street
Queensberry Street
Dudley Street
Kings Way
Clarendon Street
City Road
Power Street
Sturt Street
St. Kilda Road
Southbank Boulevard
Whiteman Street
Normanby Road
Montague Street
Ferrars Street
Park Street
Dorcas Street
Bank Street
Coventry Street
Williamstown Road
Ingles Street
Lorimer Street
North Wharf Road
Crockford Street
250
500 m

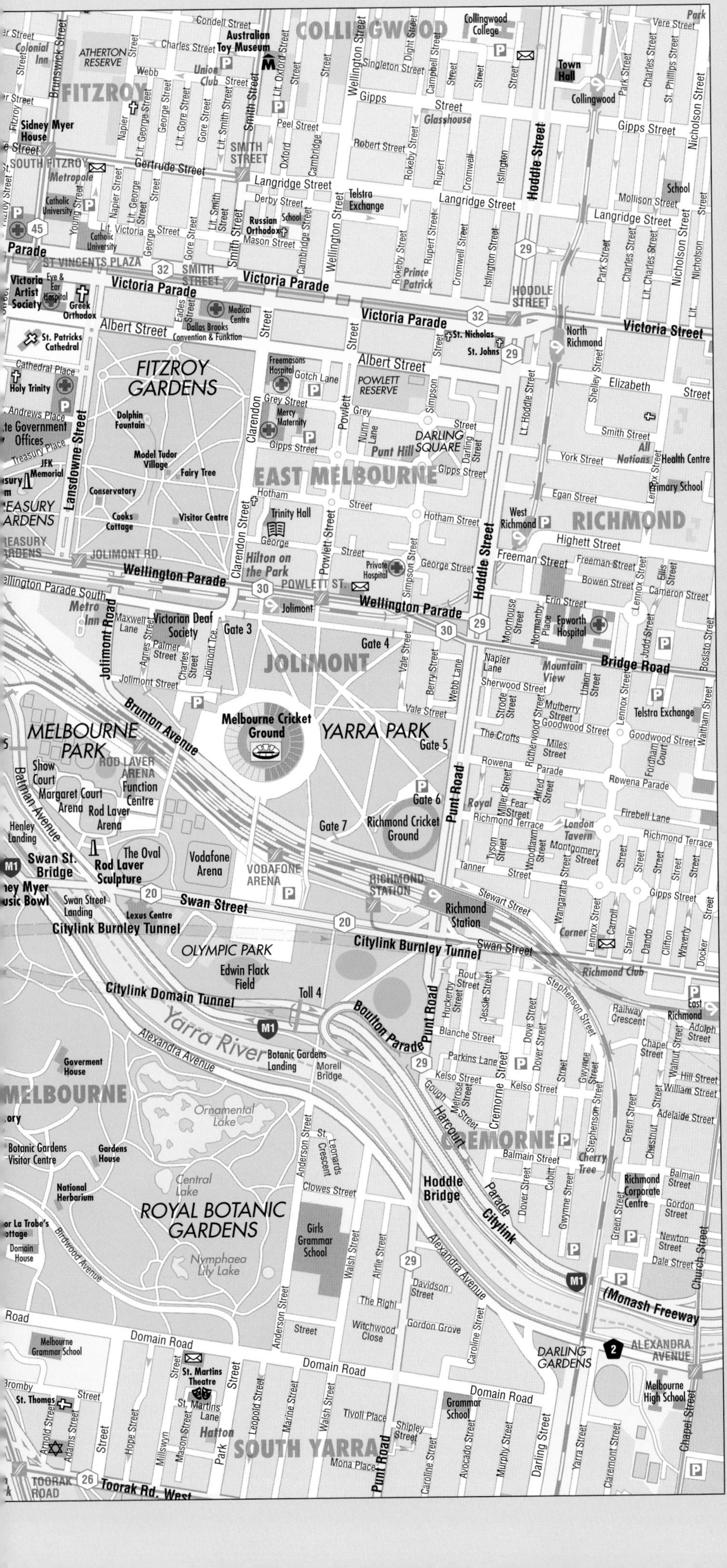

Melbourne

Melbourne calls itself the 'City of Diversity', referring to the wide range of things to see and do here. A diverse mix of nationalities has also helped to shape the city. Located in the south of Victoria, Melbourne is rich in culture and full of gardens and parks.

The whole world seems to feel at home in this city. It has, for instance, the largest Greek community outside Greece, a fact of which Melbourne people are very proud. The streets are arranged on a grid and are packed with variety: magnificent Victorian architecture, on Collins Street for example, sits comfortably alongside skyscrapers and modern glass-and-steel shopping arcades. All over the city, high-rises and shopping malls are interspersed with tranquil parks such as Queen Victoria Gardens or the Royal Botanic Gardens.

The history of this now so diverse city began rather shadily on 6 June 1835, when John Batman talked the Aborigines into transferring around 240,000 ha (593,093 acres) of land to him. 'This will be the place for a village', he wrote in his journal. The settlement expanded slowly in its early years, and the gold-rush threatened its existence by clearing entire districts, but it was soon to become much more than a 'village'. The diggers returned to Melbourne, their pockets full of gold, and by 1860 the population had grown to around 140,000. From 1901 to 1927, Melbourne was the capital of Australia. The city's cultural activity began to flourish around the same time, and Melbourne became known as the 'cultural capital of Australia'.

You will need two to three days for a visit to Melbourne if you want to see the city's many attractions. At 253 m (830 ft), the Rialto Towers are the highest buildings in the Southern hemisphere. A visit to the viewing platform at a heady 248 m (814 ft) should be your first stop on any trip to Melbourne. Nowhere else can you enjoy such a fantastic panorama over the city and its surrounds.

Among the premier attractions in the city are the 'Federation Square' building complex (which opened in 2002), the Ian Potter Centre (a gallery showing works by Australian artists), and the Queen Victoria Market. The market halls date back to 1878 and hold a huge variety of fresh produce. The Royal Exhibition Building in Carlton Gardens was built for the Melbourne International Exhibition of 1880 and inscribed on the World Heritage List in 2004, together with Carlton Gardens, which are also home to the new Melbourne Museum. The architects certainly pulled out all the stops when designing this futuristic-looking city landmark. Glass, steel and rare wood frame the 16,000 m² (172,222 sq ft) of exhibition space showcasing the history of Australia. The Royal Botanic Gardens are situated to the south of the Yarra River and offer visitors a good overview of Australia's native flora.

Above and right: The skyline over the Yarra River is the modern face of Melbourne. The city centre is dominated by huge steel-and-glass office towers, including the two 250-m (820-ft) skyscrapers at 120 and 101 Collins Street (each with roof antenna, see above). Collins Street is also Melbourne's luxury shopping boulevard.

The Great Ocean Road begins south of Geelong and heads around 300 km (186 miles) west along lengthy stretches of the coast until it reaches Princes Highway. The most spectacular section of this scenic route is in Port Campbell National Park. The park's main landmark is the 'Twelve Apostles', a group of

limestone columns that rise 65 m (213 ft) out of the surf and are constantly changing under the effects of wind and weather. Once upon a time, the West Wind Drift forced countless ships onto the rocks and into what was to become one of the world's largest ship graveyards, just off the coast here.

Wildlife on the south coast

The scenic beauty of the south coast of Australia is matched by its diverse range of fauna. Most distinctive of the mammals is the wombat. This nocturnal creature, which looks like a small bear, feeds mainly on grasses, herbs, roots and fungus and digs entire networks of underground burrows with its powerful claws.
Of all species the most unusual are the monotremes, the only egg-laying mammals on earth. The name originates from the fact that they, like birds and reptiles, have only a single opening for reproduction, defecation

The black swan is found only in Australia.

and urination. The duck-billed platypus is an example of a monotreme; it has the body of an otter, the tail of a beaver, fins for swimming and a beak-like mouth.
One of the ornithological rarities in the region is the black swan, a bird found only in Australia. With its black plumage, it was thought for a long time to be a harbinger of bad tidings. Little penguins are also found on some sections of the south Australian coast, an indication that Antarctica is not that far away.
The sea lions that inhabit some sections of beach are unperturbed by curious tourists. In deeper waters you can expect to find sharks – around a hundred species of the creatures live off the coast of eastern and southern Australia alone, some of which pose a danger to humans.

1

22 Geelong The second-largest city in Victoria, set on Corio Bay, is the first major place you come to after leaving Melbourne on the Princes Highway and driving west along the coast. The first permanent settlement here was established in 1836 and initially centred on agriculture (wool and wheat). During the gold boom, Geelong became the chief port for incoming gold-prospectors and exporting gold. Industrialization took off on a large scale at the beginning of the 20th century and is still a feature of the city today. Geelong's main attraction is the National Wool Museum in an old woodshed dating back to 1872. The museum showcases the history of sheep-breeding and the wool trade in Australia.
Between Geelong and Warrnambool you should leave the Princes Highway for the Great Ocean Road, an absolute dream of a route along the coast. The road winds like a gigantic snake along the stunning steep coastline, also known as the 'Shipwreck Coast'. Spits of land reach like fingers into the surging ocean and dark-green grassland stretches below the wisps of black storm clouds that sporadically shroud the landscape in rain. Our route passes the Mountain Ash (*Eucalyptus regnans*) of Great Otway National Park, the bizarre cliffs of the 'Twelve Apostles' and at Loch Ard Gorge a rock cave on the ocean that is bathed in myth and legend.

2

23 Warrnambool This city full of parklands and gardens marks the end of the Great Ocean Road. The Flagstaff Hill Maritime Village is a living reminder of days gone by, where visitors can view restored sailing ships and port buildings dating from the 19th century.
Apart from whale-watching, you can also take a day trip from here or from Portland, 100 km (62 miles) away at the other end of the bay, to the Grampians National Park, just two hours' drive to the north. The park is described as the most beautiful of Victoria's National Parks on account of its fascinating mountainous landscape, Aboriginal rock drawings, and the diversity of animal species that seek refuge here.
Around 100 km (62 miles) west of Warrnambool, the Princes Highway crosses the border between Victoria and South Australia. In Mount Gambier the Riddoch Highway takes you north to one of the most significant archaeological sites in the world.

24 Naracoorte Caves National Park In 1969, a team of researchers discovered a new cave among the many karst caverns found in the area. The floor of the cave was littered with bones and, in the ensuing years, tens of thousands of fragments of skull and jaw bones from mammals, marsupials, birds, lizards and monotremes were uncovered. Monotremes

are transitional forms of creatures between reptiles and mammals, and include the rare duck-billed platypus.
The Victoria Cave fossils are between 18,000 and 170,000 years old and the site was inscribed on the UNESCO World Heritage List in 1994. The bones found here come from a total of ninety-three rare species of vertebrates and include many of the Australian megafauna that inhabited the continent 100,000 years ago.

The Princes Highway continues its way along the coast; if visibility is good, you can even make out Kangaroo Island from here. Shortly before arriving in the capital of South Australia, the Highway comes upon a German settlement that looks somewhat out of place in the South Australian countryside.

25 Hahndorf Streets lined with old trees, typically German half-timbered houses and Lutheran churches with pointed spires make up Hahndorf, the second-oldest German settlement in Australia. Here you will find plenty of typically German souvenirs and a variety of German dishes on the menu of every restaurant in town – and if that is not enough, Hahndorf pays homage to German tradition with an annual Oktoberfest at the Hahndorf Inn.
Hahndorf was established in 1839 by Protestant migrants from East Prussia. The name comes from Captain Hahn, who helped the newcomers to find land. In 1988, the whole of Hahndorf was granted conservation status. Our journey continues through the stunning Adelaide Hills some 30 km (18 miles) down the road to the city of Adelaide.

26 Adelaide With its wide streets, open squares and historic arcades, visitors to Adelaide quickly forget they are in a city that is home to over a million people. The city centre, which was modelled on the Sicilian city of Catania, is arranged on a grid, making it compact and easy to get around on foot. The wide streets and boulevards are interspersed with generous areas of parkland. It is a vibrant and attractive city.
Adelaide's main attractions include the venerable buildings along the elegant North Terrace, also known as the 'Cultural Mile', and the entertainment district around Hindley Street or in the East End. It also makes a perfect base for trips to the nearby wine regions.

The Great Ocean Road

The Great Ocean Road runs 320 km (199 miles) between Torquay and Warrnambool and brings drivers face-to-face with the breathtakingly atmospheric, raw and untamed nature along the 'Shipwreck Coast'. The coast owes its rather ominous name to the 150 ships that ran aground here between 1837 and 1920. The stormy south winds regularly drove sailing ships against the dangerous cliffs and sent them to a watery grave, taking hundreds of migrants and gold-seekers down with them.

1 The strangely shaped Remarkable Rocks at Kirkpatrick Point on Kangaroo Island are just a day trip away from Adelaide.

2 Still waters at Grampians National Park.

Hobart

Hobart has a population of 200,000 and sits picturesquely beneath Mount Wellington on the south-east coast of Tasmania. To describe the capital on the Derwent River as Australia's largest open-air museum is no exaggeration, since the National Trust lists more than ninety of its buildings as historically important. Although Hobart is the capital of Tasmania, it is a tranquil and gentle city. Here you can linger in the comfortable sidewalk cafés or wander down the many historic streets for a spot of window-shopping. Mount Wellington offers a fabulous view over the wide expanse of houses, Sullivans Cove, Storm Bay and the undulating country around Hobart. The beautiful parklands to the north of the city centre, not least the Royal Botanic Gardens, are well worth visiting.

Victoria Dock is home to Hobart's fleet of fishing boats.

Its pretty houses and street cafés make Salamanca Place a very fashionable address in Hobart. The place comes alive on Saturday mornings for a large open-air market selling everything from fruit and vegetables to books and antiques. The city's shopping and business district centres on Liverpool Street and Collins Street and the two streets they cross, Elizabeth Street and Murray Street. The area around the harbour is another of Hobart's lively spots. A trip through Battery Point transports visitors back into olden times. Named after the gun emplacements that once protected the port, Battery Point used to be a working-class area. Later, well-off merchants moved in and settled here. Most houses have undergone careful restoration and create a charming atmosphere.

Art-lovers should not miss the Tasmanian Museum & Art Gallery. Sections of the building date back to 1808 and as such are among the oldest buildings in town. Collections deal with the natural world, Aboriginal culture, maritime history and the development of whaling.

1

Detour

Tasmania

Australia's smallest state is an island full of superlatives. Tasmania's population of just under 500,000 people is said to breathe the cleanest air on earth. In the forests to the south-west of the island, a 4,000-year-old Huon Pine is thought to be the oldest tree in the world. 'Tassies' are also proud of the fact that their island is home to 'Cascade', Australia's oldest brewery. And if you want to get a gourmet's heart beating faster, just mention Tasmanian fish: nowhere else in Australia can you find such excellent brown trout, pollack or trevalla as on the green island.

European discovery of the 'green corner of the red continent' actually began with a mistake. Dutch seafarer Abel Tasman first stepped ashore on the island on the morning of 2 December 1642. He named it 'Van Diemen's Land' in honour of the then governor of the Dutch East Indies colony. Tasman believed himself to be standing on the southernmost tip of the mainland. His sea charts consequently included the land bridge that had in fact been submerged under the rising ocean during the last ice age 10,000 years ago. It was not until a good 150 years later that seafarers Matthew Flinders and George Bass discovered the 240-km- (149-mile)-wide Bass Strait. The British kept a close watch over the land that Captain Cook had claimed for the crown, particularly in 1802, when French frigates sailed close to Van Diemen's Land. In 1804 a colony was founded, with Lieutenant Colonel David Collins serving as its first Lieutenant-Governor. He established the settlement that would become Hobart at Sullivans Cove on the Derwent River.

2

From 1821 onwards, Macquarie Harbour on the west coast was the end of the road for many convicts. Up to the turn of the year 1852/53, when the last deportees arrived and Van Diemen's Land was officially renamed Tasmania, thousands of people were sentenced to hard labour on the docks, in house construction and forestry, particularly in 'prison town' Port Arthur. Just a year before Van Diemen's Lane separated from New South Wales, Lieutenant George Arthur took over, governing with an iron fist from 1824 to 1836. The Arthur regime was notorious for hunting down Aborigines. None of the 5,000 Tasmanian Aborigines survived; the last Aborigine on Tasmania died in 1876.

Timber, mining, sheep breeding and a huge volume of inward tourism provide the state of Tasmania with a good living. Granny Smiths are also a major export; this green apple was named after Maria Smith, who grew the first apples of this kind in Tasmania in her small garden in Hobart in the year 1868.

Devonport

Welcome to Tasmania! Ferries from Melbourne dock early in the morning – often after a rough crossing – in Devonport, for many travellers the gateway to Tasmania. The third-largest town in Tasmania has a population of around 25,000 and is an important industrial and shipping centre for agricultural products. The Tiagarra Tasmanian Aboriginal Culture Centre presents an informative exhibition on the indigenous Aborigines of Tasmania, who died out on the island in the 19th century. The Culture Centre is situated on the Mersey Bluff, a rocky ledge on the Bass Strait, a traditional Aboriginal sacred site. The cliffs along the coast are full of Aboriginal artwork and a walking trail leads from the museum to the site. From Devonport, Highway 1 initially heads inland to the next stop, Launceston.

Launceston

This verdant city (population: 70,000) is the second-largest community in Tasmania and is set in the north-east of the island in a charming landscape of small hills and valleys. Launceston is sited at the convergence of the North Esk and South Esk rivers, and the planners who designed the town were

obviously keen on small parks and grassy areas. The protected harbour on the estuary of the Tamar River, as it is called from here, lies around 60 km (37 miles) inland and was explored by Bass and Flinders in 1798 during their circumnavigation of Tasmania. William Paterson founded the present settlement in 1805 and profitable agriculture in the surrounding area, mills and breweries ensured growing prosperity. As early as the 1820s, Launceston became northern Tasmania's most important city. Quays and warehouses were built along the river harbour. Most historic buildings can be found in St John Street and George Street, parallel to it. The shopping district centres on two pedestrian zones: the Brisbane Street Mall and the curved Quadrant Mall.

Penny Royal World is one of the city's most popular attractions. At the heart of this open-air museum are a windmill and a watermill, the Royal Gunpowder Mill and an arsenal foundry. Here you can take a trip on a historic tram or on board a paddle steamer. It's just a ten-minute walk from Penny Royal World to Cataract Gorge in the south-west of the city. Here the South Esk River has carved a wild and romantic gorge into the rock. Pathways lead through the gorge, and a chair-lift runs overhead.

Highway 3 (Tasman Highway) heads towards the north-eastern tip of the island. From Herrick take the road to Gladstone.

Mount William National Park

From Gladstone it is a further 15 km (9 miles) east to the National Park: wide expanses of eucalypt forest cover the slopes of Mount William (216 m/708 ft) and Bailey's Hill. The fauna is relatively diverse too, although the National Park was mainly set up as a sanctuary for the indigenous Forester kangaroo. The park also provides a habitat for many nocturnal creatures, and with a bit of luck you might even spot an elusive Tasmanian devil.

The Tasman Highway (Highway 3) runs from the north-eastern tip along the rugged east coast all the way to the south-east corner of the island. The mountains in the interior are often shrouded in thick mist. Our route continues through an alternating landscape of green pastures and dense beech forests, past the Freycinet National Park and its three distinctive granite cliffs and onwards to Port Arthur just under 400 km (248 miles) away.

Port Arthur

Between 1831 and 1853, more than 12,500 convicts passed through 'Tasmania's hell on earth', as the history books refer to Port Arthur. On the southern tip of the Tasman Peninsula, visitors today can view the ruins of the former 'model prison' of Port Arthur. The desolate remains of the prison walls are a sinister reminder of Tasmania's past as a penal settlement. People were often interned for no good reason: stealing a piece of bread or a horse was enough to get the *(continued p. 139)*

1 A guiding light into Tasmania: Devonport Lighthouse.

2 Once the end of the road for many convicts: the former prison of Port Arthur.

3 Freycinet Peninsula, a dramatic spit of land reaching far south.

4 Giant ferns, a typical feature of Tasmania's temperate rainforest.

Tasmanian wildlife

Tasmanian fauna feature a number of interesting species, among them the nocturnal Tasmanian devil (*Sarcophilus harrisii*). This carnivorous marsupial is around 80 cm (31½ inches) long and stockily built. It has dark fur, a terrifying set of teeth and a 'devilish' screech. Like the Tasmanian tiger and the wallaby, the Tasmanian devil has been threatened with extinction. It is now only found in Tasmania. Little penguins can be found along the coast.

Top: Tasmanian devil.
Bottom: Wallaby in the Tasmanian Highlands.

Typical features of the Tasmanian landscape include deeply fissured mountains rising to 1,500 m (4,291 ft) and plateaux bordered by steep scarps known as 'tiers'. The plateaux fall dramatically towards the sea, as seen here at the South West Cape on Tasmania's southern tip. Thousands of lakes and rivers make

large sections of Tasmania difficult to reach, which has helped to preserve the island's unspoilt natural beauty. Around a quarter of Tasmania's area is inscribed on the UNESCO World Heritage List, and around forty per cent is protected by National Parks. The South West Cape is part of the Southwest National Park.

The Southwest National Park, the largest and most remote park in Tasmania, stretches to the southernmost tip of the island and is dominated by barren shale mountains, densely wooded valleys and a superb

perpetrator shipped off to Port Arthur. Many of the deportees were repeat offenders who had been banished from the mainland. When deportations ceased in 1853, the prison complex was turned into an asylum. In 1897, a large section of the buildings burnt down.

Hobart
Lieutenant Colonel David Collins surely never dreamt that the piece of land he named in 1804 after Lord Hobart, the minister for the colonies at that time, would one day become the southernmost capital of an Australian state. Thanks to Governor Macquarie, the town was built according to a structured plan. Whaling, shipbuilding and exports of maize, high-quality wood and merino wool brought in a lot of money, and this prosperity found expression in the town's many magnificent sandstone and brick buildings constructed by convicts.

South of the city centre, Nelson Road winds up Mount Nelson. The mountain offers a panoramic view of Hobart, the harbour and the Derwent River estuary from its peak at 340 m (1,115 ft). Tasmania's scenic attractions commence to the west of the city; most are listed as National Parks and have been under the protection of UNESCO since 1982. All the parks are in easy reach of Highway 10 and the minor roads leading from it.

Southwest National Park
The largest and also the most remote National Park in Tasmania forms the southern section of the Tasmanian Wilderness World Heritage Area, taking in the entire south-west of the island. The landscape is dominated by impressive barren quartzite and slate mountains and densely wooded valleys interspersed with grassy plains. In the very south, the isolated coastline is set in magnificent scenery.

Franklin-Gordon Wild Rivers National Park
This National Park covers some 4,460 km^2 (2,052 square miles) of land and is the heart of the Tasmanian Wilderness World Heritage Area, connecting the Southwest National Park in the south with the adjoining Cradle Mountain–Lake St Clair National Park in the north, Walls of Jerusalem National Park, and Mount Field National Park. In the 1970s and 1980s, the National Park attained international fame as controversy raged over plans to build a hydro-power station and huge reservoirs in the area. The conservationists won, and the wild beauty of the Franklin River, its tributaries and the dense rainforest remain intact today.

Cradle Mountain–Lake St Clair National Park
Cradle Mountain is vaguely crib-shaped. It was given its name by a surveyor for the Van Diemen's Land Company in 1827. Joseph Fossey saw the dramatic peak of what is now the park and immediately named it Cradle Mountain. The region around the mountain and around Lake St Clair further south is a National Park and forms the northern section of the UNESCO World Heritage Area. The alpine terrain originated during the last ice age, especially at the end of the period. The glaciers retreated, leaving behind them rugged peaks, U-shaped valleys and moraine lakes. Scenic highlights are the Frenchmans Cap peak, the highlands of the Mount-La-Pérouse massif and the rugged heights of the Du Cane and Traveller Ranges. These are parts of the island's central plateau, which is made up of around twenty peaks with heights exceeding 1,300 m (426 ft); one of them, Mount Ossa, is the highest mountain in Tasmania at 1,617 m (5,305 ft). It is composed of Jurassic dolerite and is named after Mount Ossa in Greece.

1 **The waters of Franklin-Gordon Wild Rivers National Park have an austere beauty.**

2 **Green pastures border the road to Stanley on the north-west coast of Tasmania.**

Nambung National Park Some 200 km (124 miles) north of Perth stretches a bizarre desertscape; the Pinnacles are its most striking feature – thousands of sandstone peaks in an ocean of sand dunes.

Nullarbor National Park Not a tree (Latin *'nullus arbor'*) but low saltbush prevails in this monotonous-looking plain – at least in summer. Flowers and grasses bloom after the winter's rain.

Flinders Ranges National Park A rich abundance of vegetation has survived at the heart of a picturesque chain of mountains, despite harsh natural conditions. In spring the area is carpeted with wild flowers. The shapes and colours of the mountains and their deep gorges have inspired many artists.

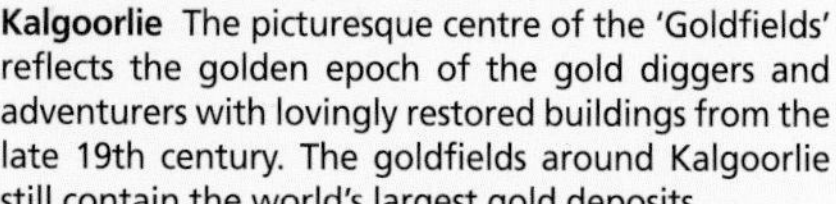

Kalgoorlie The picturesque centre of the 'Goldfields' reflects the golden epoch of the gold diggers and adventurers with lovingly restored buildings from the late 19th century. The goldfields around Kalgoorlie still contain the world's largest gold deposits.

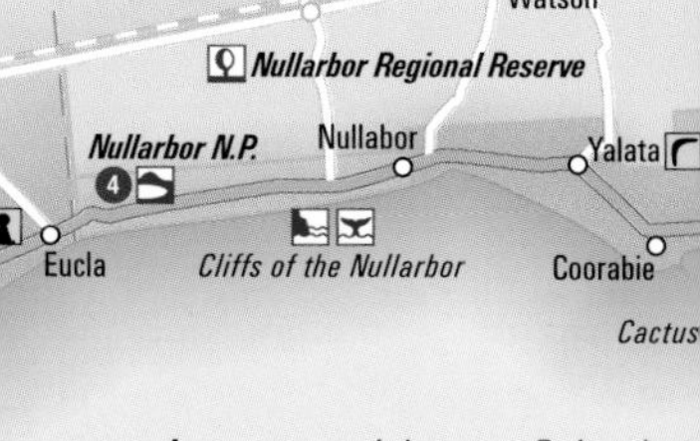

Perth The capital of Western Australia, renowned for its colourful and laid-back lifestyle, is also the water sports capital of Australia. Sights worth seeing include Kings Park and Botanic Garden, the historic London Court shopping arcade and the museums in Perth Cultural Centre.

Eucla The ruins of an important 1877 telegraph station now lie almost buried under drifting sand in this tiny outpost. The transcontinental telephone network marked the end of the line for the telegraph station.

Cliffs of the Nullarbor A virtually treeless landscape drops away to the strangely formed cliffs of the stormy Southern Ocean. These cliffs and the chance of spotting a whale offshore lend this coastline its particular charm.

Adelaide The capital of South Australia holds the largest cultural festival in the Asia-Pacific region. The South Australian Museum is worth a visit.

Melbourne Magnificent Victorian buildings stand alongside skyscrapers and shopping malls, with large areas of parkland in between. The city has a big migrant population: people from 140 nations have made Melbourne their home. Must see: Royal Botanic Gardens, Flinders Station, Victorian Arts Centre.

Kangaroo Island The third-largest Australian island is a must for nature-lovers. The photo shows the Cape du Couedic Lighthouse.

Great Otway National Park Mountain Ash grow to heights of 100 m (328 ft) here in the dense cool-temperate rainforest.

Twelve Apostles These hard limestone monoliths rise out of the landscape along the Great Ocean Road in the south of Victoria.

Freycinet National Park Situated on a peninsula on the east coast of Tasmania, this National Park boasts dreamlike bays of white sandy beaches. 'The Hazards' are three distinctive granite rocks just off the coast.

Franklin-Gordon Wild Rivers National Park Following a battle over a reservoir-building project here, Tasmania's sleepy Franklin River and its unique rainforest are now protected areas.

Mungo National Park This desert park lies 100 km (62 miles) east of Mildura at the centre of the Willandra Lakes World Heritage Area. The main attraction is the 'Walls of China', a solidified sand dune stretching some 40 km (25 miles). Archaeological finds point to 40,000 years of settlement in this area.

Blue Mountains National Park A fine mist of eucalyptus oil swathes a bizarre mountainous world to the west of Sydney in a mysterious bluish haze. Forests and gorges dominate the landscape of the National Park.

Sydney The metropolis is not only the oldest and largest city in Australia, it is also considered the most beautiful. Sydney enjoys a fabulous location in a large natural harbour basin and has kilometre-long sandy beaches (Bondi Beach). The stunning Opera House is an architectural highlight.

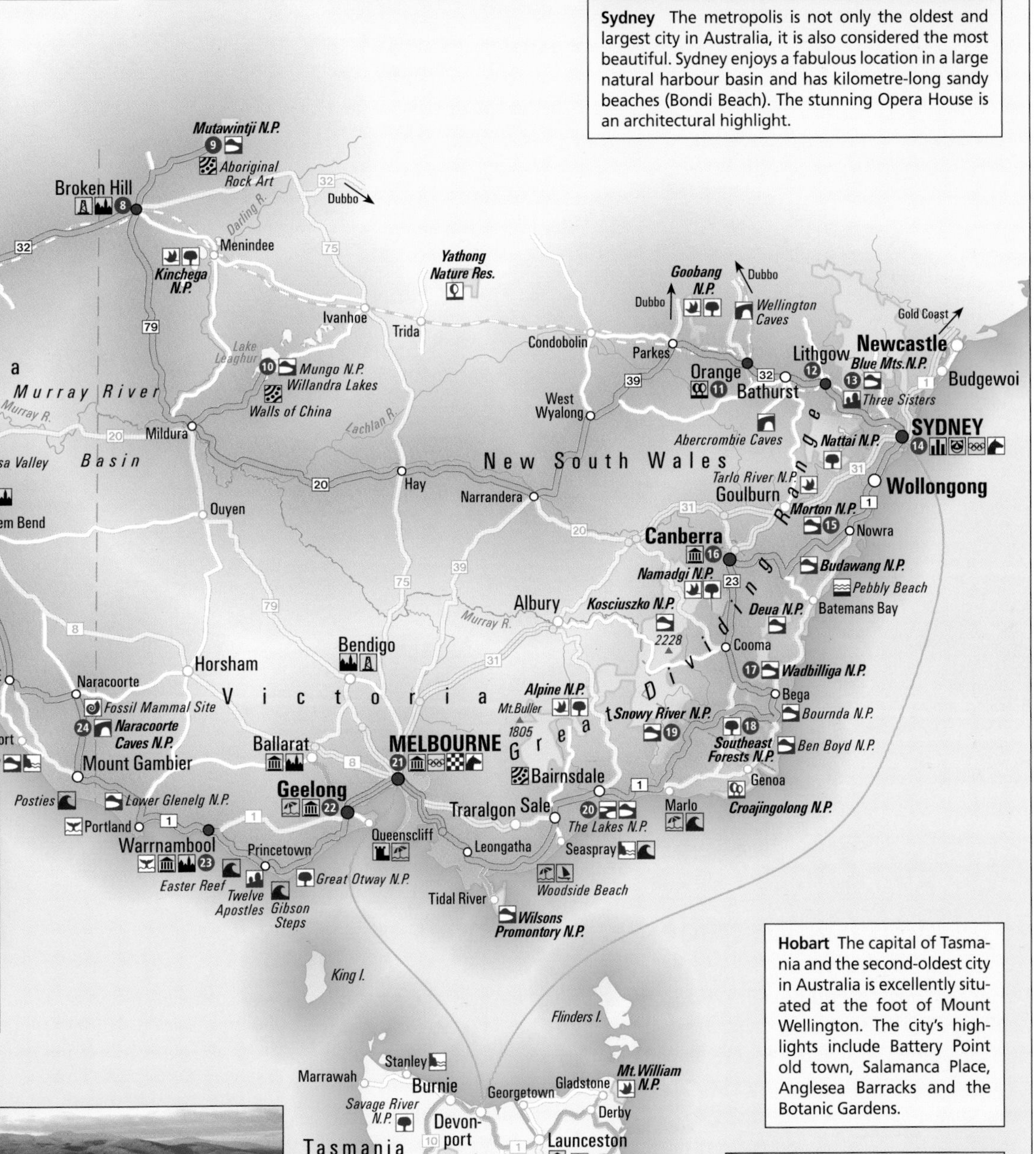

Canberra Once a ceremonial meeting place for Aborigines, today the political heart of the country: Canberra was established as the Australian capital in 1911.

Hobart The capital of Tasmania and the second-oldest city in Australia is excellently situated at the foot of Mount Wellington. The city's highlights include Battery Point old town, Salamanca Place, Anglesea Barracks and the Botanic Gardens.

Southwest National Park Barren shale mountains and densely wooded valleys alternate with wide expanses of grassy plain in Tasmania's largest National Park.

Southwest and Southeast Cape Magnificent landscapes stretch along the southern coast of Tasmania. Bizarrely shaped surf-battered cliffs and tranquil bays are the main features of Australia's southernmost tip.

Port Arthur Tasmania's 'hell on earth' is one of the most important historic sites in Australia. In 1831 a prison was established here in which convicts were forced into hard labour.

Route 6

New Zealand

The North Island: trademark volcanoes

A vineyard near Napier. New Zealand wines

Volcanoes, geysers and hot springs are the defining features of New Zealand's North Island, home to the vast majority of the country's population including most of the Maori, New Zealand's indigenous people. This is also where the country's key economic regions are located, in and around Auckland, the largest city, and Wellington, New Zealand's capital.

From Auckland, this round trip first takes us to the north, then down to Wellington at the southern tip of the island, and finally back to the point of departure. The route covers unique landscapes, all individually shaped by volcanism, impressive cities and traditional centres of Maori culture. Most cities are very cosmopolitan in character, which is hardly surprising given that three-quarters of New Zealanders are of European descent. In Auckland and in the surrounding area, many people are also of Maori and other Polynesian origin. These indigenous people, in contrast to others such as the Australian Aborigines, have been relatively successful in maintaining their cultural independence and in safeguarding their ancestral rights. In the Treaty of Waitangi, which was ratified as early as 1840, the Maori were granted the right to own their land in return for accepting British sovereignty. To this day, the Treaty, which was drafted in both English and Maori, continues to form the foundation for the relationship between Maori and white New Zealanders. Today, Maori is the country's second official language and there are numerous Maori educational and healthcare institutions.

The only two large cities on the North Island are Auckland (population 1.2 million) and Wellington (population 300,000). But the island's main attractions are its magnificent natural phenomena. In orde to protect these, several National Park have been established; these are easil accessible via numerous hiking trails. Th tremendous forces of nature that, fo example, created Mount Taranaki (2,518 m 8,262 ft), in the National Park of the sam name, can only be guessed at.

Maori in traditional war-dance pose.

This now-dormant volcano is sacred t the Maori, as are many other volcanoes In Tongariro National Park, one of th most important places of interest on th North Island, nature is more active. Here geysers project their spectacular foun tains straight up into the air. Some do thi irregularly whereas others could be use to tell the time.

Even more popular is Rotorua, a place o traditional cultural and historical signifi cance to the Maori, whose craftsmanshi can be seen along the entire route

A breathtaking view from Cape Reinga. Here, at the North Island's north-westerly tip, the Tasman Sea meets the Pacific Ocean. The lighthouse, which can withstand severe storms, was built in 1941 and stands 165 m (541 ft) above sea level on a distinctive rocky promontory.

ave earned an excellent international reputation.

ʼlaori wood carvings in particular, as ʼell as their weaving and plaiting, are of very high standard. Music also plays an nportant part in Maori life. The otorua area is rich in geothermal phe-omena such as geysers, hot springs and ud volcanoes, and it is famous for its ısh forests, rivers teeming with fish and s crystal-clear lakes. On the North land, the latter are often used for vater sports and conditions for wind-ırfing, in particular, are ideal.

he North Island's central region is one of ıe most productive agricultural regions f New Zealand. In recent decades, wine roduction has become extremely impor-ant to the economy alongside sheep arming, while the kiwifruit, the country's ational fruit, is also cultivated on a large ale. However, the economy is no longer xclusively agrarian. Auckland has established itself as a base for a large range of different industries and the city's harbour handles much of New Zealand's international trade.

Northland, the northern peninsula and the most northerly of New Zealand's sixteen administrative regions, is also called the 'cradle of the nation' because it was here that the Treaty of Waitangi, mentioned above, between the British government and the Maori was signed in 1840. The Waitangi Treaty Grounds is the country's most historic site.

The North Island's extraordinary range of different landscapes can be seen in close proximity on its northern tip. Here, virgin forests dominated by giant kauri trees, such as Waipoua Kauri Forest, alternate with dunes that reach 100 m (328 ft) in height, as can be found on the long expanse of Ninety Mile Beach.

Mount Ngauruhoe is one of three active volcanoes in Tongariro National Park.

Giant ferns

The isolation of New Zealand's islands, and the great distances between them and any larger stretches of land, have enabled the country's fauna and flora to develop independently. This has led to the development of species that occur nowhere else on earth as they would be unable to survive in other regions.

The giant ferns that enjoy ideal growing conditions in the temperate to tropical climates of New Zealand are one such botanical curiosity. These giant plants transport you to a magical fairytale forest. They are quite unbelievable. Their majestic fronds can span up to 5 m (16½ ft) and some ferns may grow as tall as trees, which is why they are sometimes also called tree ferns. It is not uncommon to find individual specimens up to 30 m (98½ ft) tall. These tree ferns have woody trunks although this is not real wood; the trunks are supported by deposits of lignin (a fibrous mass of roots). The sound of the wind rustling the fronds in such a 'fern forest' is also very impressive.

Giant ferns are not only spectacular to look at, but they also have an important ecological function. Their shade protects many flowering plants that cannot tolerate full sunlight. The ferns can also be put to practical use. Smaller ones make decorative house plants, and the fronds are also traditionally turned into fans.

Fern forests near Whangarei.

New Zealand's forests boast 190 native fern species in total. The silver fern (*Cyathea dealbata*) is the country's most recognised plant and a cornerstone of New Zealand culture. It is a symbol of national pride and as famous as the All Blacks, who wear it on their rugby shirts. You will spot the imposing black mamaku or ponga (*Cyathea medullaris*), with ease. It is the most common native tree fern and towers up to 15 m (49 ft) high. It has blackened stems and umbrellas of mid-green fronds that rise above the canopy.

1

As well as interesting towns with charming harbours and unusual architecture, this route also takes in ancient forests with 2,000-year-old trees, endless beaches and volcanoes. There are ideal opportunities for water sports in the coastal waters.

1 Auckland See page 148.

2 Waiwera Waiwera is located about 50 km (31 miles) north of Auckland. This town is famous for its hot springs, which are said to possess special healing powers. There are twenty-six pools, each with different water temperatures. Staying on Highway 1 at the major Brynderwyn road junction to the north, head for Whangarei.

3 Whangarei This modern port city is framed by forested hills and a harbour. The Clapham Clock Museum boasts a collection of 1,600 clocks, the oldest one dating from 1720. A few miles north of the city, the Whangarei Falls are an impressive natural spectacle falling in a 24 m (79 ft) cascade. North of the city, a road branches off towards the coast, where Tutukaka, not far from Ngunguru, is a popular diving resort.

4 Waitangi National Reserve At the Bay of Islands, the Waitangi National Reserve surrounds the town of Waitangi. The town itself is of historical significance, for it was here that in 1840 representatives of the Maori and of Great Britain signed the Treaty that is considered the 'birth certificate' of modern New Zealand. This event is commemorated each year on 6 February and on the 100th anniversary of the signing of the Treaty, a large Maori meeting house was inaugurated.

5 Kaitaia The coastal road to Kaitaia in the north-west is bordered with bush land and mangrove forests. The town itself is an important starting point for tours to the northernmost points of the North Island. The Far North Regional Museum houses a cast-iron anchor weighing about 1,500 kg (3,300 lb), lost by a European discovery vessel in a heavy storm in 1769. The impressive scenery in this area can best be seen from the Kaitaia track, a popular hiking trail 10 km (6 miles) long.

6 Ninety Mile Beach This description is actually misleading

2

Travel information

Route profile
Length: approx. 2,500 km/ 1,500 miles (excluding detours)
Time needed: 10–14 days
Start and end: Auckland
Itinerary (main locations): Auckland, Waitangi National Reserve, Cape Reinga, Rotorua, Taupo, Tongariro National Park, Wellington, Waitomo Caves

Traffic information
Cars drive on the left in New Zealand. The distances between individual towns are indicated in kilometres. In order to get to the more remote destinations, off-road vehicles are recommended. Many petrol stations are closed on Sundays.

When to travel
The best time to travel is from September to April. The official high season is between November and April.

Information
www.newzealand.com/travel
www.destination-nz.com
www.tourism.net.nz

as the beach is less than 60 miles (96.5 km) long. Dunes more than 100 m (328 ft) high loom alongside the road. The area used to be densely forested with kauri trees, which unfortunately were destroyed by flooding. In January, an annual fishing competition, the 'Ninety Mile Beach Surfcasting Contest', takes place, drawing thousands of anglers. Trees are now being planted in an attempt to secure the beach and the shifting sand dunes. The road to Cape Reinga, the northern tip of the island, is drivable all the way. The beach is only accessible with off-road vehicles.

7 Cape Reinga At the lighthouse, some 165 m (541 ft) above sea level, we have reached the northernmost point of our route. However, this is not the most northerly point of New Zealand , which is located further east, at the North Cape. The lighthouse was erected in 1941 and gives breathtaking views over the sea. Heading back the same way, just outside Waitangi you follow the turnoff west towards Omapere.

8 Waipoua Kauri Forest This virgin forest of around 9,000 hectares (22,239 acres) contains the largest population of kauri pines in New Zealand. The tallest tree – which the Maori call Tane Mahuta ('God of the forest') – is more than 51 m (167 ft) high and its trunk boasts a circumference of more than 14 m (46 ft). It is estimated to be around 2,000 years old. The road through the forest, which is approximately 20 km (12 miles) long, is drivable all the way.

An ideal add-on to the Waipoua Kauri Forest trip is a visit to the Kauri Museum at Matakohe on the way back to Auckland. This museum documents the importance of these giant trees in the history of New Zealand. Via Brynderwyn, Waiwera and Auckland, our route then continues on to Tauranga, which is situated south-east of Auckland at the Bay of Plenty.

9 Tauranga This town plays a major part in the economy of New Zealand as its harbour handles much of the country's foreign trade. Tauranga is considered a popular retirement community and a paradise for water sports. Its best-known building is the Elms Mission House which was built in 1838 and has been conserved almost unchanged. A few miles east of the city, Mount Maunganui rises to 232 m (761 ft). There are some hot springs at the base of this now-extinct volcano, also known as Mauao, and the coastal waters are popular for surfing. After passing Te Puke, you leave Highway 2 and carry on south towards Rotorua.

10 Rotorua This town on the southern shore of the lake of the same name is one of the North Island's most popular tourist destinations. The surrounding landscape was shaped by volcanoes and the region's thermal activity is extraordinary: geysers spray into the air, hot

(continued p.152)

1 **Muriwai Beach near Auckland is populated by a colony of Australian gannets.**

2 **Auckland's harbour and skyline form a charming contrast.**

3 **The Champagne Pool at Waiotapu Thermal Wonderland testifies to the high levels of geothermal activity in the region.**

4 **Lake Tarawera near Rotorua is one of the most scenic of the lakes surrounding the town.**

Detour

White Island

Near Whakatane, at roughly 50 km (31 miles) offshore, White Island, also known as Whakaari, rises to about 300 m (984 ft) above sea level. This is an active volcano. In fact, it is one of the most active in the entire region. It forms part of a chain of volcanoes that starts at Tongariro National Park and includes a whole row of fiery mountains on New Zealand's North Island. The eastern side of White Island's mountain was completely blasted away in a fierce eruption in 1914, with the loss of ten lives when workers in the sulphur mines were taken by surprise by the night-time disaster.

Although there have been no major eruptions since then, volcanic activity remains very high. Sulphur-infused steam and bubbling ponds testify to the extraordinary activity taking place just below the surface. The British explorer and circumnavigator James Cook first sighted the island at the end of the 18th century, although he did not recognize it as a volcano. Because of the billowing clouds of white steam pouring out, he named it White Island.

White Island rises 300 m (984 ft) out of the sea.

You can take a boat tour of the island from the harbour in Whakatane or Tauranga. Helicopters also land on White Island, with prior permission. If you would like a glimpse of this extraordinary volcano from the sky, treat yourself to a scenic flight. It will take you over the island by helicopter or small plane. From the air, the island looks like a lunar landscape, and you will really begin to appreciate the extraordinary forces of nature that are at work shaping the landscape both here and in many other parts of the country. Undeterred by such majestic forces deep within the earth, countless seabirds come to nest on the island. Gannets, in particular, form large colonies.

Sailing ships are more typical of the 'City of Sails', as Auckland is sometimes nicknamed, than of almost any other city in the world. Around 80,000 boats and yachts are moored in Auckland's seven harbours. Sailing is New Zealand's favourite national sport, and Auckland, situated on a narrow isthmus between the

Tasman Sea and the Southern Pacific, was the proud host of the world's most famous sailing regatta, the America's Cup, in both 2000 and in 2003. This view of numerous yachts in front of Auckland's skyline is dominated by the Sky Tower, the Southern hemisphere's tallest building at 328 m (1,076 ft).

Auckland

New Zealand's largest city, although not its capital, is nevertheless the country's metropolitan heartland. Roughly one-third of New Zealanders live in and around Auckland. New Zealand's ethnic diversity can be seen in this cultural melting pot. The population includes people of white and Asian backgrounds, as well as substantial numbers of Maori and other Polynesian peoples. It is this mix that gives Auckland its cosmopolitan atmosphere.

Auckland is known as the 'City of Sails', and this is hardly surprising given that, in good weather, there are huge numbers of sailing ships near the harbour and in the coastal waters. The 1-km (0.6-mile) long Harbour Bridge, built in 1959, connects Auckland and the North Shore, spanning the harbour at 43 m (141 ft) above high water. Despite the heavy traffic, it offers one of the best views in the city. Along the harbour, Quay Street has numerous food stalls offering foods from all over the world. Many visitors are drawn to Microworld, a universe of small things (micro-organisms, tiny crystals, etc.). The Ferry Building, built in 1912, is the starting point for harbour boat trips. Queen Street leads from the harbour to the commercial centre of Auckland; it is both a magnificent boulevard and the city's main artery. Many high-rise office blocks have been built here in recent years, generally occupied by banks and insurance companies. The area is paradise for anyone interested in architecture – art nouveau villas sit beside modern glass palaces and buildings dating from colonial times. West of central Queen Street is Sky Tower,

Auckland skyline with the 328-m (1,076-ft) Sky Tower.

which, at 328 m (1,076 ft), is the city's, and indeed the country's, tallest building. The futuristic tower is part of a hotel and retail area called Sky City, which was inaugurated in 1997.

A must-see is the Auckland Art Gallery Toi o Tāmaki with its impressive collections of ancient and contemporary art from New Zealand and many other countries.

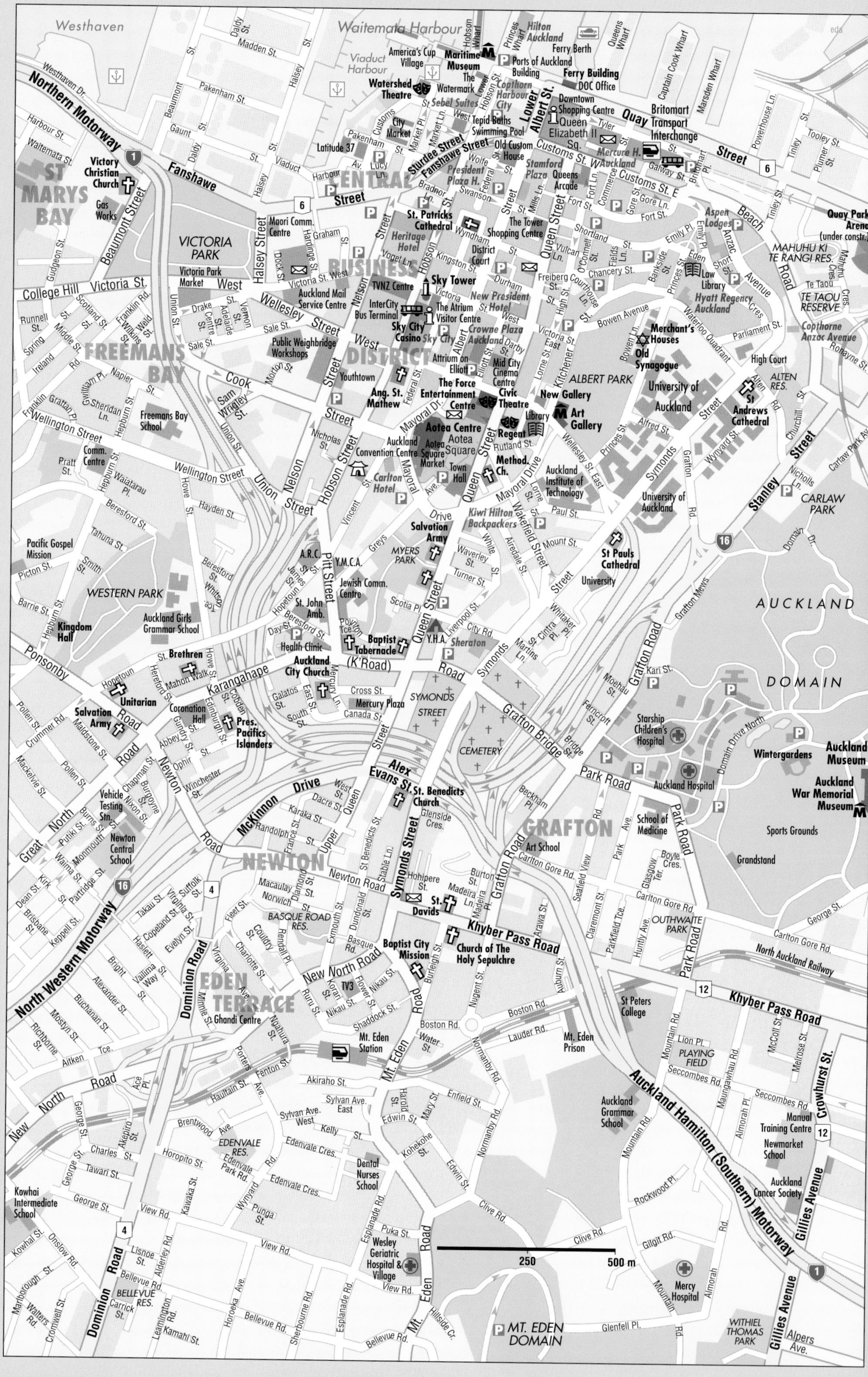

Wellington

New Zealand's capital is surrounded by uniquely beautiful scenery. It is located on one of the most picturesque bays in the world, within sight of golden beaches and snow-capped mountains. Because of its exposure to an almost incessant westerly wind, the city has been nicknamed 'Windy Wellington'.

The 19th-century centre of Wellington was unable to cope with the large influx of immigrants, so the city rapidly spread into the hilly country to the north. A mosaic of brightly coloured villas shapes these pretty suburbs, connected to the city centre by a cable car built in 1912. It's a pretty steep climb if you decide to walk up, but a breath-taking view awaits you at the top. Nearby, the Otari Botanic Garden displays some of the indigenous flora, with a small planetarium attached.
Lambton Quay in the heart of Wellington is the city's number one boulevard for retail therapy. The road, which is about 1 km (0.6 mile) long, is lined by shopping centres and boutiques, arcades and numerous restaurants. The harbour district around the spacious Civic Square has its own uniquely charming atmosphere – in particular during the summer, when the traditional regattas take place. The Wellington Maritime Museum is devoted to the history of the harbour.
Wellington replaced Auckland as the capital of New Zealand in 1865 and today the city is not only the seat of the country's parliament and government, but also plays an important role as a traffic hub. Most traffic heading to the South Island passes through the city. Since the 1980s, Wellington has developed into an ambitious cultural metropolis. It is the home of the New Zealand Symphony Orchestra and the New Zealand Dance School, among others. Important works of art from the Pacific region are displayed in the New Zealand Te Papa Tongarewa Museum. Wellington was the main location for the shooting and production of the hugely successful film trilogy, *The Lord of the Rings*, and the city's International Film Festival, which takes place annually in June, regularly draws large audiences.

Wellington at dusk.

The Waitangi Treaty Grounds is New Zealand's most historic site. The Treaty of Waitangi, which was signed here in 1840, mainly governs issues of land ownership between white settlers and the Maori. To this day, the exact interpretation of this bilingual document remains a subject of heated, legal debate.

This carved Maori meeting house, Te Whare Runanga, was built in 1940 to commemorate the centenary of the signing of the Treaty. In this room, with its elaborate wood carvings, Maori cultural groups present traditional and contemporary entertainment, including the Haka war dance, several times a week

The Maori

New Zealand's indigenous people arrived on both islands around AD 900. The arrival of the Europeans in the 18th century fundamentally changed their lives, pushing Maori culture to the background and the loss of their cultural identity led to a marginal existence for many Maori within New Zealand society. Since the early 1980s, there has been a revival

Top: Maori group at a dance festival. Bottom: Intricate Maori carving with mother-of-pearl eyes.

of Maori culture and Maori currently account for about ten per cent of the country's population.

The Maori are mainly known for their wood carving and stonemasonry, which are among the most sophisticated in the Pacific region, and their art is closely tied to religious images. The Maori have a distinctive culture of ancestor worship, central to this being the representation of human figures with pronounced heads. Ancestor worship is also evidenced in Maori architecture. The roofs of their meeting houses are typically adorned with images of their ancestors, and the windows are often shaped like eyes. Music and rhythmical dancing also form part of their traditional ceremonial, with the participants wearing garments made of flax, feathers and leather.

steam hisses from cracks in the earth and mud pools pop and bubble. Above all, however, its crystal-clear lakes and rivers as well as its fascinating hot springs make Rotorua a particularly attractive spot. The largest lake in the area is the almost-circular Lake Rotorua with the Government Gardens located on its shore. Tudor Towers is the architectural highlight of the park. This timber-framed building, a former bath house, was built in the 19th century and currently houses the Rotorua Museum featuring the natural and cultural history of the region. Behind the museum is a modern thermal/medical spa complex, including a range of hot mineral bathing pools that are fed by a number of healing springs.

Rotorua is an important Maori cultural centre and the reconstructed Tamaki Maori Village introduces visitors to Maori various traditions and performances. It is possible to stay overnight in the village.

About 20 km (12 miles) to the south-east of Rotorua, there is a blue lake (Tikitapu) and a green lake (Rotokakahi). The different colours of the two lakes are clearly visible from a narrow hill between them. Rotokakahi is sacred to the Maori and therefore not accessible, whereas Tikitapu is open to tourists.

Further to the south-east lies the buried village of Te Wairoa, which was submerged by the eruption of Mount Tarawera in 1886. Some excavated huts are open to visitors. Also close to Rotorua is Waiotapu, set in some very colourful scenery (Te Whakarewarewa with its geothermal activity). Visitors flock to its wonderful geysers, hot thermal springs and bubbling mud pools, including the Champagne Pool. On rejoining Highway 1, it's only a few kilometres to the town of Taupo at the northern tip of Lake Taupo.

⓫ Lake Taupo This lake, the country's largest inland water at 600 km² (232 square miles), is a popular holiday destination. Boat trips start from the harbour in Taupo. Many visitors are drawn here by the open-air mineral baths of the lovely Hot Springs & Health Spa, whose architecture resembles traditional Japanese bath houses. To see the whole lake at its best, it is worth spending a day driving around it. The route, which is 150 km (93 miles) long, runs directly along the eastern and southern shores of the lake, but in the west it departs from the lake shore.

For a short trip to the east coast, take Highway 5 in Taupo to Napier, 150 km (93 miles) away (see Detour, page 154). North of the Highway, you will pass Whirinaki Forest where giant Podocar-

paceae (evergreen coniferous trees) can attain more than 60 m (197 ft) in height. The main route then continues south from Taupo, along the east coast; our next destination is Tongariro National Park, that lies to the west of Highway 1.

⓬ Tongariro National Park Founded in 1887, this protected area in the North Island's central plateau is one of the oldest National Parks in the world. The 765 km² (295 square mile) park was named after Mount Tongariro (1,967 m/6,454 ft), which is flanked by Mount Ngauruhoe (2,291 m/7,517 ft) and Mount Ruapehu (2,797 m/9,177 ft). These three active volcanoes are surrounded by many geysers and near their summits lie a number of beautiful lakes that glisten like polished emeralds in the sun, hence their name Emerald Lakes. In 1991, the National Park was designated a UNESCO World Heritage Site.

From the southern edge of the National Park, it is around 120 km (75 miles) to the junction of Highway 1 and Highway 3. Before you carry on to Wellington, it is worth taking a short detour to Palmerston North.

⓭ Palmerston North This town at the junction of three rural roads is an important traffic hub. The Square, the town's central point, provides an interesting cross-section of New Zealand's architectural history. The Rugby Museum is devoted to New Zealand's national sport while the Manawata Museum documents the cultural heritage of the region. Via Highway 57, you rejoin Highway 1 and continue on to Wellington.

⓮ Wellington See page 149.

⓯ Wanganui Along the west coast, the main route now takes you along Highway 1 to Wanganui, which is known mainly for its pretty Victoria Avenue. From December through to March, a host of colourful flower baskets lines the road to celebrate the 'Wanganui in Bloom' festival. The Wanganui Museum displays Maori weapons and jewellery made from greenstone (a kind of nephrite jade), as well as a war canoe built by the indigenous people, measuring an impressive 23 m (75 ft). To drive to Whanganui National Park, which lies some 80 km (50 miles) from here, take Highway 4 in the direction of Raetihi. A few kilometres past Upokongaro, the Whanganui River Road will take you to Pipiriki.

⓰ Whanganui National Park The park was established in 1987 in the catchment area of the scenic Whanganui River, the longest navigable river in New Zealand and very popular with canoeists. After about 35 km (21 miles) on the Whanganui River Road, it is worth stopping in Atene, where a Maori meeting house built in 1886 is well worth seeing. The Atene Skyline Walk, a hiking trail that takes several hours to complete, leads to some terrific views. The mountainous landscapes are densely forested.

About 10 km (6 miles) north of the town, the road turns into an unmade track, but it is relatively good for driving. The Whanganui River Road ends in Pipiriki about 80 km (50 miles) north of Wanganui. To return to Wanganui, you can take the same route back or follow an alternative road via Raetihi. Continue along the coast from Wanganui to the Taranaki National Park.

1 **Geysers spouting at Waiotapu Fountains.**

2 **A bizarre canyon cutting across Whirinaki Forest.**

3 **Mount Ngauruhoe, 2,291 m (7,517 ft) high, one of New Zealand's active stratovolcanoes.**

Detour

Napier

After a devastating earthquake in 1931, large parts of the town were rebuilt from scratch. The many art deco buildings with their façades painted largely in subtle pastel colours are particularly eye-

Hilly landscape near Napier.

catching. You can visit some of the prettiest buildings as part of a guided tour.
Marine Parade, a shopping boulevard lined with pine trees, runs directly along the coast. Marineland, where you can watch dolphins, seals and sea lions performing their range of tricks, is a top tourist spot. Hawke's Bay Museum houses a collection of Maori arts and crafts. By car, you can take the Lighthouse road north to the Bluff Hill Lookout, which offers a breathtaking view of Napier.

17 Taranaki National Park As first point of call in the National Park, we recommend the North Egmont Visitor Centre where you can view some interesting audio-visual presentations to gain a detailed overview of the history of the National Park. It has an area of 320 km^2 (124 square miles), and Mount Taranaki (Mount Egmont), which gave the park its name. Because of its almost perfectly symmetrical cone shape, the mountain, which is 2,518 m (8,262 ft) high, is often compared to Mount Fuji in Japan, and there are several different routes to climb it. Non-climbers, however, can follow an easy route that takes them around the mountain below the summit.
Besides the volcano, the 18 m (60 ft) cascades of Dawson Falls are among the scenic attractions of the park. From the visitor centre, Egmont Road takes you into the northern part of the National Park and on to New Plymouth.

18 New Plymouth This city has the only deep-water port on New Zealand's west coast, and it is a centre for the processing and sale of agricultural produce such as dairy products and exotic woods. It is known for its large sweeping parks. Of these, Pukekura Park with its plant collections and exotic trees is especially popular.
Taranaki Museum is one of the country's oldest cultural centres, housing a whole range of different objects, ranging from Maori arts and crafts to whale skeletons. At the Govett-Brewster Art Gallery, you can see contemporary New Zealand art. St Mary's Church was consecrated in 1848, making it New Zealand's oldest stone church.

19 Waitomo Caves From Te Kuiti, a road branches off to the elaborate network of the Waitomo Caves. In these underground grottoes you can admire some bizarre dripstones with countless stalagmites and stalactites. A boat trip takes you to the main cave, where in the darkness you will glimpse extraordinary garlands of light dangling all around you. This beautiful Milky Way is created by thousands of tiny glow-worms. This is the Glowworm Cave. From the car park outside the central cave, the Waitomo Walkway takes you alongside the Waitomo River through forested areas and gorges, providing a good overview of the range of landscapes along the coastal strip.
Back on Highway 3, travel north to Hamilton to rejoin Highway 1, which after a further 130 km (81 miles) brings you back to Auckland, the starting point of this round trip.

1 Mount Taranaki's almost symmetrical shape is very impressive. A climb to its summit at 2,518 m (8,262 ft) is just one of the challenges a trip to New Zealand has to offer.

2 The Waitomo Caves attract a large number of adventurous explorers from all over the world. Here you can tackle the world's longest abseiling route.

Cape Reinga This headland with the northernmost lighthouse in New Zealand separates the Tasman Sea from the Pacific Ocean. In the Maori language, the word 'Reinga' refers to the underworld.

Waipoua Kauri Forest Kauri trees can reach almost biblical ages – some of these giants are up to 2,000 years old. Around 300 tree species grow within the protected area.

Haruru Falls The stunning and noisy Haruru Falls, shaped like a horseshoe, are well worth a visit. You can drive to them from the Haruru Falls township, located near Paihia.

White Island This privately owned scenic reserve is one of New Zealand's most active volcanic sites, but you can still walk into the crater.

Auckland Since 1997 the skyline of New Zealand's largest city has been dominated by the 328 m (1,076 ft) Sky Tower. Auckland is also the country's most important harbour.

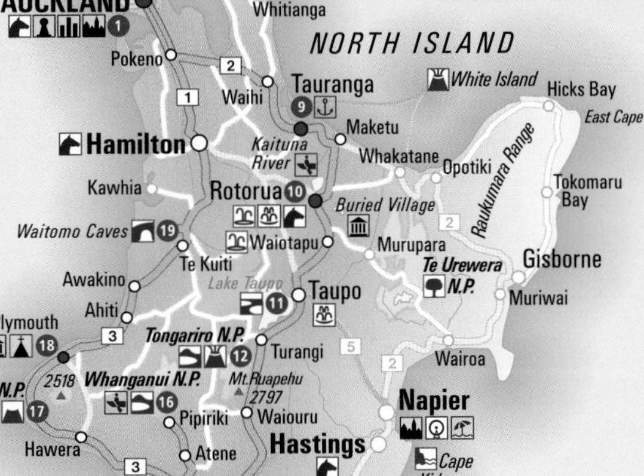

Bay of Islands A pleasant climate, long beaches and more than a hundred islands make this bay in the Waitangi National Reserve a popular holiday destination. The area is particularly suitable for all kinds of water sports.

Whirinaki Forest Located in the centre of the North Island, this is one of the highlights of New Zealand's rainforests. Some giant trees grow to more than 60 m (197 ft).

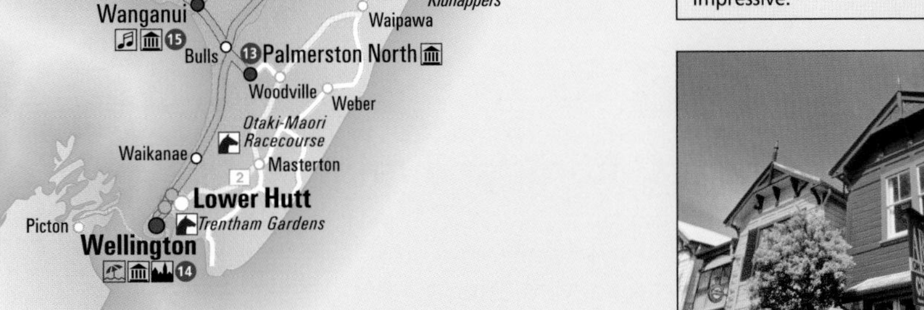

Te Whakarewarewa Thermal Reserve / Champagne Pool The hot springs near Waiotapu, with their ochre-coloured edges, are very impressive.

Maori New Zealand's Polynesian indigenous people boast a sophisticated tradition of arts and crafts, with outstanding examples of wood carving. In these carvings, the eyes of the figures are made from shiny mother-of-pearl. Maori stonemasonry and weaving are also of a very high standard.

Napier The brightly painted wooden houses of this elegant town on the south-eastern coast of North Island are considered architectural gems.

Taranaki National Park The region's landmark is the dormant volcano Mount Taranaki (2,518 m/ 8,262 ft), which is sacred to the Maori.

Wellington This cultural metropolis is located on a picturesque bay. Its main sights are the seaside walks, the Botanic Garden and the National Museum.

Whanganui National Park The park, which was established in 1987, is traversed by the Whanganui River. A canoe trip on the river is a very special experience. The area is also famous for its varieties of brightly coloured birds and its giant fern species.

Tongariro National Park Mount Tongariro is one of several active volcanoes in this park, a designated UNESCO World Heritage Site.

Route 7

New Zealand

The South Island: glaciers, fiords and rainforests

The snow-capped summit of Aoraki/Mount Cook is sacred to the Maori.

Visitors to New Zealand's South Island can expect some absolutely fabulous scenery. You will enjoy one spectacular view after another as you travel along the coast or to the highest peaks in the interior. Some of the more remote regions are difficult to reach, making for a great diversity of plant and wildlife. The island's mountains, lakes and rivers are ideal for those in search of outdoor adventures.

Many consider that New Zealand's South Island embraces the whole range of the world's landscapes in perfect harmony. In the sun-drenched north, the Tasman Sea's large waves pound the shore, while you can relax on the sandy beaches in its sheltered bays. Further south, the agricultural flatlands of Canterbury Plain spread across the eastern side of the island.

Although the South Island is much larger than its northern counterpart, it is much less densely populated. Large areas of the interior are almost uninhabited. Only five per cent of New Zealand's Maori population lives on the South Island, so there are far fewer Maori sacred sites than on the North Island. On the east coast, you will find two lively, cosmopolitan cities with a distinctly European flavour: Christchurch and Dunedin. Christchurch still boasts colonial buildings and extensive parks and is often described as the most English city outside England, with good reason. As you stroll through the port city of Dunedin with its many Victorian-Gothic buildings and its lovely parks, you will be reminded of its Scottish heritage: the very name of the city derives from the Gaelic name for the Scottish capital, while the names of some of its streets and quarters will transport you briefly to Edinburgh.

Brown kiwi.

Further to the south and west, the plains give way to more hilly country, which rises to form the snow-covered peaks of the Southern Alps. This mountainous region, which forms the backbone of the South Island, is accessible by only a few roads. The highest mountain in the Southern Alps is Aoraki/Mount Cook, originally named after Captain Cook, the British explorer. Five powerful glaciers flow from its summit (3,764 m/12,350 ft) down into the valley. In the Maori language, the mountain is known by its more poetic name Aoraki (Cloud Piercer).

Milford Sound, with its steep forest-clad rock faces, is one of the major attractions in New Zealand's South Island.

Coastal landscape near Akaroa on the Banks Peninsula, south-east of Christchurch.

The south-west of the island is one of New Zealand's most attractive regions, and Queenstown, on the northern shore of Lake Wakatipu, makes a perfect starting point for exploring it. Several fiords, such as the famous Milford Sound, penetrate deep into the island. There are some dramatic waterfalls, Sutherland Falls among them, and a number of impressive dripstone caves. Fiordland National Park at 12,000 km^2 (4,632 square miles) is the country's largest protected area and a designated UNESCO World Heritage Site, a status it certainly deserves. It is home to a wide range of bird species.

This route takes you to a number of large mountain lakes, known collectively as the Southern Lakes Region, which includes Lakes Te Anau, Wakatipu and Wanaka. A little further north, in Westland National Park, fifty-eight glaciers flow down from the mountain tops almost to the west coast. The Franz Josef and Fox Glaciers are the most famous, but the South Island has around three hundred such ice-flows, some of which can be several kilometres long. Owing to the island's high levels of precipitation, the coastal areas are usually covered in jungle-like rainforests.

Following our route northwards along the west coast, you will come across villages that look much the same as they did at the time of the New Zealand gold-rush, which lured many people to seek their fortunes in the area in the 1860s. When it came to an end, some communities, such as Greymouth, switched to coal-mining to sustain their economy. Agriculture continues to play an important role. Although the large majority of the population lives in the towns and cities, farming is vital to the economy of the South Island.

Countless islands, bays and fiords break up the coastline in the north of the South Island.

Detour

Nelson Lakes National Park

The northern tip of the South Island has some spectacular scenery in store for the traveller. Nelson Lakes National Park is one of the most impressive protected areas in the region, but Abel Tasman and Kahurangi National Parks are not far behind. On Highway 63, it is around 100 km (62 miles) from Blenheim to the St Arnaud visitor centre on the shore of Lake Rotoiti, and the road comes to an end after a further 25 km (16 miles), when you rejoin Highway 6 at Kawatiri Junction. This park in the northern foothills of the Southern Alps covers almost 1,000 km^2 (386 square miles) and encapsulates all that is beautiful about the South Island: snow-capped mountains, lush, overgrown forests, roaring waterfalls and crystal-clear lakes. The park is at its most breathtaking around the two largest glacial lakes, Lake Rotoroa and Lake Rotoiti. When the ice retreated at the end of the last ice age, valleys and depressions carved out by the glaciers filled with water, creating the

Lake Rotoiti.

park's numerous lakes. Today, these lakes are popular for fishing, water sports and hiking.
An intricate network of hiking trails traverses Nelson Lakes National Park. The most demanding is the Travers Sabine Circuit Track, a 79-km (49-mile) route that takes between six and eight days to complete. It skirts crystal-clear lakes and leads across a mountain pass up to Lake Angelus. En route, you pass the Speargrass Wetlands with their diverse flora and walk through the extensive forests of southern beech. The track's highest point is crossing the Travers Saddle at 1,780 m (5,840 ft). While ambitious climbers and skiers enjoy the mountains, they can also be explored from the lakes by water-taxi.

The South Island is full of amazing scenic contrasts. It has every imaginable variety of landscape: from sandy beaches to jagged mountains, from rocky shores to impressive glaciers and from dense rainforests and expanses of southern beech to meadows and pastures. The island also has a good road network.

1 Picton Our trip around the South Island starts from this pretty port in the far north of the island. It is here that the ferries arrive from Wellington. It usually takes around 3½ hours to travel across the Cook Strait and through Queen Charlotte Sound to reach the former whaling station of Picton. Sailing ships anchor regularly in the picturesque bays of the fiord, and you can take boat trips to the most beautiful destinations along the magical coastline around Picton.
Picton itself is more than just a stopover on the way to the heart of the South Island. The Picton Community Museum, dedicated to the discoveries of Captain Cook and to the heyday of whaling, offers an excellent introduction to the history of the island. A number of museum ships are anchored permanently in the harbour, the main attraction being the *Edwin Fox*, the last survivor of a large fleet that brought thousands of immigrants from Europe to New Zealand. The Seahorse World Aquarium gives a wonderful overview of local marine life.
There's an interesting excursion east to Robin Hood Bay, although the route involves some very steep roads, and is a challenge for both cars and drivers. It takes 20 minutes to reach the Karaka Point peninsula where the fortifications of a former Maori settlement are worth visiting.

2 Marlborough Sounds The fiords north of Picton are full of islands, bays, caves and a maze of waterways. Valleys in the area were flooded when the sea level rose after the last ice age. What were once hills are now mere islands jutting out of the sea. The coastline is 1,500 km (932 miles) long. You will enjoy constantly changing views along the hiking trails, including the Queen Charlotte Track, which is 67 km (42 miles) long and can also be tackled by mountain bike. A trip through the sounds by boat or kayak is a very special experience, and you will find several places where you can hire boats (and bikes). The region's famed Queen Charlotte Drive is the most scenic road. Allowing for stops, you should complete the winding 35-km (22-mile) route in around three hours. It is a well-signposted road, ending up in Havelock, known for its green-shelled mussels, from where you can continue to the next destination on our route, either back via Picton or via the vineyards in the Wairau Valley.

3 Blenheim This town enjoy around 2,600 hours of sunshin

Travel information

Route profile
Length: approx. 2,500 km/ 1,500 miles (excluding detours)
Time needed: 2–3 weeks
Start and end: Picton
Itinerary (main locations): Picton, Christchurch, Aoraki/ Mt Cook National Park, Invercargill, Fiordland National Park, Queenstown, Westland National Park, Karamea, Picton

Traffic information
Cars drive on the left in New Zealand. The legal blood alcohol limit for driving is 0.5 per mil. In urban areas, the speed limit is 50 km/h (31 mph); outside the towns it is 100 km/h (62 mph).

Travel season
In the southern part of the country, some higher altitude roads may become impassable during the winter (June to September) and sometimes also in early spring and late autumn. The best time to travel is December to March.

Information
www.newzealand.com
www.tourism.net.nz

Weather
www.metservice.co.nz

per year, making it one of the country's most sun-drenched spots. Almost everything in Blenheim revolves around wine and the region's mild climate is perfect for growing vines. West of Blenheim, New Renwick Road, Middle Renwick Road and Old Renwick Road take you to some of New Zealand's most famous vineyards, such as Highfield Estate, Allan Scott Wines and Estates and Stoneleigh Vineyards. Blenheim hosts a famous wine festival during the second week of February, featuring wine, food and entertainment. New Zealand's only salt production plant is located 35 km (22 miles) south of Blenheim; its salt heaps are visible for miles. Highway I now hugs the water, running between the shore and the Seaward Kaikoura Range, parallel to the coastline.

❹ **Kaikoura** In the 19th century, this town was a famous whaling station. Nowadays, only a few whalebones serve as a reminder of bygone days, such as those you can see in the Garden of Memories. Fyffe House has carvings made of whale teeth. Kaikoura Bay itself is spectacular, set against the backdrop of the coastal mountains reaching nearly 3,000 m (10,000 ft). It is a perfect spot for whale watching. Warm and cold ocean currents meet in the coastal waters, and you can enjoy spotting sperm whales, orcas and several species of dolphin, all of which come to feed on the plentiful supplies of fish. Remember to look up from time to time to spot great albatrosses with wingspans extending to more than 3 m (10 ft).

Only a few miles south of Kaikoura, you come to the Maori Leap Cave. Large numbers of bird and seal skeletons were discovered in this lovely dripstone cave. As you travel further south you will begin to notice more and more vineyards.

❺ **Waipara** This town is now the centre of a relatively new wine-growing area. Vines have only been cultivated here successfully since the 1980s. Many vineyards are located along the smaller roads leading off the main route. If you are coming from Kaikoura, the Main North Road takes you to Glenmark Wines and Torlesse Wines. Take Reeces Road to Daniel Schuster Wines and MacKenzies Road to Fiddler's Green Wines. Chardonnay, Pinot Noir and Sauvignon Blanc grapes are cultivated in the area, together with Gewürztraminers.

Many vineyards offer wine tastings. At Christchurch Information Centre, you can even book a trip in a horse-drawn carriage through the vineyards.

❻ **Christchurch** The largest city on the South Island was founded as recently as 1850. Today, it is the political, economic and cultural hub of the island. Thanks to its lovely, sweeping parks and well-kept gardens, it is also known as the 'garden city'. Its clubs and cricket grounds and late 19th-century English-style architecture make Christchurch the 'most English town outside England'. Try to park your car on the outskirts as, despite its size, the centre of town is easily manageable on foot. Enjoy a sightseeing tour on one of the lovingly restored trams that make regular stops in the city centre.

The city is laid out in a grid pattern, and as a result it is quite easy to find your way around. Cathedral Square is dominated by the massive cathedral (1864–1904), the city's landmark. Inside this monumental church, you'll find an exhibition on the history of the Anglican Church in New Zealand. You can climb halfway up the steeple (65 m/ 215 ft) to enjoy a beautiful view of the city. South of Cathedral Square is City Mall, the city's main shopping street. Many visitors also take a boat trip on the River Avon which winds its way across the city in numerous loops, with lovely weeping willows growing along its banks. In marked contrast to Christchurch itself is the mountainous Banks Peninsula just south of the city on the Canterbury Plains; the region is volcanic in origin. The port town of Lyttleton and the summer resort of Akaroa with its quiet beaches are also worth visiting.

❼ **Aoraki/Mount Cook National Park** This National Park is one of the absolute highlights of a trip to the South Island of New Zealand, and not simply because of its altitude. The park was established in

1 The Inland Kaikoura Range runs parallel to the Seaward Kaikoura Range from north-east to south-west. The Clarence River divides the ranges.

2 Historic trams in Christchurch city centre.

3 The mountains of the Seaward Kaikoura Range on the Kaikoura Peninsula run all the way down to sea level.

Southern Alps

New Zealand's longest and highest mountain range extends across most of the South Island, from the north-east to the south-west. In the Pleistocene or ice age, glaciers flowed down from these snow-covered mountain peaks, carving out a truly striking landscape with numerous fiords, lakes and rivers.
This mountain range is known as the Southern Alps – and this is no mere accident as the mountains resemble the European Alps in many ways. At 3,764 m (12,350 ft), the range's highest peak, Aoraki/Mount Cook challenges the Alps in altitude and is also

Top: Ski-touring on Fox Glacier. Bottom: A view of Upper Fox Glacier.

the highest in Australasia. The peaks are jagged and serrated, and at lower altitudes the slopes are covered with beech forests.
The Southern Alps were formed as a result of tectonic forces. They are located at the point of contact between two mighty tectonic plates – the Pacific Plate and the Australian Plate, which slides beneath it. Many millions of years ago, the land began to be uplifted on a large scale, culminating in the creation of this mighty mountain range, the backbone of the South Island. The plate continues to rise to this day at a rate of 10 mm (0.4 in) per year. Similar forces shaped other 'younger' mountain ranges such as the Alps, the Himalayas, the Andes and the Rocky Mountains.
The Southern Alps divide the wetter western regions of the island from its drier eastern parts. They are the most-visited winter sports region in the country.

1

2

1953 and covers an area of 700 km² (270 square miles). In addition to Aoraki/Mount Cook itself (3,764 m/12,350 ft), there are thirteen mountains, all at altitudes of more than 3,000 m (9,843 ft), including some famous peaks such as Mount Tasman (3,498 m/11,477 ft). Forty per cent of the park's surface area is covered in glaciers and high levels of precipitation around the mountain peaks provide a continuous supply of snow and ice. The Tasman Glacier flows directly from the summit of Aoraki/Mount Cook. It is some 27 km (17 miles) long and up to 3 km (2 miles) wide, making it the longest glacier in the country.
It will take you some time to get here from Christchurch, but you will find spectacular scenery along the way. Driving across the Canterbury Plains, you first reach Timaru, where you turn north-west onto Highway 8. From Twizel, take Aoraki/Mount Cook Road (Highway 80) to Aoraki/Mount Cook village. This access road is sealed and generally in good condition. It climbs slowly, taking you along the western shore of Lake Pukaki in which, on a clear day, you can see the reflections of the park's giant mountains. The village sits at an altitude of 762 m (2,500 ft) amid the fabulous mountain scenery, and has all the amenities you are likely to need, including an information centre. An alternative route takes you inland from Christchurch via Sheffield and Mount Hutt to Fairlie along Highway 8, and then follows the route already described. One of the highlights of the National Park is a visit to the lower part of the Tasman Glacier, which you can reach via the road to Blue Lake. After about 8 km (5 miles), park your vehicle and climb for around 30 minutes until you reach the Tasman Glacier viewpoint. From here, you can see the Aoraki/Mount Cook range in all its glory. At higher altitudes, skiers can enjoy a number of ski resorts that remain open throughout the year. The visitor centre can provide you with detailed information on what to do in the National Park. Several hiking trails start here, too, and they are well signposted although very stony in places.

8 Twizel This town at the junction of Aoraki/Mount Cook Road and Highway 8 started out as a builder's campsite erected to service the construction of a hydroelectric dam. As part of this project, several lakes were created, including Lake Pukaki and Lake Tekapo in the north-east. The dam was highly controversial at the time, but one positive consequence was the development of the Mackenzie Hydro Lakes recreational area which now provides ideal conditions for water sports. The lakes are full of fish, and you can hire boats from various places. A further attraction of Twizel is the Kaki Visitor Hide where ornithologists can observe the wading kaki (black stilt), one of the country's rarest birds undisturbed.
Just 25 km (16 miles) south of Twizel, you reach Omarama whose north-west thermals make it a perfect spot for gliders and paragliders. The 'Clay Cliffs' 10 km (6 miles) west of

Omarama are a geological phenomenon but this jagged, rocky landscape with its many stone pinnacles is relatively difficult to get to. Our route now follows Highway 8 south to Cromwell at the eastern flank of the Southern Alps.

9 Cromwell This town is located at the point where the Kawarau and Clutha rivers meet and started out as a settlement for gold-diggers. The gold-rush arrived in Cromwell in the 1860s but quickly moved on to the west coast. At the end of the 19th century, the last of the pioneers left town. Part of the settlement was flooded when the dam was built, but some buildings of historical significance were moved to higher ground and restored to create Old Cromwell Town.

At a few kilometres west of Cromwell is the Goldfields Mining Centre, which gives you a real flavour of just how labour-intensive the process of gold-mining can be. You can also enjoy a trip along the Kawarau River in a kayak or rubber dinghy.

From Cromwell, Highway 8 follows the valley of the Clutha River for the most part. It rejoins Highway I in Milton. It is worth taking a detour north to Dunedin along the south-east coast (see side panel, page 168). Heading south, at Balclutha you will join Highway 92 to Invercargill, located on the southern tip of the island. The Cathedral Caves are worth a quick stop along the way, as are the Purakaunui Falls, where the Purakaunui River cascades from a height of over 20 m (66 ft).

10 Invercargill New Zealand's most southerly town boasts tree-lined avenues and sweeping parks, including Queen's Park, which has an area of 1 km² (4 square miles). The town's Scottish heritage is clearly visible today, and many roads are named after Scottish rivers. The Southland Museum and Art Gallery is renowned throughout the country and includes Maori works of art and a natural history exhibition that includes impressive fossils and petrified tree trunks. Next stop is Bluff, around 30 km (18½ miles) south of Invercargill. This small village at the southern tip of the island is home to a large fishing fleet and terminus for the ferries to Stewart Island. The Bluff Maritime Museum houses objects related to the history of whaling. Our next destination is the country's largest National Park, covering 12,000 km² (4,632 square miles) of the island's south-westerly tip.

11 Fiordland National Park (see side panel, page 165).

Its wide lakes, fourteen deep fiords and snow-capped mountains have made this National Park world famous. The park's protected area is traversed by around 500 km (311 miles) of hiking trails, among them the spectacular Milford Track. Our first port of call is Te Anau on the shore of Te Anau Lake. From here, a two-hour boat trip takes us to the fascinating underground world of the Te Anau Caves ('Glowworm Caves'). A drive along the Milford Road (120 km/75 miles) between Te Anau in the south and Milford Sound in the north, one of the scenic highlights of New Zealand, is an unforgettable experience. On both sides of the road, you can see the diverse landscapes of New Zealand's southern tip in all their glory and variety: luxuriant forests, jagged mountains, torrential mountain rivers, roaring waterfalls and tranquil lakes. The Milford Track passes Sutherland Falls which, at 580 m (1,900 ft), was once thought to be the world's tallest waterfall.

A trip to the south to see Doubtful Sound is well worth while, although the journey from Manapouri to Doubtful Sound involves two boat trips and a drive across Wilmot Pass. Several dolphin species live in the coastal waters.

12 Milford Sound This fiord is 16 km (10 miles) long and becomes wider as it makes its way inland. Tall mountains surround the coastline of the South West New Zealand World

(continued p.169)

1 Aoraki/Mount Cook National Park is part of the UNESCO World Heritage Site Te Wahipounamu.

2 Lake Tekapo, east of the Aoraki/Mount Cook range, is surrounded by forests and high mountains.

3 The fiords and forests of the Fiordland National Park are quite breathtaking.

The Hooker Valley Trail along the Hooker River offers many spectacular views of the southern side of Aoraki/Mount Cook and the glaciers surrounding the mountain. The river is fed mainly by snowmelt from the Mueller and Hooker Glaciers. The latter is now melting rapidly, leading to the formation of

a lake at its lower end. The Hooker River runs along extensive scree slopes piled up by the glaciers over time. The two hanging footbridges that span the river

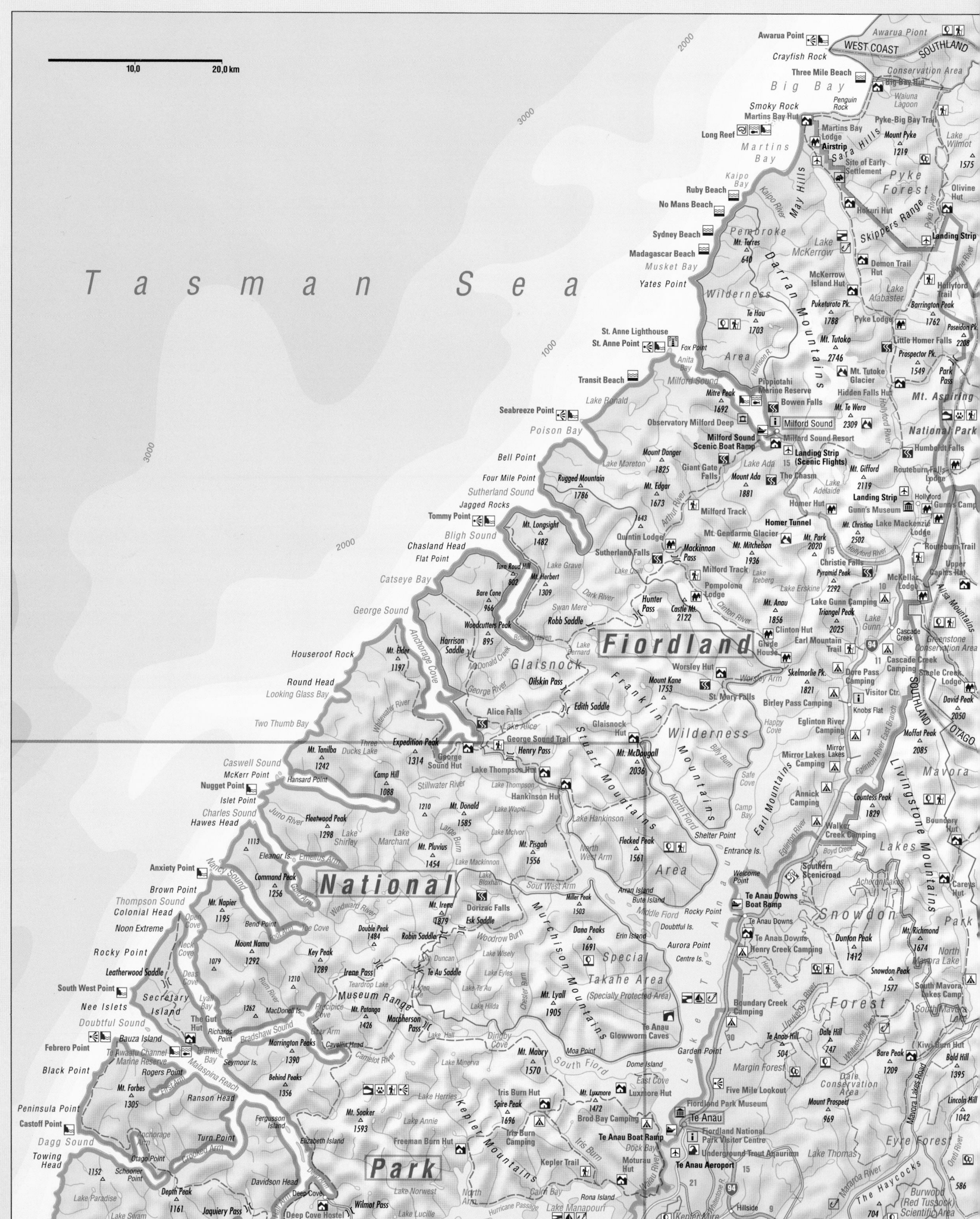
10,0
20,0 km
Tasman Sea
Fiordland
National
Park
Glaisnock
Wilderness
Area
Franklin Mountains
Stuart Mountains
Murchison Mountains
Kepler Mountains
Museum Range
Darran Mountains
Livingstone Mountains
Earl Mountains
Special
Takahe Area
(Specially Protected Area)
Snowdon
Forest
Eyre Forest
Pyke Forest
Mavora
Lakes
WEST COAST
SOUTHLAND
OTAGO
Conservation Area
Awarua Point
Crayfish Rock
Three Mile Beach
Big Bay
Big Bay Hut
Penguin Rock
Waiuna Lagoon
Smoky Rock
Martins Bay Hut
Long Reef
Martins Bay
Martins Bay Lodge
Airstrip
Sara Hills
Site of Early Settlement
Pyke-Big Bay Trail
Mount Pyke
1219
Lake Wilmot
1575
Olivine Hut
Kaipo Bay
Kaipo River
May Hills
Ruby Beach
No Mans Beach
Hokuri Hut
Skippers Range
Pyke River
Landing Strip
Sydney Beach
Pembroke
Mt. Terres
640
Lake McKerrow
Madagascar Beach
Musket Bay
Demon Trail Hut
Yates Point
McKerrow Island Hut
Lake Alabaster
Hollyford Trail
Barrington Peak
1762
Te Hau
1703
Puketuroto Pk.
1788
Pyke Lodge
Poseidon Pk.
2208
St. Anne Lighthouse
St. Anne Point
Fox Point
Anita Bay
Mt. Tutoko
2746
Little Homer Falls
Prospector Pk.
1549
Park Pass
Transit Beach
Milford Sound
Piopiotahi Marine Reserve
Mt. Tutoke Glacier
Hidden Falls Hut
Mt. Aspiring
Lake Bonald
Mitre Peak
1692
Bowen Falls
Mt. Te Wera
2309
Hollyford River
Seabreeze Point
Poison Bay
Observatory Milford Deep
Milford Sound Resort
National Park
Milford Sound Scenic Boat Ramp
Landing Strip (Scenic Flights)
Humboldt Falls
Bell Point
Lake Moreton
Mount Danger
1825
Giant Gate Falls
Lake Ada
Mt. Gifford
2119
Routeburn Falls Lodge
Four Mile Point
Rugged Mountain
1786
Mt. Edgar
1673
Mount Ada
1881
The Chasm
Lake Adelaide
Sutherland Sound
Arthur River
Jagged Rocks
Milford Track
Homer Hut
Landing Strip
Gunn's Museum
Hollyford
Gunn's Camp
Tommy Point
Mt. Longsight
1482
1643
Homer Tunnel
Mt. Christina
2502
Lake Mackenzie Lodge
Bligh Sound
Quintin Lodge
Mt. Gendarme Glacier
Mt. Park
2020
Chasland Head
Flat Point
Sutherland Falls
Mackinnon Pass
Mt. Mitchelson
1936
Routeburn Trail
Turn Road Hill
802
Mt. Herbert
1309
Lake Grave
Lake Quill
Milford Track
Christie Falls
Pyramid Peak
2292
Upper Caples Hut
Catseye Bay
Bare Cone
966
Pompolona Lodge
Lake Iceberg
Lake Erskine
McKellar Lodge
Ailsa Mountains
Dark River
Swan Mere
Hunter Pass
Castle Mt.
2122
Mt. Anau
1856
Lake Gunn Camping
George Sound
Woodcutters Peak
895
Robb Saddle
Clinton River
Triangel Peak
2025
Lake Gunn
Cascade Creek
Greenstone Conservation Area
Anchorage Cove
Harrison Saddle
Lake Bernard
Clinton Hut
Glade House
Earl Mountain Trail
Houseroof Rock
Mt. Elder
1197
McDonald Creek
Cascade Creek Camping
Worsley Hut
Worsley Arm
Skelmorlie Pk.
1821
Dore Pass Camping
Steele Creek Lodge
Round Head
Looking Glass Bay
George River
Oilskin Pass
Mount Kane
1753
St. Mary Falls
Visitor Ctr.
David Peak
2050
Edith Saddle
Birley Pass Camping
Knobs Flat
Whitewater River
Alice Falls
Lake Alice
Two Thumb Bay
Glaisnock Hut
Happy Cove
Eglinton River Camping
Moffat Peak
2085
Mt. Tanilba
1242
Three Ducks Lake
Expedition Peak
1314
George Sound Hut
George Sound Trail
Henry Pass
Mt. McDougall
2036
Billy Burn
Mirror Lakes
Caswell Sound
McKerr Point
Hansard Point
Camp Hill
1088
Lake Thompson Hut
Lake Thompson
Mirror Lakes Camping
Eglinton River East Branch
Nugget Point
Islet Point
Stillwater River
Hankinson Hut
Safe Cove
Annick Camping
Charles Sound
Hawes Head
Juno River
1210
Mt. Donald
1585
Lake Wapiti
North Fiord
Camp Bay
Countess Peak
1829
Fleetwood Peak
1298
Lake Shirley
Lake Marchant
Large Burn
Lake McIvor
Lake Hankinson
Shelter Point
Eglinton River
Walker Creek Camping
Boundary Hut
1113
Mt. Pluvius
1454
Mt. Pisgah
1556
North West Arm
Flecked Peak
1561
Entrance Is.
Boyd Creek
Anxiety Point
Eleanor Is.
Emelius Arm
Lake Mackinnon
Nancy Sound
Command Peak
1256
Lake Bloxham
Welcome Point
Southern Scenicroad
Acheron Lakes
Careys Hut
Brown Point
Thompson Sound
Sout West Arm
Arran Island
Bute Island
Te Anau Downs Boat Ramp
Colonial Head
Mt. Napier
1195
Windward River
Mt. Irene
1879
Dorizac Falls
Miller Peak
1503
Middle Fiord
Rocky Point
Open Cove
Bend Point
Esk Saddle
Doubtful Is.
Te Anau Downs
Noon Extreme
Gold Arm
Tee Cove
Double Peak
1484
Robin Saddle
Woodrow Burn
Dana Peaks
1691
Erin Island
Dunton Peak
1412
Mt. Richmond
1674
Neck Cove
Mount Nama
1292
Key Peak
1289
Lake Wisely
Aurora Point
Henry Creek Camping
North Mavora Lake
Rocky Point
1079
Deas Cove
Duncan
Centre Is.
Henry Creek
Leatherwood Saddle
Rum River
Irene Pass
Te Au Saddle
Lake Eyles
Snowdon Peak
1577
1210
Teardrop Lake
Lake Te Au
Chester Burn
South West Point
Secretary Island
Lyall Bay
Hidden Lake
Lake Hilda
Mt. Lyall
1905
South Mavora Lakes Camp
Nee Islets
1262
MacDonell Is.
Mt. Patanga
1426
Precipice Cove
Boundary Creek Camping
Doubtful Sound
The Gut Hut
Bradshaw Sound
Macpherson Pass
Te Anau Glowworm Caves
South Mavora
Uruwhenua River
Bauza Island
Richards Point
Gaer Arm
Lake Hall
Whitestone River
Dale Hill
747
Febrero Point
Te Awaatu Channel Marine Reserve
Blanket Bay
Seymour Is.
Marrington Peaks
1390
Cavellia Head
Camelot River
Dingby Cove
Moa Point
Te Anau Hill
504
Kiwi Burn Hut
Bald Hill
1395
Black Point
Rogers Point
Malaspina Reach
Mt. Mabry
1570
South Fiord
Garden Point
Bare Peak
1209
Mt. Forbes
1305
First Arm
Lake Minerva
Dome Island
Margin Forest
Dale Conservation Area
Ranson Head
Behind Peaks
1356
East Cove
Luxmore Hut
Lake Te Anau
Five Mile Lookout
Mavora Lakes Road
Peninsula Point
Lake Herries
Iris Burn Hut
Mt. Luxmore
1472
Fiordland Park Museum
Mount Prospect
969
Lincoln Hill
1042
Castoff Point
Mt. Soaker
1593
Spire Peak
1696
Ferguson Island
Anchorage Cove
Dagg Sound
Lake Annie
Iris Burn Camping
Brod Bay Camping
Te Anau
Turn Point
Elizabeth Island
Freeman Burn Hut
Te Anau Boat Ramp
Dock Bay
Fiordland National Park Visitor Centre
Underground Trout Aquarium
Lake Thomas
Towing Head
Otago Point
Crooked Arm
Iris Burn
Moturau Hut
Te Anau Aeroport
Oreti River
1152
Schooner Point
Kepler Trail
Waiau River
The Haycocks
Mararoa River
586
Davidson Head
Deep Cove
Lake Norwest
Whitestone R.
Burwood (Red Tussock) Scientific Area
Depth Peak
1161
Lake Paradise
Lake Swan
Jaquiery Pass
Deep Cove Hostel
Wilmot Pass
Lake Lucille
North Arm
Hurricane Passage
Calm Bay
Rona Island
Lake Manapouri
Kepler Mire
Hillside
704
1000
2000
3000
94
15
11
10
7
21
30
9

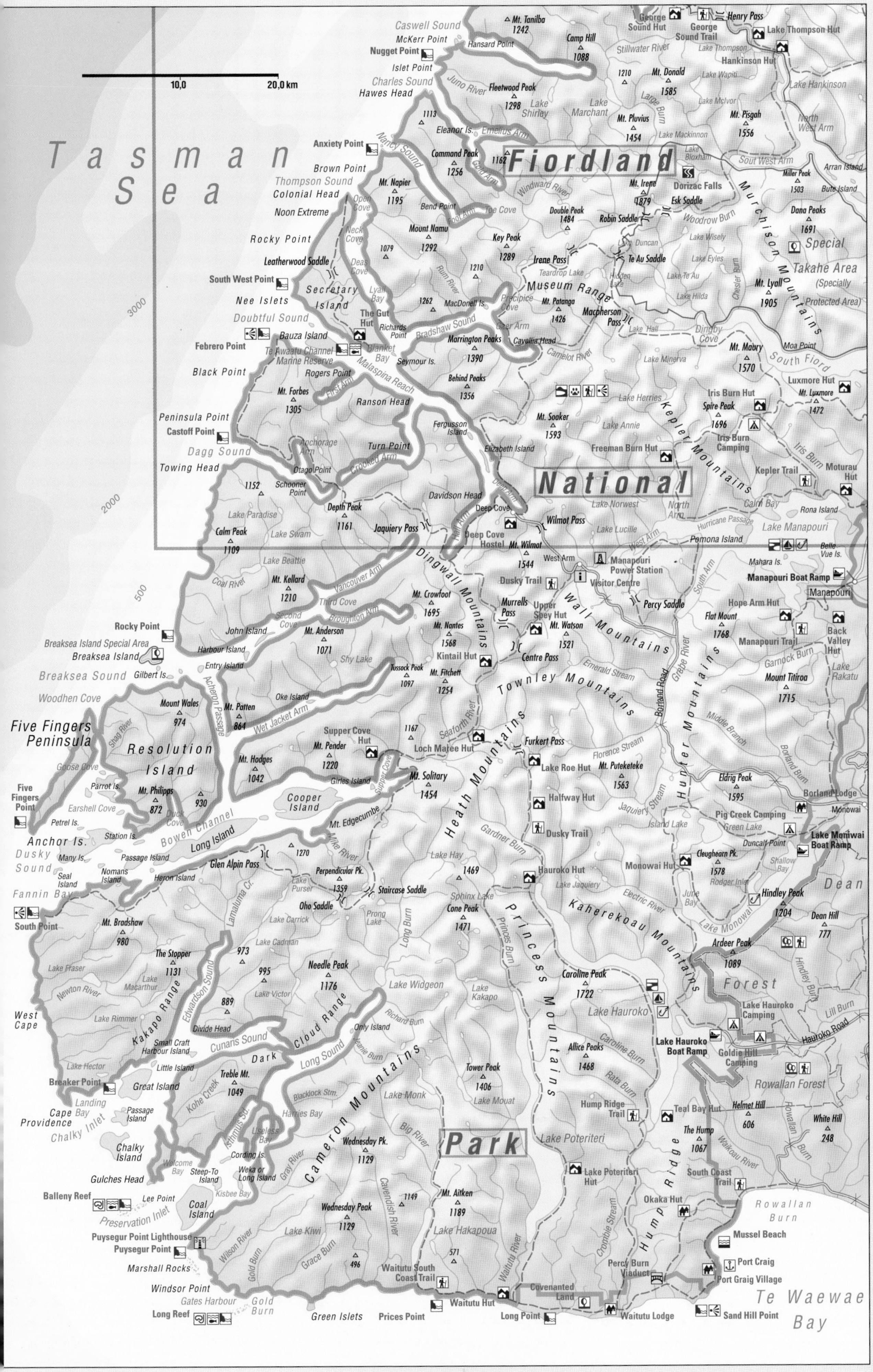

Fiordland National Park

This park, which is New Zealand's largest National Park by far – at 12,000 km² (4,632 square miles) – is also considered the most beautiful National Park in the country.

Its snow-capped mountains are the backdrop to extensive beech forests with giant moss-covered 500-year-old trees, valleys with crystal-clear rivers and quiet lakes and, of course, the majestic fiords of the west coast. Only one of these, Milford Sound, is accessible by road. In this area, there are 700 endemic plant species as well as kakapos, a curious kind of flightless parrot. This masterpiece of natural creation (which includes the three National Parks of Aoraki/Mount Cook and Westland) definitely merits its status as a UNESCO World Heritage Site.

The sealed road to Milford Sound is spectacular. One hundred and twenty km (75 miles) long, it runs along the shore of Lake Te Anau and then across virtually untouched primeval landscapes, with magnificent views of Mount Christiana (2,502 m/8,209 ft). The route takes you through Hollyford Valley, past stunning natural features such as Mirror Lakes until you reach Homer Tunnel. At the western side of the tunnel, some steep hairpin bends take you down to Milford Sound. Mitre Peak (1,692 m/6,437 ft) rises up abruptly out of the sea.

Lake Manapouri is located south of Te Anau; its islands and peaceful, bush-clad shores are best explored by kayak.

Top: On the way to Milford Sound, Bottom: Lake Te Anau.

At the lake's western arm, there is a hydroelectric power plant buried 200 m (650 ft) deep in the rocks.

When this power plant was built, an access road also needed to be constructed. This road now connects the lake to Deep Cove on Doubtful Sound via Wilmot Pass – you can take it to reach the cruise boats on New Zealand's deepest fiord.

An unusual view of Mitre Peak (1,692 m/6,437 ft), which is more commonly seen from Milford Sound where it is a familiar landmark. Its jagged, conical peak

The Track, which is about 54 km (33 miles) long, starts at Lake Te Anau and follows Mackinnon Pass, past Sutherland Falls to Milford Sound. Time and again, there are breathtaking views along the way.

Dunedin

The city has close ties to the Scottish city of Edinburgh – and not simply because Dun Edin is the Gaelic name for Scotland's capital. New Zealand and Scottish elements mingle in the town's cultural life. The Octagon is the city centre, a circular thoroughfare area bisected by the city's main streets, with an inner pedestrian area surrounded by some of Dunedin's most important buildings, including the

Statue of Robert Burns outside Dunedin Cathedral.

Anglican St Paul's Cathedral and Dunedin Public Art Gallery with its collection of European art. The Octagon itself is the venue for several festivals and markets.

Dunedin's railway station is also architecturally interesting; the Flemish-style building with its 37-m (121-ft) tower is considered one of New Zealand's most beautiful stone buildings. Its magnificent mosaic floors were created from more than 700,000 pieces of porcelain.

Detour

The south-east coast

Milton is the ideal starting point for a trip north, taking you to some of the scenic and cultural highlights of the South Island's south-east. Via Clarendon, this route first goes to Dunedin and then to the Otago Peninsula, which is 25 km (16 miles) long. The most northerly point of this excursion is Oamaru, from which you retrace the route back to Milton on Highway I, also known as SH1.

Otago Peninsula

The 60 km (37 miles) of the Highcliff Road take you past the most important sights, with spectacular, ever-changing views of the sea. This thinly populated, hilly peninsula boasts a surprisingly varied range of fauna and flora. The northernmost tip (Taiaroa Head) is especially suited to wildlife watching. It is the only mainland breeding site of the royal albatross, and colonies of seals, sea lions and penguins make their home in the immediate vicinity. In the coastal waters, you can see orcas and other whales. Boat trips to these impassable cliffs can be booked in Dunedin. The small harbour village of Portobello is known for its aquarium, which gives visitors an interesting introduction to maritime life. Glenfallochs Woodland is a park with ancient trees, rhododendrons and azaleas.

Larnach Castle is an architectural highlight. This impressive mansion was built for a banker, William Larnach, between 1871 and 1885. When Larnach committed suicide, the surrounding land was sold and the building fell derelict until it was restored some forty years ago; it is now a hotel and conference centre.

The castle, with its beautiful painted ceilings and its floating staircase, is open to visitors. It also has a 250-m^2 (2,690-sq ft) ballroom.

Moeraki Boulders

When you continue your journey on Highway 1, it is well worth stopping at the Moeraki Boulders. These mighty stone spheres, measuring up to 3 m (10 ft) across, provided the Maori with the inspiration for many legends. For a long time, they were believed to be petrified food storage containers (Te Kai-hinaki), thrown ashore by their ancestors from their canoes. The scientific explanation, however, is much less colourful – the spheres were formed at the bottom of the sea from lime deposits that built up around a hard core. When the land rose above the sea the stones were exposed and now lie on a fine stretch of sandy beach. Today, the nearby fishing village of Moeraki is populated mainly by Maori.

Oamaru

Our excursion to the southeast terminates in the small town of Oamaru. Most of the town's historic buildings were built from the pale limestone found in the surrounding area and some have been renovated several times. Particularly noticeable are the colonnaded porticoes framing many buildings such as the Courthouse and Forrester Gallery. South Hill Walkway above the harbour gives you a good view of the town. It is surrounded by impressive mountain ranges and if you arrive at sunset, you will enjoy some spectacular views.

1 At high tide the Moeraki Boulders are partly submerged and sink into the soft sand.

2 Sheep in the mountains north of Dunedin: pastureland as far as the eye can see.

3 Winding roads open up the charming hills along the south-east coast.

Heritage Site, known in Maori as Te Wahipounamu, and rise suddenly above the waterline, their slopes covered in rainforests. Mitre Peak (1,692 m/6,437 ft), with its remarkable conical shape, is one of the most-photographed spots in New Zealand. The mountain peaks are reflected in the clear, still waters of the fiord.

From the town of Milford, located on the south-eastern shore of Milford Sound, you can arrange a boat trip on the fiord, or even book a cruise for a few days and really explore the area from the sea. From a zoological point of view, the diversity of fish species is very interesting. The heavy rains in the area mean that above the water that flows into the fiord from the sea there is a permanent layer of fresh water, several metres deep, providing an extraordinary environment in which both freshwater and saltwater fish can thrive.

Milford Track (54 km/33 miles) is one of the most famous hiking trails in the country. It begins at Glade House at the northern tip of Lake Te Anau and runs through the Clinton Valley, past Sutherland Falls and up to the fiord. When booking, do bear in mind that the track is only walkable from November to March. From Milford Sound, you return to Te Anau, where you pick up the eastbound Highway 94. The rivers near Lumsden are famous for their wealth of trout. From Lumsden, you follow Highway 6 to the north. In Kingston, at the southern shore of Lake Wakatipu, you can take a 75-minute ride on the Kingston Flyer, a vintage steam train.

⑬ **Queenstown** This town at the northern shore of Lake Wakatipu is one of the South Island's biggest tourist attractions. The town centre is spread out around the Queenstown Bay. Queenstown Gardens are located on a peninsula that extends far into the lake. If you are looking for an oasis of peace and tranquillity in what is a very busy town, you have come to the right place: the gardens' fir-tree-lined lawns and rose beds are a quiet haven. The Mall is a popular meeting point for locals and visitors alike. Along this bustling shopping street, you will see some well-preserved colonial buildings, among them Eichardt's Tavern (1871). At Underwater World, you can observe some of the local marine life. The Kiwi and Birdlife Park shelters several endangered bird species. The Skyline Gondola takes you up to Bob's Peak (450 m/1,475 ft), with its fantastic view of the town and the surrounding area.

⑭ **Wanaka** This lakeside town lies around 55 km (34 miles) as the crow flies from Queenstown and sits at the southern tip of Lake Wanaka. Its proximity to Mount Aspiring National Park and to the lake itself makes this a very attractive spot. The

1 Mist drifts over Lake Wanaka.

2 View from Bob's Peak over Queenstown and Queenstown Gardens on Lake Wakatipu

South Island wildlife

Thanks to the island's low population density, local fauna live in relative peace and there are many bird breeding-sites, giving the island its nickname of 'seabird paradise'. As well as albatrosses, waders such as black-winged stilts find suitable habitats in this area. Along the coast, you can find several species of penguin. The South Island's coastal waters are home to many whales and dolphins. Wild boar, red deer, rabbits, martens and possums were introduced to the country by European settlers.

Red deer roam freely in the solitude of the Southern Alps.

Transport and Toy Museum located near the airport is definitely worth visiting – its collection of vehicles and toys comprises more than 13,000 exhibits. And if you want to take a break from all this wonderful scenery, you can head for Stuart Landsborough's Puzzling World in Wanaka.

15 Mount Aspiring National Park Wanaka is the gateway to this National Park. North-west of the town, a small road follows the Matukituki river right into the park which, at 3,555 km^2 (1,372 square miles) is New Zealand's third largest. At its heart is Mount Aspiring (3,027 m/9,932 ft), shaped like a pyramid, hence its nickname of 'New Zealand's Matterhorn'. The scenery consists of tall, snow-capped mountains. There are numerous densely forested valleys and picturesque river plains. Several hiking trails allow you to explore the beauty of the park on foot. The Dart Rees Track is well-known and makes an ideal trek lasting several days through mountainous terrain. However, do note that you have to be in very good physical shape if you plan to attempt it. Less demanding but still worth doing is a hike on the Rob Roy Valley Trail along the Matukituki River. Keas, a species of mountain parrot, and timberline wrens are just two of the bird species you might spot in the park. You may be lucky enough to see keas at close range but the wrens tend to stick to higher altitudes. Many waterbirds live along the rivers and lakes.

16 Lake Hawea From Wanaka, on the next leg of our journey to the coast, Highway 6 runs between Lake Wanaka and Lake Hawea (140 km^2/54 square miles). Surrounded as it is by impressive scenery, this lake, with its clear blue waters, is one of the most beautiful on the South Island. It is 410 m (1,345 ft) deep, which means it is actually below sea level. Its abundance of trout and salmon makes it one of New Zealand's most popular fishing grounds. You might want to stop en route for a rest and enjoy the view at the Cameron Creek Lookout. On the far side of the Haast Pass (563 m/1,847 ft), you will pass Thunder Creek Falls, at a height of 30 m (98 ft). The road now runs along the Haast River, and once you get to Haast you'll have made it to the west coast.

17 Westland National Park This park (1,176 km^2/454 square miles) stretches from the Okarito Lagoon on the west coast inland to Mount Tasman (3,498 m/11,475 ft), one of the highest mountains in the New Zealand Alps. Its variety of wetlands, lakes, rainforests, glaciers and rocky landscapes make this National Park particularly attractive. The west coast still bears witness in places to the 1860s gold-rush. Gillespies Beach on the coast is a former goldminers' settlement, and traces of the era are still visible today. A beautiful hike along a former mining track leads down to a beach with a seal colony.
Access roads such as Docherty Creek Road and Forks Okarito Road link Highway 6 to the west coast. The shore of Lake Mapourika is a popular spot for a picnic on the main road. Further south, you will find Lake Matheson, which is probably New Zealand's most photographed lake.

18 Franz Josef Glacier Like Fox Glacier to the south, this glacier stretches from its feeding point at more than 3,000 m (9,840 ft) to about 300 m (984 ft) above sea level, where the coastal rain-

forests grow right up to the edge of the glacier. Named after the Austrian Emperor Franz Josef, it is around 13 km (8 miles) long and forms part of Westland National Park. There are some dangerous crevices, so hiking across the glacier is only permitted as part of a guided tour. During the last two centuries, the ice has advanced on a number of occasions, but then always receded to its current level. The melt waters form the Waiho River, on which Franz Josef Village is located. A road takes you to a car park, and from there it is a one-hour tramp to the glacier gate at the lowest point of the ice flow.

⑲ **Hokitika** In this charming town, which you reach via Highway 6, the Hokitika Heritage Walk will take you to some interesting 19th-century buildings. An old ship is also open for visits. The West Coast Historical Museum is dedicated to the gold-rush era, as is the historical open-air museum at the recreated 1860s gold-mining town, known as Shantytown, located 10 km (6 miles) south of Greymouth.

⑳ **Greymouth** This town flourished during the 19th-century gold-rush. When the region's deposits were exhausted, coal mining replaced gold digging as the town's principal source of revenue. However, Greymouth's development was severely restricted by recurrent heavy flooding. The History House Museum displays some interesting photographic documentation of the town's history and the Left Bank Art Gallery features Maori arts and crafts. If you are looking for something a bit more exciting, why not try floating through the network of the Taniwha Caves on inflated inner tubes.

㉑ **Paparoa National Park** This National Park (300 km²/116 square miles) protects the karst formations of the Paparoa Range, which runs parallel to the coast. Its most popular attractions are the Pancake Rocks and the blowholes close to Punakaiki, a coastal village. The Pancake Rocks are huge limestone pillars, so-named because they look like pancakes piled one on top of the other. Heavy seas force water through the blowholes – funnels carved

1 Dense lowland rainforest covers the karst formations of the Paparoa National Park.

2 The Pancake Rocks near Punakaiki are one of the geological highlights of Paparoa National Park.

3 Ocean waves breaking on the cliffs at Woodpecker Bay north of Punakaiki.

The South Island rainforests

In the wettest parts of the South Island, annual precipitation levels reach 6,000–7,000 mm (232–270 in) ideal conditions for the development of species-rich rainforests. In particular, the wind-exposed western flanks of the New Zealand Alps, with their ascending rains, provide ideal growing conditions for this type of vegetation. In places like the Fox and Franz Josef Glaciers, forests often grow right up to the glacier tongues — a surprising sight for Europeans.
One of the trademarks of the South Island's evergreen rainforests is their jungle-like fern thickets in the undergrowth. These ferns thrive here even though only a tiny fraction of the sunlight filters through the dense roof canopy.

Luxuriant growth in the rainforest.

Detour

Arthur's Pass

An impressive mountain road (Highway 73) takes you across the Southern Alps between Springfield in the south-east and Kumara Junction on the north-west coast (Highway 6). The road's highest point is at Arthur's Pass (920 m/3,019 ft), named after Arthur Dudley Dobson, who was the first European to scale it in 1864. Five km (3 miles) south of the pass, the village of the same name serves as a base camp for climbers and skiers and is also the administrative centre for Arthur's Pass National Park, which was established here in 1929, making it the South Island's oldest National Park. Its main attraction is the kea, a type of parrot. The pass road is sometimes closed after heavy snow.

Mountain lake at Arthur's Pass.

out by the surf – and it shoots up into the air in powerful jets. This karst area is entirely covered in subtropical rainforests that flourish thanks to the warm ocean currents in this part of the west coast. Dolomite Point Walk is a hiking trail that takes you right to the heart of this virgin forest and just 15 minutes down Truman Track you come to a wild and romantic piece of coastline with a waterfall and several caves.

Continuing to the north, you reach Westport, which serves as an ideal base for a range of outdoor activities in the area. For thrill-seekers, the local underground rafting is particularly spectacular; accompanied by a guide, you can drift along underground waterways and visit hidden caves. A three-hour hike on Cape Foulwind Walkway takes you to a seal colony in Tauranga Bay.

22 Karamea In Westport, you leave Highway 6 and take Highway 67 to the north. The coastal town of Karamea is the starting point for several hikes into the Kahurangi National Park, of which Heaphy Track (15 km/9 miles) is one of the best known. North of Karamea, you reach the Oparara Basin with its monumental limestone cliffs. There is also an extensive and intricate network of caves known as the Honeycomb Hill Caves. Inside the caves are the bones of nine species of the now extinct wingless – and therefore flightless – moa bird. It boasts the most varied collection of subfossil bird bones ever found in New Zealand. The caves have some huge passages and enormous chambers to explore. Prior booking of a guided tour is essential.

Another scenic highlight is Oparara Arch, a natural rock

arch, some 43 m (141 ft) high and 220 m (241 yds) long.

From Karamea, take Highway 67 back to Westport and then follow Highway 6 to Matupiko and Nelson. From either place, you can pick up a road to Abel Tasman National Park and Cape Farewell. Eroded granite sculptures, sandy bays and estuaries all feature in this National Park.

Return to Picton by following the shore of the Tasman Bay.

1 Rocky coastline at Wharakiri Beach near Cape Farewell.

2 At Tasman Bay near Nelson.

3 Coastal landscape at Marlborough Sounds.

Abel Tasman National Park Endless beaches and jungle-like rainforests – this National Park named after the Dutch explorer boasts some spectacular contrasts.

Marlborough Sounds Quiet bays and green hills are typical of the scenery at the South Island's northernmost tip. There are also some impressive dripstone caves on the coast.

Kaikoura Range In the north-east of the South Island the land gradually rises up from the coast to jagged mountains — a hiker's paradise.

Paparoa National Park In the course of millennia, wind and waves have carved out the bizarre shapes of the Pancake Rocks – a breathtaking landscape.

Nelson Lakes National Park This National Park with an area of nearly 1,000 km² (386 square miles) is located at the northern end of the Southern Alps, the South Islands geological backbone. It boasts two spectacular glacier lakes at its centre .

Christchurch The impressive Christchurch Cathedral is located in the centre of this city with its many typical parks.

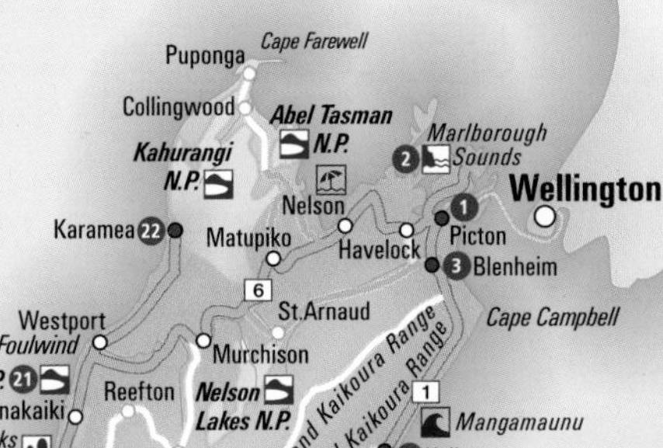

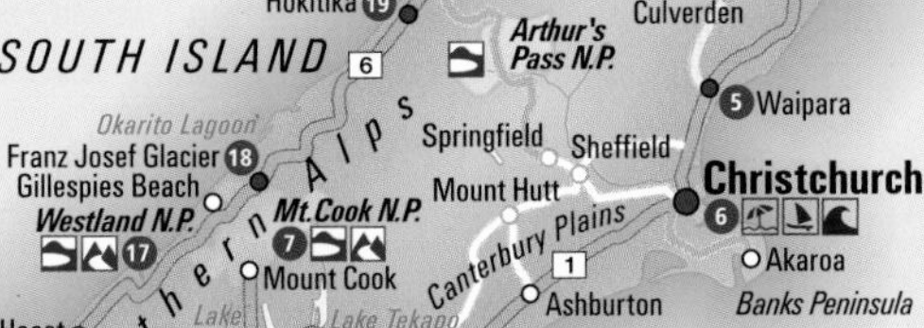

Westland National Park Massive glaciers – among them the famous Franz Josef and Fox Glaciers – extend down the slopes of the Southern Alps.

Aoraki/Mount Cook National Park Much of this park, named after New Zealand's highest mountain (3,764 m/12,350 ft), is covered by glaciers.

Keas These mountain parrots are at home in the South Island's high country. Keas were named after the typical hooting noise they make while flying.

Te Wahipounamu The coastal scenery of the South Island's south-west is incredibly varied and intricate. In places rainforests run all the way down to the shoreline; elsewhere, steep cliffs border fiords stretching far inland.

Dunedin A touch of Scotland in New Zealand: magnificent town houses, massive churches and extensive parks make Dunedin so attractive. The railway station with its 37 m-/121 ft-clock tower is one of the country's most impressive stone buildings.

Lake Wanaka This is one of several lakes at the eastern slopes of the Southern Alps. In summer, it is a popular water sports resort.

Milford Sound One of the landmarks of Fiordland National Park is the distinctive shape of Mitre Peak (1,692 m/6,437 ft), with its steep rock faces rising abruptly out of Milford Sound.

Queenstown Sloping down to Lake Wakatipu, in front of the 'Remarkables' – this is Queenstown. This former gold-diggers' settlement is now a popular holiday resort.

Purakaunui Falls The falls cascade down more than 20 m (66 ft) to make a deafening roar here.

Route 8

Fiji, Tonga and Samoa

Island hopping in Western Polynesia

The island states of Fiji, Tonga and Samoa are made up of a number of islands and beaches spread over a wide expanse of sea. Mountain ranges criss-cross volcanic islands covered in virgin forests, and in contrast there are also many flat coral islands and atolls. The cultural diversity of Western Polynesia is equally fascinating.

On average, the Pacific Ocean seabed lies at a depth of 4,000 m (13,124 ft). This unimaginably vast expanse is punctuated by numerous volcanic islands, coral reefs and atolls; these island chains were formed by movement of the earth's tectonic plates. The Pacific Plate slowly slid towards the Australian and Philippine Plates and, where these plates met, the Pacific Plate was submerged, creating deep sea rifts, such as the Tonga Rift: these are among the lowest points of the earth's crust. The submerged rock then melted deep down in the earth's mantle, expanded again and, through powerful volcanic eruptions, was thrown back up to the surface, creating the volcanic islands that make up the so-called 'Pacific Ring of Fire'. These volcanic islands can reach considerable altitudes. By contrast, the coral reefs and atolls are often only a few metres above sea level.

The first settlers to the islands came from Australia and New Guinea. They arrived in Fiji around 1500 BC, reaching Tonga and Samoa a little later. Their vast knowledge of wind and weather conditions, ocean currents, stars and bird migration routes

Tattooed male hips and stomachs are a cultural tradition in Samoa.

Fiji's bright white beaches and turquoise coastal waters attract many sunbathers and divers; favourable winds also provide excellent conditions for surfing.

The Fijian archipelago comprises numerous small islands, of which many are uninhabited.

enabled Polynesians to undertake extensive voyages of discovery through which they gradually established settlements on most of the Polynesian islands.

Fiji comprises around three hundred islands, although only one hundred or so are permanently inhabited. Its scenic diversity sets Fiji apart from other South Sea islands. Fijians are very traditional and set great store on maintaining their cultural values. They see themselves as the ambassadors of a 'Pacific Way', a political and cultural way of life the essence of which is quite different from that of the West. However, there is also a large population of Fiji Indians, who were originally imported as plantation workers by the islands' British colonial rulers.

Roughly 500 km (310 miles) to the east, the kingdom of Tonga is Fiji's neighbour. Tongans are hospitable people, polite and reserved. Proud of their traditions, they enjoy a laid-back lifestyle. Tonga is made up of some 150 islands, mostly strung out at quite some distance from each other. Its gems can be found in the north – the islands of the Vava'u group are among the most beautiful in the South Seas.

In Samoa, the Polynesian way of life has been preserved in its purest form. 'Fa'a Samoa', meaning ´the Samoan Way', a traditional system of behaviour and responsibilities, is still a strong influence and Samoans have so far succeeded in defending it against Western incursions. It manages to fulfil most tourists' romantic expectations of life in the South Seas. As a result of former colonial days, Samoa is now divided into Western Samoa and American Samoa to the east. Culturally, however, the islands continue to form a unified whole.

Barracudas armed with frightening sets of teeth dart through the coastal waters of Polynesia.

Wildlife of the Fiji islands

Fiji's reptiles include not only crocodiles but two remarkable iguanas – the banded iguana and the larger Fijian crested iguana, which can grow up to 1 m (over 3 ft) long. Birds include sunbirds, kingfishers, several species of parrot and dove, as well as many native birds, including the Fiji goshawk and the Fiji bar-winged rail, which are threatened with extinction or may already be extinct. Red-tailed nightingales and Indian myna were introduced to Fiji in 1890 in order to combat coconut pests, but they have proliferated considerably and are now considered to be pests in their own right because of their noise and numbers.

Top: The collared lory (*Phygis solitarius*) is one of Fiji's parrot species. Bottom: Banded iguanas (*Brachylophus fasciatus*) live in the temperate forests of the Fiji archipelago.

Our South Seas route takes us through the western part of the Polynesian islands, starting out in Viti Levu, Fiji's main island, site of the capital, Suva. Via Vanua Levu (Fiji), we travel eastwards to Tonga and then continue to the north. After around 2,300 km (1,430 miles), our journey ends in Samoa.

❶ **Suva (Viti Levu)** Its population of around 150,000 inhabitants makes Suva the largest city in the South Pacific. It has been Fiji's capital since 1877, and it is also home to the University of the South Pacific, which is jointly maintained by eleven Pacific island states. From Suva's central market, head south on foot to a road junction known as 'The Triangle'. This marks the beginning of Victoria Parade, Suva's main street. At its southern end, you will find the Fiji Museum, which houses a large collection of Fijian historical artefacts.

❷ **Colo-i-Suva Forestry Reserve (Viti Levu)** Leave Suva on the northbound Princess Road; after about 12 km (8 miles), you will reach this small rainforest reserve. Its altitude (120–200 m/ 400–650 ft above sea level) makes it a refreshingly cool spot. Further to the north, our route passes the Tomaniivi range, Fiji's highest mountains. At Rakiraki, you reach Viti Levu's northernmost point. Here, the road heads west, arriving after another 50 km (31 miles) at Latuoka, the island's second largest town.

❸ **Koroyanitu National Heritage Park (Viti Levu)** This nature and culture park in the Koroyanitu mountain range behind Latuoka is accessible via a number of hiking trails. Local guides can take you to the mountain gardens of this wild, rocky landscape where once bloody tribal feuds were fought. The way to the park is not signposted and is relatively hard to find, so it is advisable to book a guided tour from Latuoka. Back in town, it is only 20 km (12 miles) to Nadi on the southbound island road.

❹ **Nadi (Viti Levu)** Located in the drier western part of the

Travel information

Route profile
Length: approx. 2,300 km/ 1,430 miles (excluding detours)
Time needed: min. 3 weeks
Start: Suva (Fidschi)
End: Aganoa Beach (Samoa)
Itinerary (main locations): Suva, Savusavu, Nuku'alofa, Vava'u, Apia

Traffic information
Some roads may become impassable after heavy rains. A national or international driving licence is required. On Fiji and Tonga, you drive on the left, on Samoa on the right. Cargo-boats and passenger ships are the islander's main method of transport and are relatively cheap. Boats also go to some of the more remote islands on a regular basis.

Information
Fiji:
www.bulafiji.com

Tonga:
www.tongaholiday.com
www.vacations.tvb.gov.to

Samoa:
www.visitsamoa.ws

island, Nadi is close to Fiji's main international airport, through which the majority of visitors arrive. The town has a population of around 30,000, with a large Indian presence, hence the predominance of Indian markets and restaurants. Nadi is also the starting point of the Queen's Road, the coastal road back to Suva that takes you through some extremely varied scenery. About 35 km (22 miles) south of Nadi, the small Maro Road takes you to one of the most beautiful beaches of the island. Recently, Natadola Beach has become a favourite surfing spot.

5 Sigatoka Sand Dunes National Park (Viti Levu) Travel a further 35 km (22 miles) along Viti Levu's southern coastline, known as the Coral Coast, to the charming town of Sigatoka, on the shores of a river of the same name. Just outside Sigatoka are some giant sand dunes, not immediately recognizable as such because they are covered in grass. The area, which is also of archaeological significance, reaches right down to the coast and became the island's first National Park in 1989. After around 100 km (62 miles), the Queen's Road ends in Suva. From here, there are regular ferries to Vanua Levu.

6 Savusavu (Vanua Levu) Without doubt, Vanua Levu's second largest town is one of the

1 **The clear waters off Fiji's beaches are a wonderful way to discover the underwater world of the South Seas.**

2 **Fish sellers are a common sight offering their wares on many beaches on the Fiji Islands.**

3 **Viti Levu is Fiji's main island. Its mountainous interior with steep volcanic slopes and its narrow coastal stretches are typical of many islands in the group.**

4 **Many islands in Fiji are volcanic in origin. They are often protected by offshore coral reefs.**

5 **Vanua Levu is Fiji's second largest island. It is sparsely populated and its natural delights remain almost unspoilt.**

Life on the reef

The magnificent shapes and colours of diverse marine life are one of the key attractions of the Pacific islands. Most impressive are the countless coral reefs that provide a habitat for a huge variety of species and represent the most complex ecosystem on earth. The tropical rainforests come a close second.

Among the many reef dwellers are turtles, rays, sharks, swordfish and tuna. Snorkelling and diving give splendid opportunities for observing the sheer size and beauty of these coral gardens and their astonishing biodiversity. Admire the intricate patterns and colours of the many fish, including doctor fish, triangle butterflies, angel fish, parrotfish, clownfish, cuttlefish, pipefish, sweetlips, trigger fish and moray eels. Gaze at the multicoloured sea urchins and starfish, seashells, snails, octopuses, sea anemones and punkfish. Last but by no means least, feast your eyes on the coral. Larger fish that you may encounter close to the coast include rays and some harmless reef sharks. Some sea creatures, however, may sting; these include coelenterates such as some corals, sea anemones and jellyfish, as well as some cone shells, sea urchins and starfish.

Red lionfish are not at all shy but they are venomous.

The volcanic island of Tofua

Covering 56 km² (22 square miles), Tofua is the largest island in the Tongan archipelago of Ha'apai. The Lofia volcano at its centre is 500 m (1,640 ft) high and visible from great distances.

The volcanic island of Tofua was the scene of the famous 'Mutiny on the *Bounty*'.

Since it is an active volcano, a cloud of smoke constantly rises from it. Tofua's caldera (a large, circular depression at the summit of the volcano) is 4 km (2½ miles) across and the crater lake is 230 m (755 ft) deep. It made history in 1789, when mutinous sailors on the *Bounty*, among them Fletcher Christian, abandoned William Bligh, their captain, and a number of crew members in a small boat in the waters just off the island.

most attractive spots in Fiji. This small town, situated on the beautiful Savusavu Bay, has around five thousand inhabitants. Savusavu is famous for its hot springs, of which there are more than twenty on this island. From here, it's 150 km (93 miles) by boat to Fiji's third largest island, Taveuni.

❼ **Bouma National Park, Taveuni** Because of its luxuriant vegetation, Taveuni is also known as the Garden Island. Its mountain ranges, which reach altitudes of up to 1,000 m (3,280 ft), are covered in jungle-like rainforests. In addition, there are coconut plantations that reach all the way down to sea level. Bouma National Park has picturesque waterfalls, some of them cascading from heights of up to 24 m (78 ft). Travelling south-eastwards and crossing the international dateline, you will reach the neighbouring island state of Tonga.

❽ **Nuku'alofa (Tongatapu)** In Tonga's early history, the 'place of love' (as Nuku'alofa, Tonga's capital, literally translates) was a fortified settlement from which Tongan kings ruled the surrounding islands. These days, the town still looks like a 19th-century colonial settlement, with largely wooden buildings. The

principal landmark is the Royal Palace, built in 1867 from prefabricated wooden elements made in New Zealand. Nuku'alofa makes an ideal starting point for a tour around Tongatapu. The coastal road takes you to the most attractive beaches and key sights of Tonga's main island.

❾ **Ha'amonga Trilithon (Tongatapu)** This massive stone archway stands at roughly 32 km (20 miles) from the capital, near Niutoua and at Tongatapu's most northerly point. Legend has it that the Polynesian demigod Maui carried this monument on his shoulders all the way to Tonga from the island of Wallis. This also explains the name of the trilithon, known as Ha'amonga'a Maui, or 'Maui's burden'. It consists of three huge rectangular stones, weighing more than 100 ton (110 tonnes) in total. It is thought that it served as a solar calendar for astronomical calculations. On 21 June, the shortest day of the year in the Southern hemisphere, the sunrise is in direct alignment with the trilithon. Our route now takes you past the Haveluliku dripstone caves and the Tongan Wildlife Centre (featuring the Aviary and Botanical Gardens) to Houma in the west of Tongatapu.

❿ **Houma (Tongatapu)** Along the rocky coast of Houma with its terraced slopes, sea spray is forced through hundreds of rock holes, spouting up to 20 m (66 ft) in the air. When viewed at high tide in particular, it soon becomes clear why in Tonga these blowholes are called Mapu'a a Vaca ('King's Pipes'). The high pressure generated by the water

makes a truly deafening noise. After 15 km (9 miles) east on the coastal road, you make your way back to the capital of Nuku'a-luofa, where you can catch a ferry to the Vava'u islands, about 275 km (170 miles) away.

11 Vava'u Vava'u The Vava'u group consists of thirteen inhabited islands and twenty-one uninhabited ones, all of them densely forested. Extensive coconut and vanilla plantations blanket the hills of Vava'u, the main island, which covers an area 90 km² (35 square miles) in size. The main town of Neiafu with its numerous colonial wooden buildings is Tonga's second largest settlement, with a population of five thousand. A walk up Mount Talau (Mo'unga), 131 m (430 ft) high, offers the best views of Neiafu's harbour and the surrounding islands. From here, you can also see the island of Pangaimotu, which is some 9 km² (3½ square miles) in size.
Around 750 km (465 miles) to the north of the Vava'u islands lies the neighbouring island state of Samoa, whose largest island is Savai'i.

12 Mu Pagoa Falls (Savai'i) The ferries dock at Salelologa, and it is not far from the airport, making it an ideal starting point for a tour around the island. Since the interior of Savai'i is inaccessible, the best way to see the island is along the coastal road. Around 10 km (6 miles) west of the town, you reach the prehistoric Pulemelei pyramid near Vailoa. This large stone mound is 61 m (200 ft) in diameter and 50 m (164 ft) wide, and reaches a height of 12 m (39½ ft). You can then visit the nearby Mu Pagoa waterfalls and their idyllic natural pool.

13 Taga (Savai'i) Near Taga, about 25 km (16 miles) further west along the coastal road, you will encounter more blowholes, where sea is forced through narrow openings in the coral rocks and spurts upwards like a fountain. These blowholes really are a spectacular sight, especially at high tide and in high winds. The coastal area is a popular surfing spot, in particular between May and October.

14 Safotu (Savai'i) The island's north coast is notable for its huge lava fields that reach all the way to the shoreline. They were created by a series of eruptions from Mount Matavanu (433 m/1,421 ft) that took place between 1905 and 1911. Several legends recount how the lava flow miraculously divided and then rejoined around the grave of a Samoan nun. This 'virgin's grave' is still visible at the base of a rectangular depression in the lava flow. The coastal road takes you back to Salelologa, from where you can take the ferry to the island of 'Upolu, arriving after 45 km (28 miles) at Apia, capital of this island state.

1 The Vava'u islands, Tonga's most beautiful island group, are breathtaking, even when viewed from the air. The thirteen inhabited islands and twenty-one uninhabited islands are a paradise for swimmers and divers.

2 The scenic attractions of the Vava'u islands include their rocky coastline with its many caves.

3 Savai'i boasts wonderful waterfalls, including Mu Pagoa, and lava fields from nearby volcanoes.

4 Savai'i also has the most amazing blowholes. When high waves crash against the shoreline, water is forced through holes in the rock and spurts skyward like a fountain.

Most South Sea islands are surrounded by fringing or barrier reefs, lying respectively just a few metres from the coast or at several kilometres offshore. They are made of coral, which is created by billions of mi

leaf corals shown above. When stimulated, individual corals light up like fluorescent lamps. Corals can live at depths of 10–40 metres (33–130 ft), but they grow best at around 10 m (33 ft) below the surface. They need clear water at a temperature of 27°C (80° F) in order to survive.

Detour

American Samoa

This US outpost in the South Pacific comprises five main islands of volcanic origin and two low coral atolls. Rainforests cover more than two-thirds of the land mass. One of

Rugged rock faces are typical of the southern coast of Tutuila. Its northern coast is even more inhospitable.

the attractions of American Samoa is the town of Pago Pago, located on Tutuila at the base of Mount Pioa. Due to the mountain winds, Pago Pago Bay receives up to 7,000 mm (270 in) of rainfall per year.

15 Apia ('Upolu) Around a quarter of the Samoan population lives in the state capital on 'Upolu's northern coast. Apia is made up of several individual villages. You can admire some typical wooden buildings dating from colonial times, such as the Palace of Justice and the Congregational Christian Church. Samoa was a German colony from 1900 to 1914, when New Zealand took administrative control until independence in January 1962. A pyramid-shaped monument on the Mulunu'u peninsula marks the spot where the colony was declared in 1900. South of the island, along Falealili Road you will reach the estate of Robert Louis Stevenson, author of *Treasure Island*. The summit of Mount Vaea (475 m/ 1,558 ft) provides a splendid view over the island's north coast. From Apia, you can take an excursion to American Samoa (see side panel, this page).

16 Sopoaga Falls ('Upolu) All island tours start in Apia and travel around 'Upolu in a clockwise direction. First up are the beaches beloved by surfers on account of their wonderful high waves. At Falefa, the road heads into the interior of the island and to the Lemafa Pass. This takes you to the Sopoaga Falls, located in the midst of magnificent tropical vegetation. Following the southern coastal road to the west, you then have to take a track running north of the waterfalls, if you want to make your way to Siuniu. This track is suitable for all-terrain vehicles only. One picturesque village follows another all along the south coast.

17 Aganoa Beach ('Upolu) The southern coast of 'Upolu is noted for its immaculate beaches where you can enjoy a swim and a chance to relax. This is also where the Samoan National Park of O Le Pupu Pu'e is located. A walk on the O Le Pupu Trail gives an excellent overview of the variety of local flora. The main road takes you back to the north coast and to Apia, the capital.

1 **The beaches of Savai'i, Samoa's largest island, are fringed with palm trees. Its mountainous interior is mostly inaccessible.**

2 **Between 'Upolu and Savai'i lie a number of tiny islands and islets; their beaches are protected by coral reefs.**

3 **'Upolu, Samoa's second largest island, has many idyllic beaches, and also some picturesque waterfalls, such as the Sapoaga Falls, in the interior.**

Viti Levu This island boasts a huge range of different scenery: wild, volcanic mountain landscapes alternate with narrow coastal strips with beautiful sandy beaches.

Savai'i The attractions of Samoa's largest island include Mu Pagoa Falls, a climb up Mount Matavanu, and the blowholes with their dramatic seawater fountains.

'Upolu Samoa's second largest island is overlooked by gentle volcanic hills up to 1,000 m (3,200 ft) high. The beautiful beaches in its south are renowned.

Suva Since 1877, the South Pacific's largest town, with a population of 150,000, has been the capital of the Republic of Fiji. It is located on Viti Levu, the archipelago's main island. It is also of cultural significance as the University of the South Pacific is also based here. The Fiji Museum and the Orchid Island Cultural Centre will give you a good overview of Fiji's many traditions and cultural practices.

Tutuila This island forms part of American Samoa and has some truly impressive scenery to offer. Highlights include tropical rainforests with their luscious vegetation, white sandy beaches and the American Samoa National Park in the north. You can enjoy wonderful panoramic views from several places on this mountainous island.

Great Sea Reef
Vanua Levu
Yasawa
Bligh Water
Naravuka
Lagalaga
Viti Levu
Mamanuca
Nabouwalu
Savusavu
6
Tavua
Rakiraki
Somosomo
Lautoka
3
7
Taveuni
Nadi 4
Koroyanitu N.P.
Lawaki
Koro
Bouma N.P.
Sigatoka
Colo-i-Suva Forest Res.
Northern Lau Group
Sigatoka Sand Dunes N.P. 5
2
Lomaloma
Korolevu
Koro Sea
Suva 1
Gau
Vatulele
Cicia
Great Astrolab Reef
FIJI
Lakeba Passage
Lakeba
Tavuki
Moala
Kadavu
Southern Lau Group
Matuku
Kabara
Fulaga
Niuatoputapu

Apia Samoa's capital, located in the north of 'Upolu, developed from a large number of small villages and has a population of 40,000. Numerous colonial-style wooden buildings have given way to more modern architecture. Among the architectural sights in this lively city are the Palace of Justice and the Congregational Christian Church. Robert Louis Stevenson spent the last years of his life here and is buried on Mount Vaea.

Sigatoka Sand Dunes National Park Sigatoka is a good starting point for a trip along the Sigatoka River, which is bordered by high, overgrown sand dunes. The region has been a National Park since 1989.

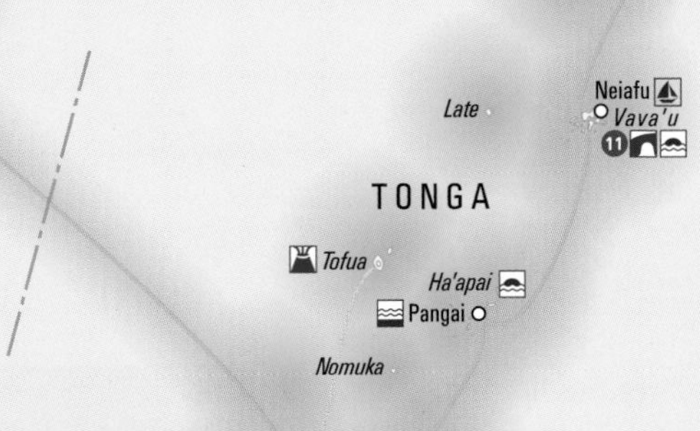

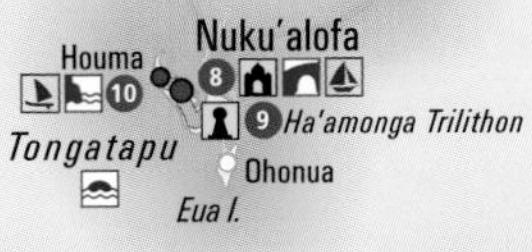

Vava'u The paradise islands of Vava'u – Tonga's most beautiful archipelago, according to some – comprises thirteen inhabited and twenty-one uninhabited islands. Extensive coconut and vanilla plantations flourish on the hills of its densely forested main island, which covers 90 km² (35 square miles).

Taveuni The 420 km² (162 square miles) of this island are rich in vegetation, making it 'Fiji's Garden Island'. At the heart of the island lies the crater lake of Tagimaucia.

The kingdom of Tonga This island kingdom, once called 'The Friendly Islands', is the only state in the South Pacific never to have been a true colony. However, it is part of the British Commonwealth, and, curiously enough, is governed by a dynasty of kings who have been in power since 1845. Tonga is currently ruled by King George Tupou V, who will be officially crowned in 2008. His wooden palace, built in 1867, is located in Nuku'alofa, the capital.

Tongatapu In contrast to the archipelago's smaller islands, Tonga's larger ones, including Tongatapu, are coral islands that have surfaced from the sea and are sheltered by the coral-laden barrier reefs that form a protective barrier against the high waves. Apart from the ubiquitous coconut palms, agricultural crops account for most of the vegetation on the main island.

Route 9

Polynesia

From the Marquesas to the Cook Islands

Fabulous tales of the South Seas have been told since the first explorers returned with reports of a lost paradise rediscovered. The myth has been perpetuated by many a writer. Descriptions abound of hospitable islanders, endless sunshine, blue lagoons, white beaches and a relaxed, carefree lifestyle.

Within the continental grouping known as Oceania, Polynesia ('many islands') is the largest group of small island nations, followed by Melanesia and Micronesia. Geologically, there are two very distinct types of island in the area – those of volcanic origin and flat coral ones. The existing islands are in fact simply the summits of mountains from a continent that was submerged in prehistoric times. Atolls represent a very distinct type of island, formed when a coral reef grows around a volcanic island that later subsides into the ocean, leaving only a circular reef above sea level. A chain of sandbanks and overgrown islets then develops, known in the Polynesian language as 'motus'. These islets enclose the lagoon of an atoll.
The climate in the southern Pacific is tropical and heavily influenced by the sea and the trade winds. There is every kind of island you could imagine, from flat, hot and dry coral islands to humid, warm, mountainous and densely forested ones. The trade winds blow endlessly from a south-easterly direction, bringing welcome freshness. Each island has its own ecosystem, with its particular combination of flora and fauna. Native species of plants and animals have developed on most islands, some of them unique to the environment in which they flourish.

Traditional Polynesian flower garlands.

Our route through the island world of eastern Polynesia starts on the Marquesas Islands, approximately 1,200 km (745 miles) north-east of Tahiti. These are the first islands in French Polynesia and were populated around 300 BC by Polynesians from Samoa and Tonga. In 1595 the Spaniard Alvaro de Mendana was the first European to discover them. He named them after the Marqués de Cañete, then viceroy of Peru.
Captain Cook arrived some two hundred years later and after him came the whale hunters and slave traders, bringing with them diseases that reduced the native

Volcanic and mountainous Huahine, one of the Society Islands, is 680 m (2,230 ft) high and wholly enclosed by a reef.

The main attraction of Bora-Bora is its lagoon with crystal-clear waters and fascinating marine life.

population from 50,000 to around 1,000. Today, around 7,000 people live on the islands, the largest of which are Nuku Hiva and Hiva Oa. Both have rocky, partly inaccessible coasts unprotected by reefs. The Marquesas are a popular stopover for yachts en route from the west coast of America to Tahiti.

From the Marquesas Islands, the route takes you south to the Society Islands and to Tahiti, the main island in the group. Tahiti epitomizes all our romantic dreams of the South Seas. The concept of an earthly paradise originated with the fabulous accounts of early explorers and was perpetuated by the Hollywood versions of *Mutiny on the Bounty*.

Today, Tahiti still has much to offer: picturesque volcanic islands with steep slopes, flat atolls with turquoise lagoons, wonderful scuba-diving sites and sailing resorts, along with delightful Polynesian dance and song. It is a unique mix that puts French Polynesia in a different league to other island groups in the South Seas.

Heading west, the route finally takes you to the Cook Islands, in effect a miniature version of Polynesia. The Cook Islands comprise eight larger volcanic islands and numerous small coral atolls; many of the motus (islets) are uninhabited. Rarotonga is the main island, and with its volcanic, jagged mountain tops it is a smaller version of Tahiti, whereas Aiutaki, a mixture of atoll and volcanic island, is more like Bora-Bora.

Travelling in the Polynesian islands is a dream journey, but most of these very beautiful islands have not remained untouched by the trappings of modern life. You will still find paradise, but it is a modern-day version.

Paul Gaugin's *Mountains of Tahiti* (1893) is now in the Minneapolis Institute of Art.

Most of our South Seas journey, from the Marquesas via the Tuamotu Archipelago and the Society Islands, takes us through the wide, seemingly endless island world of Polynesia. After some 3,500 km (2,175 miles) we at last reach the Cook Islands, which are linked with New Zealand.

1 Taiohae (Nuku Hiva) The largest island in the northern archipelago, Nuku Hiva, is also home to the Marquesas Island's administrative and economic centre, Taiohae, a small town located at the foot of Mount Muake (864 m/2,835 ft). Nuku Hiva covers 330 km² (127 square miles) and has a population of 2,100, making it the largest island in the archipelago. The harbour in Taiohae Bay is protected by two small islands often used as a stopover by long-distance sailors. The church of Notre Dame, built in 1974 and now the seat of a Catholic archbishop, was constructed with different-coloured stones from six different islands in the Marquesas group. The sculptures inside this church demonstrate the great skill of woodcarvers from the archipelago. On a headland at the eastern end of Taiohae Bay, the remains of Fort Collets testify to the occupation of the island by French soldiers, following its annexation in 1842.

2 Hakaui-Tal (Nuku Hiva) After heading south-west along the coastal road from Taiohae for about 15 km (9 miles), you reach the Hakaui Valley, where you will see some traditional houses and ceremonial platforms. The valley is famous for its waterfall, which is 350 m (1,150 ft) high. The western side of the gorge is flanked by 1,000-m (3,200-ft) high vertical cliffs rising dramatically from the river edge. On the next part of our journey we head north, through the rocky, dry terrain of the western part of Nuku Hiva, passing the fertile Plateau de Toovii in the centre of the island.

3 Hatiheu Bay (Nuku Hiva) A number of important, partly restored cultural sites are located near Hatiheu Bay, on the northern coast of the island. This was a favourite spot of the famous Scottish writer, Robert Louis Stevenson, and it is one of the prettiest parts of the Marquesas Islands. On a basalt peak, some 300 m (984 ft) above the bay, stands a statue of the Virgin Mary. The coastal road now takes us along the eastern coast, which is rocky and inaccessible in places. Back in Taiohae, we take the ferry across to the island of Ua Pou, located around 50 km (31 miles) to the south.

4 Ua Pou The name means 'two pillars' and refers to the spectacular backdrop of its dramatic sugarloaf mountain peaks, which look like church spires. Ua Pou inspired the Belgian songwriter Jacques Brel to compose his *chanson* 'La Cathédrale'. Its highest mountain is Oave at 1,232 m (4,042 ft) and the main town is Haka Hau in the north-west. The island has around 1,200 inhabitants. The most notable building in this pretty settlement, with its many flowering trees and shrubs, is the church of St Stephen, designed in traditional Polynesian style. It contains some very impressive wood carvings.

The island's interior is covered in dense rainforests and is only partly accessible by road and path. In several valleys, there are abandoned settlements, which you can recognize by their over-

Travel information

Route profile
Length: 3,500 km/2,175 miles (including sea crossings)
Time needed: at least 4 weeks
Start: Nuku Hiva (Marquesas Islands)
End: Aitutaki (Cook Islands)
Itinerary (main locations): Nuku Hiva, Bora-Bora, Tahiti, Rarotonga, Aitutaki

Traffic information
In French Polynesia, cars drive on the right and seatbelts are compulsory; on the Cook Islands cars drive on the left. The speed limit is 40 km/h (25 mph) inside towns, 60 km/h (31 mph) outside towns and 80 km/h (50 mph) on multi-lane highways. There are regular sea and air connections between the larger islands.

Information
www.tahiti-tourisme.co.nz
www.tahiti-tourisme.com
www.tahitinow.com.au
www.cook-islands.com
http://au.franceguide.com/what-to-do/overseas-france/destinations

Tikis: ancestral images

Tikis are sculptures that depict the islanders' ancestors; they are usually carved in palm-wood, but sometimes also hewn from stone. In some South Seas cultures, ancestors are worshipped like gods. The term 'tiki' comes from the Marquesas language; it is also used by the Maori, the Polynesian first settlers in New Zealand, and it has been suggested that 'hei-tiki' are fertility charms representing the human embryo. 'Hei-tiki' are often carved out of pounamu (greenstone or New Zealand nephrite jade) and worn on a string around the neck as talismans. After World War II, during which many American and Japanese soldiers encountered the Pacific way of life while serving in the South Sea islands, tiki became known in the West, first mainly on the west coast of the United States, and subsequently throughout the world. Following a general rise in interest in the South Seas and in exotic fashions, tiki became a term for all sorts of primitive likenesses of gods, and also for imitations, either produced in the Islands specifically for Western tourists or made by Western artists, sometimes bearing only a tenuous resemblance to South Seas art.

Tiki at the Gauguin Museum, Papeari, Tahiti.

The acceptance of tikis in western popular culture was fostered by modern art when, in the early 20th century, artists like Pablo Picasso and Georges Braque discovered the art of so-called 'primitive' peoples and Impressionism merged into 'primitivism'. The term gained world-wide currency in 1947 thanks to the Norwegian explorer Thor Heyerdahl, who travelled from Ecuador to the Polynesian islands of Tuamotu by wooden raft in order to prove that the South Seas could have been settled from South America. The diary of his expedition, *Kon-Tiki*, was a worldwide bestseller.

grown 'paepae' or house platforms. Very little has been excavated or restored in any way. The site of Te Menaha Takaoa in the Hakamoui Valley is worth visiting. This compound has many house and ceremonial platforms and is almost entirely overgrown. It covers a large area of a wild, romantic valley where coconut palms, giant banyan trees, mango and pandanus grow. From Haka Hau, it is around 100 km (62 miles) by ferry to Atuona, the main town on the island of Hiva Oa.

5 Hiva Oa This island covers 320 km² (124 square miles), making it the largest and most important island in the southern Marquesas archipelago. It features a jagged mountain range that runs from south-west to north-east, some peaks being up to 1,100 m (3,600 ft) high. Hiva Ova has a population of 1,800 and the largest settlement is the village of Atuona on the southern coast. Its sheltered bay allows medium-sized vessels to call at the island, which became famous thanks to the French painter Paul Gauguin. On his second sojourn in the South Seas, the artist fled to Hiva Oa after unhappy experiences in Tahiti, which he described as 'paradise lost'. Following a long illness, he died on 8 May 1903 and now lies buried in a cemetery north of Atuona.
Archaeological digs have led to the reconstruction of an ancient village in the Upeke Valley, one of many excavation sites on Hiva Oa. Near the village of Puamau on the northern coast, amid tropical rainforest, is Marae Takii, the largest ceremonial site in the Marquesas Islands. Its eleven expressive stone figures stand on carefully constructed stepped stone platforms and are up to 2 m (6½ ft) high.

1 A typical jagged coastline at Nuku Hiva (Marquesas Islands).

2 The island of Hiva Oa (Marquesas Islands) has many ceremonial sites, including the MeAe Oipona temple.

3 On most of the islands in the Marquesas group (such as Nuku Hiva) you will find ancient ceremonial sites with tikis and a variety of sculptures.

4 The rocky shore of Hiva Oa is broken up by many small bays; it is partly inaccessible.

Marae Taputapuatea

Ancient Polynesian culture involved ceremonies that entailed sacrifices to the gods, such as food, animals and sometimes even humans. These rites were enacted on stone platforms called 'marae'. These sacred sites also

Temple ruins on Raiatea, one of the Society Islands.

documented the property rights and social standing of families. Today, the remains of these marae can mainly be found in eastern Polynesia, although they are generally no more than a few centuries old. The largest marae in Polynesia, Marae Taputapuatea, is located on the remote island of Raiatea, around 250 km (155 miles) to the north-east of Tahiti and around 100 km (62 miles) south of Bora-Bora.

6 Fatu Hiva This island covers an area of around 80 km² (31 square miles) and has a population of 500. Located around 60 km (37 miles) south of Hiva Oa, it is the southernmost island in the archipelago and receives more rain than any of the other islands in the Marquesas group. The explorer and archaeologist Thor Heyerdahl was inspired to write his famous work, *Fatu Hiva,* describing his stay of several months here in the 1930s. The Hanavave Valley and the village of the same name in the Bay of Virgins are famous for their tropical beauty. Tapa, a type of cloth made from the bark of the paper mulberry tree, is today produced only on Fatu Hiva. From the Marquesas Islands, the northernmost archipelago in French Polynesia, it is around 1,000 km (620 miles) south-west to the Society Islands.

7 Rangiroa On the 1,000-km (620-mile) voyage from the Marquesas to the Society Islands, you will pass the Rangiroa atoll, which forms part of the Tuamotu Islands. Its lagoon, at just under 80 km (50 miles) long and up to 25 km (16 miles) wide, makes Rangiroa the world's largest fully enclosed atoll. There are three inhabited motus at the northern ring of the lagoon but most of the population lives in the two pretty villages of Avatoru and Tiputa.

8 Bora-Bora This island, also known as 'Pearl of the Pacific', is one of the most famous of the Society Islands. Its mountains rise like pinnacles above the deep blue and sunlit turquoise waters of the lagoon. The mountains are the remnants of a volcanic crater, as are the two hilly islets off the island's west coast. A long chain of sandy motus surrounds the reef to the north and the east.
In World War II, Bora-Bora served as a supply station for the American navy and air force. Its military airport later served to open up the island to tourists. This beautiful South Sea island has often been used as a location by film directors. With the exception of Anau to the east of the island, most villages and hotels are located along its western coast and on the southern tip of Bora-Bora. From Vaitape, you can take a challengingly steep hiking trail across forested slopes up to Mount Pahia, but beware – the starting point for this hike of several hours' duration is almost impossible to find without a guide.

9 Huahine Around 200 km (124 miles) south-east of Bora-Bora, and halfway to Tahiti, you will come to the island of Huahine, which, until now, has largely been spared the mixed blessings of mass tourism. Like most of the Society Islands, Huahine is completely enclosed by a reef, encircling a lagoon as well as several motus. Excavations have unearthed the Society Islands' most ancient relics to date. In 1972, the ruins of an entire village were discovered north of Fare. These indicate that the island was populated around AD 650–850 by voyagers from the Marquesas Islands. The Maeva temples are most impressive in documenting the original cultural significance of the island. From Huahine, it is around 100 km (62 miles) to the south-east to Tahiti, the island that epitomizes everyone's idea of the South Seas.

10 Papeete (Tahiti) When Captain Cook landed on Tahiti, Papeete was nothing more than a sparsely populated, boggy

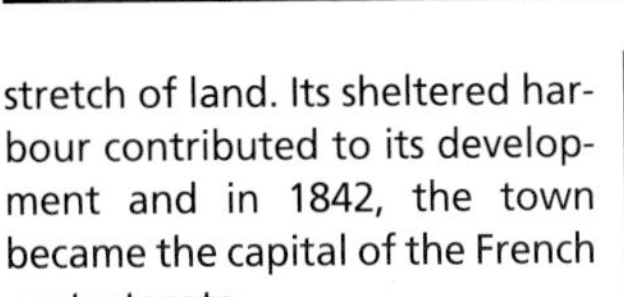

stretch of land. Its sheltered harbour contributed to its development and in 1842, the town became the capital of the French protectorate.

Today, houses and apartments increasingly encroach on the surrounding hills. Papeete is both the economical and political centre of French Polynesia, and three-quarters of the island's population lives in and around the town.

The tourist information centre at Boulevard Pomare is a good starting point for a tour of Papeete. This building is notable for its characteristic traditional Polynesian style, rarely found in Tahiti these days.

⑪ Pointe Venus (Tahiti) In 1769 Captain Cook chose the island's northernmost point, some 10 km (6 miles) east of Papeete, to carry out the astronomical observations that were the main reason for his journey to the Pacific. He wanted to observe and measure the transit of Venus through the sun, hoping that it would help calculate the earth's distance from the sun. Pointe Venus is a popular excursion destination. To reach it, turn left off the main road in Mahina. Back on the island road, drive south past the Fa'arumai waterfalls and the fountains at the cliffs of Pointe d'Arahoho to

1 Bora-Bora lagoon – the quintessential South Seas fantasy.

2 Turquoise waters and tropical vegetation on Bora-Bora.

3 Huahine's beautiful scenery is easy to explore by bicycle or boat.

4 The Rangiroa atoll (Tuamotu Islands) is one of the world's largest.

5 The Kia Ora Village Hotel on Rangiroa is an oasis of tranquillity.

Exotic flowers

Flowers have always played a big part in the culture of the South Seas islands. They are given to guests when they arrive and when they leave. Flower arrangements and palm fronds are used for decoration at festivities. Polynesians use flowers to decorate their bodies and hair, and wear them around their necks for fragrance. Bright flowers generally signify hospitality and *joie de vivre*, and have thus become a trademark of the South Seas.

Most flowers used for decoration grow throughout the year on trees and shrubs, such as gardenias (Polynesian: *tiare*), hibiscus or frangipani (*tipani*). Hibiscus, which probably originated in China, and of which there are many hybrids in different shapes and colours, is among the best-known decorative plants of the tropics. Frangipani are easily recognized by their strong scent and striking white, yellow, pink or red flowers. The red flame tree or flamboyant, an unmistakable part of the island scenery, flowers only from December through to March. It provides useful shade and is therefore planted along many of the roads and pathways. Heliconias and bird-of-paradise (*Strelitzia reginae*) are some of the other beautiful flowers of the South Seas.

Top: The pink-and-white cup-shaped frangipani flowers have a powerful fragrance.
Bottom: Many scented plants such as hibiscus, heliconias and bird-of-paradise are native to the Society Islands.

Polynesian dance festivals

Above all, dance is an expression of the Polynesian way of life and the joy of living. As legs and hips twirl, hands and faces tell entire stories. They are all variations on a theme – gods and legends, Tane and Wahine (Man and Woman), love, separation, longing, flowers and birds, voyages, fishing and adventures, as well as stars, wind and waves. Both men and women dance in groups, either together or taking turns. The dancers form lines, each dancing individually but with every man and woman moving in perfect harmony with everyone else. The women's basic movement is a rhythmical swaying of the hips, the men's a scissor-like opening and closing of the knees. Upper bodies hardly move, arms and hands make gesture-like movements.

Top: Polynesian dancers tell a story with their body language.
Bottom: Fire dancers on Moorea.

The obvious sexual connotations of many dances led missionaries to banish them from Polynesian life. Only in the last few decades have they been revived, thanks partly to tourism. The art of dancing is taken very seriously, mainly on the Cook Islands and in French Polynesia, and is much more than a tourist magnet. Children learn basic dance movements at school and there are nationwide contests to find the best groups and individual dancers.

1

reach Taravao, and from there the Tahiti Iti peninsula.

⓬ Tahiti Iti (Tahiti) This peninsula is linked to the main island via a very narrow stretch of land and has less remarkable mountains than its bigger sister, but boasts some impressive scenery. The Plateau de Taravo is one of the most beautiful viewpoints. To the east, a small road winds its way up to the plateau from Afaahiti through farmland and scrub. Fresh mountain air and a fantastic view of Tahiti Nui await visitors, as well as magnificent gardens and picturesque villages along the road to the remote area of Vairao. Just before you reach the village from the north, you'll see a large footprint on the reef, which, according to legend, was left by the Polynesian demi-god Maui.
In the south-east of the peninsula, the cliffs of Te-Pari rise dramatically from the water and are considered the highlight of the local scenery.

⓭ Papeari (Tahiti) From Taravao, the coastal road takes us back towards Papeete. The area around Papeari is particularly attractive due to its colourful gardens and the many fruit and vegetable stalls lining the road. Back in Papeete, you take a ferry to Moorea, only 40 km (25 miles) to the north-west.

2

⓮ Moorea The jagged mountain range and the deep, picturesque bays to the north make the scenery of this island particularly attractive. Mount Rotui (900 m/2,953 ft) sits on the peninsula separating the two bays. Its proximity to Papeete makes Moorea a popular tourist destination alongside Tahiti and Bora-Bora. Tourists mainly visit Paopao in Cook's Bay and the north-west coast with its choice of sandy beaches.

White milestones shaped like the outline of Moorea itself indicate the sealed road around the island, which is 60 km (37 miles) long. Halfway between Temae and Cook's Bay, near Maharapa, is Maison Blanche. Located at the foot of verdant hills, this well-maintained, colonial-style building from the early 20th cen-

tury was once owned by a plantation farmer. Such farmers used to make a fortune from growing vanilla. Past the hotels and restaurants on the eastern shore of Cook's Bay, you will come to Paopao, situated at the end of the bay. Further inland is a fertile plain with fields of taro, tapioca and pineapple. The road then makes a few hairpin bends on the way up to the Belvedere viewpoint, Moorea's most visited panoramic spot. About 3 km (2 miles) south of Hauru, you will reach Tiki Théâtre-Village, a reconstructed Polynesian village. Further along the southern and eastern coast, small villages, tropical gardens and fishing nets laid out to dry underline the laid-back, idyllic atmosphere.

⓯ **Tetiaroa** This atoll, located around 40 km (25 miles) east of Moorea, comprises thirteen motus, the largest of which is 3.2 km (2 miles) long. Tetiaroa used to be a summer retreat for the royal family of Pomare. On the Rimatuu motu, a giant tuu tree still marks the royal picnic spot. The tree is so large that it creates a patch of shade one hectare (2½ acres) wide. Female members of noble families were brought here and, according to Polynesian tradition, fattened up before their weddings.

⓰ **Manuae** This is the most westerly island of the Society Islands group also known as the Leeward Islands ('islands under the wind'). Manuae is located 550 km (342 miles) west of Tahiti and 350 km (217 miles) west of Bora-Bora. The atoll measures some 11 km (7 miles) across, and its area of dry land is under 4 km² (1½ square miles). If you want to visit Manuae, you need to have your own boat or charter one. These days the atoll is not inhabited year-round, but fishermen from Raiatea call here on a regular basis. There are many species of turtle on Manuae that return to the beaches every year to lay their eggs.

⓱ **Motu One** This atoll is also called Bellinghausen and is located 150 km (93 miles) north of Manuae. The German explorer Otto von Kotzebue named the atoll in honour of the Russian explorer Fabian Gottlieb von Bellinghausen. It consists of four islands with an area of 2.3 km² (0.9 square miles) and makes a good starting point for exploring the underwater world of the South Seas.

⓲ **Rarotonga** From the western group of the Society Islands

(continued p. 194)

1 Moorea's serene bays set against a jagged backdrop are a popular stopover point for ocean-going yachts.

2 Moorea's interior is wild and mountainous, but its bays are peaceful and quiet.

3 Tahiti: On the way from Papeari to Papeete, it is worth visiting Vaipahi Gardens, which has tropical plants and a small waterfall.

Gauguin on Tahiti

Paul Gauguin arrived in Tahiti on 9 June 1891, at a time when Polynesian culture had already vanished almost entirely. In Papeete in particular, the capital of the French colony, life ticked on just as it would in any small town in Europe. Gauguin had set off in search of the 'noble savage', but instead he encountered men decorously wrapped in loincloths while women wore the frilly dresses introduced by the missionaries.

So Gauguin soon decided to move to the country. In Mataiea on Tahiti's southern coast he found a home and also the company of a Tahitian woman. But even here, little Polynesian culture remained.

Paul Gauguin: *Ea Haere ia Oe* – Where are you going? (1893)

After two years, financial problems and poor health forced Gauguin to return to Paris. His last European years (1893–5) convinced him that his place was no longer in the Old World, so he boarded another ship to Tahiti. In order to escape the vagaries of life in the colonies, he decided in 1901 to relocate to the mythical Marquesas Islands. His time on Hiva Oa, however, was anything but paradisiacal. Worn out by disease, he managed to create some outstanding works of art before, alone and bitter, he died on 8 May 1903.

Dance performance in Papeete, French Polynesia. If you open up your eyes and your heart, you will soon appreciate why Polynesian culture reached its highest level of sophistication in these islands, why a sense of beauty is given

when, for example, a young Tahitian spontaneously stops delivering breakfasts to the guest bungalows in a honeymoon resort because he is so enthralled by the sight of a young woman that he goes off to pick orchids to decorate her room.

Traditional fishing

Alongside tourism, fishing is one of the South Sea islands' most important economies. For millennia the fish-laden waters have contributed to the islanders' diet. Even now, traditional fishing methods are used. For example, in the lagoons, intricate

Top: Tahitian fish traps.
Bottom: Parrot fish in the market at Papeete.

canal systems weighed down by stones are created, so that fish cannot find their way out. Such fish traps have been constructed for centuries.

to the main island of the Cook Islands is a distance of 1,000 km (620 miles). Rarotonga is known, deservedly, as 'the island of flowers', and its narrow fertile coastal strip, planted with a variety of tropical crops, looks very much like a large garden. The steep mountains in the interior are covered in dense vegetation. There are two main roads on the island: you can circle it on a sealed coastal road, around 32 km (20 miles) long, or take an inland route along a road, built more than a thousand years ago and hewn directly from the coral rock. Along the latter, you will find remains of several marae, sacred places destroyed when the island was Christianized.
The lagoon near the picturesque village of Titikaveka offers some excellent snorkelling opportunities. Muri Beach is the island's most beautiful beach with some spectacular views of the lagoon and its motus. Some of the Polynesian stone buildings on the island are up to 800 years old, the most sacred places being the marae of Arai-te-Tonga. To this day, the Ariki, the highest-ranking local chieftains, are enthroned on this marae.

⑲ **Aitutaki** This island lies 225 km (140 miles) north of Rarotonga. Aiutaki is surrounded by what many consider to be the Pacific's most beautiful lagoon and has some wonderful white beaches on the twelve uninhabited motus in the east and south. There are many activities to choose from when staying on Aitutaki – boat trips to the motus, reef hikes, a bicycle tour around the island, which is around 7 km (4½ miles) long, or a walk up Mount Maungapu, 124 m (407 ft) high.

1 A key factor in the abundant vegetation on the Cook Islands is the high average temperature of 26°C (79°F); even in winter the temperature rarely drops below 22°C (72°F).

2 The Cook Islands comprise eight larger volcanic islands and numerous small coral atolls; many motus (islets) are uninhabited.

Nuku Hiva The largest of the volcanic Marquesas Islands (330 km²/127 square miles) has around 2,100 inhabitants. The highest mountain on the island is Mount Muake (864 m/2,835 ft).

Hiva Oa This mountainous island in the Marquesas is famous for its sacred sites. Here, the stone temple of MeAe Oipona, with tikis. Painter Paul Gauguin died in Atuona on Hiva Oa.

Fatu Hiva With its densely overgrown rainforests and abundant vegetation, Fatu Hiva in the south of the archipelago is the wettest of the Marquesas Islands.

Society Islands The majority of the population of French Polynesia lives on this group of islands. The islands and islets are mostly of volcanic origin. The turquoise lagoons are wonderful for diving. The Society Islands are divided into the Windward Islands ('islands of the wind') and the Leeward Islands ('islands under the wind'). The capital, Papeete, is located on Tahiti, the main island. The islands and their diverse fauna and flora were first discovered and charted in 1768. Most of the population lives on the coastal strips of these volcanic islands. The climate is tropical and hot and also very humid.

Rangiroa This atoll between the Marquesas and the Society Islands, which forms part of the Tuamotu Islands, 350 km (217 miles) northwest of Tahiti, is the largest of its kind in the world, being some 80 km (50 miles) long and up to 25 km (16 miles) wide. At the northern end of its 35-m (115-ft) deep lagoon are several small fishing villages of about 2,300 inhabitants.

Rarotonga The main island of the Cook Islands, Rarotonga is characterized by flat, fertile coastal plains and therefore also nicknamed 'Island of flowers'. The interior, by contrast, is made up of steep mountains which are densely forested. The lagoons, mainly those near the village of Titikaveka, are wonderful for snorkelling and diving.

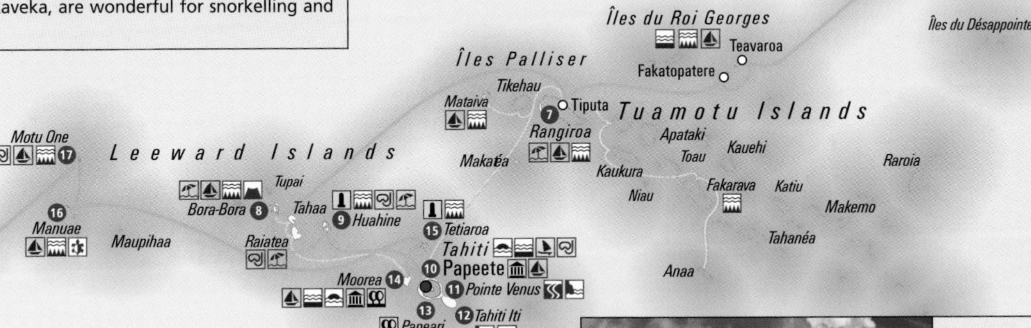

Cook Islands These fifteen islands were discovered by the Spanish in 1595, Located between American Samoa and French Polynesia, they are a self-governing democracy in free association with New Zealand. Their capital is Avarua on the island of Rarotonga. The islands are divided into a northern and a southern group. Some are flat coral-reef islands that are difficult to access, others are high, densely overgrown islands as well as (mainly in the north) atolls.

Huahine This Society Island, which has as yet had very little tourism, is located around 200 km (124 miles) from Bora-Bora. It is surrounded by a complete fringing reef which contains a lagoon and some motus. The mountainous island, which is volcanic in origin, reaches an altitude of up to 680 m (2,230 ft). Its beautiful scenery is best explored by boat.

Bora-Bora The 'Pacific Pearl' is probably the best-known of the Society Islands and famous for its giant volcanic mountains rising up from the blue and turquoise waters.

Moorea This island is only 40 km (25 miles) from Tahiti; it has a distinctive jagged mountain range and bays reaching deep into the interior.

Papeete Tahiti, the very essence of the South Seas, developed from two extinct volcanoes. Three-quarters of its population lives in Papeete, the capital.

Route 10

Hawaii

Dream beaches, tropical flowers and volcanoes – from Big Island to Kauai

Fantastic pure-white beaches, the gentle murmur of palm trees, hula dancers and bright garlands of flowers, together with tropical rainforests, cascading waterfalls, active and dormant volcanoes, Honolulu city life and the magic of the indigenous people: these are just some of the many faces of Hawaii. The largest island in the archipelago, and its namesake, trumps almost any other island on the planet with its magnificent and extraordinary lava landscape.

On arrival at the airport you'll be greeted with the words 'Aloha komo mai!': 'Welcome to Hawaii'. Wherever you go in these dreamlike Pacific islands, you'll discover the 'aloha spirit' and enjoy the islanders' infectious friendliness. The sky is a deeper blue here, the beaches wider and cleaner than anywhere else, and the wind rustles gently in the palms and along the magical cliffs on Na Pali Coast. In the language of the Polynesians, who came to Hawaii around AD 500, the island's name means 'heaven' or 'paradise'. Every visitor is greeted with a 'lei', a traditional Polynesian garland of flowers, and the warm air seems to echo with the romantic chants that rang out over the islands when kings still reigned and before white people arrived.

The Silversword grows only on Maui.

The Hawaiian Islands extend some 2,436 km (1,513 miles) across the northern Pacific, meaning that travel between them is possible only by plane or boat. Island-hopping is certainly the right term for it, since the best-known islands in the archipelago are within hopping distance of each other: Kauai, Oahu, Molokai, Lanai, Maui and Hawaii (Big Island). The islands are as varied as their names: Kauai is a surprising mix of tropical rainforests, beautiful gardens, the Waimea Canyon and the stunning Na Pali Coast, the backdrop to films like *King Kong* and *Jurassic Park*. On Oahu, the most developed of the islands, the main attractions are Honolulu, the legendary Waikiki Beach and the metre-high breakers in the surfers' paradise on the North Coast. The history of Molokai is both moving and interesting, with Father Damien at its centre: in the late 19th century, he cared for those suffering from leprosy on the Kalaupapa Peninsula. Lanai, one of the smallest Hawaiian Islands, is a paradise for golfers and has the most isolated beaches. Maui, the favourite haunt of American holidaymakers, boasts luxurious hotels, a tropical wilderness on both sides of the legendary Hana Road, and Haleakala, one of the largest and most colourful volcanoes on earth. Big Island, the main island in the south, also has its fair share of active volcanoes and tropical flowers.

A jewel of nature on Kauai: the legendary Na Pali Coast was the setting for Steven Spielberg's film *Jurassic Park*.

At the Akaka Falls west of Hilo on Big Island, the water pours 130 m (426 ft) down the green rock face.

The turbulent past of the islands lives on in Pu'uhonua o Honaunau and a series of other villages. Before the arrival of white settlers, the larger islands were ruled by kings who reigned with absolute power over their subjects. They paraded before their people in dazzling robes, surrounded themselves with pomp and ceremony and lived in awe of supernatural beings. Hula dance, originally reserved exclusively for men, was a Hawaiian way of worshipping the gods. Kahunas, the priests of the people, were responsible for enforcing 'kapus' or rigid taboos; death was the penalty for anyone who transgressed them. Professional storytellers still tell of these turbulent times and in the cities statues are a reminder of powerful kings like Kamehameha I.

In 1778, Captain Cook discovered the islands for the western world. A monument to him at Kealakekua Bay bears the inscription, 'In memory of the great circumnavigator, Captian James Cook, RN, who discovered the islands on the 10th January, AD 1778 and fell near this spot on the 14th February, AD 1779'. White settlers and missionaries followed and there has been a recent influx of Asian migrants. The colourful mix of peoples on the islands has resulted in a particularly tolerant society. Hawaii became the fiftieth US state in 1959, and tourism has helped it develop into a popular and flourishing destination. In spite of everything, the language of the islands has been preserved in Hawaii, and if there was a prize for the friendliest and most beautiful state in the US, Hawaii would undoubtedly be up there among the top contenders. Even the relentless spread of commercialism on some islands is no match for that aloha spirit.

Mauna Loa, one of the world's largest active volcanoes, last erupted in 1984.

Pu'uhonua o Honaunau National Historic Park

The first Polynesians arrived on Hawaii around AD 500, crossing the seas in ocean-going canoes. Once on the islands, they continued to practise their belief in the supernatural. The leaders rigidly enforced the strict 'kapus' and their subjects were forced to live by those laws. The term comes from the Tahitian 'tapu', the origin of the word 'taboo'. Anyone who broke a 'kapu', e.g. by standing so that his shadow fell on the king, could expect certain death. Only the temple at Pu'uhonua o Honaunau could offer fleeing offenders a 'place of refuge' with the priests.

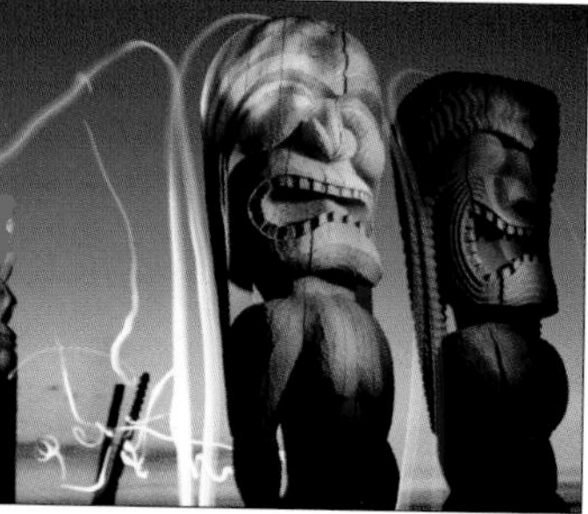

Statues of gods on Big Island.

From Hilo, Hawaii's main port, our island journey initially crosses barren terrain, where lava still spills out of the earth. The winding roads pass through thick forests and along steep coasts, while the snow-capped peak of Mauna Kea shines like a beacon in the distance. Our route heads north-west along the curve of the islands to Kauai.

1 Hilo, Hawaii Planes land on the east coast of Big Island in Hilo, the island's largest settlement (population: 40,000) and the southernmost city in the US. In the mid-19th century, missionaries arrived in Hilo Bay and built churches. The town owed its expansion to the sugar plantations. In 1929, a tsunami devastated the area around Hilo Bay. When the sugar plantations closed down in the 1990s, Hilo became known as a cultural centre.

2 Hawaii Volcanoes National Park, Hawaii This National Park in the south of Big Island is a UNESCO World Heritage Site. It includes part of Mauna Loa, the active crater of Kilauea and parts of the rugged coastline. For an eye-opener of a drive, take the 16-km (10-mile) Crater Rim Drive on Kilauea and the Chain of Craters Road, past lavascapes and fern thickets to the coast, where lava flows occur every few years. Here you can get a view of the fires of Halemaumau, a crater cone on Kilauea. In the rainforest, lava has solidified into what is known as the Thurston Lava Tube.

3 Kailua-Kona, Hawaii This small and bustling city, full of hotels and restaurants, lies on a sunlit coast, complete with black lava cliffs and white sand beaches. The highways lead you through a lunar landscape. Head back to Hilo via Waimea in the north. The beautiful Scenic Drive passes through the jungle along the steep coast; rising above it all is Mauna Kea, a dormant volcano.

4 Kahului, Maui The commercial centre of the island of Maui has all the conveniences

1 The peak of Mauna Kea (4,205 m/ 13,796 ft) is snow-clad, sometimes even in the summer months.

2 The Thurston Lava Tube Trail passes through the wilderness beyond the volcanic crater on Big Island.

Travel information

Route profile
Length: approx. 2,500 km/ 1,554 miles (excluding detours)
Time needed: approx. 14 days
Start and end: Hilo (Hawaii)
Itinerary (main locations): Hawaii, Maui, Lanai, Molokai, Oahu, Kauai

Transport information
Public transport on the islands (apart from in Honolulu) is not very reliable. It is advisable to hire a car for touring. Tours by bus are possible but take a long time.

Best time to travel
The best time to travel to the islands is in late spring, when you will encounter pleasantly warm temperatures, flowers in bloom and fewer tourists, since it is also before US school holidays begin (mid-June to early September). Prices rise in summer and over Christmas and the New Year.

Accommodation
Many hotels are cheaper than you might imagine; affordable accommodation is available on all the islands.

Information
www.hawaii-tourism.co.uk
www.hawaiitourism.com.au

Nature at its most spectacular: what seems to be an endless flow of bubbling molten lava spurts out into the Pacific Ocean from Kilauea on Big Island. This crater next to Mauna Loa is one of the world's most active volcanoes and covers an area of around 10 km^2 (4 square miles).

Whales

Whale-watching is very popular with visitors to Hawaii. If you want a closer view of these giant mammals, you will need to head out to sea. Choose from one of the many boat trips on offer from a range of companies. You will only manage a sighting of the mighty humpback whales between December and April, when they leave the cool waters of Alaska to mate and give birth in the southern Pacific. Whale-watchers are often lucky enough to see baby whales with their mothers. The calves put on around 45 kg (100 lb) in weight per day while they learn to swim, hunt and breathe. Whaling was an important industry in the 19th century. Whale oil was exported all over the world as fuel for lamps and as a lubricant. The flesh,

Top: Huge as they are, humpback whales can perform out-of-the-water acrobatics.
Bottom: The humpback whale's tail fluke has a span of up to 3 m (10 ft).

blubber, baleen and teeth or beards of whales were also put to practical use. More than five hundred whaling boats sailed between the Aleutians and Hawaii in the Pacific, spending winters in Lahaina harbour. The sailors who poured into the town clearly left their morals on the other side of the cape, and turned the Hawaiian coastal town into 'one of the breathing holes of Hell'. This is how the puritanical missionaries who arrived in Lahaina in 1823 described the rowdy town. They imposed a curfew, persuaded the governor to place a 'kapu' on the whaling boats, declaring them officially forbidden, and even commissioned the construction of a fort as protection. Even when the whalers resorted to violence, the single-minded Christians pursued their mission with determination.

1

2

3

(and excesses) of America, including several shopping centres and the island's only cinema. Just a few kilometres away, in the Iao Valley State Park, the Iao Needle juts sharply out of the lush vegetation to a height of 675 m (2,214½ ft) above sea level. Legend has it that the demigod Maui turned an unwanted suitor of the beautiful Iao into this stone pinnacle.

5 Lahaina, Maui This is where history and commerce come together, where business flourishes in the shade of historic buildings that date back to the whaling era. Things were much the same centuries ago, when the Hawaiian kings and nobility frequented the west coast as a retreat. In the 19th century, Lahaina became a major whaling port. Over five hundred ships were moored in the town's harbour over the winter. Post-1850, crude oil took over from whale oil and the demise of whaling hit Lahaina hard. It became a sleepy plantation town once more and did not reawaken until 1966. Part of historic Front Street was declared a National Historic Landmark and luxurious hotels and leisure centres sprang up north of Lahaina. The whales swimming offshore – once a much sought-after commodity – became a star attraction, and whale-watching is now an important feature of every visitor's itinerary. The actors Errol Flynn and Spencer Tracy both enjoyed the fabulous view from the legendary Pioneer Inn, which dates back to 1901. The massive banyan tree, planted in memory of the missionaries, goes back even further. Just behind it you will spot the old court building and jail. From Lahaina our route leads back to Kahului.

Hana Road

The road to Hana on Maui was carved out of the volcanic coastal rock in 1927. It has some 617 bends and 56 single-lane bridges and winds through forests and past waterfalls to the lava beaches in the east, clinging to steep mountainous slopes, descending into valleys and allowing glimpses of the ocean every few metres.

6 Haleakala, Maui Drive up to the crater of Haleakala before sunrise and you will be rewarded for your efforts with a spectacular view of the natural world. The journey up follows Routes 37 (Haleakala Highway), 377 (Upper Kula Road) and 378 (Haleakala Crater Road), a winding road popular with mountain-bikers. The islanders of Maui call Haleakala the 'house of the sun' and watch with

reverence as the fiery star seems to rise out of the crater in the morning and sink back into it at the close of day. The crater covers an area of just under 52 km² (20 square miles) with a perimeter of 34 km (20 miles). Add the 7,000 m (22,966 ft) lying below sea level and you have before you one of the world's biggest mountains. The volcano last erupted 200 years ago.

7 Nahiku, Maui Nahiku has the dubious honour of being one of the wettest places on earth. Fewer than a hundred people live in this tropical little nest where ex-Beatle George Harrison once made his home. Near Wailua, Hana Road takes you to the Waikani Falls on the Puaa Kaa State Wayside and the Waianapanapa State Park, one of nature's gems, with tropical hala trees, temples and a wide beach of black lava sand.
The route returns to Hana and from there along the north coast and back to Kahului for the plane trip to Lanai.

8 Lanai This exclusive island is the preserve of multimillionaires on holiday. The Lodge at Koele, located in an idyllic spot in the mountains, and the Manele Bay Hotel, a luxurious beach resort boasting one of the best golf courses in the world, are two of the top hotels on the islands.
Sights worth seeing on Lanai include the Kaunolu, a huge rock massif that rises out of the ocean around a natural harbour, and the Munro Trail, a steep track that is often shrouded in mist and winds its way for around 10 km (6 miles) through the tropical rainforest.

9 Hoolehua, Molokai This sleepy little place on the island of Molokai is the gateway to another world. Aloha spirit is very much alive and kicking here. The fifth-largest island in the archipelago has remained virtually untouched by tourism. There are no skyscrapers, no gourmet restaurants and not even a set of traffic lights. Instead, the island boasts wide expanses of beach and is imbued with the essence of 'Hawaii as it once was'.

10 Kalaupapa, Molokai Visitors can only reach this infamous peninsula by helicopter or on the back of a mule. Kalaupapa is *(continued p.204)*

1 Nature's drama: sunrise over Haleakala on Maui.

2 Beyond Hana Road at Wailua the Waikani Falls cascade 70 m (230 ft) into the depths below.

3 Cooler and more refreshing than the Pacific – a dip in the waterfalls.

4 The only place in the world where the Silversword grows is on Suu Kukui and the crater of Haleakala on Maui.

5 Craters in Haleakala National Park.

Surfing

The 'Duke', a direct descendant of Hawaiian royalty, became a folk hero in the early 20th century when he introduced surfing to the world and made it famous. It is now an extremely popular sport. In fact, surfing existed before the arrival of white people on the islands. Ancient Hawaiians called it

A surfer's 'perfect wave'.

'he'enalu' or wave-sliding. 'To have a neat floatboard, well-kept, and dried, is to a Sandwich islander what a tilbury or cabriolet, or whatever light carriage may be in fashion is to a young English man', wrote Captain the Rt. Hon. Lord Byron (cousin of the poet) as HMS *Blonde* lay at anchor off the Hawaiian coast in 1820. Back then Hawaiians used wooden boards strong enough for the powerful waves. Modern fibreglass boards take surfers on their elaborate and dangerous rides through the 'Pipelines' off the North Coast of Oahu.

Sometimes the waves on the North Coast of the Hawaiian Islands swell to a dangerous height. On these occasions, and particularly in winter, people indulge in two kinds of surfing. Windsurfing originated in New Zealand and the US and is more akin to sailing than surfing. Hookipa Beach on Maui is a popular meeting

place for windsurfers, who traverse the waves on their sailboards at speeds of up to 40 km/h (25 mph). Hawaiian wave-riding needs less equipment.

Honululu and Waikiki

Honolulu, a busy metropolis (around 380,000 inhabitants) in the Pacific, is the only big city on the islands. Formerly the seat of the Hawaiian kings, it is now the centre of government and the hub of all social and political life. Honolulu was once a major port and an important supply base for the American troops during World War II. Nowadays the city makes its living from trade with Asia and from tourism.
The very heart of the city can be found on King Street, a bustling area right at the centre of Honolulu. A statue commemorating King Kamehameha I stands here.
Nestled among parkland boasting palms and tropical trees, the Iolani

Top: Waikiki beach.
Bottom: Honolulu skyline.

Palace is the US's only royal palace. The US flag was raised here on 12 August 1898. Opposite the Iolani Palace are the Kawaiahao Church and the Mission Houses. This was the first Christian church on the island. Built between 1836 and 1842 by the Reverend Hiram Bingham, it is made of 14,000 slabs of coral rock. The three houses next door are a reminder of the early missionary years and various attempts to bring the Polynesians into the Christian fold. Waikiki is one of the best-known beachside cities in the world. This Honolulu neighbourhood is bordered in the north by the Ala Wai Canal and in the south by the Pacific. Plush luxury hotels, eateries and shops line Kalakaua Avenue and Kuhio Avenue. After extensive renovation, the beach resort has resumed its reputation as a top location.

1

2

3

isolated from the outside world by high cliffs and rough seas. For almost a century it served as a detention centre for more than eight thousand lepers.
The next stop on our route is Honolulu on the island of Oahu.

⓫ **Honolulu, Oahu** See side panel, left.

⓬ **Pearl Harbor, Oahu** See side panel, right.

⓭ **Haleiwa, Oahu** Haleiwa, the former mission station at the mouth of the Anahulu River, has become a mecca for ageing hippies, New Age travellers, North Coast surfers and others in search of an alternative lifestyle. The surfing beaches along the legendary North Shore are less than 100 m (109 yds) from the two-lane road that leads to the ocean in Haleiwa and ends on the surfers' beaches.
Just a few miles further up the road is Banzai Pipeline, which ranks among the most famous surfing beaches in the world. It was the location for the 1950s film *Surf Safari*, which attained cult status and brought worldwide fame to the tunnel-shaped breakers on the North Coast. Only the most experienced surfers brave the 'Pipeline', which is thrown up by a flat tabletop reef.
Next door is Sunset Beach with its long (3 km/2 mile) stretch of sand, packed with surfers' cars during the winter. According to surfing pros, this is where you'll find the best waves. Beginners should look for calmer waters before trying their hand at the sport, however. The breakers here are extremely dangerous and should be braved only by skilled surfers with years of experience.

⓮ **Polynesian Cultural Center, Oahu** Students admitted to the Mormon Brigham Young University in Laie swear that they will never grow a beard and promise to lead a wholly moral life, free of alcohol and drugs. They earn their pocket money in the nearby Polynesian Cultural Center, an informative 'pleasure park' with a touch of Disneyland about it in the early evening. Later in the evening the park explodes into a kitschy but spectacular and opulent show, in which Polynesian musicians, singers and dancers perform the history and myths of the South Seas. Volcanoes spewing fire, rushing waterfalls and palm-roofed huts are the backdrop to a spectacle that not even the IMAX Polynesia Theater's big screen can rival.
The Polynesian Cultural Center was built in 1963 and many people expected it to flop. Few believed that tourists would travel from Waikiki to Laie to visit a cultural park. They thought that people visiting Hawaii would want to do little else but lie on the sand and swim in the sea. How wrong they

were. The 'PCC', as most locals call it, has become a real tourist magnet. Profits go to Brigham Young University and the 'Latter-day Saints'.

The Center's seven villages represent the cultures of Samoa, New Zealand, Fiji, Hawaii, the Marquesas, Tahiti and Tonga. Polynesian students, mainly from the same islands, sing traditional songs, play historical instruments, cook their native dishes and relate the stories and legends of their home. Their houses are situated on the banks of a man-made river and lectures and concerts are held in the public square.

⑮ Valley of the Temples, Oahu The Valley of the Temples, a non-denominational place of worship, is set against the dramatic backdrop of the verdant mountain slopes of Oahu's Windward Coast, which are usually covered in cloud. It offers magnificent views over the coastline.

The Byodo-In Temple is a faithful replica of the 900-year-old Byodo-In in Uji, Japan. It was built in 1968 to commemorate the centenary of the arrival of the first Japanese immigrants to Hawaii. Kiichi Sano, a famous landscape architect from Kyoto, designed the colourful garden refuge at a distance from the hustle and bustle of Honolulu. The sound of a 3-ton brass bell spreads the word of Amidha Buddha and calls people to meditation while peacocks fan out their bright tail feathers along the pathways.

⑯ Kailua, Oahu The journey along the Windward Coast heads south and through the old part of Kailua, past the beach homes of the rich and famous. Kailua Beach Park, a wide expanse of sandy beach with perfect conditions for surfing, is the meeting place for Hawaii's bravest and most experienced surfers. The only place you will see more colourful sails is on the North Coast of Maui. Windsurfing is relatively rare on the islands, since any surfer worth his salt would prefer to take to the waves aboard a 'proper' surfboard.

Sparse woodland separates the white strip of sand from the inland area and provides some extremely welcome shade during the midday heat. The beach is relatively quiet – by Oahu's standards it is virtually deserted – and particularly popular with families. Kailua Beach is one of the safest beaches on Oahu, since it shelves further out to sea and there is no strong current; the only danger is at the weekend, when the bay is packed with surfers and you might get hit by the sharp end of a surfboard.

Further south is Lanikai Beach, which slopes even more gently into the sea and is not widely known. The place has managed to hold out against the spread of commercialism. Its key attractions include soft sand and clear blue water, making it the perfect spot for a picnic.

As you head back to Honolulu, just some 20 minutes away on the Pali Highway, it is worth making a slight detour along the coast via Kahala. This is Honolulu's smart suburb, filled with luxurious villas.

⑰ Lihue, Kauai Our tour of Kauai begins in Lihue, the island's capital, and as a result of the impassable cliffs on the north-west coast the route is best described as fork-shaped. Lihue has a busy shopping centre and many commercial outlets.

(continued p.208)

1 Stormy weather on Oahu's Windward Coast.

2 Molokai remains relatively untouched by civilization.

3 A young Hawaiian woman greets the sunrise.

4 Lush nature and a dramatic crater in the Oahu interior.

Pearl Harbor

On 7 December 1941, Japanese bombers, torpedo jets and fighter-planes attacked the US naval base of Pearl Harbor. It was one of the great defining moments in world history. The Americans were taken utterly by surprise, even though intelligence services had cracked the Japanese secret code months before. Some people still maintain that the US President withheld his knowledge of the forthcoming attack to pave the way for his country's entry into war following the catastrophe. The US Pacific Fleet was unprepared: seven of its battleships lay anchored like open targets in Battleship Row. Japanese planes appeared over Pearl Harbor at 7.55am and launched their

Top: The Arizona Memorial was erected in remembrance of the dead. Bottom: The USS *Arizona*.

deadly attack. At 8.10am the USS *Arizona* was hit by a huge bomb. The massive vessel sank in less than nine minutes, with 1,177 crew on board. The USS *Oklahoma* was hit in the side and rolled over, trapping 400 men inside. The USS *Utah* also keeled over in the water and other ships were seriously damaged. The Japanese ceasefire came at 10am, leaving a scene of devastation and destruction in its wake. In total, 2,395 soldiers were lost, 164 planes destroyed, and the proud ships of the Pacific Fleet lay sunk or severely damaged in the harbour. The USS Arizona Memorial marks the spot where the battleship went down and is a reminder of this horrific event in history. The white, open-air shrine displays the names of all the men lost on the *Arizona* and remains one of Hawaii's most visited historic sites.

Sunrise on one of Oahu's dream beaches. In 1866, Mark Twain described Hawaii as 'the loveliest fleet of islands that lies anchored in any ocean'.
For the American writer as for many others, the Hawaiian Islands are the ultimate idyllic South Sea paradise, with endless white beaches, palms swaying

softly in the breeze, exotic fragrances, hula dancers, tropical rainforest and impossibly romantic waterfalls. Situated in the outer tropics, the islands enjoy

The Kauai Museum provides information on the island's past. Kalapaki Beach and the palm-flanked Kauai Lagoon are just a few kilometres away.

18 Kapaa, Kauai The route to Na Pali Coast takes us via Kapaa, a small town with an attractive shopping centre. The 'Sleeping Giant', a gigantic stone in the mountains, lies just inland. Legend has it that the giant once helped to build a temple and ate so much during the ensuing festivities that he fell asleep, never to wake again.
One of the must-dos in this region is a boat trip on the Wailua River to Fern Grotto, a romantic cavern covered in ferns. The Wailua Falls are not far from here.

19 Hanalei, Kauai This sleepy fishing village serves as a base camp for trips to Na Pali Coast. Several artists have settled here and there's a lively nightlife in the few local pubs and bars. A luxury hotel is situated on nearby Hanalei Bay, and Hanalei Lookout offers fantastic views over the ocean and the lush tropical landscape.

20 Na Pali Coast, Kauai The rugged mountain slopes on this legendary coast are one of the world's most amazing natural wonders. The sun creates bizarre images on the furrowed rock face that rises high above the ocean and casts a long shadow. Most of Na Pali Coast is a conservation area. Above the coastline, the Kalalau Trail passes through forests and over ridges to the Kalalau Valley. The trail ends at Kalalau Beach.

21 Poipu Beach, Kauai The route initially heads south via Lihue and then west to the most popular beach on Kauai. A massive reef protects the sandy beach against the raging waves. This is where half of the island's inhabitants meet at the weekend. A bumpy sand track leads to nearby Mahaulepu, the collective name given to Gillin's Beach, Kawailoa Bay and Haula Beach, all of which are usually peaceful and deserted.

22 Waimea Canyon, Kauai Waimea means 'red water' and the glistening red river of the same name lies embedded here in the volcanic earth.
Above the river, the winding Waimea Canyon Drive heads up into the mountains. With its fabulously colourful valleys and emerald-green forests highlighted oasis-like against the red, brown and purple rock, the Waimea Canyon is the largest in the Pacific and is a dramatic, awe-inspiring sight. It is the Pacific's answer to the Grand Canyon and, although smaller, it is just as spectacular. There are numerous lookouts offering fabulous panoramic views. The canyon brings our journey to a spectacular close.

1 The wildly romantic Na Pali Coast in the north of Kauai.

2 The Wailua Falls, not far from Kapaa, cascade 30 m (99 ft) down the rock face.

3 The dramatic colours of the Waimea Canyon.

Na Pali Coast (Kauai) Fabulous sandy beaches line the rugged slopes – most of which are conservation areas – in the north of Kauai.

Molokai Just 8,000 people live on the fifth-largest Hawaiian island. The absence of tourist facilities has helped to keep the whole island relatively unspoilt.

Maui The north of the island features excellent conditions for surfers. Winter months are best for stunning views of huge breakers rolling onto the shore.

Pearl Harbor (Oahu) Since 7 December 1941, the harbour on the island of Oahu has been remembered for a traumatic event in modern US history. Japanese planes bombarded the battleships anchored there, leaving a scene of devastation behind them. The harbour town has many modern warships, a museum and a number of memorials.

Haleakala National Park (Maui) A charming road winds up to the crater of Haleakala, the imposing 'house of the sun'.

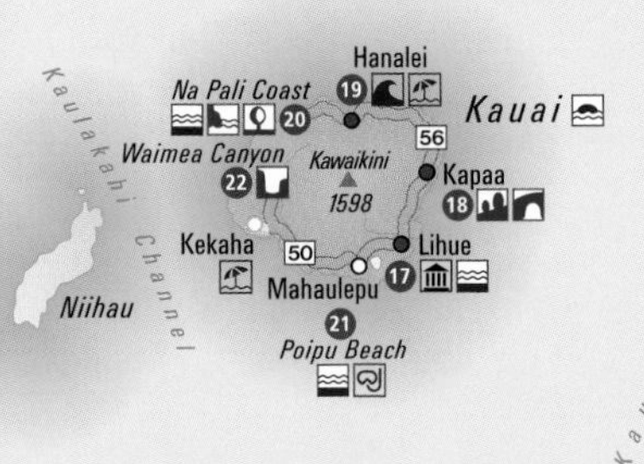

Waikiki Beach (Oahu) The world-famous city shoreline in the south of Oahu is a neighbourhood of Honolulu. Many restaurants, hotels, boutiques and bars vie for tourist trade.

Mauna Kea (Hawaii) Few vistas can beat the view over Hawaii from this peak. Its name – 'white mountain' – refers to the snow that usually cloaks its peak.

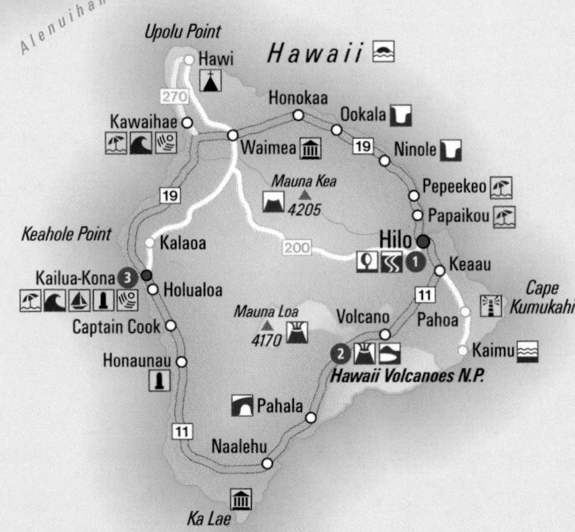

Pu'uhonua o Honaunau Historical Park (Hawaii) The Ku-Kaili and Ku-Ki'i-Akua statues belong to the temple gardens in the park where breakers of 'kapu' once sought sanctuary.

Hilo (Hawaii) This bustling city lies at the most southerly point of the US and is the main settlement on Big Island, as the largest island in the archipelago is also known. The sugar-cane industry that made Hilo its fortune has now all but vanished, but with its Caribbean ambience and brightly coloured houses, the city is now a centre for arts and culture. It also has a number of dockyards and tourists come here to enjoy its great variety of tropical flowers.

Hawaii Volcanoes National Park This park, located in the south of Hawaii, has been designated a UNESCO World Heritage Site, as are parts of Mauna Loa, Kilauea and the coast. Molten lava can often be found flowing through the dark and primeval-looking scree landscape. A journey along the 16-km (10-mile) Crater Rim Drive on Kilauea is an extraordinary experience.

Atlas

Overview of maps and explanation of symbols

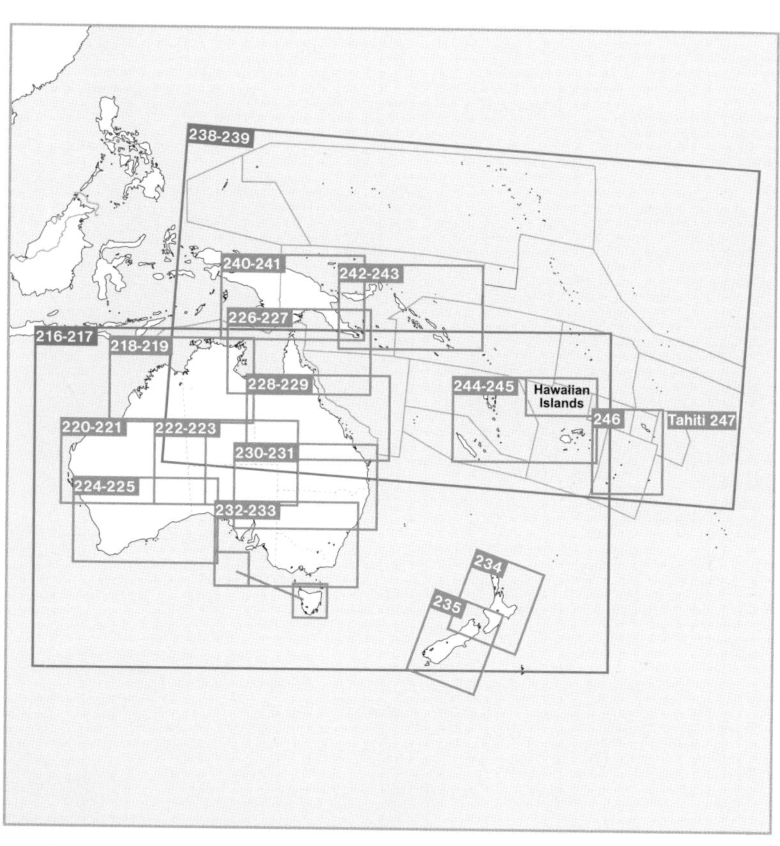

- Motorway/Tollway
- Multi-lane highway
- Highway
- Primary main road
- Secondary main road
- Side road
- Track
- Railway
- International border
- Regional border
- Border of a National Park/Protected area
- Reserve
- Main airport
- Airport

Scale: 1 : 18 000 000 (green) — 0 160 320 Kilometres

1 : 4 500 000 (orange) — 0 40 80 Kilometres

Previous page: The Great Ocean Road on Australia's southern coast has some truly breathtaking views of the 'Twelve Apostles' limestone formations, which are up to 65 m (213 ft) high.

Top: Melbourne skyline against the Yarra River. Australia's second largest city is characterized by a colourful mix of different peoples from more than 140 nations.

Principal travel routes
- Auto route
- Rail road
- Highspeed train
- Shipping route

Remarkable landscapes and natural monuments
- UNESCO World Natural Heritage
- Mountain landscape
- Extinct volcano
- Active volcano
- Rock landscape
- Ravine/canyon
- Depression
- Cave
- Glacier
- Desert
- River landscape
- Waterfall/rapids
- Lake country
- Geyser
- Oasis
- National Park (landscape)
- National Park (fauna)
- National Park (flora)
- National Park (culture)
- Nature park
- Biosphere reserve
- Coastal landscape
- Island
- Beach
- Coral reef
- Underwater reserve
- Spring
- Zoo/safari park
- Fossil site
- Wildlife reserve
- Whale watching
- Turtle conservation area
- Protected area for sea-lions/seals
- Protected area for penguins
- Crocodile farm

Remarkable cities and cultural monuments
- UNESCO – World Cultural Heritage
- Remarkable cities
- Pre- and early history
- Prehistoric rockscape
- Places of Jewish cultural interest
- Places of Islamic cultural interest
- Places of Buddhist cultural interest
- Places of Hindu cultural interest
- Pl. of cult. interest to other religions
- Pl. of cult. interest to indig. peoples
- Places of Christian cultural interest
- Christian monastery
- Places of Abor. cultural interest
- Aborigine reservation
- Cultural landscape
- Historical city scape
- Impressive skyline
- Castle/fortress/fort
- Palace
- Mine (in service)
- Mine (abandoned)
- Technical/Industrial monument
- Memorial
- Monument
- Tomb/grave
- Space mission launch site
- Space telescope
- Tourist information centre
- Festivals
- Museum
- Theatre/theater
- World exhibition
- Olympics
- Market
- Theatre of war/battlefield
- Dam
- Remarkable lighthouse
- Remarkable bridge

Sport and leisure destinations
- Race course
- Golf course
- Arena/stadium
- Skiing
- Sailing
- Canoeing/rafting
- Diving
- Wind surfing
- Surfing
- Deep-sea fishing
- Seaport
- Mineral/thermal spa
- Beach resort
- Leisure pool
- Amusement/theme park
- Casino
- Horse racing
- Campground
- Hill resort
- Lodge
- Mountain hut
- Aerial tramway
- Hiking region
- Lookout point

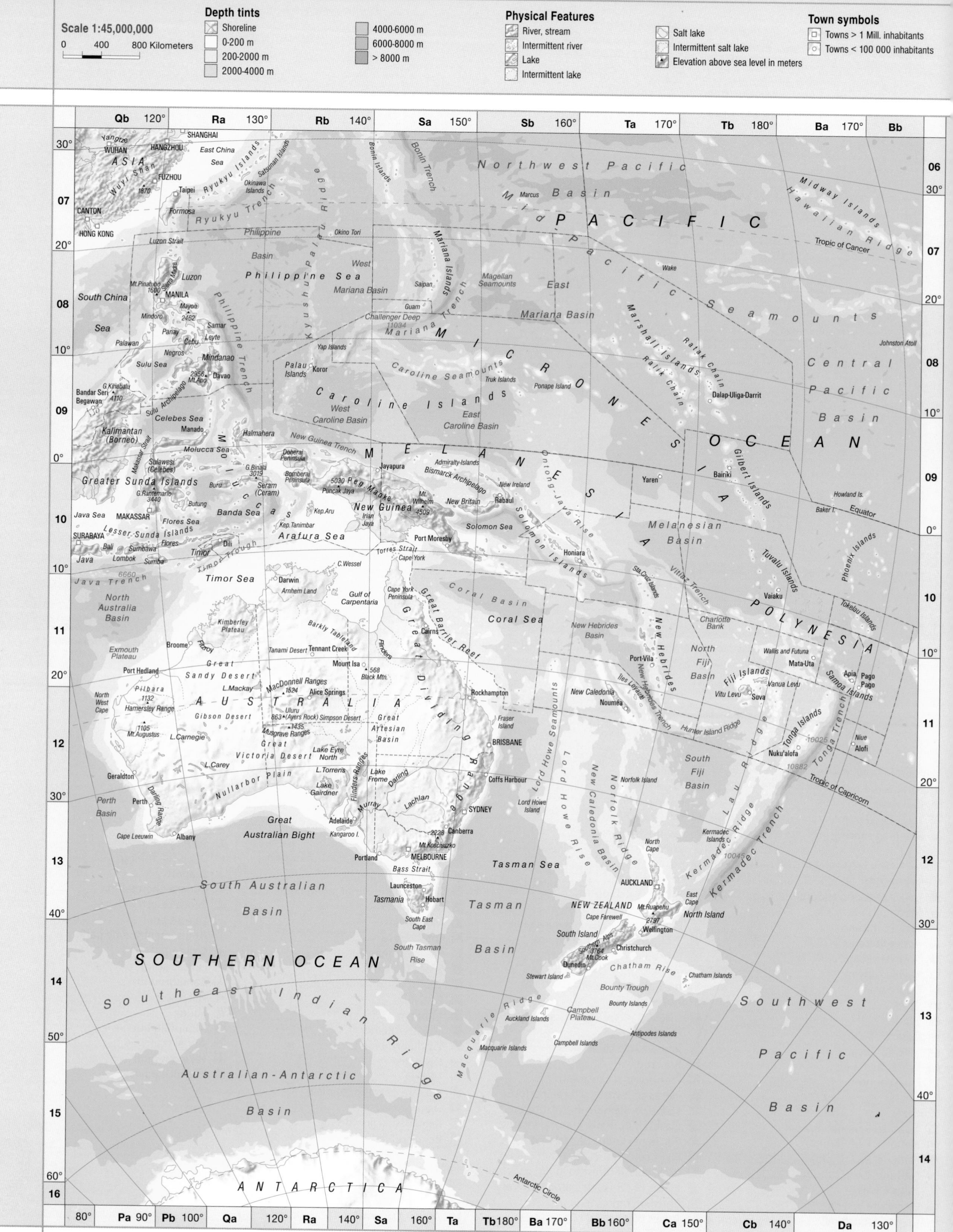
Scale 1:45,000,000
0 400 800 Kilometers
Depth tints
Shoreline
0-200 m
200-2000 m
2000-4000 m
4000-6000 m
6000-8000 m
> 8000 m
Physical Features
River, stream
Intermittent river
Lake
Intermittent lake
Salt lake
Intermittent salt lake
Elevation above sea level in meters
Town symbols
Towns > 1 Mill. inhabitants
Towns < 100 000 inhabitants
ASIA
SHANGHAI
WUHAN
HANGZHOU
FUZHOU
Taipei
Formosa
CANTON
HONG KONG
East China Sea
Ryukyu Islands
Ryukyu Trench
Philippine Basin
Philippine Sea
Luzon
MANILA
South China Sea
Mindanao
Davao
Sulu Sea
Celebes Sea
Kalimantan (Borneo)
Sulawesi (Celebes)
Greater Sunda Islands
Java Sea
MAKASSAR
SURABAYA
Java
Banda Sea
Flores Sea
Timor
Timor Sea
Arafura Sea
New Guinea
Port Moresby
Solomon Sea
Bismarck Archipelago
Mariana Trench
Mariana Islands
Guam
Challenger Deep
Caroline Islands
Northwest Pacific Basin
PACIFIC OCEAN
MICRONESIA
MELANESIA
POLYNESIA
Marshall Islands
Gilbert Islands
Central Pacific Basin
Tropic of Cancer
Equator
Tuvalu Islands
Fiji Islands
Samoa Islands
Tonga Islands
Tonga Trench
Kermadec Trench
Tropic of Capricorn
AUSTRALIA
Darwin
Gulf of Carpentaria
Great Barrier Reef
Great Dividing Range
Great Sandy Desert
Gibson Desert
Great Victoria Desert
Great Artesian Basin
Lake Eyre North
Nullarbor Plain
Great Australian Bight
Perth
Adelaide
MELBOURNE
SYDNEY
BRISBANE
Canberra
Coral Sea
Tasman Sea
Tasmania
Hobart
NEW ZEALAND
North Island
South Island
AUCKLAND
Wellington
Christchurch
Dunedin
South Australian Basin
Tasman Basin
SOUTHERN OCEAN
Southeast Indian Ridge
Australian-Antarctic Basin
Southwest Pacific Basin
Macquarie Ridge
Antarctic Circle
ANTARCTICA

Scale 1:45,000,000

0 400 800 Kilometers

Political Boundaries

- International
- International disputed
- Main administrative

Capitals of political units

- WASHINGTON D.C. — Independent
- Saint-Denis — State/province

Town symbols

- Capital > 1 Mill. inhabitants
- Capital < 1 Mill. inhabitants
- State capital > 1 Mill. inhabitants
- State capital < 1 Mill. inhabitants
- Towns > 1 Mill. inhabitants
- Towns < 100 000 inhabitants

Qb 120° Ra 130° Rb 140° Sa 150° Sb 160° Ta 170° Tb 180° Ba 170° Bb

SHANGHAI
WUHAN
HANGZHOU
CHINA
FUZHOU
Taipei
CANTON
Taiwan
HONG KONG
Bonin Islands (Japan)
Okinawa (Japan)
Okino Tori (Japan)
Midway Islands (USA)
PACIFIC OCEAN
Wake (USA)
Laoag
Philippine Sea
South China Sea
San Carlos
MANILA
PHILIPPINES
Northern Mariana Islands (USA)
Garapan
Guam (USA)
Agana
Johnston Atoll (USA)
MICRONESIA
Cebu
Iloilo
Butuan
Cagayan de Oro
Zamboanga
Davao
General Santos
Colonia
Mohen
Palikir
MARSHALL ISLANDS
Dalap-Uliga-Darrit
Koror
PALAU
Caroline Islands
Bandar Seri Begawan
BRUNEI
Sandakan
MALAYSIA
Tawau
Manado
Gorontalo
Sorong
Manokwari
MELANESIA
Samarinda
Palu
Balikpapan
Banjarmasin
MAKASSAR
Kendari
Ambon
Fakfak
Nabire
Sarmi
Jayapura
Amampare
Kiunga
Madang
Mt.Hagen
Rabaul
PAPUA NEW GUINEA
Morehead
Port Moresby
Yaren
NAURU
Bairiki
Howland Is. (USA)
Baker I. (USA)
KIRIBATI
INDONESIA
SURABAYA
Ende
Dili
EAST TIMOR
Denpasar
Kupang
Arafura Sea
Timor Sea
Honiara
SOLOMON ISLANDS
Phoenix Islands
TUVALU
Vaiaku
POLYNESIA
Tokelau Islands (NZ)
Darwin
Weipa
Katherine
Wyndham
Cairns
Coral Sea
Coral Sea Islands Territory
VANUATU
Wallis and Futuna (F)
Mata-Uta
SAMOA
Apia
Pago Pago
Broome
Tennant Creek
Townsville
Mount Isa
Northern Territory
Port-Vila
Port Hedland
Mackay
Queensland
Alice Springs
Rockhampton
New Caledonia (F)
Nouméa
Suva
FIJI
American Samoa (USA)
Emerald
AUSTRALIA
Bundaberg
TONGA
Niue (NZ)
Alofi
Nuku'alofa
Oodnadatta
Western Australia
Denham
Coober Pedy
Cunnamulla
BRISBANE
Moree
South Australia
Broken Hill
Coffs Harbour
Geraldton
Kalgoorlie-Boulder
Port Augusta
New South Wales
Newcastle
Norfolk Island (AUS)
Lord Howe Island (AUS)
Cook Islands (NZ)
Perth
Esperance
Port Lincoln
Adelaide
Mildura
Orange
SYDNEY
Wollongong
Bunbury
Great Australian Bight
Wagga Wagga
Canberra A.C.T.
Albany
Bendigo
Victoria
Kermadec Islands (NZ)
Portland
Geelong
MELBOURNE
Tasman Sea
Whangarei
AUCKLAND
Hamilton
Rotorua
Launceston
Tasmania
Hobart
NEW ZEALAND
Napier
Nelson
Wellington
Queenstown
Christchurch
SOUTHERN OCEAN
Invercargill
Dunedin
Chatham Islands (NZ)
Bounty Islands (NZ)
Auckland Islands (NZ)
Antipodes Islands (NZ)
Macquarie Islands (AUS)
Campbell Islands (NZ)
ANTARCTICA

80° Pa 90° Pb 100° Qa 120° Ra 140° Sa 160° Ta Tb Ba 170° Bb 160° Ca 150° Cb 140° Da 130°

Scale 1:18,000,000
0 160 320 Kilometers
Depth tints
Shoreline
0-200 m
200-2000 m
2000-4000 m
4000-6000 m
6000-8000 m
> 8000 m
Physical Features
River, stream
Intermittent river
Lake
Intermittent lake
Salt lake
Intermittent salt lake
Elevation above sea level in meters
Qc 115° Qd 120° Ra 125° Rb 238 130° Rc 135° Rd 140° Sa 145°
Qa 105° Qb 110° Qc 115° Qd 120° Ra 236 125° Rb 130° Rc 135° Rd 140° Sa 145° Sb
20 21 15° 22 20° 23 25° 24 30° 25 35° 26 40° 27 45°
10°
Probolinggo
Denpasar
Mataram
Banyuwangi
Java
Bali
Lombok
Sumbawabesar
Taliwang
Sumbawa
Selat Sumba
Flores
Memboro
Waingapu
Sumba
Baing
Kefamenanu
Besikama
Timor
Soe
Kupang
P.Sawu
Baa
P.Roti
Ashmore Is.
Cartier Is.
Scott Reef
Bonaparte Archipelago
Cape Londonderry
Joseph Bonaparte Gulf
Kalumburu
Wyndham
Kununurra
Mt.Hann 779
KIMBERLEY
Kimberley
PLATEAU
936
Mt.Ord
King Leopold Ranges
Bungle Bungle Ranges
L.Argyle
C.Leveque
Sunday Strait
Dampier Land
Derby
Fitzroy Crossing
Halls Creek
Broome
Rowley Shoals
La Grange
Sturt
Larrey Pt.
Sandfire Flat Roadhouse
De Grey
Dampier Archipelago
Port Hedland
Montebello Is.
Barrow I.
Dampier
Roebourne
Marble Bar
Nullagine
Telfer
Percival Lakes
L.Dora
Mary Anne Passage
Pilbara
North West C.
Onslow
Exmouth
Hamersley Range
Nanutarra Roadhouse
1132
Tom Price
Paraburdoo
Ashburton
Newman
L.Disappointment
North
West
Basin
Mt.Augustus 1105
Mt.Essendon 906
Geographe Chan.
L.MacLeod
Gascoyne
Carnarvon
Shark Bay
Denham
Wooramel Roadhouse
Dirk Hartog I.
Mt.Hale 732
Murchison
Wiluna
L.Way
Meekatharra
L.Carnegie
L.Wells
Zuytdorp Cliffs
Dalgaranga Hill 652
Yalgoo
L.Austin
Mount Magnet
Sandstone
Agnew
Cosmo Newbery Mission
Laverton
L.Carey
Leonora
Yeo Lake
Jubilee L.
Kalbarri
Northampton
Geraldton
Dongara
Mullewa
Morawa
Paynes Find
L.Barlee
Menzies
L.Minigwal
Plumridge Lakes
Eneabba
L.Moore
Wubin
L.Rebecca
Kalgoorlie-Boulder
Coolgardie
Zanthus
Rawlinna
Badgingarra
Moora
Goomalling
Southern Cross
Merredin
The Johnston Lakes
L.Cowan
Norseman
Belladonia Motel
L.Dundas
Pt.Culver
Twilight Cove
Perth
Fremantle
Kwinana
Northam
Darling Range
Narrogin
Lake Grace
Wagin
Ravensthorpe
Esperance
Israelite Bay
C.Pasley
Archipelago of the Recherche
Bunbury
Geographe Bay
C.Naturaliste
Busselton
Kojonup
Bridgetown
Manjimup
Jerramungup
C.Knob
Augusta
C.Leeuwin
Flinders Bay
Walpole
Albany
Bald Head
Melville I.
Bathurst I.
C.Croker
Goulburn Is.
Van Diemen Gulf
Beagle Gulf
Darwin
Jabiru
Maningrida
Adelaide River
Pine Creek
Katherine
Mataranka
Roper
Roper Bar
Larrimah
Timber Creek
Top Springs
Daly Waters
Kalkaringi
Elliott
Limmen Bight
Limmen Bight R.
C.Wessel
Marchinbar I.
Wessel Islands
Nhulunbuy (Gove)
Gove Pen.
Bickerton I.
Groote Eylandt
Maria I.
Sir Edward Pellew Group
Borroloola
Calvert
Barkly Tableland
Barkly Homestead Roadhouse
Tennant Creek
Camooweal
Wauchope
Lander
L.White
L.Mackay
Sandover
L.MacDonald
Mt.Liebig 1524
Mt.Zeil 1511
MacDonnell Ranges
Alice Springs
Hale
L.Hopkins
L.Amadeus
Yulara
Uluru (Ayers Rock)
Erldunda
Mt.Olga 1066
863
Kulgera
Finke
Tomkinson Ranges
Mt.Woodroffe 1435
Musgrave Ranges
Mt.Sir Thomas 772
Marla
Peera Peera Poolanna L.
Macumba
Oodnadatta
Warburton
Lake Eyre North
-16
Coober Pedy
Lake Eyre South
Marree
L.Blanche
L.Maurice
Maralinga
Tarcoola
L.Torrens
Kingoonya
L.Everard
Woomera
Pimba
Lake Gairdner
Flinders Ranges
Deakin
Eucla Motels
Head of Bight
Coorabie
Penong
Ceduna
Port Augusta
Iron Knob
Kimba
Streaky Bay
Anxious Bay
Flinders I.
Kyancutta
Eyre Peninsula
Whyalla
Port Pirie
Wallaroo
Spencer Gulf
Port Wakefield
Mount Hope
Port Lincoln
Adelaide
Inneston
Gulf St.Vincent
C.Spencer
Cape Borda
Kingscote
Kangaroo I.
Victor Harbor
Tailem Bend
Kingston SE
Beachport
Mount Gambier
Portland
C.Nelson
Prince of Wales I.
Cape York
Weipa
Albatross Bay
Lockhart River
Princess Charlotte Bay
C.Melville
Silver Plains
Edward River
C.Flattery
Cooktown
Mitchell
Mossman
Cairns
Wellesley Islands
Gununa
Mornington I.
Gilbert
Karumba
Normanton
Burketown
Flinders
Croydon
Forsayth
Ingham
Townsville
Mount Isa
Cloncurry
Black Mtn. 568
Julia Creek
Richmond
Hughenden
Dajarra
Winton
Boulia
Muttaburra
Longreach
Barcaldine
Thomson
Diamantina
Blackall
Windorah
Tambo
Birdsville
L.Yamma Yamma
Charleville
Quilpie
Sturt Stony Desert
Grey Range
Thargomindah
Cunnamulla
Warrego
Milparinka
Paroo
Bourke
Lake Frome
White Cliffs
Louth
Darling
Wilcannia
Cobar
Broken Hill
Menindee
Olary
Ivanhoe
Roto
Murray River
Basin
Lake Gampung
Booligal
Griffith
West Wyalong
Wentworth
Mildura
Balranald
Hay
Narrandera
Renmark
Murray
Riverina
Quyen
Deniliquin
Wagga Wagga
Pinnaroo
Swan Hill
Albury-Wodonga
Lascelles
Keith
Shepparton-Mooroopna
Charlton
Mt. Kosciuszko
Horsham
Bendigo
Wangaratta
Naracoorte
Castlemaine
Hamilton
Ballarat
Sunbury
MELBOURNE
Geelong
Cranbourne
Sale
Warrnambool
Morwell
C.Otway
Port Welshpool
South East Pt.
King Island
Currie
Kent Group
Flinders I.
Cape Barren I.
Burnie-Somerset
Smithton
Devonport
Launceston
Rosebery
Great L.
Queenstown
L.Gordon
Hobart
L.Pedder
Bruny I.
South West Cape
South East Cape
Eastern Fields
Jericho
4865
715
6660
2280
1555
3475
55
140
18
9
2435
355
6840
5
25
70
1445
65
5525
235
2085
65
735
5025
6035
5080
3725
2640
505
65
1390
55
5705
2500
6320
2500
5030
5030
5670
5605
5485
3725
3905
4530
3595
4610
3865
3870
770

Political Boundaries
International
International disputed
Main administrative

Transportation
Interstate Hwy./Motorway
Main road
Railway
Airport

Capitals of political units
WASHINGTON D.C. Independent
Richmond State/province

Town symbols
Capital > 1 Mill. inhabitants
Capital < 1 Mill. inhabitants
State capital > 1 Mill. inhabitants
State capital < 1 Mill. inhabitants
Towns > 1 Mill. inhabitants
Towns 100 000 to 1 Mill. inhabitants
Towns < 100 000 inhabitants

150° Sc 155° Sd 160° Ta 165° 239 Tb 170° Tc 175° Td 180° Ua

5° 20 10° 21 15° 22 20° 23 25° 24 30° 25 35° 26

Fergusson I. d'Entrecasteaux Islands Salamo Alotau Normanby I. Misima I. The Calvados Chain Louisiade Archipelago Pocklington Reef Tagula I. Yela I.

Russell Is. Auki Malaita Stewart Is. Honiara Guadalcanal Maramasike San Cristóbal Bellona I. Rennell I. Hauraha Indispensable Reefs

Reef Islands Duff Is. Nendo Sta.Cruz Islands Utupua Vanikolo Cherry I. Tikopia Fataka Torres Is./Îles Torres Banks Is./Îles Banks Vanua Lava/Île Vanoua Lava Santa Maria I./I.Gaua Tabwemasana 1879 Espíritu Santo/Île Santo Obe/I.Aoba Maewo/Île Aurora Luganville Pentecost I./Île Pentecôte Sarmette Ambrim/I.Ambrym Malakula/I.Mallicolo Epi/Île Epi Efate/Île Vaté Port-Vila Eromanga I./I.Erromango Unpongkor Tana/I.Tanna Aneityum/I.Anatom

Nanumanga Niutao Nui Vaitupu Nukufetau Atoll Funafuti Atoll Vaiaku Nukulaelae Atoll Niulakita Rotuma Île Futuna Île Alofi Mata Utu Îles Wallis

Lihou Reefs and Cays Mellish Reef Marion Reef Récifs et Chesterfields Île de Sable Récifs Bellona Swain Reefs Saumarez Reef Wreck Reef Cato Island

Récifs d'Entrecasteaux Grand Récif de Cook Îles Belep Récifs des Français Poum Touho Koné Ouvéa Lifou Thio Nouméa Mont-Dore Maré Île des Pins Grand Récif Sud Île Matthew Île Hunter

Yasawa Group Vanua Levu Cikobia Labasa Nabouwalu Rakiraki Naitauba Lautoka Nadi Tomanivi 1323 Koro Taveuni Viti Levu Suva Vatulele Gau Vanua Balavu Kadavu Lakeba Matuku Lau Group Vatoa Ono-i-Lau Tuvana-i-Ra Niuafo'ou Fonualei Late Tofua Ha'apai Group Otu Tolu Group Nuku'alofa Tongatapu 'Eua Tongatapu Group

Yeppoon Curtis I. Gladstone Monto Hervey Bay Bundaberg Fraser I. Maryborough Gympie Kingaroy Caloundra Dalby Moreton I. Toowoomba Ipswich BRISBANE Warwick Gold Coast Goondiwindi Lismore Ballina Casino Grafton Glen Innes Coffs Harbour Armidale Tamworth Port Macquarie 1555 Singleton C.Hawke Maitland Newcastle SYDNEY Wollongong

Middleton Reef Elizabeth Reef Norfolk Island Lord Howe I. Ball's Pyramid Raoul I. Macauley I. Curtis I. L'Esperance Rock

Three Kings Is. North Cape Great Exhibition Bay Awanui Omapere Kawakawa Whangarei Great Barrier I. Takapuna AUCKLAND Coromandel Pen. Hamilton Tauranga Bay of Plenty Te Araroa East Cape North Taranaki Bight Rotorua New Plymouth Taupo Opotiki Mt.Taranaki 2518 Mt.Ruapehu 2797 Hawera Napier Gisborne South Taranaki Bight Hawke Bay Wanganui Hastings C.Farewell Tasman Bay Palmerston North Westport Nelson Picton C.Foulwind Greymouth Blenheim Lower Hutt Wellington Harihari Southern Alps Kaikoura Haast Mt.Cook 3764 Waipara Pegasus Bay Milford Sound Ashburton Christchurch Queenstown Timaru Canterbury Bight Banks Peninsula Cromwell Resolution I. Te Anau Oamaru Invercargill Gore Foveaux Strait Dunedin Halfmoon Bay Balclutha Stewart I. Chatham I.

155° Sd 160° Ta 165° Tb 170° Tc 175° Td 236 180° Ua 175° Ub 170° Uc 165° Ud

Principal travel routes
Auto route
Rail road
Shipping route
Remarkable landscapes and natural monuments
UNESCO World Natural Heritage
Mountain landscape
Rock landscape
Ravine/canyon
Geyser
Cave
River landscape
Waterfall/rapids
National park (landscape)
National park (flora)
National park (fauna)
National park (culture)
Wildlife reserve
Crocodile farm
Coastal landscape
Underwater reserve
Scale 1:4,500,000
0 40 80 Kilometers
Timor Sea
INDIAN OCEAN
INDONESIA
Timor Trench
Kimberley Coast
Kimberley Plateau
Western Australia
Great Sandy Desert
Joseph Bonaparte Gulf
Broome
Derby
Wyndham
Kununurra
Halls Creek
Fitzroy Crossing
Great Northern Highway
King Leopold Ranges
Drysdale River National Park
Mitchell River N.P.
Prince Regent Nature Reserve
Purnululu N.P.
Eighty Mile Beach

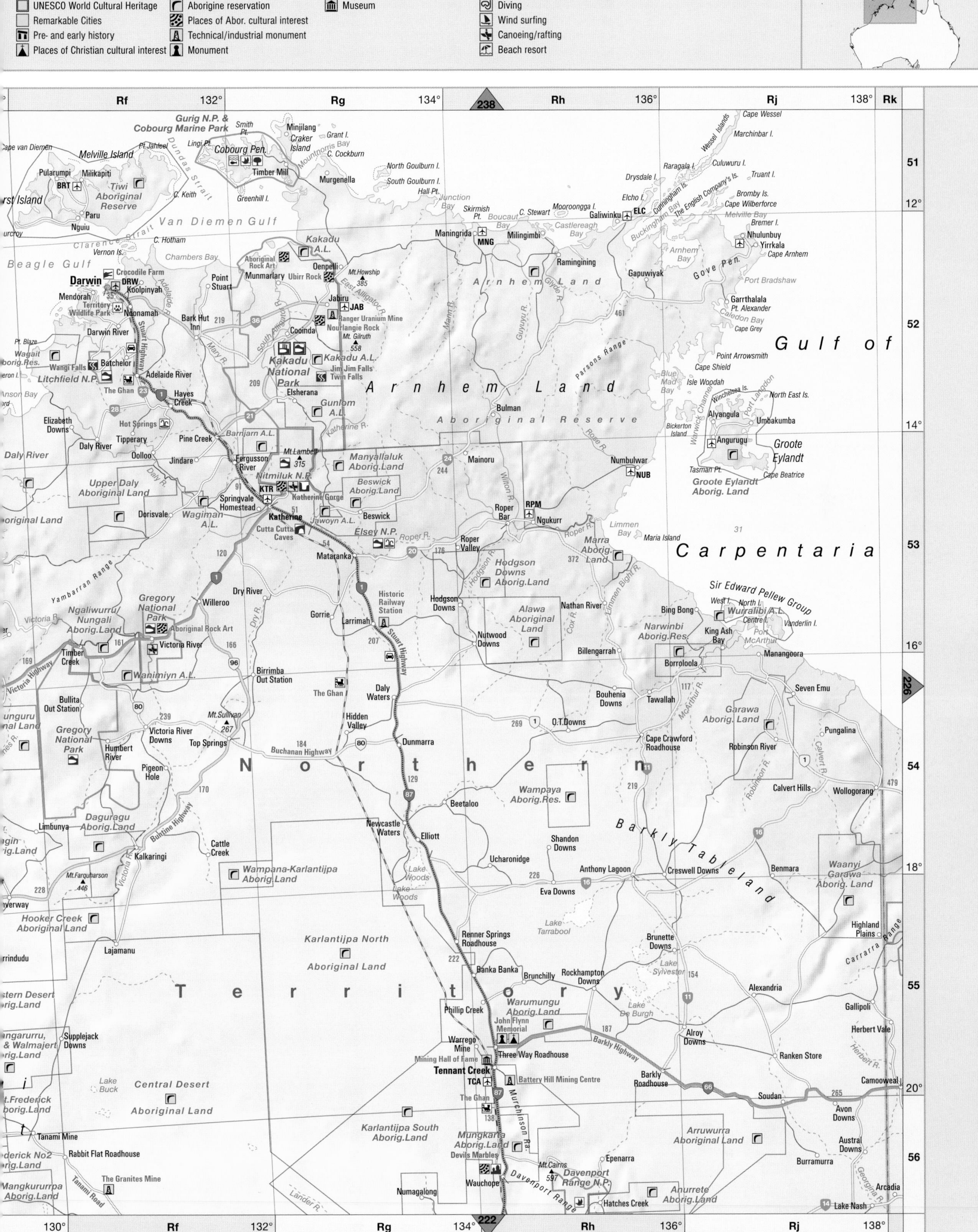
Remarkable Cities and Cultural monuments
UNESCO World Cultural Heritage
Remarkable Cities
Pre- and early history
Places of Christian cultural interest
Aborigine reservation
Places of Abor. cultural interest
Technical/industrial monument
Monument
Museum
Sport and leisure destinations
Diving
Wind surfing
Canoeing/rafting
Beach resort
Rf
132°
Rg
134°
238
Rh
136°
Rj
138°
Rk
51
12°
52
14°
53
16°
226
54
18°
55
20°
56
130°
222
Gurig N.P. & Cobourg Marine Park
Cobourg Pen.
Melville Island
Tiwi Aboriginal Reserve
Van Diemen Gulf
Beagle Gulf
Darwin
Kakadu National Park
Arnhem Land
Aboriginal Reserve
Gulf of Carpentaria
Groote Eylandt
Groote Eylandt Aborig. Land
Sir Edward Pellew Group
Litchfield N.P.
Nitmiluk N.P.
Katherine
Elsey N.P.
Gregory National Park
Upper Daly Aboriginal Land
Hodgson Downs Aborig.Land
Alawa Aboriginal Land
Narwinbi Aborig.Res.
Borroloola
Garawa Aborig. Land
Wampaya Aborig.Res.
Barkly Tableland
Daguragu Aborig.Land
Wampana-Karlantijpa Aborig.Land
Hooker Creek Aboriginal Land
Karlantijpa North Aboriginal Land
Northern Territory
Warumungu Aborig.Land
Central Desert Aboriginal Land
Karlantijpa South Aborig.Land
Arruwurra Aboriginal Land
Waanyi Garawa Aborig. Land
Mungkarta Aborig.Land
Davenport Range N.P.
Anurrete Aborig.Land
Stuart Highway
Victoria Highway
Buchanan Highway
Buntine Highway
Barkly Highway
Tanami Road
Tennant Creek
Mining Hall of Fame
Battery Hill Mining Centre
Three Way Roadhouse
John Flynn Memorial
Devils Marbles
Wauchope
Elliott
Newcastle Waters
Dunmarra
Daly Waters
Larrimah
Mataranka
Cape Wessel
Marchinbar I.
Wessel Islands
Nhulunbuy
Yirrkala
Cape Arnhem
Gove Pen.
Maningrida
Milingimbi
Ramingining
Oenpelli
Jabiru
Cooinda
Batchelor
Adelaide River
Pine Creek
Roper Bar
Ngukurr
Numbulwar
Bulman
Kalkaringi
Lajamanu
Timber Creek
Victoria River Downs
Top Springs
Cattle Creek
Tanami Mine
Rabbit Flat Roadhouse
The Granites Mine
Camooweal
Soudan
Alexandria
Brunette Downs
Anthony Lagoon
Creswell Downs
Calvert Hills
Wollogorang
Seven Emu
Robinson River
Cape Crawford Roadhouse
Renner Springs Roadhouse
Banka Banka
Barkly Roadhouse
Lake Nash
Arcadia
Epenarra
Hatches Creek

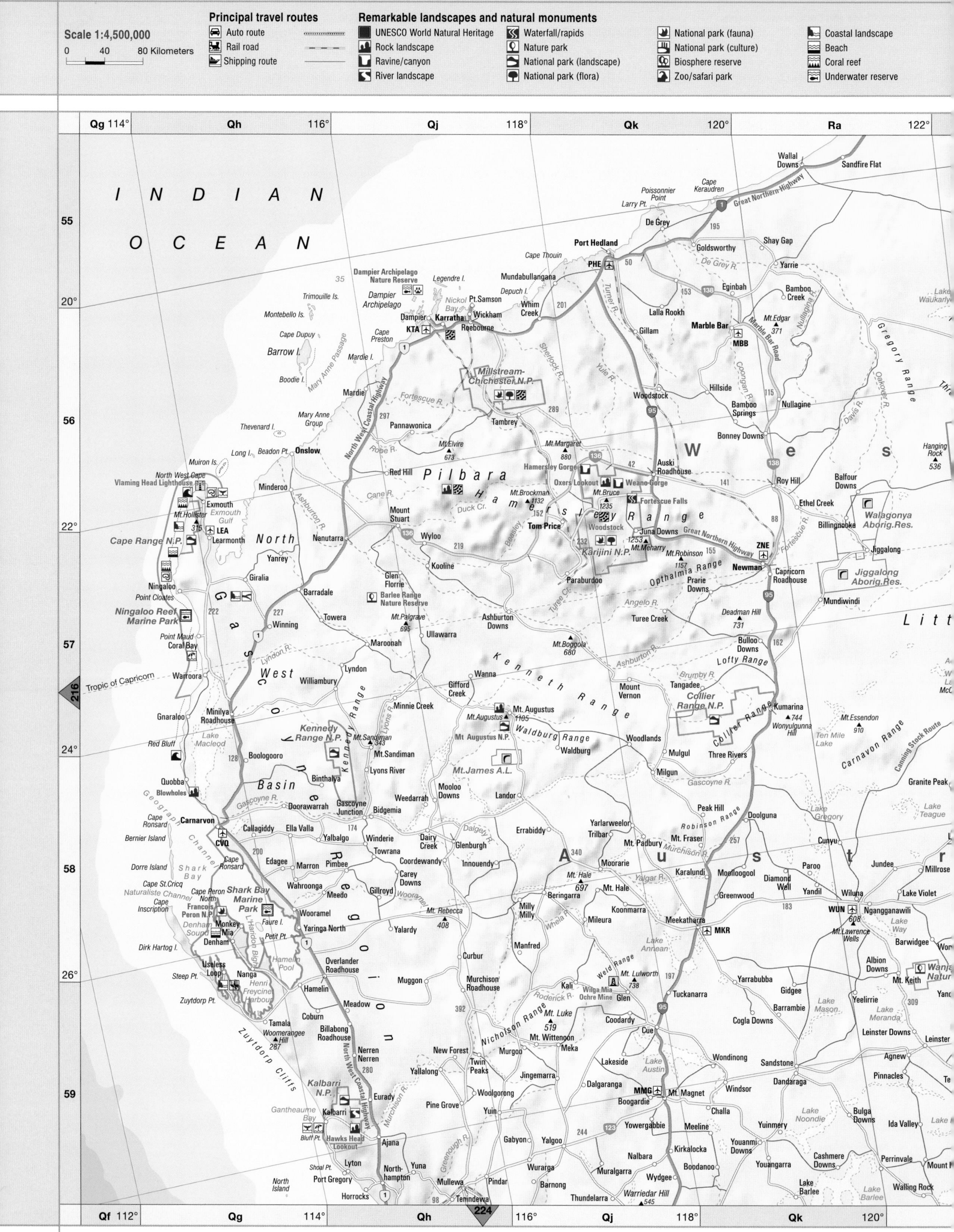
Scale 1:4,500,000
0 40 80 Kilometers
Principal travel routes
Auto route
Rail road
Shipping route
Remarkable landscapes and natural monuments
UNESCO World Natural Heritage
Rock landscape
Ravine/canyon
River landscape
Waterfall/rapids
Nature park
National park (landscape)
National park (flora)
National park (fauna)
National park (culture)
Biosphere reserve
Zoo/safari park
Coastal landscape
Beach
Coral reef
Underwater reserve
Qg 114° Qh 116° Qj 118° Qk 120° Ra 122°
INDIAN OCEAN
55
56
57
58
59
20°
22°
24°
26°
Tropic of Capricorn
216
Port Hedland
PHE
Karratha
KTA
Dampier
Wickham
Roebourne
Pt.Samson
Dampier Archipelago Nature Reserve
Millstream-Chichester N.P.
Pilbara
Hamersley Range
Karijini N.P.
Tom Price
Paraburdoo
Newman
ZNE
Marble Bar
MBB
Nullagine
Onslow
Exmouth
LEA
Learmonth
Cape Range N.P.
Ningaloo
Ningaloo Reef Marine Park
Coral Bay
North West Cape
Vlaming Head Lighthouse
Great Northern Highway
North West Coastal Highway
Gascoyne
North West
Kenneth Range
Kennedy Range N.P.
Collier Range N.P.
Mt. Augustus
Mt Augustus N.P.
Mt.James A.L.
Carnarvon
CVQ
Shark Bay
Shark Bay Marine Park
Denham
Monkey Mia
Francois Peron N.P.
Dirk Hartog I.
Zuytdorp Cliffs
Kalbarri N.P.
Kalbarri
Northampton
Port Gregory
Mullewa
Meekatharra
MKR
Wiluna
WUN
Mt. Magnet
MMG
Cue
Sandstone
Murchison Roadhouse
Robinson Range
Gregory Range
Opthalmia Range
Wannarra
Collier Range
Carnavon Range
Canning Stock Route
Lake Gregory
Lake Carnegie
Nicholson Range
Weld Range
Lake Austin
Lake Annean
Lake Way
Lake Mason
Walagonya Aborig.Res.
Jiggalong Aborig.Res.
Qf 112° Qg 114° Qh 116° Qj 118° Qk 120°
224

Remarkable Cities and Cultural monuments
UNESCO World Cultural Heritage
Remarkable Cities
Aborigine reservation
Places of Abor. cultural interest
Historical city scape
Technical/industrial monument
Remarkable lighthouse
Monument
Museum
Sport and leisure destinations
Diving
Wind surfing
Surfing
Deep-sea fishing
Beach resort
Great Sandy Desert
Gibson Desert
Great Victoria Desert
Northern Territory
South Australia
Balgo Aboriginal Land
Mangkururrpa Aborig.Land
Yiningarra Aborig.Land
Lake Gregory
Mt.Cornish 363
Lake Dennis
Lake White
Lake Wills
Stansmore Range
Wilbrunga Range
Mala Aborig.Land
Chilla Well
Tanami Road
Lake Mackay Aboriginal Land
Central Australia Aboriginal Land
Truer Range
Vaughan Springs
Percival Lakes
Tobin Lake
Canning Stock Route
No.35 Well
Lake Auld
Lake Dora
Lake Blanche
Lake Mackay
Yunkanjini Aborig.Land
Gurner
Lake Bennett
Kiwirrkurra Aborig.Land
Walungurru
Lake Macdonald
Mt.Leisler 901
Kintore Range
Tropic of Capricorn
Haasts Bluff Aboriginal Land
No.24 Well
Ngaanyatjarra Land Council Aboriginal Land
Watarrka N.P.
Carmichael Craig 906
Lake Dissapointment
Lake Neale
Lake Hopkins
Bloods Range
Mt.Harris 840
Petermann Aboriginal Land
Lake Amadeus Aboriginal Land
Lake Amadeus
Lake Cobb
Lake Christopher
Rawlinson Ra.
Schwerin Mural
Giles Meteorological Station
Docker Creek
Great Central Road
Mt.Deering 1219
Petermann Ranges
Katiti Aborig.Land
The Olgas (Kata Tjuta)
AYQ
Yulara
Mt.Olga 1066
Uluru 863
Uluru (Ayers Rock)
Uluru - Kata Tjuta National Park
Stevensons Peak 1319
Mt.Madley 534
Gary Highway
Gibson Desert Nature Reserve
Lake Newell
Warakurna
Central Reserve Aboriginal Land
Everard Junction
Mungilli Aborig.Land
Lake Burnside
Gunbarrel Highway
Mann Ranges
Papulankutja
Mt.Morris 1307
Amata
Lake Buchanan
Carnegie
Lake Breaden
Herbert Wash
Southern Central Reserve Aboriginal Land
Warburton
Warburton Aborig.Land
Warburton Range
Mt.Hinkley 1053
Pipalyatjara
Mt.Davis 1053
Tomkinson Ranges
Lake Carnegie
Anangu Pitjantjatjara Aboriginal Land
Windidda
Prenti Downs
Lake Baker
Yapuparra Aborig.Land
Cheeseman Peak 654
Lake Wells
Sykes Bluff 490
De La Poer Range Nature Res.
Lake Throssel
Mt.Maiden 690
Bandya
Yeo Lake Nature Reserve
Cosmo Newberry Aboriginal Land
Cosmo Newbery
Yeo Lake
Yamarna
Neale Junction Nature Reserve
Neale Junction
Anne Beadell Highway
Unnamed Conservation Park
Pt.Salvation 508
Point Salvation Aboriginal Land
White Cliffs
Serpentine Lakes
Maralinga Tjarutja Aboriginal Land
Wyola Lake
Lake Dey Dey
Erlistoun
Laverton Downs
Rason Lake
LVO
Laverton
Merolia
Jubilee Lake
Forrest Lakes
Lake Maurice
Mt. Margaret
Bartlet Bluff
Great Victoria Desert Nature Reserve
Lake Carey
Yundamindra
Plumridge Lakes Nature Reserve
Connie Sue Hwy.
Lake Minigwal
Yerilla
Mount Gelia
Rb Rc Rd Re Rf
122° 124° 126° 128° 130°
22° 24° 26° 28° 30°
56 57 58 59 60 61
218 222 225

Scale 1:4,500,000
0 40 80 Kilometers
Principal travel routes
Auto route
Rail road
Shipping route
Remarkable landscapes and natural monuments
UNESCO World Natural Heritage
Rock landscape
Ravine/canyon
Geyser
Cave
Desert
Nature park
National park (landscape)
National park (flora)
National park (fauna)
National park (culture)
Biosphere reserve
Zoo/safari park
Rc 126° Rd 128° Re 219 130° Rf 132° Rg 134°
56
22°
57
24°
58
221
26°
59
28°
60
Rc 126° Rd 128° 225 Re 130° Rf 132° Rg
Mt.Cornish 363
Lake Gregory
Balgo Aboriginal Land
Mangkururrpa Aborig.Land
The Granites Mine
Tanami Road
356
Lander R.
Numagalong
Wirliyajarrayi Aborig.Land
Willowra
Yiningarra Aborig.Land
Lake Dennis
611
N o r t h
Barrow Creek
Stansmore Range
Lake Wills
Lake White
Wilbrunga Range
Chilla Well
Mala Aborig.Land
Pawu Aborig.Land
Mt.Leichhardt 1140
Stirling
Tobin Lake
Canning Stock Route
Lake Mackay Aboriginal Land
Central Australia Aboriginal Land
Mount Denison
Ahakeye (Ti-Tree) Aborig.Land
Ti-Tree
Truer Range
Yuendumu
Yalpirakinu Aborig.Land
Reynolds Range
Vaughan Springs
Yuendumu Aborig.Land
Napperby
The Ghan
Aileron
Lake Mackay
No.35 Well
Gibson Desert
Yunkanjini Aborig.Land
Gurner
Lake Bennett
Ngalurrtja Aborig.Land
1094
Central Mt.Wedge
Stuart Bluff Ra.
152
130
540
Kiwirrkurra Aborig.Land
T e r r i
Papunya
110
255
Mt.Liebig 1524
Mt.Edward 1416
Mt.Zeil 1511
West MacDonnell N.P.
Mt.Hay 1250
136
68
Haast Bluff
ASP
Museum of Central Australia
Walungurru
Lake Macdonald
Mt.Leisler 901
Kitmbre Range
Haasts Bluff Aboriginal Land
MacDonnell Ranges
Hermannsburg
Tropic of Capricorn
Ngaanyatjarra Land Council Aboriginal Land
364
Watarrka N.P.
Palm Valley
Finke Gorge N.P.
331
Carmichael Craig 906
George Gill Ra.
Kings Canyon
Urrampinyu Iliyjiltjarri Aborig.Land
James Range
Orange Creek
Henbury Meteorite Craters
201
Henbury
Lake Neale
Lake Hopkins
Bloods Range
Mt.Harris 840
Petermann Aboriginal Land
Lake Amadeus
Lake Amadeus Aboriginal Land
Wallara Ranch Roadhouse
Chambers Pillar
Lake Cobb
Gary Highway
Lake Christopher
Rawlinson Ra.
Schwerin Mural
Giles Meteorological Station
Docker Creek
Great Central Road
Angas Downs
Mt.Ebenezer Roadhouse
Gibson Desert Nature Reserve
Lake Newell
Warakurna
Mt.Deering 1219
Petermann Ranges
259
The Olgas (Kata Tjuta)
AYQ
Yulara
Katiti Aborig.Land
137
110
Erldunda
Mt.Olga 1066
Uluru (Ayers Rock)
Uluru 863
Curtin Springs
Stevensons Peak 1319
Uluru - Kata Tjuta National Park
74
Central Reserve Aboriginal Land
Everard Junction
W e s t e r n
Great Central Road
Kulgera Roadhouse
Mulga Park
Mann Ranges
227
Papulankutja
Mt.Morris 1307
Amata
Musgrave Range
Mt.Woodroffe 1435
Pukatja
Lake Breaden
Southern Central Reserve Aboriginal Land
Warburton Aborig.Land
Warburton
Warburton Range
Mt.Hinkley 1053
Pipalyatjara
Mt.Davis 1053
Tomkinson Ranges
Agnes Creek
179
Aparawatatja (Fregon)
Everard Park
Iwantja
Mt. Illbillee 917
Mimili
Everard Ranges
Mintable
Lake Baker
Yapuparra Aborig.Land
Anangu Pitjantjatjara Aboriginal Land
Cheeseman Peak 654
S o
524
Great Central Road
Sykes Bluff 490
307
Great Victoria Desert
Yeo Lake Nature Reserve
Yeo Lake
Neale Junction Nature Reserve
Neale Junction
Anne Beadell Highway
638
Unnamed Conservation Park
Tallaring Conservation Park
Anne Beadell Highway
325
Serpentine Lakes
Maralinga Tjarutja
A u s t r a l i a
Rason Lake
Wyola Lake
Lake Dey Dey
A u s t
Jubilee Lake
Forrest Lakes
Wilkinson Lakes
Lake Maurice
Aboriginal Land
Indoor
Bartlet Bluff
Great Victoria Desert Nature Reserve
Lake Anthony
Plumridge Lakes Nature Reserve
Connie Sue Hwy.
344
Ooldea Range
Maralinga
Ooldea
665
Trans Australian Railway
Wynbring

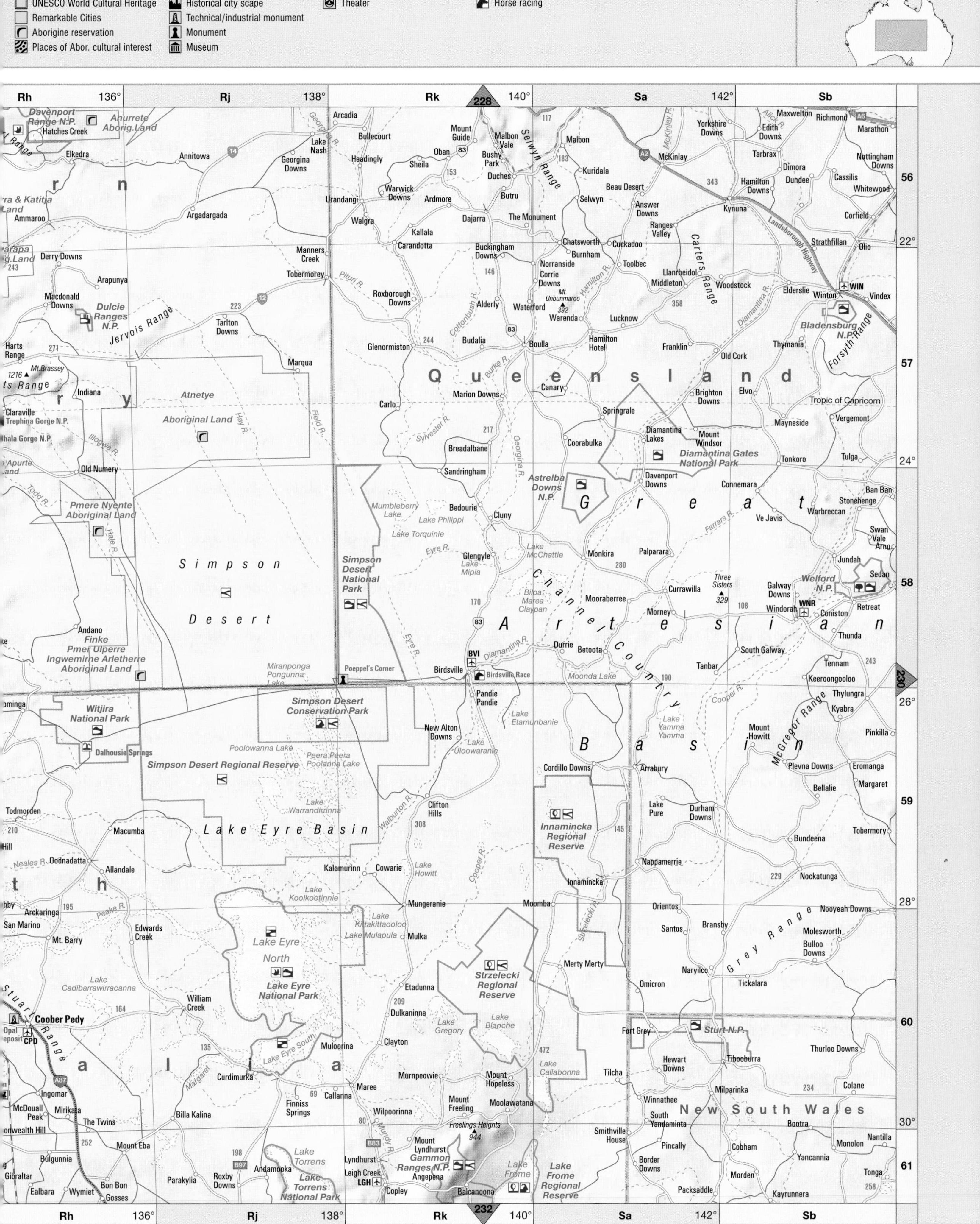
Remarkable Cities and Cultural monuments
UNESCO World Cultural Heritage
Remarkable Cities
Aborigine reservation
Places of Abor. cultural interest
Historical city scape
Technical/industrial monument
Monument
Museum
Theater
Sport and leisure destinations
Horse racing
Rh
136°
Rj
138°
Rk
228
140°
Sa
142°
Sb
232
230
56
57
58
59
60
61
22°
24°
26°
28°
30°
Queensland
Great Artesian Basin
Simpson Desert
Lake Eyre Basin
Channel Country
New South Wales
Davenport Range N.P.
Hatches Creek
Anurrete Aborig.Land
Elkedra
Annitowa
Georgina Downs
Lake Nash
Arcadia
Bullecourt
Headingly
Urandangi
Warwick Downs
Sheila
Oban
Mount Guide
Malbon Vale
Bushy Park
Duches
Butru
Selwyn Range
Malbon
Kuridala
Selwyn
Beau Desert
McKinlay
Answer Downs
Ranges Valley
Carters Range
Yorkshire Downs
Edith Downs
Alick R.
Maxwelton
Richmond
Marathon
Tarbrax
Dimora
Dundee
Hamilton Downs
Kynuna
Nottingham Downs
Cassilis
Whitewood
Corfield
Landsborough Highway
Strathfillan
Olio
Ammaroo
Argadargada
Walgra
Ardmore
Dajarra
The Monument
Kallala
Carandotta
Buckingham Downs
Chatsworth
Cuckadoo
Burnham
Norranside
Corrie Downs
Toolbec
Llanrheidol
Middleton
Woodstock
Elderslie
Winton
WIN
Vindex
Derry Downs
Manners Creek
Tobermorey
Pituri R.
Arapunya
Macdonald Downs
Dulcie Ranges N.P.
Jervois Range
Tarlton Downs
Roxborough Downs
Alderly
Waterford
Mt. Unbunmaroo
392
Warenda
Hamilton R.
Lucknow
Diamantina R.
Bladensburg N.P.
Forsyth Range
Harts Range
Mt.Brassey
1216
Marqua
Glenormiston
Budalia
Boulla
Hamilton Hotel
Franklin
Old Cork
Thymania
Indiana
Atnetye Aboriginal Land
Carlo
Marion Downs
Burke R.
Canary
Brighton Downs
Elvo
Tropic of Capricorn
Claraville
Trephina Gorge N.P.
Springrale
Mayneside
Vergemont
Hay R.
Field R.
Sylvester R.
Breadalbane
Georgina R.
Coorabulka
Diamantina Lakes
Mount Windsor
Diamantina Gates National Park
Old Numery
Sandringham
Davenport Downs
Tonkoro
Tulga
Todd R.
Pmere Nyente Aboriginal Land
Hale R.
Mumbleberry Lake
Lake Philippi
Lake Torquinie
Bedourie
Cluny
Astrelba Downs N.P.
Connemara
Farrars R.
Ve Javis
Warbreccan
Stonehenge
Ban Ban
Swan Vale
Arno
Eyre R.
Glengyle
Lake Mipia
Lake McChattie
Monkira
Palparara
Jundah
Simpson Desert National Park
Three Sisters
329
Currawilla
Galway Downs
Welford N.P.
Sedan
Bilpa Marea Claypan
Mooraberree
Morney
Windorah
WNR
Coniston
Retreat
Thunda
Andado
Finke
Pmer Ulperre Ingwemirne Arletherre Aboriginal Land
Diamantina R.
Durrie
Betoota
South Galway
Tanbar
Tennam
Keeroongooloo
Miranponga Pongunna Lake
Poeppel's Corner
Birdsville
BVI
Birdsville Race
Moonda Lake
Cooper R.
Thylungra
Kyabra
McGregor Range
Witjira National Park
Dalhousie Springs
Simpson Desert Conservation Park
Pandie Pandie
Lake Etamunbanie
Lake Yamma Yamma
Mount Howitt
Pinkilla
Poolowanna Lake
Peera Peera Poolanna Lake
Simpson Desert Regional Reserve
New Alton Downs
Lake Uloowaranie
Cordillo Downs
Arrabury
Plevna Downs
Eromanga
Margaret
Bellalie
Lake Warrandirinna
Clifton Hills
Warburton R.
Innamincka Regional Reserve
Lake Pure
Durham Downs
Todmorden
Macumba
Tobermory
Bundeena
Neales R.
Oodnadatta
Allandale
Kalamurinn
Cowarie
Lake Howitt
Nappamerrie
Innamincka
Nockatunga
Lake Koolkootinnie
Mungeranie
Moomba
Orientos
Nooyeah Downs
Arckaringa
Peake R.
Lake Kittakittaooloo
Lake Mulapula
Mulka
Strzelecki R.
Santos
Bransby
Molesworth
Bulloo Downs
Grey Range
San Marino
Edwards Creek
Mt. Barry
Lake Eyre North
Lake Eyre National Park
Strzelecki Regional Reserve
Merty Merty
Naryilco
Tickalara
Omicron
Lake Cadibarrawirracanna
Etadunna
William Creek
Stuart Range
Coober Pedy
CPD
Opal
Dulkaninna
Lake Gregory
Lake Blanche
Fort Grey
Sturt N.P.
Thurloo Downs
Lake Eyre South
Muloorina
Clayton
Hewart Downs
Tibooburra
Curdimurka
Margaret
Murnpeowie
Mount Hopeless
Lake Callabonna
Tilcha
Milparinka
Colane
Ingomar
Maree
Callanna
Finniss Springs
Mount Freeling
Moolawatana
Winnathee
McDouall Peak
Mirikata
The Twins
Billa Kalina
Wilpoorinna
Freelings Heights
944
South Yandaminta
Bootra
Smithville House
Mount Lyndhurst
Gammon Ranges N.P.
Mundy R.
Pincally
Cobham
Monolon
Nantilla
Yancannia
Mount Eba
Bulgunnia
Gibraltar
Ealbara
Wymiet
Bon Bon
Gosses
Parakylia
Roxby Downs
Andamooka
Lake Torrens
Lake Torrens National Park
Lyndhurst
Leigh Creek
LGH
Copley
Angepena
Balcanoona
Lake Frome
Lake Frome Regional Reserve
Border Downs
Morden
Packsaddle
Tonga
Kayrunnera

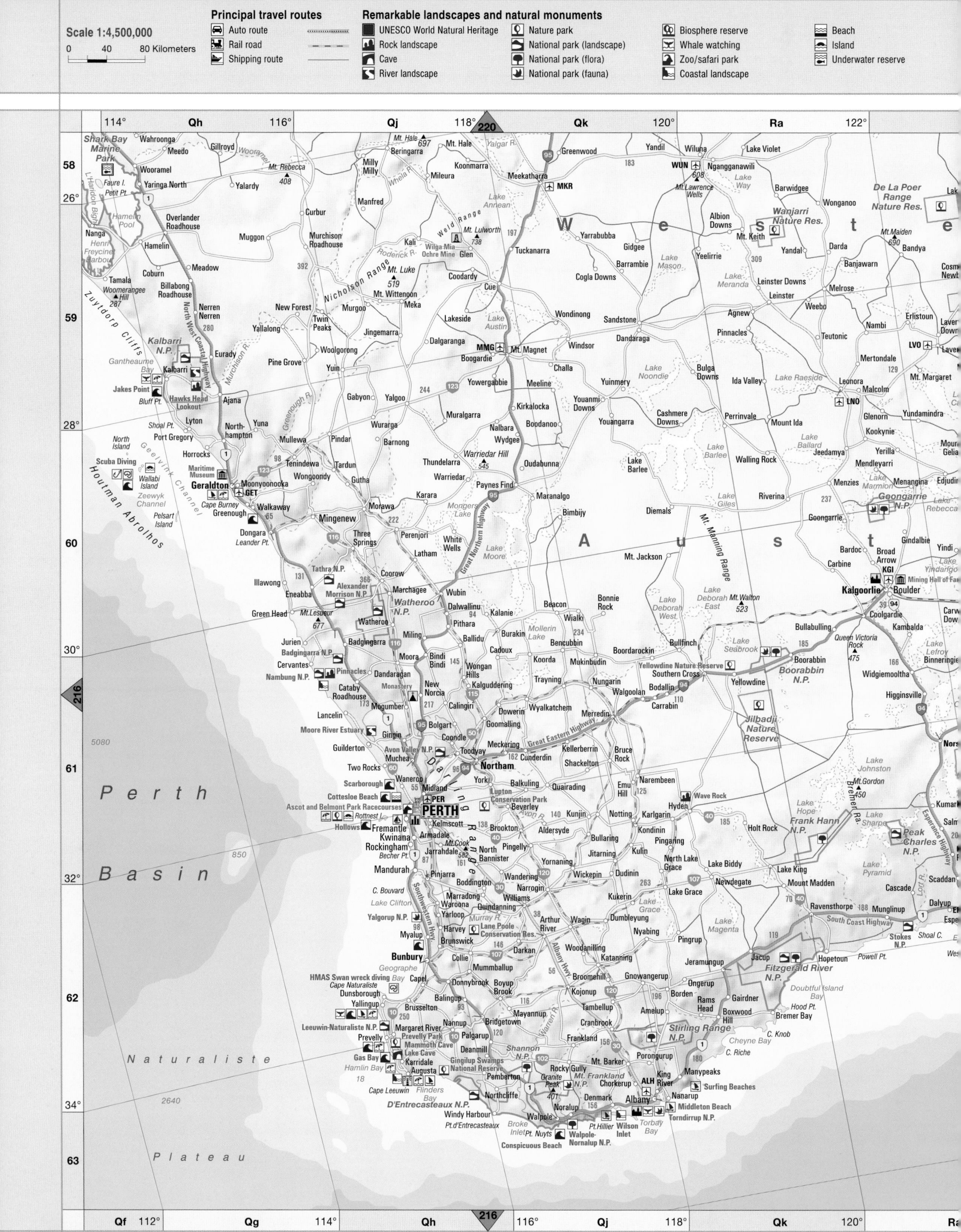
Scale 1:4,500,000
0
40
80 Kilometers
Principal travel routes
Auto route
Rail road
Shipping route
Remarkable landscapes and natural monuments
UNESCO World Natural Heritage
Rock landscape
Cave
River landscape
Nature park
National park (landscape)
National park (flora)
National park (fauna)
Biosphere reserve
Whale watching
Zoo/safari park
Coastal landscape
Beach
Island
Underwater reserve
114°
Qh
116°
Qj
118°
220
Qk
120°
Ra
122°
58
26°
59
28°
60
30°
216
61
32°
62
34°
63
Qf
112°
Qg
114°
Qh
216
116°
Qj
118°
Qk
120°
Shark Bay Marine Park
Wahroonga
Meedo
Gillroyd
Wooramel
Yaringa North
Yalardy
Mt. Rebecca
408
Mt. Hale
697
Beringarra
Mt. Hale
Milly Milly
Mileura
Koonmarra
Meekatharra
MKR
Greenwood
Yandil
Wiluna
WUN
Lake Violet
Ngangganawili
Mt. Lawrence Wells
608
Lake Way
Barwidgee
Wonganoo
De La Poer Range Nature Res.
Faure I.
Petit Pt.
Hamelin Pool
Overlander Roadhouse
Nanga
Hamelin
Curbur
Manfred
Lake Annean
Murchison Roadhouse
Muggon
Weld Range
Mt. Lulworth
738
Kali
Wilga Mia Ochre Mine
Glen
Tuckanarra
Yarrabubba
Gidgee
Lake Mason
Albion Downs
Wanjarri Nature Res.
Mt. Keith
Yeelirrie
Yandal
Darda
Mt. Maiden
690
Bandya
Banjawarn
Coburn
Meadow
Tamala
Woomerangee Hill
287
Billabong Roadhouse
Roderick R.
Mt. Luke
519
Mt. Wittenoon
Coodardy
Barrambie
Cogla Downs
Lake Meranda
Leinster Downs
Leinster
Melrose
Zuytdorp Cliffs
Nerren Nerren
280
New Forest
Nicholson Range
Murgoo
Meka
Cue
Twin Peaks
Lakeside
Lake Austin
Wondinong
Sandstone
Agnew
Weebo
Erlistoun
Kalbarri N.P.
Yallalong
Jingemarra
Dalgaranga
Dandaraga
Pinnacles
Nambi
Teutonic
Gantheaume Bay
Kalbarri
Eurady
Woolgorong
MMG
Mt. Magnet
Boogardie
Windsor
Challa
Pine Grove
Yuin
Lake Noondie
Bulga Downs
Ida Valley
Lake Raeside
Leonora
Mertondale
LVO
Jakes Point
Bluff Pt.
Hawks Head Lookout
Ajana
Gabyon
Yalgoo
Yowergabbie
Meeline
Yuinmery
LNO
Malcolm
Mt. Margaret
Shoal Pt.
Port Gregory
Lyton
Northampton
Yuna
Mullewa
Pindar
Wurarga
Muralgarra
Nalbara
Wydgee
Kirkalocka
Youanmi Downs
Boodanoo
Youangarra
Cashmere Downs
Perrinvale
Mount Ida
Glenorn
Yundamindra
North Island
Horrocks
Barnong
Lake Ballard
Jeedamya
Kookynie
Yerilla
Scuba Diving
Wallabi Island
Maritime Museum
Geraldton
Moonyoonooka
GET
Tenindewa
Wongoondy
Tardun
Thundelarra
Warriedar Hill
545
Warriedar
Oudabunna
Lake Barlee
Walling Rock
Mendleyarri
Houtman Abrolhos
Geelvink Channel
Zeewyk Channel
Pelsart Island
Cape Burney
Greenough
Walkaway
Gutha
Paynes Find
Menzies
Lake Marmion
Menangina
Karara
Maranalgo
Lake Giles
Riverina
Goongarrie N.P.
Mingenew
Morawa
Mongers Lake
Bimbijy
Diemals
Goongarrie
Dongara
Leander Pt.
Three Springs
Perenjori
White Wells
Lake Moore
Great Northern Highway
Mt. Manning Range
Gindalbie
Bardoc
Broad Arrow
Carbine
KGI
Mining Hall of Fame
Latham
Mt. Jackson
Tathra N.P.
Coorow
Alexander Morrison N.P.
Illawong
Eneabba
Marchagee
Watheroo N.P.
Wubin
Dalwallinu
Beacon
Bonnie Rock
Lake Deborah West
Lake Deborah East
Mt. Walton
523
Kalgoorlie
Boulder
Coolgardie
Green Head
Mt. Lesueur
677
Watheroo
Kalanie
Pithara
Wialki
Mollerin Lake
Burakin
Bullabulling
Kambalda
Jurien
Badgingarra N.P.
Badgingarra
Miling
Ballidu
Cadoux
Bencubbin
Boordarockin
Bullfinch
Lake Seabrook
Queen Victoria Rock
475
Lake Lefroy
Binneringie
Cervantes
Nambung N.P.
Pinnacles
Dandaragan
Moora
Bindi Bindi
Wongan Hills
Koorda
Mukinbudin
Yellowdine Nature Reserve
Southern Cross
Boorabbin
Boorabbin N.P.
Yellowdine
Widgiemooltha
Cataby Roadhouse
Monastery
New Norcia
Kalguddering
Trayning
Nungarin
Walgoolan
Bodallin
Carrabin
Higginsville
Lancelin
Mogumber
Calingiri
Dowerin
Wyalkatchem
Merredin
Jilbadji Nature Reserve
Moore River Estuary
Gingin
Bolgart
Goomalling
Coondle
Guilderton
Avon Valley N.P.
Toodyay
Meckering
Great Eastern Highway
Kellerberrin
Bruce Rock
Two Rocks
Muchea
Northam
Cunderdin
Shackelton
Lake Johnston
Darling Range
Perth Basin
Scarborough
Wanero
Midland
York
Balkuling
Quairading
Emu Hill
Narembeen
Wave Rock
Mt. Gordon
450
Bremer Ra.
Cottesloe Beach
PER
PERTH
Lupton Conservation Park
Beverley
Ascot and Belmont Park Racecourses
Rottnest I.
Hollows
Fremantle
Kelmscott
Kwinana
Armadale
Brookton
Kunjin
Notting
Karlgarin
Hyden
Lake Hope
Frank Hann N.P.
Holt Rock
Lake Sharpe
Peak Charles N.P.
Esperance Highway
Rockingham
Becher Pt.
Mt. Cook
Jarrahdale
North Bannister
Pingelly
Aldersyde
Bullaring
Kondinin
Pingaring
Mandurah
Pinjarra
Yornaning
Jitarning
Kulin
North Lake Grace
Lake Biddy
Lake King
Mount Madden
Lake Pyramid
Scaddan
C. Bouvard
Lake Clifton
Boddington
Wandering
Wickepin
Dudinin
Newdegate
Marradong
Waroona
Narrogin
Williams
Kukerin
Lake Grace
Cascade
Yalgorup N.P.
Yarloop
Quindanning
Lake Grace
Ravensthorpe
Munglinup
Dalyup
Harvey
Murray R.
Lane Poole Conservation Res.
Arthur River
Wagin
Dumbleyung
Lake Magenta
South Coast Highway
Stokes N.P.
Shoal C.
Myalup
Brunswick
Nyabing
Pingrup
Bunbury
Collie
Darkan
Woodanilling
Katanning
Jeramungup
Jacup
Hopetoun
Powell Pt.
Geographe Bay
Capel
Mumballup
Broomehill
Gnowangerup
Fitzgerald River N.P.
HMAS Swan wreck diving
Cape Naturaliste
Dunsborough
Donnybrook
Boyup Brook
Kojonup
Ongerup
Borden
Rams Head
Gairdner
Doubtful Island Bay
Yallingup
Balingup
Tambellup
Amelup
Boxwood Hill
Hood Pt.
Bremer Bay
Busselton
Mayannup
Leeuwin-Naturaliste N.P.
Margaret River
Prevelly Park
Nannup
Bridgetown
Cranbrook
Stirling Range N.P.
C. Knob
Prevelly
Mammoth Cave
Palgarup
Frankland
Cheyne Bay
C. Riche
Gas Bay
Lake Cave
Karridale
Deanmill
Shannon N.P.
Mt. Barker
Porongurup
Naturaliste Plateau
Hamlin Bay
Augusta
Gingilup Swamps National Reserve
Pemberton
Granite Peak
401
Rocky Gully
Mt. Frankland N.P.
Chorkerup
ALH
King River
Manypeaks
Cape Leeuwin
Flinders Bay
Northcliffe
Surfing Beaches
Nanarup
D'Entrecasteaux N.P.
Denmark
Albany
Middleton Beach
Windy Harbour
Walpole
Noralup
Torndirrup N.P.
Pt. d'Entrecasteaux
Broke Inlet
Pt. Nuyts
Pt. Hillier
Wilson Inlet
Torbay Bay
Walpole-Nornalup N.P.
Conspicuous Beach
Western Australia
5080
850
2640

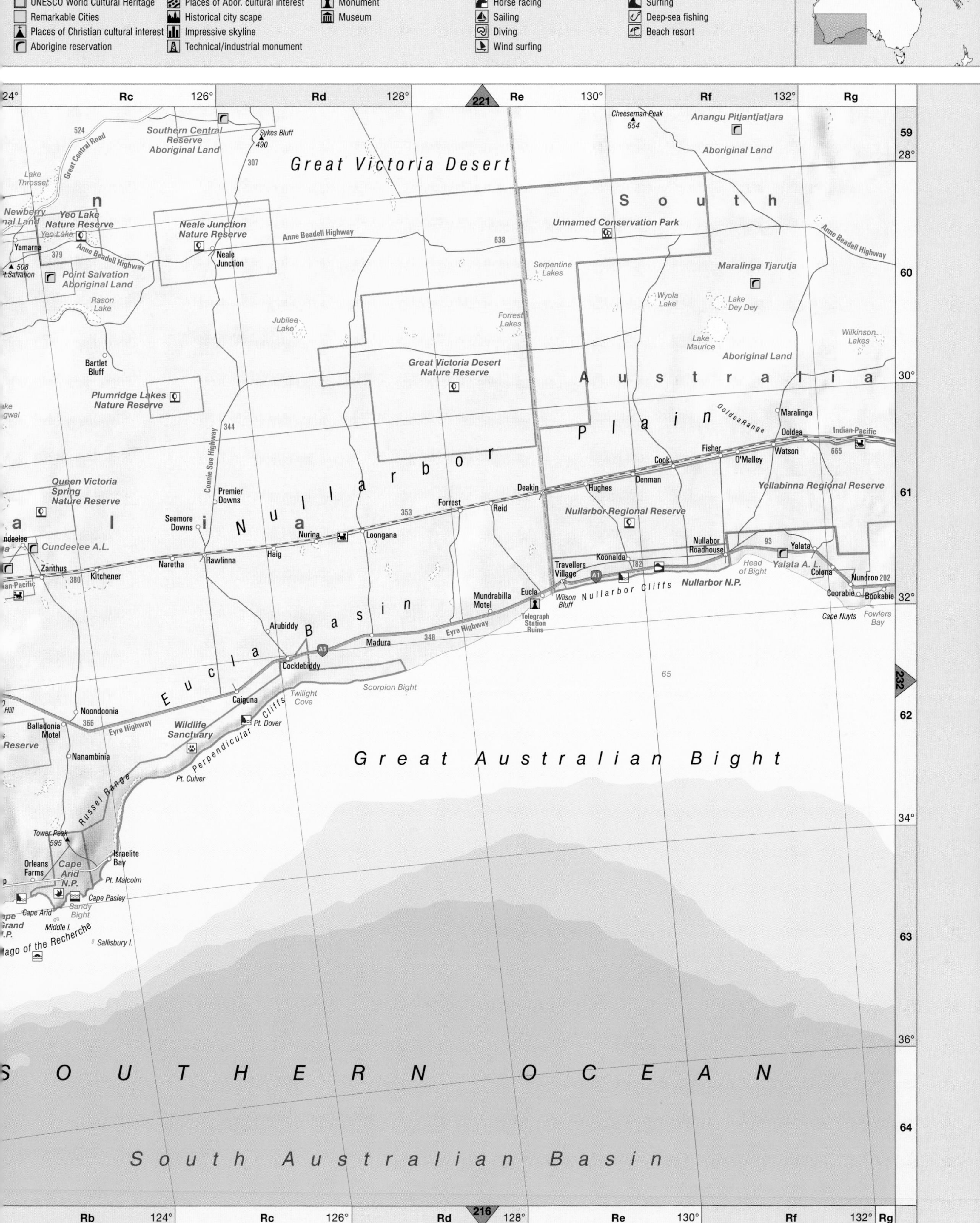

Remarkable Cities and Cultural monuments
UNESCO World Cultural Heritage
Remarkable Cities
Places of Christian cultural interest
Aborigine reservation
Places of Abor. cultural interest
Historical city scape
Impressive skyline
Technical/industrial monument
Monument
Museum
Sport and leisure destinations
Horse racing
Sailing
Diving
Wind surfing
Surfing
Deep-sea fishing
Beach resort
Rc
126°
Rd
128°
221
Re
130°
Rf
132°
Rg
59
28°
60
30°
61
32°
62
34°
63
36°
64
Great Victoria Desert
Southern Central Reserve Aboriginal Land
Sykes Bluff
490
Great Central Road
Lake Throssel
Newberry
Yeo Lake Nature Reserve
Yamarna
Pt.Salvation
Point Salvation Aboriginal Land
Rason Lake
Neale Junction Nature Reserve
Neale Junction
Anne Beadell Highway
Cheeseman Peak
654
Anangu Pitjantjatjara
Aboriginal Land
South
Unnamed Conservation Park
Serpentine Lakes
Maralinga Tjarutja
Wyola Lake
Lake Dey Dey
Lake Maurice
Aboriginal Land
Wilkinson Lakes
Jubilee Lake
Forrest Lakes
Great Victoria Desert Nature Reserve
Bartlet Bluff
Plumridge Lakes Nature Reserve
Connie Sue Highway
Premier Downs
Queen Victoria Spring Nature Reserve
Seemore Downs
Australia
Nullarbor Plain
Ooldea Range
Maralinga
Ooldea
Indian-Pacific
Watson
O'Malley
Fisher
Cook
Denman
Hughes
Deakin
Forrest
Reid
Yellabinna Regional Reserve
Nullarbor Regional Reserve
Nurina
Loongana
Haig
Rawlinna
Naretha
Cundeelee A.L.
Zanthus
Kitchener
Nullabor Roadhouse
Koonalda
Travellers Village
Yalata
Yalata A. L.
Colona
Head of Bight
Nullarbor N.P.
Nundroo
Coorabie
Bookabie
Cape Nuyts
Fowlers Bay
Eucla
Wilson Bluff
Nullarbor Cliffs
Telegraph Station Ruins
Mundrabilla Motel
Eyre Highway
Madura
Arubiddy
Eucla Basin
Cocklebiddy
Scorpion Bight
Caiguna
Twilight Cove
Noondoonia
Balladonia Motel
Nanambinia
Wildlife Sanctuary
Pt. Dover
Perpendicular Cliffs
Pt. Culver
Russel Range
Great Australian Bight
Tower Peak
595
Israelite Bay
Orleans Farms
Cape Arid N.P.
Pt. Malcolm
Cape Pasley
Cape Arid
Sandy Bight
Middle I.
Sallisbury I.
Archipelago of the Recherche
232
SOUTHERN OCEAN
South Australian Basin
Rb
124°
Rc
126°
Rd
216
128°
Re
130°
Rf
132°
Rg

Scale 1:4,500,000
0 40 80 Kilometers
Principal travel routes
Auto route
Rail road
Shipping route
Remarkable landscapes and natural monuments
UNESCO World Natural Heritage
River landscape
Waterfall/rapids
Nature park
National park (landscape)
National park (flora)
National park (fauna)
Coastal landscape
Beach
Coral reef
Island
Underwater reserve
Rh
136°
Rj
138°
240
Rk
140°
Sa
142°
49
8°
50
10°
51
12°
219
52
14°
53
16°
54
228
Arafura Sea
Arafura Shelf
INDONESIA
P. Dolak
Kiworo
Kimaan
Yawimu
Okaba
Wamal
Welab
Kladar
Tg. Vals
P.Komoran
Mombum
Tg. Cool
Kurik
Sarore
Kumbe
Merauke
MKQ
Kembapi
Tamarike
Daub
Yangga
Wasur National Park
Sakiramke
Suki
Goe
Kaniya
Kenalia
Kiriwa
Weam
Morehead
Dimissi
Buk
Malam
Wipim
Arufi
Wando
Tonda
Mari
Bula
Sibidiri
Togo
Talbot I.
Buru I.
SBR
Saibai I.
Torres Strait
Orman Reef
Gabba I.
Zagai I.
Mabuiag I.
Badu I.
Sassie I.
Moa I.
Hammond I.
Wednesday I.
Horn I.
Thursday Island
Prince of Wales I.
Cape York
Somerset
Bamaga
Newcastle Bay
ABM
Endeavour Strait
Slade Point
Cowal Creek
Mapoon Aboriginal Land
Jardine R.
Port Musgrave
Mapoon
Cape York Peninsula
Bramwell
Moreton
Andoom
Weipa
WEI
Weipa South
Duyfken Point
Albatross Bay
Batavia Downs
Thud Point
Merluna
Archer Bay
Aurukun
Archer Bend N.P.
Archer River Roadhouse
Rokeby
Peret
Kendall River
Merapah
Aurukun Aboriginal Land
Ti Tree
Cape Keer-weer
Edward River
Strathgordon
Kowanyama Aboriginal Land
Pormpuraaw
Strathmay
Kowanyama
Mitchell and Alice Rivers N.P.
Rutland Plains
Koolatah
Dunbar
Inkerman
Galbraith
Macaroni
Staaten River N.P.
Vanrook
Delta Downs
Stirling
Miranda Downs
Karumba
Maggieville
Gulf of Carpentaria
AUSTRALIA
Cape Wessel
Wessel Islands
Marchinbar I.
Raragala I.
Drysdale I.
Culuwuru I.
Truant I.
Elcho I.
Bromby Is.
Cape Wilberforce
Mooroongga I.
Galiwinku
ELC
Cunningham Is.
The English Company's Is.
Melville Bay
Bremer I.
Castlereagh Bay
Buckingham Bay
Nhulunbuy
Yirrkala
Cape Arnhem
Milingimbi
Ramingining
Arnhem Bay
Gove Pen.
Gapuwiyak
Port Bradshaw
Garrthalala
Pt. Alexander
Caledon Bay
Cape Grey
Glyde R.
Parsons Range
Point Arrowsmith
Cape Shield
Blue Mud Bay
Isle Woodah
Arnhem Land Aboriginal Reserve
Winchelsea Is.
Port Langdon
North East Is.
Alyangula
Umbakumba
Bickerton Island
Angurugu
Groote Eylandt
Tasman Pt.
Cape Beatrice
Groote Eylandt Aborig. Land
Numbulwar
NUB
Rose R.
Ngukurr
Roper R.
Limmen Bay
Maria Island
Marra Aborig. Land
Limmen Bight R.
Sir Edward Pellew Group
Nathan River
West I.
North I.
Wurralibi A.L.
Centre I.
Vanderlin I.
Bing Bong
Narwinbi Aborig.Res.
King Ash Bay
Port McArthur
Alawa Aboriginal Land
Cox R.
Billengarrah
Borroloola
Manangoora
Northern Territory
Bouhenia Downs
Tawallah
McArthur R.
Seven Emu
Garawa Aborig. Land
O.T.Downs
Cape Crawford Roadhouse
Pungalina
Robinson River
Calvert R.
Wampaya Aborig.Res.
Calvert Hills
Wollogorang
Westmoreland
Mornington Is. Aborig. Land Trust
Mornington I.
Gununa
Cape van Diemen
Denham I.
Forsyth I.
Bountiful Is.
Wellesley Islands
Allen I.
Bentinck I.
Sweers I.
Nicholson River Delta
Queensland

Remarkable Cities and Cultural monuments
UNESCO World Cultural Heritage
Museum
Remarkable Cities
Aborigine reservation
Places of Abor. cultural interest
Sport and leisure destinations
Sailing
Diving
Wind surfing
Canoeing/rafting
Deep-sea fishing
Beach resort
PAPUA NEW GUINEA
Gulf of Papua
Solomon Sea
Owen Stanley Range
Port Moresby
National Museum
Loloata Resort
Trobriand Islands
d'Entrecasteaux Islands
Goschen Strait
Ward Hunt Strait
Great Barrier Reef
Great Barrier Reef Marine Park
Coral Sea
Coral Basin
Coral Sea Island Territory
Osprey Reef
Bougainville Reef
Holmes Reefs
Willis Group
Magdelaine Cays
Heralds Cays
Coringa Islets
Cooktown
James Cook Museum
Quinkan and Regional Cultural Centre
Lakefield N.P.
Cedar Bay N.P.
Wet Tropics
Daintree N.P.
Port Douglas
Cairns
Tjapukai Aboriginal Cultural Centre
Atherton Tableland
Bellenden Ker N.P.
of Queensland

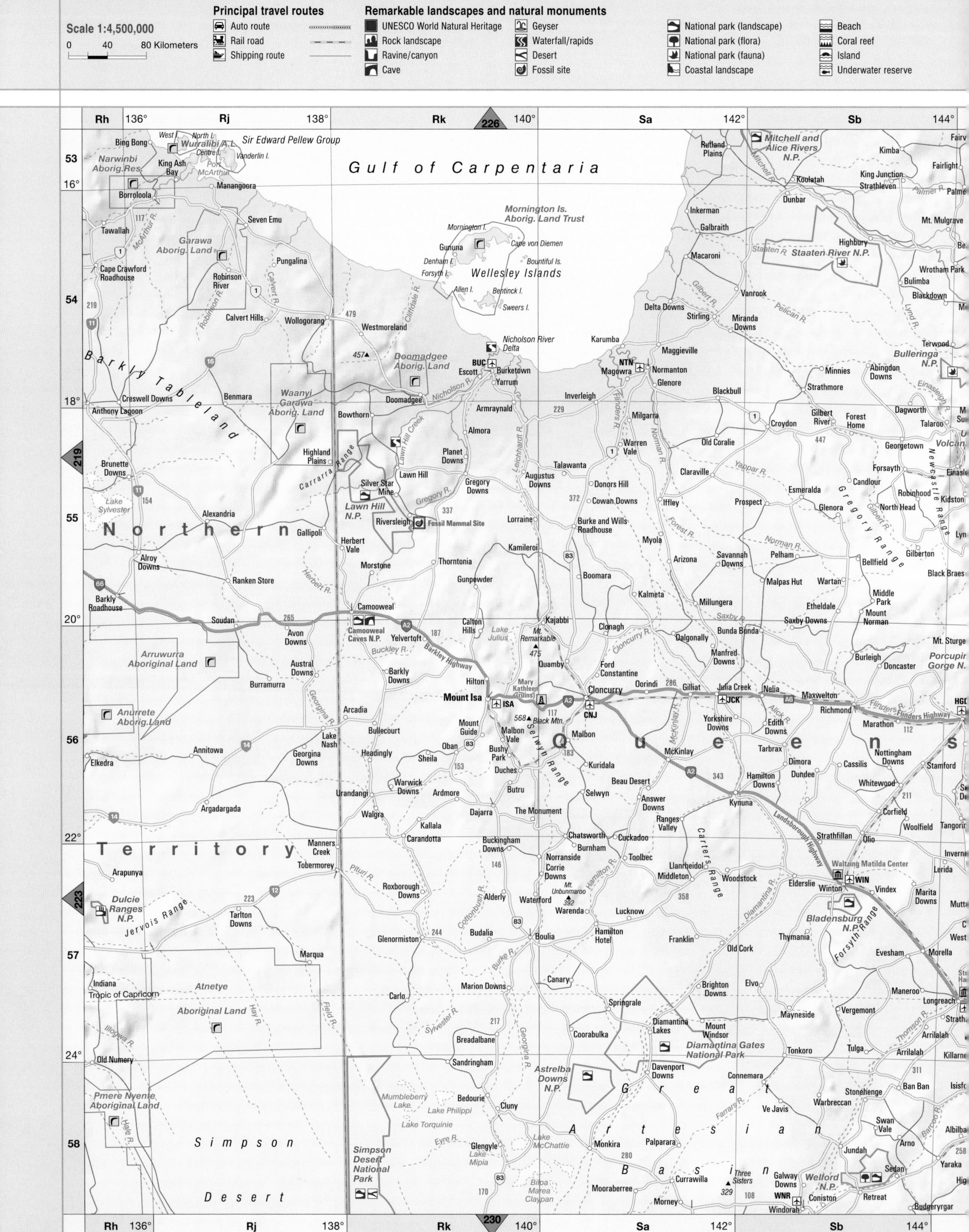

Scale 1:4,500,000
0 40 80 Kilometers
Principal travel routes
Auto route
Rail road
Shipping route
Remarkable landscapes and natural monuments
UNESCO World Natural Heritage
Rock landscape
Ravine/canyon
Cave
Geyser
Waterfall/rapids
Desert
Fossil site
National park (landscape)
National park (flora)
National park (fauna)
Coastal landscape
Beach
Coral reef
Island
Underwater reserve
Rh 136° Rj 138° Rk 226 140° Sa 142° Sb 144°
53
16°
54
18°
55
20°
56
22°
57
24°
58
219
223
Sir Edward Pellew Group
Gulf of Carpentaria
West I.
North I.
Wurralibi A.L.
Centre I.
Vanderlin I.
Bing Bong
Narwinbi Aborig. Res.
King Ash Bay
Port McArthur
Borroloola
Manangoora
Seven Emu
Tawallah
McArthur R.
Garawa Aborig. Land
Pungalina
Cape Crawford Roadhouse
Robinson River
Calvert R.
Robinson R.
Calvert Hills
Wollogorang
Westmoreland
Cliffdale R.
Barkly Tableland
Creswell Downs
Anthony Lagoon
Benmara
Waanyi Garawa Aborig. Land
Doomadgee Aborig. Land
Doomadgee
Nicholson R.
Bowthorn
Highland Plains
Carrarra Range
Lawn Hill Creek
Lawn Hill
Silver Star Mine
Lawn Hill N.P.
Riversleigh
Fossil Mammal Site
Gregory R.
Gregory Downs
Planet Downs
Almora
Armraynald
Brunette Downs
Lake Sylvester
Alexandria
Northern Territory
Gallipoli
Herbert Vale
Morstone
Alroy Downs
Ranken Store
Herbert R.
Barkly Roadhouse
Soudan
Camooweal
Camooweal Caves N.P.
Avon Downs
Yelvertoft
Buckley R.
Barkly Highway
Barkly Downs
Arruwurra Aboriginal Land
Austral Downs
Burramurra
Anurrete Aborig. Land
Georgina R.
Arcadia
Lake Nash
Bullecourt
Annitowa
Georgina Downs
Elkedra
Headingly
Argadargada
Urandangi
Walgra
Manners Creek
Tobermorey
Arapunya
Dulcie Ranges N.P.
Jervois Range
Tarlton Downs
Marqua
Indiana
Tropic of Capricorn
Atnetye Aboriginal Land
Hay R.
Field R.
Illogwa R.
Old Numery
Pmere Nyente Aboriginal Land
Hale R.
Simpson Desert
Mornington Is. Aborig. Land Trust
Mornington I.
Gununa
Cape von Diemen
Denham I.
Forsyth I.
Bountiful Is.
Wellesley Islands
Allen I.
Bentinck I.
Sweers I.
Nicholson River Delta
BUC
Escott
Burketown
Yarrum
457
Leichhardt R.
Augustus Downs
Talawanta
Lorraine
Kamileroi
Thorntonia
Gunpowder
Calton Hills
Lake Julius
Mt. Remarkable 475
Kajabbi
Quamby
Hilton
Mary Kathleen (ruins)
Mount Isa
ISA
568 Black Mtn.
Selwyn Range
Mount Guide
Malbon Vale
Oban
Sheila
Bushy Park
Duches
Warwick Downs
Ardmore
Butru
Dajarra
The Monument
Kallala
Carandotta
Buckingham Downs
Pituri R.
Roxborough Downs
Cottonbush R.
Alderly
Waterford
Glenormiston
Budalia
Boulia
Burke R.
Carlo
Marion Downs
Canary
Sylvester R.
Breadalbane
Georgina R.
Sandringham
Astrelba Downs N.P.
Mumbleberry Lake
Lake Philippi
Lake Torquinie
Bedourie
Cluny
Eyre R.
Glengyle
Lake Mipia
Lake McChattie
Simpson Desert National Park
Bilpa Marea Claypan
Karumba
Gilbert R.
Delta Downs
Stirling
Miranda Downs
Maggieville
NTN
Magowra
Normanton
Glenore
Inverleigh
Flinders R.
Milgarra
Norman R.
Blackbull
Croydon
Warren Vale
Old Coralie
Claraville
Donors Hill
Cowan Downs
Burke and Wills Roadhouse
Iffley
Myola
Forest R.
Arizona
Savannah Downs
Boomara
Kalmeta
Millungera
Clonagh
Cloncurry R.
Ford Constantine
Cloncurry
CNJ
Oorindi
Gilliat
Julia Creek
JCK
Nelia
Malbon
McKinlay R.
McKinlay
Kuridala
Beau Desert
Selwyn
Answer Downs
Ranges Valley
Carters Range
Chatsworth
Cuckadoo
Burnham
Norranside
Corrie Downs
Toolbec
Hamilton R.
Mt. Unbunmaroo 392
Warenda
Lucknow
Hamilton Hotel
Llanrheidol
Middleton
Woodstock
Diamantina R.
Franklin
Old Cork
Brighton Downs
Springvale
Coorabulka
Diamantina Lakes
Mount Windsor
Diamantina Gates National Park
Davenport Downs
Great Artesian Basin
Monkira
Palparara
Currawilla
Mooraberree
Morney
Three Sisters 329
Rutland Plains
Mitchell and Alice Rivers N.P.
Mitchell R.
Koolatah
Dunbar
Inkerman
Galbraith
Macaroni
Staaten R.
Staaten River N.P.
Vanrook
Pelican R.
Highbury
Kimba
Fairlight
King Junction
Strathleven
Palmer R.
Mt. Mulgrave
Wrotham Park
Bulimba
Blackdown
Lynd R.
Terwood
Bulleringa N.P.
Minnies
Abingdon Downs
Strathmore
Einasleigh R.
Gilbert River
Forest Home
Dagworth
Talaroo
Georgetown
Forsayth
Newcastle Range
Candlour
Esmeralda
Robinhood
Kidston
Glenora
North Head
Gregory Range
Prospect
Yappar R.
Norman R.
Pelham
Gilberton
Bellfield
Black Braes
Malpas Hut
Wartan
Middle Park
Etheldale
Mount Norman
Saxby R.
Saxby Downs
Bunda Bunda
Dalgonally
Manfred Downs
Mt. Sturgeon
Burleigh
Doncaster
Porcupine Gorge N.P.
Maxwelton
Richmond
Flinders R.
Flinders Highway
Marathon
Alick R.
Edith Downs
Yorkshire Downs
Tarbrax
Nottingham Downs
Stamford
Dimora
Dundee
Cassilis
Hamilton Downs
Whitewood
Kynuna
Landsborough Highway
Corfield
Woolfield
Tangorin
Strathfillan
Olio
Waltzing Matilda Center
WIN
Elderslie
Winton
Vindex
Marita Downs
Bladensburg N.P.
Forsyth Range
Thymania
Evesham
Morella
Elvo
Maneroo
Longreach
Vergemont
Mayneside
Thomson R.
Arrilalah
Tonkoro
Tulga
Connemara
Farrars R.
Ve Jarvis
Stonehenge
Warbreccan
Ban Ban
Swan Vale
Barcoo R.
Arno
Jundah
Galway Downs
Welford N.P.
WNR
Windorah
Coniston
Sedan
Retreat
Yaraka
Budgerygrar
Rh 136° Rj 138° Rk 230 140° Sa 142° Sb 144°

Remarkable Cities and Cultural monuments
UNESCO World Cultural Heritage
Remarkable Cities
Aborigine reservation
Places of Abor. cultural interest
Historical city scape
Technical/industrial monument
Monument
Museum
Theater
Sport and leisure destinations
Sailing
Diving
Wind surfing
Canoeing/rafting
Deep-sea fishing
Beach resort
Sc
146°
Sd
148°
Se
227
150°
Sf
152°
Sg
154°
231
217
53
54
55
56
57
58
16°
18°
20°
22°
24°
Coral Sea
Islands Territory
Great Barrier Reef
Great Barrier Reef Marine Park
Tropic of Capricorn
Cooktown
James Cook Museum
Cedar Bay N.P.
Bloomfield River
Daintree N.P.
Cape Tribulation
Cape Kimberly
Trinity Bay
Port Douglas
Mossman
Mount Molloy
Palm Cove
Yorkeys Knob
Tjapukai Aboriginal Cultural Centre
Cairns
Cape Grafton
Fitzroy I.
Kuranda
Mareeba
Edmonton
Gordonvale
Atherton
Yungaburra
Belleden Ker
Bellenden Ker N.P.
Babinda
Malanda
Herberton
Millaa Millaa
Innisfail
Ravenshoe
Johnstone
Silkwood
Atherton Tableland
Koombooloomba
Mission Beach
Dunk I.
Tully
Wet Tropics
Rockingham Bay
Kennedy
Goold I.
Cape Sandwich
Girringun N.P.
Cardwell
Hinchinbrook I. N.P.
Hinchinbrook I.
Abergowrie
Wallaman Falls
Oak Hills
Halifax
Ingham
Trebonne
Orpheus I.
Palm Islands
Great Palm I.
Toobanna
Bambaroo
Halifax Bay
Mutarnee
Rollingstone
Magnetic I. N.P.
Magnetic I.
Toomula
Hidden Valley
Bluewater
Cape Cleveland
Museum of Tropical Queensland
Bowling Green Bay
Townsville
Mt. Elliot
Giru
Bowling Green Bay N.P.
Dotswood
Woodstock
Clarke River
Maryvale
Bluff Downs
Great Basalt Wall N.P.
Eumara Springs
Fanning River
Ayr
Inkerman
Cape Upstart
Cape Upstart N.P.
Abbot Bay
Clare
Mingela
Charters Towers
Gumlu
Guthalungra
Mt. Abbot
Bowen
Gloucester I.
Ravenswood
Millaroo
Mt. Stewart
Balfes Creek
Homestead
Powlathanga
Brookeville
Dalberg
Clark Range
Binbee
Airlie
Shute Harbour
Hook I.
Whitsunday
Whitsunday Is. N.P.
Whitsunday I.
Whitsunday Passage
Hamilton I.
Whitsunday Group
Proserpine
Conway
Conway N.P.
Lindeman Group
Lindeman Is. N.P.
Strathmore
Wambiana
Pentland
Lake Dalrymple
Campaspe
Harvest Home
Collinsville
Leichhardt Range
Bowen R.
Repulse Bay
Sir J. Smith Group
Bloomsbury
Cumberland Is.
Torrens Creek
Longton
Mt. Elsie
Havilah
Eungella N.P.
Mt. Dalrymple
Seaforth
Scawfell I.
St. Bees Is.
Oxenhope
Natal Downs
Hidden Valley
Finch Hatton
Eungella
Marian
Bucasia
Mackay
Mirani
Walkerston
Bakers Creek
Hay Point
Prudhoe I.
Ulva
Mirtna
Yarrowmere
Mount Douglas
Mount Coolon
Glenden
Homevale N.P.
Sarina
Northumberland Is.
Cape Palmerston
Aberfoyle
Elphinstone
Colston Park
Koumala
Ilbilbie
Middle I.
Percy Is.
South I.
Swain Reefs
Carmichael
Moray Downs
Disney
Avon Downs
Riverside
Goonyella Mine
Nebo
Carmila
Doongmabulla
Coppabella
Deveril
Duke Is.
Long I.
Broad Sound Channel
Arthur Pt.
Shuttleworth
Frankfield
Collaroy
Clairview
Broad Sound
The Alps
St. Lawrence
Shoal Water Bay
Townshend I.
Saumarez Reefs
Adelong
Lou Lou Park
Epping Forest
Cumberland Downs
Batheaston
Eastmere
Laglan
Monteagle
Dysart
Broadsound Range
Merino Downs
Clare
Rangers Valley
Dunrobin
Albro
Belyando R.
Blair Athol
Gilberts Dome
May Downs
Ogmore
Double Mtn.
Cape Clinton
Cape Manifold
Clermont
German Creek
Junee
Marlborough
Byfield
Byfield N.P.
Oaky Creek
Rosedale
Surbiton
Capella
Tierir
Mt. Etna Caves N.P.
Yeppoon
Keppel Bay Is. N.P.
Great Keppel I.
Richmond Hill
Carfield
Florence Vale
Tressillian
Fairhill
Leura
Yaamba
The Caves
Fitzroy R.
Tree of Knowledge
Rubyvale
Mackenzie R.
Dreamtime Cultural Centre
Emu Park
Heron Island
Jericho
Mt. Tabletop
Emerald
Blackwater
Bluff
Rockhampton
Keppel Sands
Keppel Bay
Wistari Reef
Alice R.
Capricorn Hwy.
Alpha
Bogantungan
Anakie
Comet
Gindie
Stanwell
Gracemere
Westwood
Cape Capricorn
Summerdell
Fairbairn Reservoir
Kinrola
Dingo
Duaringa
Gogango
Mount Morgan
Port Alma
Bajool
Curtis I.
Yalleroi
Durandella
Laleham
Blackdown Tableland N.P.
Wowan
Dululu
Mount Larcom
Gladstone
Port Curtis
Tannum Sands
Elsie Hills
Drummond Range
Springsure
Woorabinda
Rannes
Mt. Alma
Calliope
Bustard Head
Blackall
Mantuan Downs
Nandowrie
Baralba
Eurimbula N.P.
Agnes Waters
Birkenhead
Castlevale
Rolleston
Expedition Range
Bauhinia Downs
Banana
Banana Range
Callide
Biloela
Dawes Range
Miriam Vale
Killarney Park
Carnarvon N.P.
Moura
Thangool
Bruce Highway
Landsborough Highway
Tambo
Carwell
Carnarvon
Cathedral Cave
Warrinilla
Mt. Nicholson
Palmgrove N.P.
Watalgan
Handsworth
Wyseby
Coorada
Theodore
Cracow
Monto
Yandaran
Moore Park
Burnett Heads
Sandy Cape
Minnie Downs
Babbilora
Aboriginal Rock Art
Camboon
Mulgildie
Lake Monduran
Bundaberg
Hervey Bay
Fraser Island
Great Sandy N.P.
Great Dividing Range
Bougainville Reef
Holmes Reefs
Willis Group
Magdelaine Cays
Herald Cays
Coringa Islets
Flinders Reefs
Tregrosse Islets
Lihou Reefs and Cays
Marion Reefs

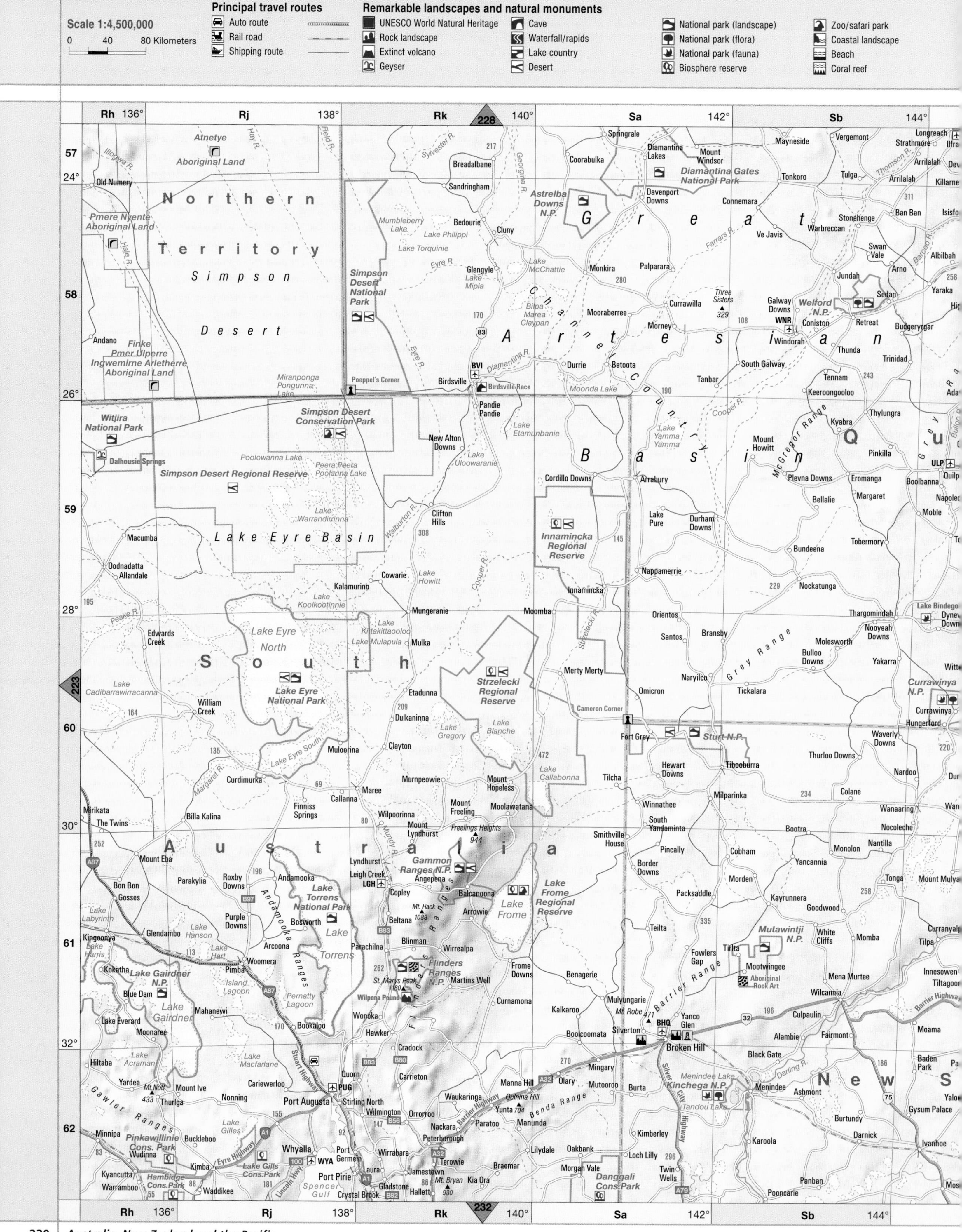
Scale 1:4,500,000
0 40 80 Kilometers
Principal travel routes
Auto route
Rail road
Shipping route
Remarkable landscapes and natural monuments
UNESCO World Natural Heritage
Rock landscape
Extinct volcano
Geyser
Cave
Waterfall/rapids
Lake country
Desert
National park (landscape)
National park (flora)
National park (fauna)
Biosphere reserve
Zoo/safari park
Coastal landscape
Beach
Coral reef
Rh 136° Rj 138° Rk 228 140° Sa 142° Sb 144°
57 58 59 60 61 62
24° 26° 28° 30° 32°
Northern Territory
Simpson Desert
Atnetye Aboriginal Land
Pmere Nyente Aboriginal Land
Finke Pmer Ulperre Ingwemirne Arletherre Aboriginal Land
Simpson Desert National Park
Simpson Desert Conservation Park
Witjira National Park
Dalhousie Springs
Simpson Desert Regional Reserve
Lake Eyre Basin
Great Artesian Basin
Channel Country
Astrebla Downs N.P.
Diamantina Gates National Park
Welford N.P.
Innamincka Regional Reserve
Strzelecki Regional Reserve
Sturt N.P.
Lake Eyre North
Lake Eyre National Park
South Australia
Gammon Ranges N.P.
Lake Torrens National Park
Lake Frome Regional Reserve
Flinders Ranges N.P.
Lake Gairdner N.P.
Mutawintji N.P.
Kinchega N.P.
Currawinya N.P.
Pinkawillinie Cons. Park
Lake Gilles Cons. Park
Hambidge Cons. Park
Danggali Cons. Park
Birdsville
Poeppel's Corner
Innamincka
Moomba
Cameron Corner
Tibooburra
Broken Hill
Port Augusta
Whyalla
Port Pirie
Woomera
Quorn
Wilcannia
Menindee
Barrier Range
Grey Range
Andamooka Ranges
Gawler Ranges
New South Wales
Queensland
223 232

Remarkable Cities and Cultural monuments
UNESCO World Cultural Heritage
Remarkable Cities
Aborigine reservation
Places of Abor. cultural interest
Historical city scape
Technical/industrial monument
Remarkable lighthouse
Monument
Space telescope
Museum
Sport and leisure destinations
Horse racing
Sailing
Diving
Wind surfing
Surfing
Canoeing/rafting
Beach resort
Amusement/theme park
146°
Sd
148°
Se
229
150°
Sf
152°
Sg
154°
57
24°
58
26°
59
28°
217
60
30°
61
32°
62
233
Sh
Rockhampton
Emerald
Gladstone
Tropic of Capricorn
Great Barrier Reef Marine Park
Bundaberg
Hervey Bay
Fraser Island
Maryborough
Gympie
Sunshine Coast
BRISBANE
Ipswich
Toowoomba
Gold Coast
Coolangatta
Lismore
Grafton
Coffs Harbour
Port Macquarie
Tamworth
Newcastle
Maitland
Dubbo
Moree
Bourke
Charleville
Mitchell
Roma
Miles
Dalby
Warwick
Armidale
Glen Innes
PACIFIC
OCEAN
Great Dividing Range
Darling Downs
Carnarvon N.P.
Carnarvon Range
Blackdown Tableland N.P.
Expedition N.P.
Chesterton Range N.P.
Culgoa N.P.
Gundabooka N.P.
Warrumbungle N.P.
Mt. Kaputar N.P.
Wollemi N.P.
Barrington Tops N.P.
Central Eastern Rainforest Reserves
Great Sandy N.P.
Cooloola N.P.
Yuraygir N.P.
Myall Lakes N.P.
New England Plateau
Liverpool Range
Nandewar Range
Wales

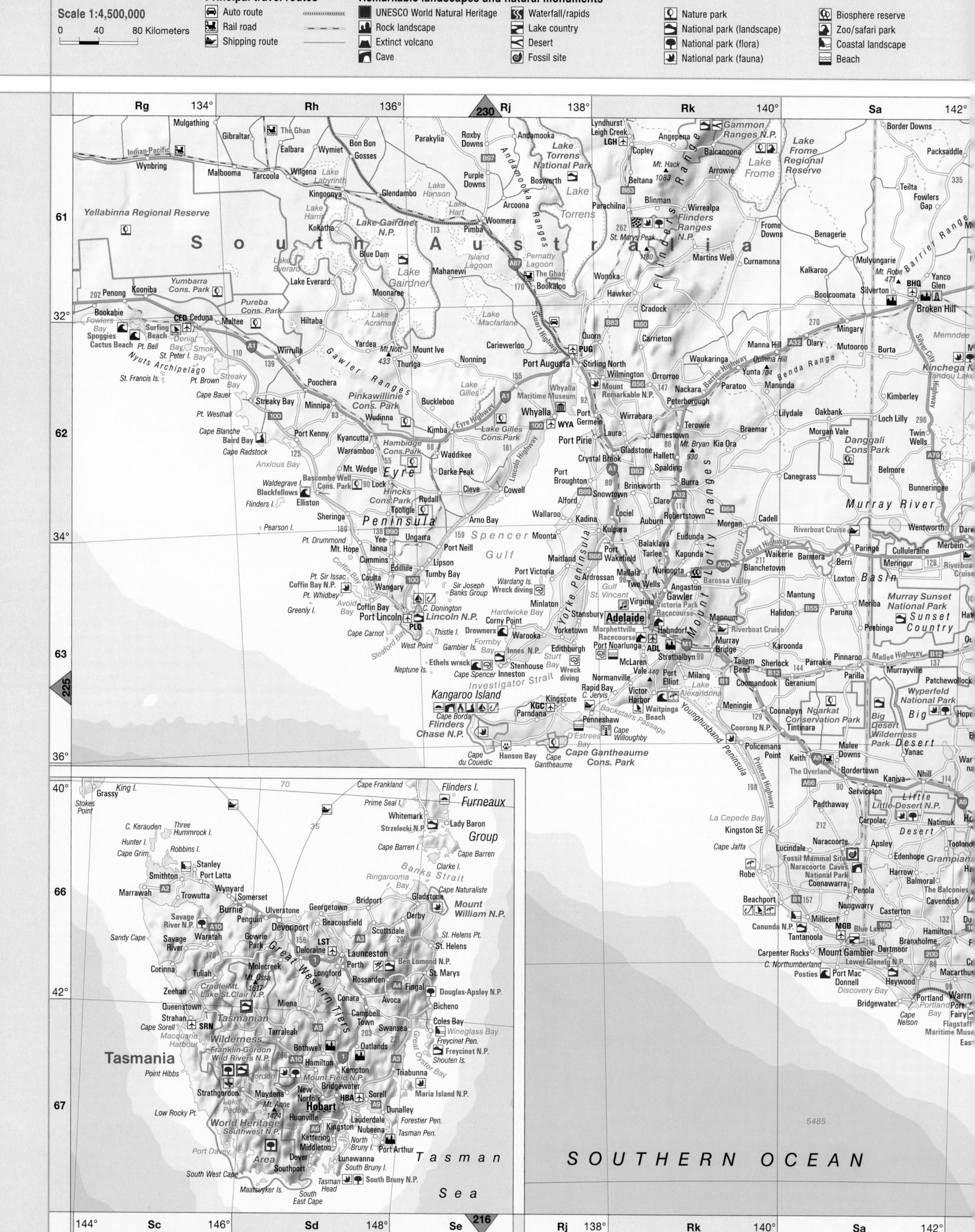

Scale 1:4,500,000
0 40 80 Kilometers
Principal travel routes
Auto route
Rail road
Shipping route
Remarkable landscapes and natural monuments
UNESCO World Natural Heritage
Rock landscape
Extinct volcano
Cave
Waterfall/rapids
Lake country
Desert
Fossil site
Nature park
National park (landscape)
National park (flora)
National park (fauna)
Biosphere reserve
Zoo/safari park
Coastal landscape
Beach
Rg
134°
Rh
136°
230
Rj
138°
Rk
140°
Sa
142°
61
62
63
34°
36°
32°
225
South Australia
Yellabinna Regional Reserve
Yumbarra Cons. Park
Pureba Cons. Park
Lake Gairdner N.P.
Lake Gairdner
Lake Torrens National Park
Lake Torrens
Andamooka Ranges
Gammon Ranges N.P.
Lake Frome
Lake Frome Regional Reserve
Flinders Ranges
Flinders Ranges N.P.
Barrier Range
Gawler Ranges
Pinkawillinie Cons. Park
Eyre Peninsula
Hambidge Cons. Park
Hincks Cons. Park
Lake Gilles Cons. Park
Spencer Gulf
Gulf St. Vincent
Yorke Peninsula
Mount Lofty Ranges
Murray River
Murray Basin
Danggali Cons. Park
Murray Sunset National Park
Sunset Country
Riverboat Cruise
Investigator Strait
Kangaroo Island
Flinders Chase N.P.
Cape Gantheaume Cons. Park
Backstairs Passage
Lake Alexandrina
Younghusband Peninsula
Coorong N.P.
Ngarkat Conservation Park
Big Desert Wilderness Park
Big Desert
Wyperfeld National Park
Little Desert N.P.
Little Desert
Naracoorte Caves National Park
Fossil Mammal Site
Grampians
Lower Glenelg N.P.
Discovery Bay
Canunda N.P.
Lincoln N.P.
Coffin Bay N.P.
Innes N.P.
Mount Remarkable N.P.
Whyalla Maritime Museum
Port Augusta
Whyalla
Port Pirie
Port Lincoln
Adelaide
Gawler
Murray Bridge
Mount Gambier
Broken Hill
Ceduna
Streaky Bay
Kadina
Victor Harbor
Kingscote
SOUTHERN OCEAN
5485
Tasmania
Furneaux Group
Flinders I.
Cape Barren I.
Banks Strait
King I.
Stanley
Burnie
Devonport
Launceston
Great Western Tiers
Cradle Mt. Lake St.Clair N.P.
Tasmanian Wilderness
Franklin-Gordon Wild Rivers N.P.
Mount Field N.P.
Southwest N.P.
World Heritage Area
Ben Lomond N.P.
Douglas-Apsley N.P.
Freycinet N.P.
Maria Island N.P.
South Bruny N.P.
Hobart
Queenstown
Tasman Sea
Great Oyster Bay
144°
Sc
146°
Sd
148°
Se
216
40°
42°
66
67

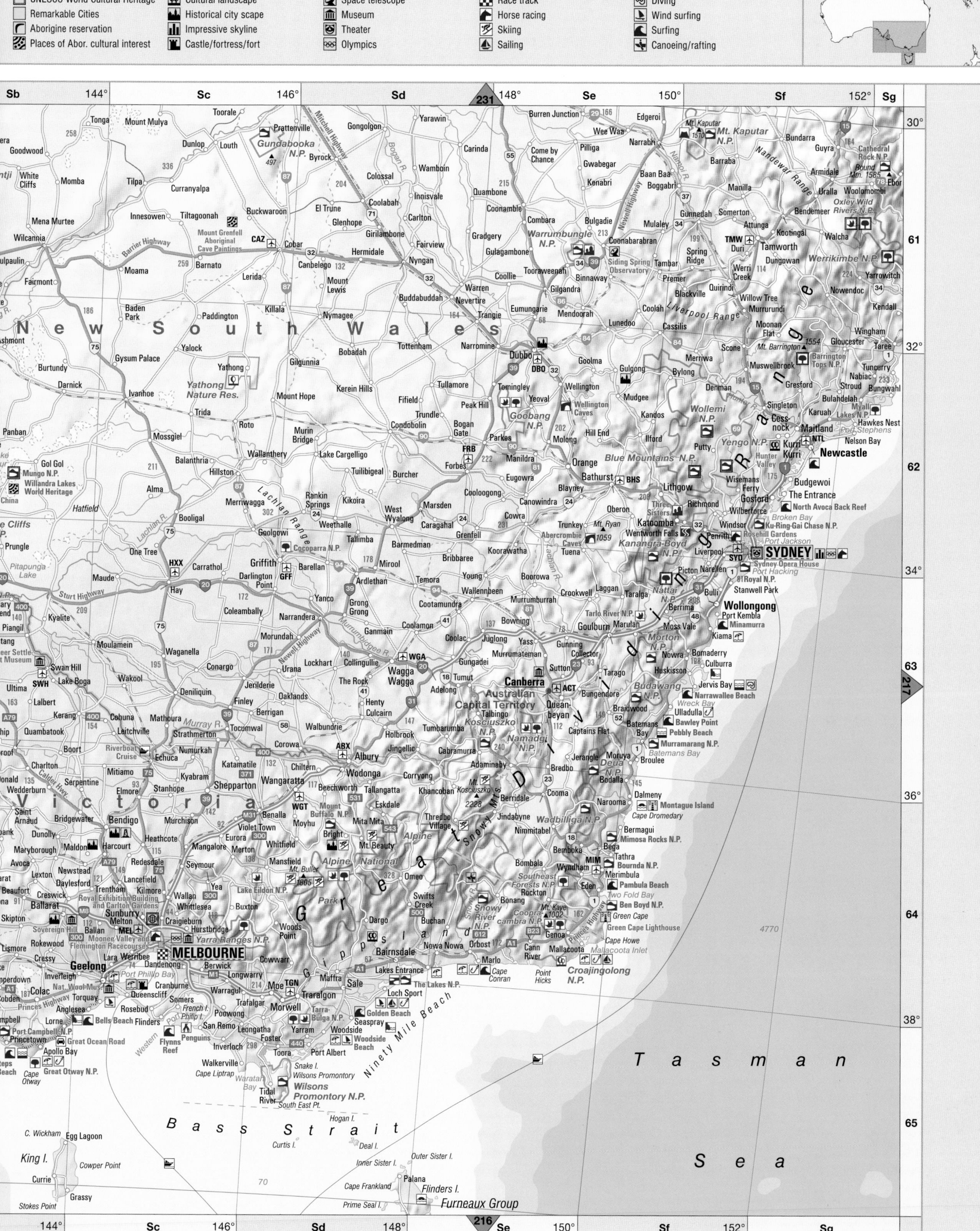
Remarkable Cities and Cultural monuments
UNESCO World Cultural Heritage
Remarkable Cities
Aborigine reservation
Places of Abor. cultural interest
Cultural landscape
Historical city scape
Impressive skyline
Castle/fortress/fort
Space telescope
Museum
Theater
Olympics
Sport and leisure destinations
Race track
Horse racing
Skiing
Sailing
Diving
Wind surfing
Surfing
Canoeing/rafting
New South Wales
Victoria
Australian Capital Territory
Great Dividing Range
Gippsland
Tasman Sea
Bass Strait
SYDNEY
MELBOURNE
Canberra
Newcastle
Wollongong
Geelong
Dubbo
Orange
Bathurst
Wagga Wagga
Albury
Wodonga
Bendigo
Ballarat
Shepparton
Griffith
Tamworth
Gosford
Katoomba
Blue Mountains N.P.
Warrumbungle N.P.
Mt. Kaputar N.P.
Gundabooka N.P.
Mungo N.P.
Willandra Lakes World Heritage
Yathong Nature Res.
Kosciuszko N.P.
Namadgi N.P.
Alpine National Park
Snowy Mts.
Wilsons Promontory N.P.
Croajingolong N.P.
Ninety Mile Beach
Flinders I.
Furneaux Group
King I.
Sydney Opera House
Great Ocean Road
Great Otway N.P.
Sb
Sc
Sd
Se
Sf
Sg
144°
146°
148°
150°
152°
30°
32°
34°
36°
38°
61
62
63
64
65
231
216
217

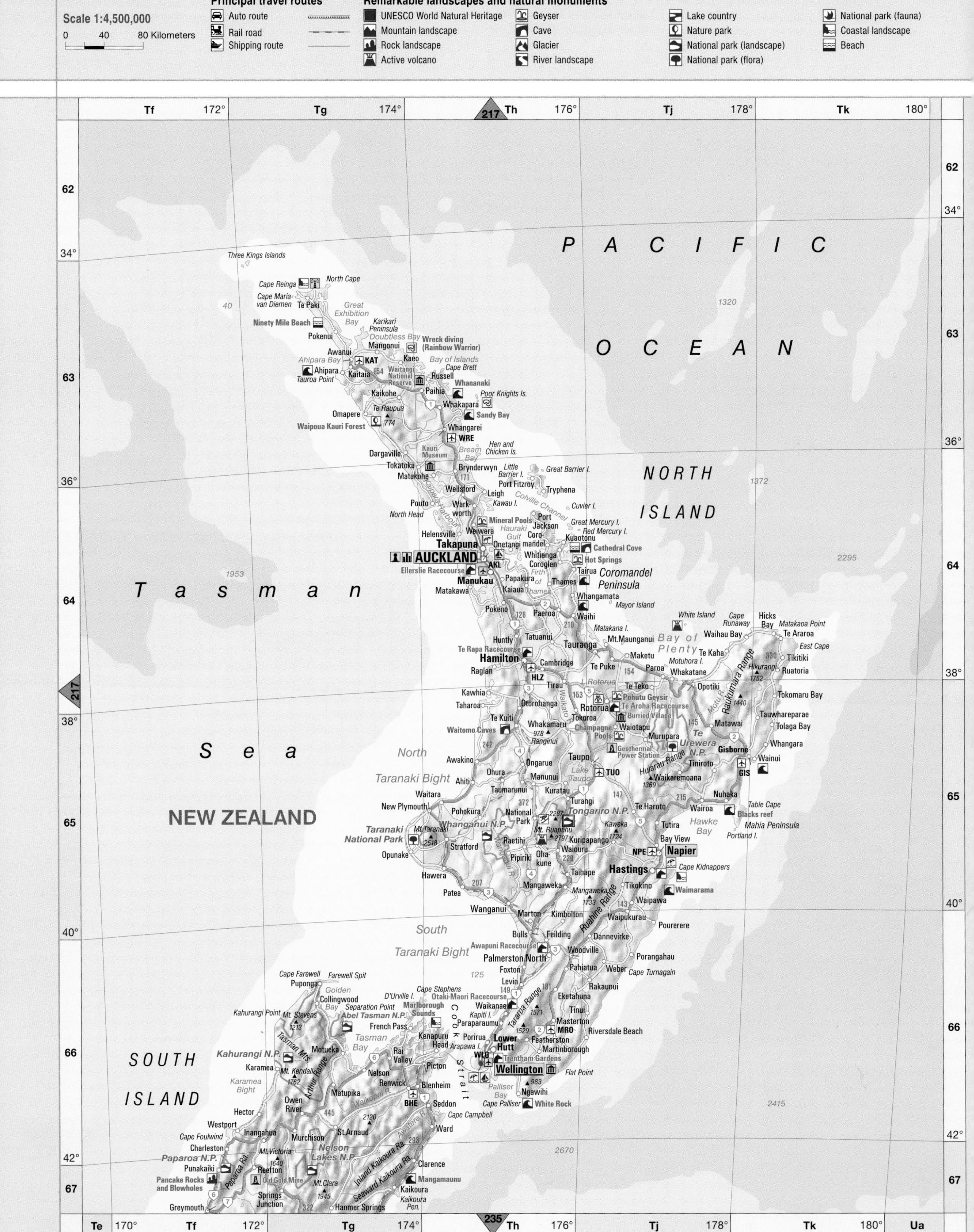
Scale 1:4,500,000
0 40 80 Kilometers
Principal travel routes
Auto route
Rail road
Shipping route
Remarkable landscapes and natural monuments
UNESCO World Natural Heritage
Mountain landscape
Rock landscape
Active volcano
Geyser
Cave
Glacier
River landscape
Lake country
Nature park
National park (landscape)
National park (flora)
National park (fauna)
Coastal landscape
Beach
Tf 172° Tg 174° 217 Th 176° Tj 178° Tk 180°
62
63
64
65
66
67
34°
36°
38°
40°
42°
P A C I F I C
O C E A N
NORTH
ISLAND
T a s m a n
S e a
NEW ZEALAND
SOUTH
ISLAND
Three Kings Islands
Cape Reinga
North Cape
Cape Maria van Diemen
Te Paki
Great Exhibition Bay
Ninety Mile Beach
Karikari Peninsula
Pokenui
Doubtless Bay
Mangonui
Wreck diving (Rainbow Warrior)
Awanui
Ahipara Bay
KAT
Kaeo
Bay of Islands
Ahipara
Kaitaia
Tauroa Point
Waitangi National Reserve
Cape Brett
Russell
Whananaki
Kaikohe
Paihia
Poor Knights Is.
Whakapara
Te Raupua
Omapere
Sandy Bay
Waipoua Kauri Forest
774
Whangarei
WRE
Hen and Chicken Is.
Kauri Museum
Bream Bay
Dargaville
Tokatoka
Matakohe
Brynderwyn
Little Barrier I.
Great Barrier I.
Port Fitzroy
Wellsford
Leigh
Tryphena
Colville Channel
Kawau I.
Pouto
North Head
Warkworth
Cuvier I.
Kaipara Harbour
Mineral Pools
Port Jackson
Great Mercury I.
Red Mercury I.
Helensville
Waiwera
Hauraki Gulf
Coromandel
Kuaotunu
Takapuna
Onetangi
Cathedral Cove
AUCKLAND
AKL
Whitianga
Coroglen
Hot Springs
Ellerslie Racecourse
Manukau
Papakura
Firth of Thames
Thames
Tairua
Coromandel Peninsula
Matakawa
Kaiaua
Whangamata
Mayor Island
Pokeno
Paeroa
Waihi
White Island
Cape Runaway
Hicks Bay
Matakaoa Point
Matakana I.
Te Araroa
Huntly
Tatuanui
Tauranga
Mt.Maunganui
Bay of Plenty
Waihau Bay
East Cape
Te Rapa Racecourse
Hamilton
Maketu
Te Kaha
Motuhora I.
Tikitiki
Cambridge
Te Puke
Raglan
Paroa
Whakatane
Hikurangi
Ruatoria
HLZ
L. Rotorua
1752
Raukumara Range
Tirau
Te Teko
Opotiki
Kawhia
Pohutu Geysir
Te Aroha Racecourse
Taharoa
Otorohanga
Rotorua
Burried Village
Tokomaru Bay
Te Kuiti
Tokoroa
Motu R.
1440
Waitomo Caves
Whakamaru
Champagne Pools
Waiotapu
Tauwhareparae
978
Rangiinui
Murupara
Matawai
Tolaga Bay
North
Taranaki Bight
Awakino
Ongarue
Taupo
Geothermal Power Station
Te Urewera N.P.
Gisborne
Whangara
Ohura
Lake Taupo
TUO
Huiarau Range
Tiniroto
Wainui
Ahiti
Manunui
Waikaremoana
GIS
Waitara
Taumarunui
Kuratau
1369
New Plymouth
Turangi
Nuhaka
Pohokura
National Park
Tongariro N.P.
Te Haroto
Wairoa
Table Cape
Blacks reef
Taranaki National Park
Mt.Taranaki
2518
Whanganui N.P.
2287
Mt. Ruapehu
2797
Kaweka
Tutira
Hawke Bay
Mahia Peninsula
Portland I.
Raetihi
Kuripapango
1724
Bay View
Opunake
Stratford
Pipiriki
Ohakune
Waiouru
NPE
Napier
Hawera
Taihape
Hastings
Cape Kidnappers
Patea
Mangaweka
Tikokino
Waimarama
Mangaweka 1733
Wanganui
Ruahine Range
Waipawa
Marton
Kimbolton
Waipukurau
Pourerere
South Taranaki Bight
Bulls
Feilding
Awapuni Racecourse
Dannevirke
Woodville
Palmerston North
Porangahau
Foxton
Pahiatua
Weber
Cape Turnagain
Cape Farewell
Farewell Spit
Puponga
Levin
Golden Bay
Collingwood
D'Urville I.
Cape Stephens
Otaki-Maori Racecourse
Eketahuna
Separation Point
Marlborough Sounds
Waikanae
Kahurangi Point
Mt. Stevens
Abel Tasman N.P.
Kapiti I.
1571
Tararua Range
Tinui
1213
French Pass
Paraparaumu
Cook Strait
1529
Masterton
MRO
Riversdale Beach
Tasman Bay
Tasman Mts.
Motueka
Kenepuru Head
Porirua
Arapawa I.
Lower Hutt
Featherston
Martinborough
Kahurangi N.P.
Rai Valley
WLG
Trentham Gardens
Karamea
Mt. Kendall
Nelson
Picton
Wellington
Flat Point
Karamea Bight
Arthur Range
1762
Renwick
Blenheim
983
Ngawihi
Matupika
Palliser Bay
Owen River
Waikopai R.
BHE
Seddon
Cape Palliser
White Rock
Hector
445
Cape Campbell
Westport
2120
Cape Foulwind
Inangahua
St.Arnaud
Ward
Charleston
Murchison
Awatere R.
Nelson Lakes N.P.
Paparoa N.P.
Mt.Victoria
1640
293
Punakaiki
Reefton
Clarence
Pancake Rocks and Blowholes
Paparoa Ra.
Old Gold Mine
Mt.Clara
Inland Kaikoura Ra.
Seaward Kaikoura Ra.
Mangamaunu
1945
Kaikoura
Springs Junction
Kaikoura Pen.
Greymouth
Hanmer Springs
Te 170° Tf 172° Tg 174° 235 Th 176° Tj 178° Tk 180° Ua
40
1320
1372
1953
2295
125
2415
2670

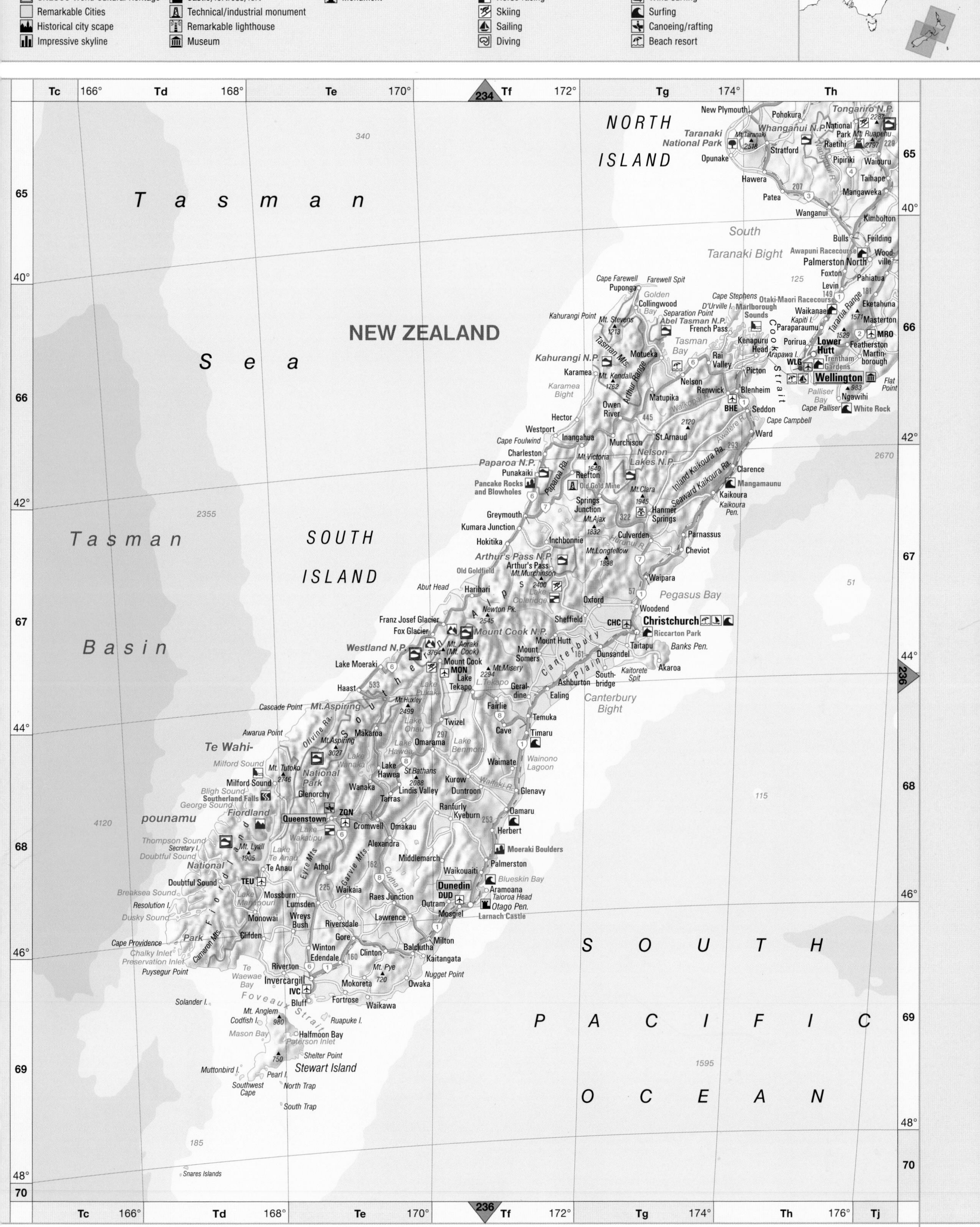

Remarkable Cities and Cultural monuments
UNESCO World Cultural Heritage
Remarkable Cities
Historical city scape
Impressive skyline
Castle/fortress/fort
Technical/industrial monument
Remarkable lighthouse
Museum
Monument
Sport and leisure destinations
Horse racing
Skiing
Sailing
Diving
Wind surfing
Surfing
Canoeing/rafting
Beach resort
NEW ZEALAND
Tasman Sea
Tasman Basin
NORTH ISLAND
SOUTH ISLAND
SOUTH PACIFIC OCEAN
Southern Alps
Cook Strait
Foveaux Strait
Te Wahi-pounamu
Fiordland National Park
Mount Cook N.P.
Westland N.P.
Mt.Aspiring National Park
Arthur's Pass N.P.
Paparoa N.P.
Kahurangi N.P.
Abel Tasman N.P.
Nelson Lakes N.P.
Taranaki National Park
Tongariro N.P.
Whanganui N.P.
South Taranaki Bight
Tasman Bay
Golden Bay
Karamea Bight
Pegasus Bay
Canterbury Bight
Canterbury Plain
Banks Pen.
Otago Pen.
Stewart Island
Wellington
Christchurch
Dunedin
Queenstown
Invercargill
Nelson
Blenheim
Timaru
Oamaru
Greymouth
Hokitika
Westport
Kaikoura
Palmerston North
New Plymouth
Wanganui
Lower Hutt
Porirua
Masterton
Picton
Te Anau
Wanaka
Twizel
Haast
Franz Josef Glacier
Fox Glacier
Milford Sound
Mt. Aoraki (Mt. Cook) 3764
Mt.Aspiring 3027
Moeraki Boulders
Larnach Castle
Riccarton Park
Pancake Rocks and Blowholes
Old Gold Mine
Southerland Falls
Snares Islands

Scale 1:54,000,000

0 400 800 Kilometers

Depth tints

- Shoreline
- 0-200 m
- 200-2000 m
- 2000-4000 m
- 4000-6000 m
- 6000-8000 m
- > 8000 m

Pb 100° | Qa 110° | Qb 120° | Ra 130° | Rb | Sa 150° | Sb 160° | Ta 170° | Tb 180° | Ba 170°

04 | 50° | 05 | 40° | 06 | 30° | 07 | 20° | 08 | 10° | 09 | 0° | 10 | 10° | 11 | 20° | 12 | 30° | 13 | 40° | 14

Stanovoy Khrebet
Sea of Okhotsk
Kamchatka Peninsula
Bering Sea
Aleutian Islands
Aleutian Trench
Komandorskie o-va
Bratsk
Irkutsk
Lake Baikal
Amur
Khrebet Dzhugdzhur
Lesser Hinggan Range
Sakhalin
mys Lopatka
Ulan Bator
Chabarowsk
Altai Mountains
Gov' Altayn Nuruu
Greater Hinggan Range
Manchuria
Sikhote-Alin
Kuril Islands
Kuril Trench
Obruchev Rise
GOBI DESERT
Hokkaido
Vladivostok
Sea of Japan
Northwest Pacific Basin
Peking
Qilian Shan
ASIA
Seoul
Korea
Yellow Sea
Honshu
Japan Trench
Lanzhou
Xi'an
Huang He
Huabei
Fujisan
Tokyo
Korea Strait
Shikoku
Kyushu
Bonin Trench
Wuhan
Shanghai
East China Sea
Gongga Shan 7576
Yangtze
Ryukyu Islands
Ryukyu Trench
South Honshu Ridge
Bonin Islands
PACIFIC
Hawaii
Kure
Midway Islands
Kunming
Hongshui He
Canton
Hong Kong
Taiwan Strait
Taipei
Formosa
Kyushu-Palau Ridge
Minami-Tori-Shima
Mid-Pacific Seamounts
Irrawaddy
Hanoi
Gulf of Tonkin
Philippine Sea
Luzon Strait
Hainan
West Mariana Basin
Asuncion Island
Wake I.
Johnston Atoll
Vientiane
Rangoon
Indochina Peninsula
South China Basin
Philippine Basin
Alamagan
East Mariana Basin
Mekong
Bay of Bengal
Bangkok
Luzon
Manila
Saipan
Garapan
Trieste Deep
Taongi Atoll
Challenger Deep
Agana
Vitiaz I Deep
Central Pacific Basin
Christmas Ridge
Gulf of Thailand
Saigon
South China Sea
Mindoro
Panay
Philippine Trench
MICRONESIA
Eniwetok Atoll
Bikini Atoll
Cape Ca Mau
Palawan
Negros
Yap Islands
Koror
Ulithi-Atoll
Faraulep Atoll
Hall Islands
Ujelang Atoll
Ujae Atoll
Ratak Chain
Maloelap Atoll
Malay Peninsula
Strait of Malacca
Kinabalu 4101
Mindanao
Woleai-Atoll
Truk Islands
Pulap Atoll
Senyavin Islands
Palikir
Ailinglapalap Atoll
Dalap-Uliga-Darrit
Bandar Seri Begawan
West Caroline Basin
Caroline Islands
East Caroline Basin
Mortlock Islands
Kosrae
Majuro Atoll
Sumatra
Singapore
Borneo
Celebes Sea
Kapingamarangi Atoll
Gilbert Islands
Bairiki
Howland-Islands
Kapuas
Halmahera
Bismarck Archipelago
Yaren
Banaba I.
Onotoa Atoll
Canton Atoll
Banjarmasin
Celebes
Moluccas
Jayapura
Bismarck Sea
New Ireland
Melanesian Basin
Nikumaroro
Orona
Phoenix Islands
Greater Sunda Islands
Java Sea
Makassar
Buru
Ceram
Banda Sea
Puncak Jaya 5050
Mount Wilhelm 4508
New Guinea
New Britain
Lae
MELANESIA
Tuvalu Islands
Niutao
POLYNESIA
Jakarta
Lesser Sunda Islands
Kepulauan Aru
Bougainville I.
Choiseul
Java
Java Trench
Bali
Lombok
Sumbawa
Flores
Dili
Timor
Dolak
Arafura Sea
Torres Strait
Port Moresby
D'Entrecasteaux Islands
Honiara
Guadalcanal
San Cristobal
Vitiaz Trench
Funafuti Atoll
Vaiaku
Planet Deep 7450
Sumba
Timor Trough
Cape York
Solomon Sea
Nendo
Swains Atoll
Darwin
Cartier Island
Timor Sea
Arnhem Land
Groote Eylandt
Cape York Peninsula
Louisiade Archipelago
Rennell I.
Santa-Cruz Islands
Rotuma
North Fiji Basin
Mata Uta
Savai'i I.
Apia
Pago Pago
Samoa Islands
North Australia Basin
Gulf of Carpentaria
Barkly Tableland
Coral Sea
Espiritu Santo
Malakula
Vanua Levu
Tafahi
Derby
Kimberley Plateau
New Hebrides
Efate
Port Vila
Fiji Islands
Northwest Australian Basin
Broome
Récifs d'Entrecasteaux
Iles Loyauté
Tana
Viti Levu
Suva
Tonga Islands
Ha'apai Group
Alofi
Port Hedland
Great Sandy Desert
Tanami Desert
Townsville
Récifs et Chesterfield
New Hebrides Trench
Ile Matthew
Tongatapu
Nuku'alofa
Tonga Trench
North West Cape
Hamersley Range
MacDonnell Ranges
Alice Springs
Great Dividing Range
Nouméa
South Fiji Basin
Vitiaz II Deep
Carnarvon
Gibson Desert
Ayers Rock 868
Simpson Desert
Fraser Island
AUSTRALIA
Great Artesian Basin
Charleville
Brisbane
Cape Byron
Lau Ridge
Raoul I.
Great Victoria Desert
Lake Eyre
Norfolk Ridge
Norfolk Island
Kermadec Islands
Geraldton
Three Kings Ridge
L'Esperance Rock
Perth
Nullarbor Plain
Flinders Ranges
Broken Hill
Darling
Lord Howe Island
Lord Howe Rise
Vitiaz III Deep
Kermadec Trench
Diamantina Deep
Cape Leeuwin
Great Australian Bight
Adelaide
Sydney
Albany
Diamantina Trench
Kangaroo Island
Murray
Mt. Kosciuszko
Canberra
North Cape
Auckland
South Australian Basin
Melbourne
Tasman Sea
North Island
Bass Strait
Furneaux Group
King Island
Cook Strait
Wellington
Tasmania
Hobart
Tasman Basin
South Island
New Zealand
Chatham Rise
Chatham Islands
SOUTHERN OCEAN
South East Cape
South Tasman Rise
Mt. Cook
Christchurch
Dunedin
Stewart Island
Bounty Islands

Pb 100° | Qa 110° | Qb 120° | Ra 130° | Rb | Sa 150° | Sb 160° | Ta 170° | Tb 180° | Ba 170°

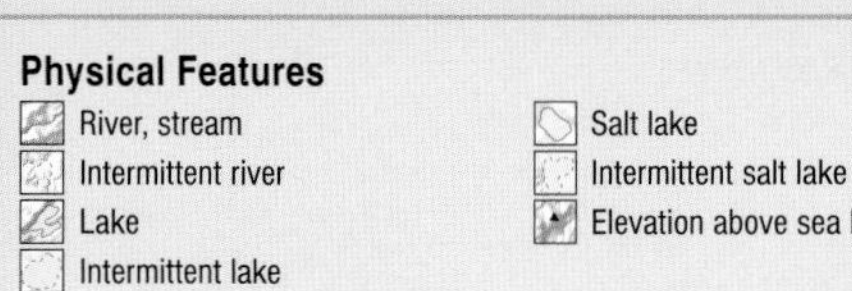

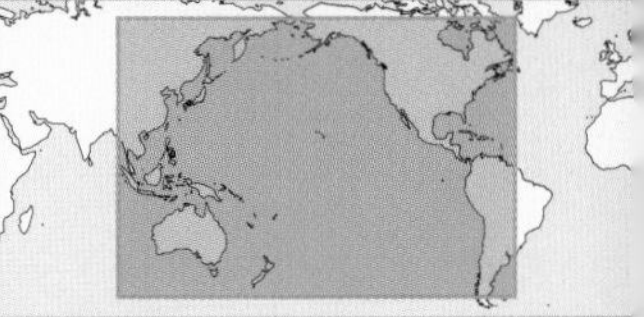

Ca 150°	Cb 140°	Da 130°	Db 120°	Ea 110°	Eb 100°	Fa 90°	Fb 80°	Ga 70°	Gb 60°

04 50° 05 40° 06 30° 07 20° 08 10° 09 0° 10 10° 11 20° 12 30° 13 40° 14

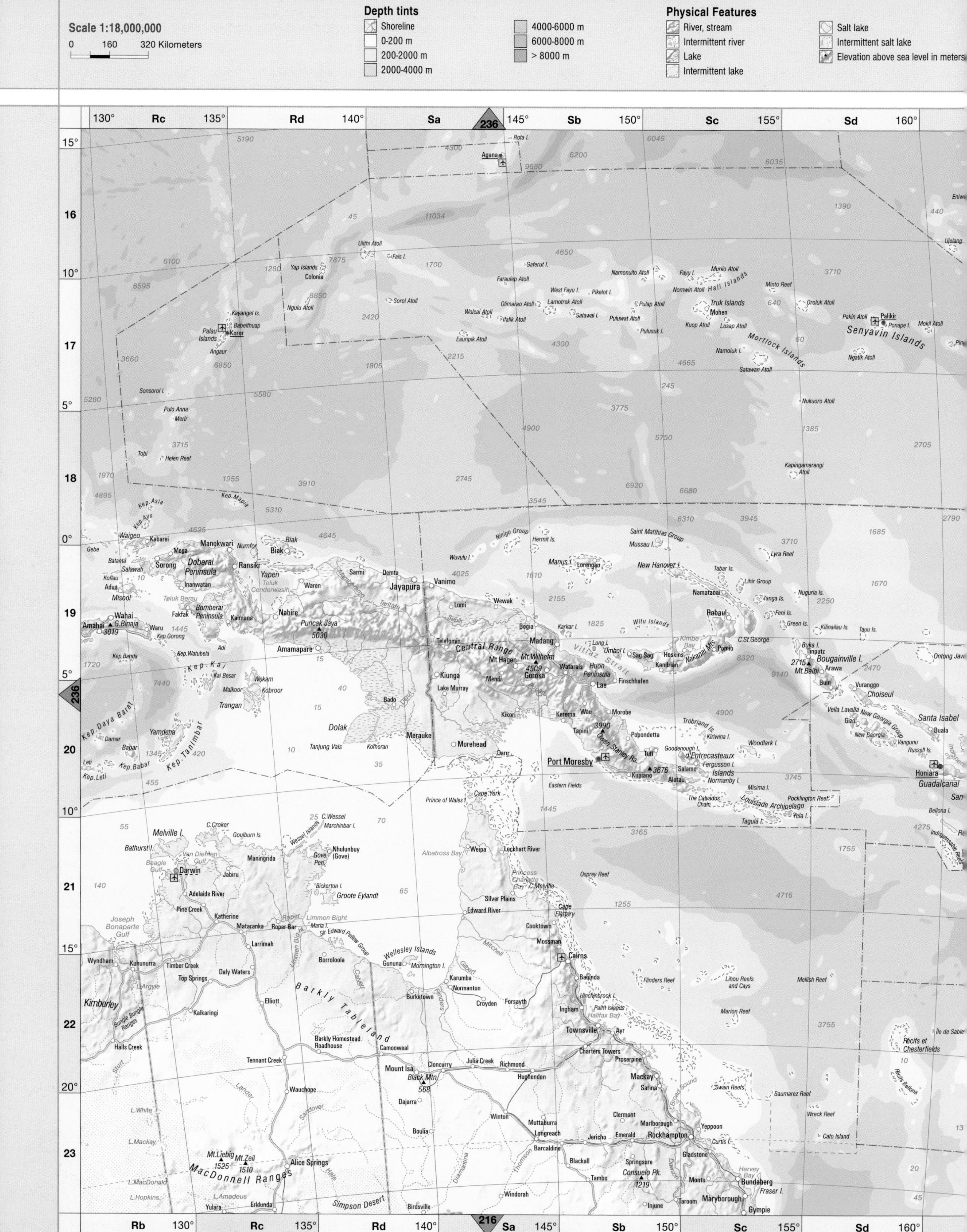
Scale 1:18,000,000
0 160 320 Kilometers
Depth tints
Shoreline
0-200 m
200-2000 m
2000-4000 m
4000-6000 m
6000-8000 m
> 8000 m
Physical Features
River, stream
Intermittent river
Lake
Intermittent lake
Salt lake
Intermittent salt lake
Elevation above sea level in meters
130° Rc 135° Rd 140° Sa 236 145° Sb 150° Sc 155° Sd 160°
15° 16 10° 17 5° 18 0° 19 5° 20 10° 21 15° 22 20° 23
Rota I.
Agana
Ulithi Atoll
Fais I.
Gaferut I.
Yap Islands
Colonia
Ngulu Atoll
Sorol Atoll
Faraulep Atoll
West Fayu I.
Pikelot I.
Lamotrek Atoll
Olimarao Atoll
Ifalik Atoll
Woleai Atoll
Satawal I.
Eauripik Atoll
Namonuito Atoll
Pulap Atoll
Puluwat Atoll
Pulusuk I.
Fayu I.
Murilo Atoll
Nomwin Atoll
Hall Islands
Truk Islands
Mohen
Kuop Atoll
Losap Atoll
Mortlock Islands
Namoluk I.
Satawan Atoll
Minto Reef
Oroluk Atoll
Pakin Atoll
Palikir
Ponape I.
Mokil Atoll
Senyavin Islands
Ngatik Atoll
Nukuoro Atoll
Kapingamarangi Atoll
Ujelang
Kayangel Is.
Babelthuap
Palau Islands
Koror
Angaur
Sonsorol I.
Pulo Anna
Merir
Tobi
Helen Reef
Kep. Asia
Kep. Ayu
Kep. Mapia
Waigeo
Kabarei
Gebe
Batanta
Salawati
Sorong
Kofiau
Adua
Misool
Manokwari
Numfor
Biak
Mega
Doberai Peninsula
Ransiki
Inanwatan
Yapen
Teluk Cenderwasih
Waren
Sarmi
Demta
Jayapura
Vanimo
Teluk Berau
Bomberai Peninsula
Fakfak
Kaimana
Nabire
Wahai
Amahai
G.Binaja 3019
Waru
Kep. Gorong
Puncak Jaya 5030
Amamapare
Kep. Watubela
Kep. Banda
Kep. Kai
Kai Besar
Wokam
Maikoor
Kobroor
Trangan
Kep. Aru
Bado
Dolak
Merauke
Kolhoran
Tanjung Vals
Morehead
Kep. Daya Barat
Damar
Yamdena
Kep. Tanimbar
Babar
Kep. Babar
Leti
Kep. Leti
Lumi
Wewak
Sepik
Bogia
Madang
Karkar I.
Telefomin
Central Range
Mt.Hagen
Mt.Wilhelm 4509
Goroka
Mendi
Kiunga
Lake Murray
Watarais
Huon Peninsula
Lae
Finschhafen
Kikori
Kerema
Wau
Morobe
Tapini
Popondetta
3990
Owen Stanley Ra.
Port Moresby
Kupiano
3676
Tufi
Daru
Eastern Fields
Ninigo Group
Hermit Is.
Wuvulu I.
Manus I.
Lorengau
Saint Matthias Group
Mussau I.
New Hanover I.
Tabar Is.
Lihir Group
Namatanai
Tanga Is.
Feni Is.
Green Is.
Nuguria Is.
Kilinailau Is.
Tauu Is.
Witu Islands
Rabaul
Long I.
Umboi I.
Sag Sag
Vitiaz Strait
Hoskins
Kimbe Bay
Kandrian
Nakanai Mts.
Pomio
C.St.George
Buka I.
Tinputz
Bougainville I.
2715 Mt.Balbi
Arawa
Buin
Ontong Java
Vuranggo
Choiseul
Vella Lavella
New Georgia Group
Gizo
New Georgia
Vangunu
Santa Isabel
Buala
Russell Is.
Honiara
Guadalcanal
Trobriand Is.
Kiriwina I.
Woodlark I.
Goodenough I.
d'Entrecasteaux Islands
Fergusson I.
Normanby I.
Salamo
Alotau
Misima I.
The Calvados Chain
Louisiade Archipelago
Pocklington Reef
Yela I.
Tagula I.
Bellona I.
Indispensable Reefs
Cape York
Prince of Wales I.
C.Wessel
Marchinbar I.
Wessel Islands
C.Croker
Goulburn Is.
Melville I.
Bathurst I.
Van Diemen Gulf
Beagle Gulf
Darwin
Jabiru
Maningrida
Nhulunbuy (Gove)
Gove Pen.
Bickerton I.
Groote Eylandt
Adelaide River
Pine Creek
Katherine
Mataranka
Roper Bar
Roper
Limmen Bight
Maria I.
Sir Edward Pellew Group
Larrimah
Joseph Bonaparte Gulf
Wyndham
Kununurra
L.Argyle
Timber Creek
Top Springs
Daly Waters
Borroloola
Wellesley Islands
Gununa
Mornington I.
Kimberley
Bungle Bungle Ranges
Kalkaringi
Elliott
Barkly Tableland
Burketown
Karumba
Normanton
Croydon
Forsayth
Halls Creek
Barkly Homestead Roadhouse
Camooweal
Tennant Creek
Mount Isa
Black Mtn 568
Cloncurry
Julia Creek
Richmond
Hughenden
Wauchope
Dajarra
Boulia
Winton
Muttaburra
Longreach
Barcaldine
Jericho
Emerald
Clermont
Blackall
Tambo
Springsure
Consuelo Pk. 1219
Injune
Taroom
L.White
L.Mackay
Mt.Liebig 1525
Mt.Zeil 1510
Alice Springs
MacDonnell Ranges
L.MacDonald
L.Hopkins
L.Amadeus
Yulara
Erldunda
Simpson Desert
Birdsville
Windorah
Weipa
Albatross Bay
Lockhart River
Princess Charlotte Bay
C.Melville
Silver Plains
Edward River
Cape Flattery
Cooktown
Mossman
Cairns
Babinda
Hinchinbrook I.
Palm Islands
Halifax Bay
Ingham
Townsville
Ayr
Charters Towers
Proserpine
Mackay
Sarina
Broad Sound
Marlborough
Rockhampton
Yeppoon
Curtis I.
Gladstone
Monto
Hervey Bay
Bundaberg
Fraser I.
Maryborough
Gympie
Osprey Reef
Flinders Reef
Lihou Reefs and Cays
Mellish Reef
Marion Reef
Récifs et Chesterfields
Île de Sable
Récifs Bellona
Saumarez Reef
Swain Reefs
Wreck Reef
Cato Island
Rb 130° Rc 135° Rd 140° 216 Sa 145° Sb 150° Sc 155° Sd 160°

Political Boundaries	Transportation	Capitals of political units		Town symbols	
International	Interstate Hwy./Motorway	WASHINGTON D.C.	Independent	Capital > 1 Mill. inhabitants	Towns > 1 Mill. inhabitants
International disputed	Main road	Richmond	State/province	Capital < 1 Mill. inhabitants	Towns 100 000 to 1 Mill. inhabitants
Main administrative	Railway			State capital > 1 Mill. inhabitants	Towns < 100 000 inhabitants
	Airport			State capital < 1 Mill. inhabitants	

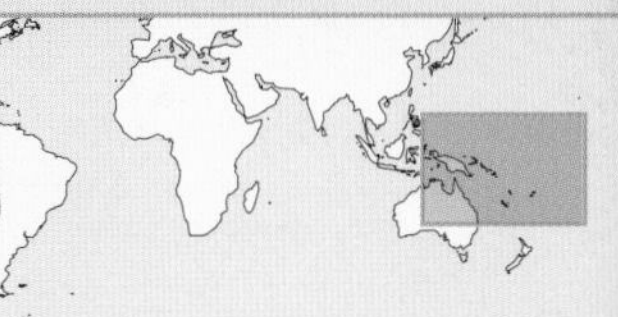

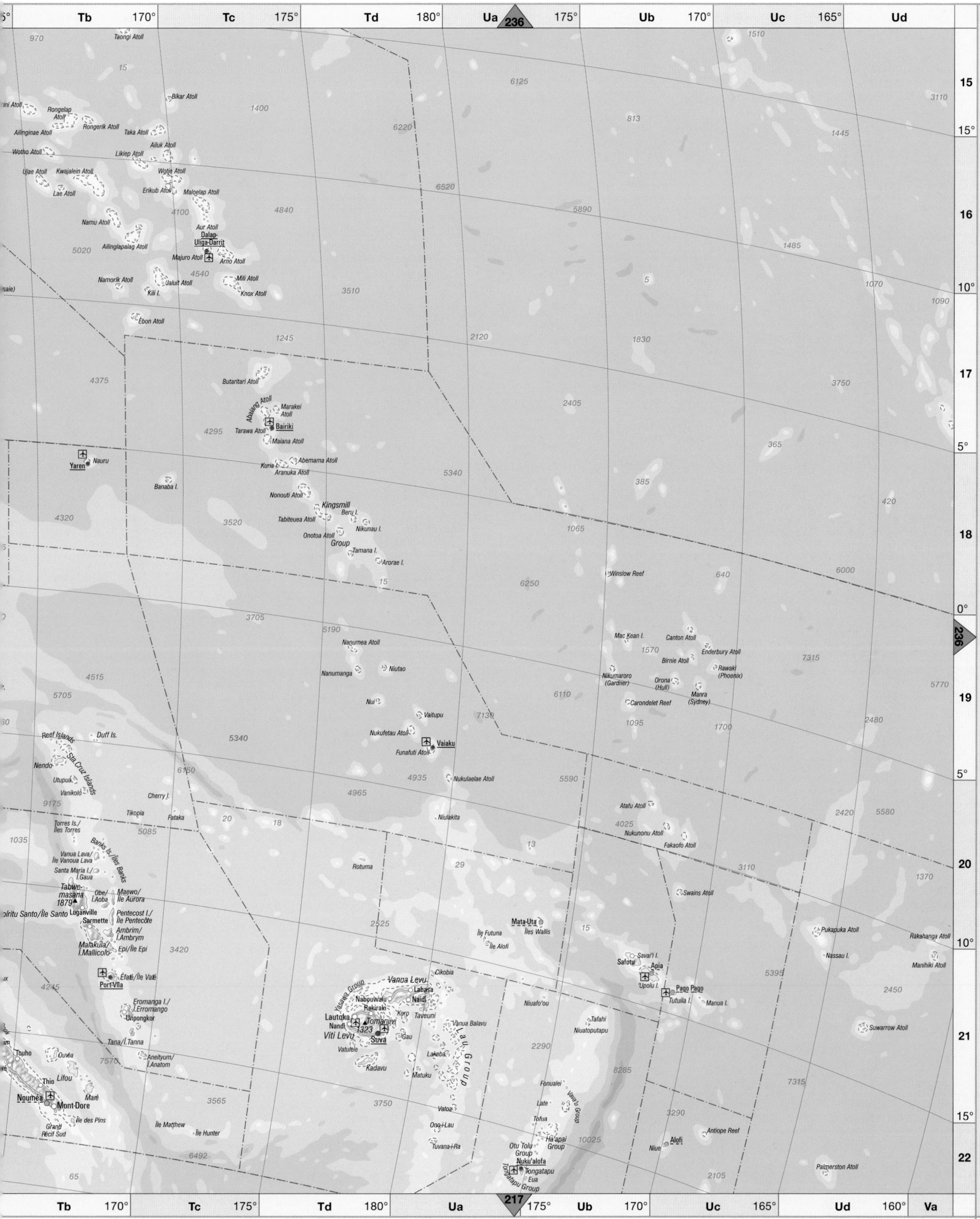

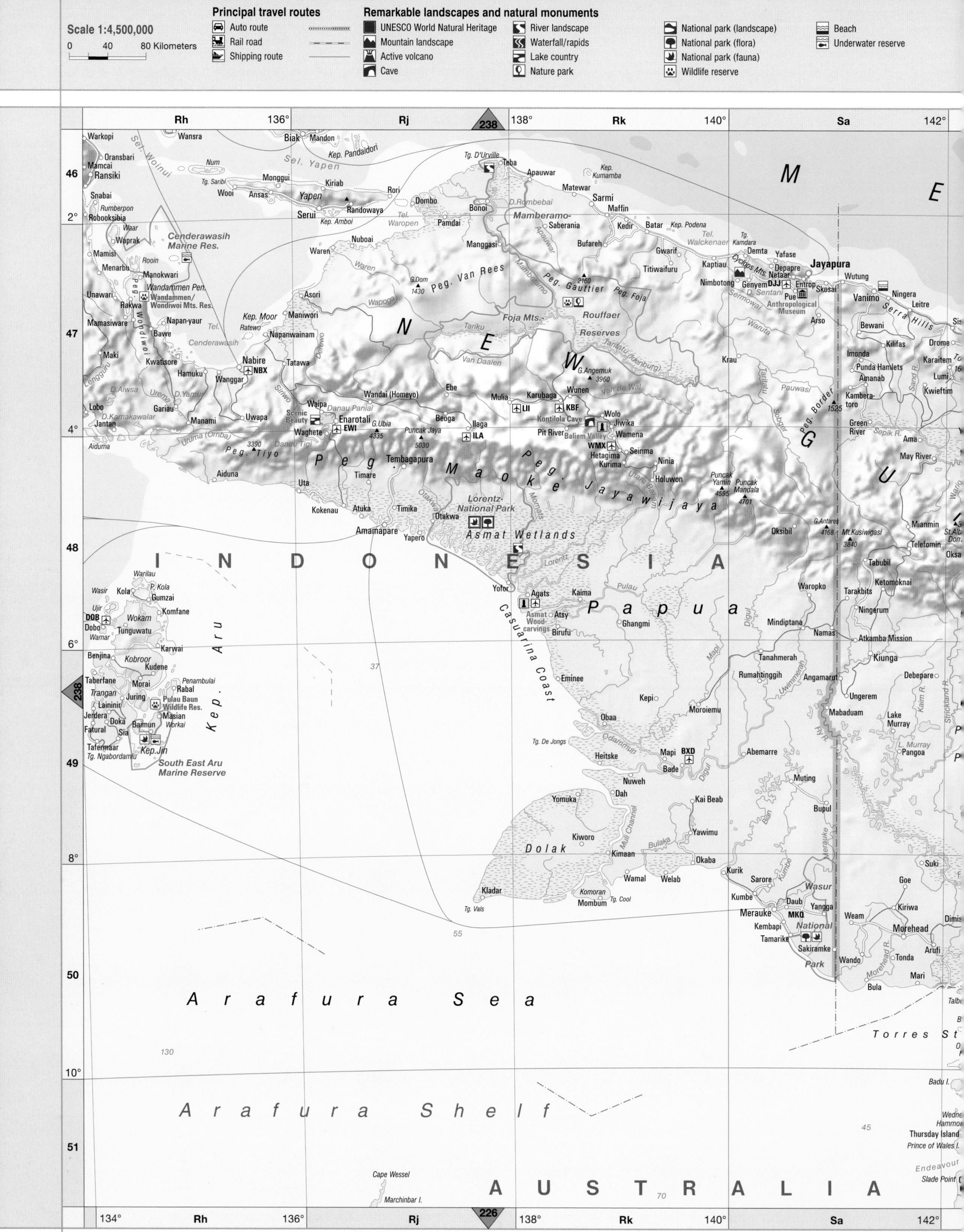
Scale 1:4,500,000
0 40 80 Kilometers
Principal travel routes
Auto route
Rail road
Shipping route
Remarkable landscapes and natural monuments
UNESCO World Natural Heritage
Mountain landscape
Active volcano
Cave
River landscape
Waterfall/rapids
Lake country
Nature park
National park (landscape)
National park (flora)
National park (fauna)
Wildlife reserve
Beach
Underwater reserve
Rh
136°
Rj
238
138°
Rk
140°
Sa
142°
46
47
48
49
50
51
2°
4°
6°
8°
10°
134°
226
Sel. Yapen
Yapen
Biak
Serui
Cenderawasih Marine Res.
Wandammen Pen.
Wandammen/ Wondiwoi Mts. Res.
Manokwari
Nabire
Enarotali
Mamberamo-
Peg. Van Rees
Peg. Gauttier
Foja Mts.
Rouffaer Reserves
Jayapura
Vanimo
Cyclops Mts.
Sentani
Anthropological Museum
Peg. Border
Peg. Maoke
Peg. Jayawijaya
Puncak Jaya 5030
Puncak Mandala 4701
Puncak Yamin 4595
G.Angemuk 3960
Tembagapura
Timika
Amamapare
Lorentz-National Park
Asmat Wetlands
Baliem Valley
Wamena
Kontilola Cave
Agats
Casuarina Coast
Papua
M
E
N
E
W
G
U
I N D O N E S I A
Kep. Aru
Dobo
Kep. Jin
South East Aru Marine Reserve
Pulau Baun Wildlife Res.
Dolak
Kimaan
Merauke
Wasur National Park
Mapi
Bade
Muting
Bupul
Tanahmerah
Kiunga
Lake Murray
Morehead
Ningerum
Tabubil
Oksibil
Arafura Sea
Arafura Shelf
A U S T R A L I A
Torres St
Thursday Island
Prince of Wales I.
Badu I.
Cape Wessel
Marchinbar I.
Slade Point

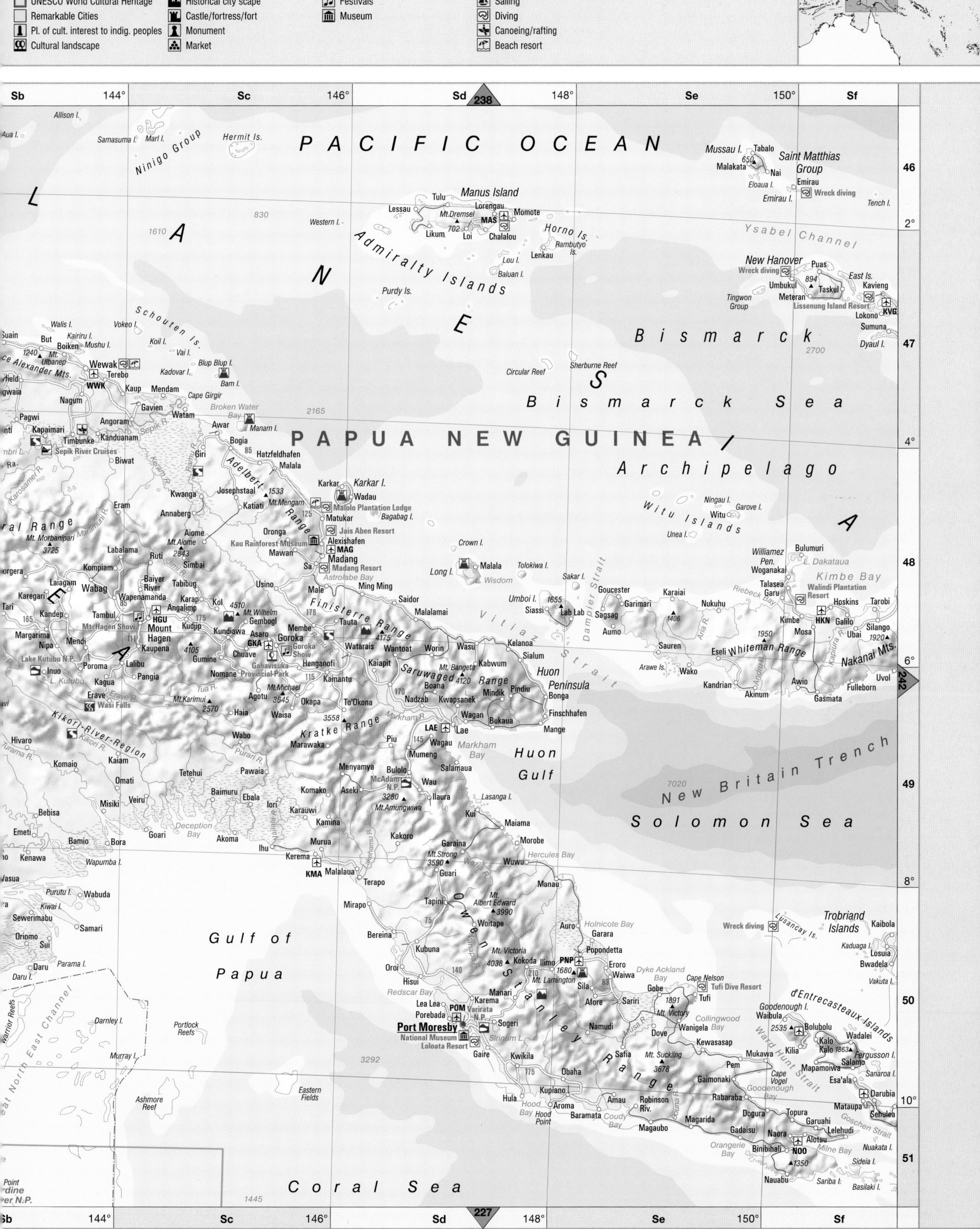

Remarkable Cities and Cultural monuments
UNESCO World Cultural Heritage
Remarkable Cities
Pl. of cult. interest to indig. peoples
Cultural landscape
Historical city scape
Castle/fortress/fort
Monument
Market
Festivals
Museum
Sport and leisure destinations
Sailing
Diving
Canoeing/rafting
Beach resort
Sb
144°
Sc
146°
Sd
238
148°
Se
150°
Sf
PACIFIC OCEAN
PAPUA NEW GUINEA
Bismarck Sea
Bismarck Archipelago
MELANESIA
Solomon Sea
Gulf of Papua
Coral Sea
Huon Gulf
New Britain Trench
Admiralty Islands
Manus Island
Lorengau
Momote
MAS
Mt.Dremsel
702
Lessau
Tulu
Likum
Loi
Chalalou
Horno Is.
Rambutyo Is.
Lenkau
Lou I.
Baluan I.
Purdy Is.
Western I.
Hermit Is.
Ninigo Group
Allison I.
Samasuma I.
Marl I.
Aua I.
Mussau I.
Tabalo
650
Malakata
Nai
Saint Matthias Group
Emirau
Eloaua I.
Emirau I.
Wreck diving
Tench I.
Ysabel Channel
New Hanover
Puas
894
Taskul
Umbukul
Meteran
Tingwon Group
Lissenung Island Resort
East Is.
Kavieng
KVG
Lokono
Sumuna
Dyaul I.
2700
Schouten Is.
Vokeo I.
Koil I.
Vai I.
Walis I.
Kairiru I.
Mushu I.
But
Boiken
Wewak
WWK
Terebo
Kaup
Mendam
Kadovar I.
Blup Blup I.
Bam I.
Cape Girgir
Broken Water Bay
Manam I.
Watam
Gavien
Nagum
Angoram
Kanduanam
Timbunke
Kapaimari
Pagwi
Sepik River Cruises
Sepik R.
Biwat
Awar
Bogia
Giri
Hatzfeldhafen
Malala
Adelbert Range
Josephstaal
1533
Katiati
Kwanga
Mt.Mengam
Annaberg
Eram
Aiome
Mt.Aiome
2843
Ruti
Simbai
Labalama
Kompiam
Wabag
Laiagam
Mt. Wilhelm
4510
Gembogl
Kundiawa
Kol
Mt. Hagen Show
Mount Hagen
HGU
Tambul
Kandep
Mendi
Margarima
Nipa
Lake Kutubu N.P.
Inuo
Poroma
Kagua
Erave
Wasi Falls
Ialibu
Pangia
Mt.Karimui
2570
Kikori-River-Region
Kikori R.
Hivaro
Komaio
Kaiam
Omati
Misiki
Veiru
Bebisa
Emeti
Bamio
Bora
Kenawa
Wapumba I.
Purutu I.
Wabuda
Kiwai I.
Sewerimabu
Samari
Oriomo
Sui
Daru
Daru I.
Parama I.
Darnley I.
Murray I.
Portlock Reefs
Ashmore Reef
Eastern Fields
Karkar
Karkar I.
Wadau
Malolo Plantation Lodge
Bagabag I.
Matukar
Jais Aben Resort
Kau Rainforest Museum
Alexishafen
MAG
Madang
Madang Resort
Astrolabe Bay
Oronga
Mawan
Usino
Ming Ming
Saidor
Malalamai
Finisterre Range
4175
Tauta
Goroka
GKA
Goroka Show
Asaro
Chuave
Gahavisuka Provincial Park
Henganofi
Kainantu
Watarais
Wantoat
Worin
Wasu
Kaiapit
Saruwaged Range
Mt. Bangeta
4120
Boana
Kabwum
Mindik
Pindiu
Nadzab
Kwapsanek
Wagan
Bukaua
LAE
Lae
Markham R.
Markham Bay
Kratke Range
3558
Mt.Michael
3645
Okapa
To'Okona
Agotu
Waisa
Haia
Wabo
Piu
Wagau
Mumeng
Marawaka
Menyamya
Bulolo
Salamaua
McAdam N.P.
Wau
3280
Mt.Amungwiwa
Aseki
Ilaura
Komako
Karauwi
Kamina
Pawaia
Tetehui
Baimuru
Ebala
Iori
Goari
Deception Bay
Akoma
Ihu
Kerema
KMA
Malalaua
Murua
Kakoro
Garaina
Mt.Strong
3590
Guari
Terapo
Mirapo
Tapini
Mt. Albert Edward
3990
Woitape
Bereina
Kubuna
Oroi
Hisui
Redscar Bay
Lea Lea
Porebada
POM
Port Moresby
National Museum
Loloata Resort
Varirata N.P.
Sogeri
Gaire
Kwikila
Owen Stanley Range
Mt. Victoria
4038
Kokoda
Ilimo
PNP
1680
Mt. Lamington
Popondetta
Eroro
Waiwa
Sila
Afore
Sariri
Manari
Karema
Namudi
Safia
Obaha
Hula
Hood Bay
Hood Point
Kupiano
Aroma
Baramata
Coudy Bay
Magaubo
Amau
Robinson Riv.
Magarida
Dove
Wanigela
Collingwood Bay
Mt. Suckling
3678
Kewasasap
Gobe
Tufi
Cape Nelson
Tufi Dive Resort
1891
Mt. Victory
Dyke Ackland Bay
Auro
Holnicote Bay
Garara
Manau
Wuwu
Hercules Bay
Morobe
Maiama
Kui
Lasanga I.
Huon Peninsula
Bonga
Finschhafen
Mange
Sialum
Kelanoa
Vitiaz Strait
Dampier Strait
Umboi I.
Siassi
1655
Lab Lab
Tolokiwa I.
Sakar I.
Long I.
Malala
Wisdom
Crown I.
Gaimonaki
Pem
Mukawa
Cape Vogel
Goodenough Bay
Rabaraba
Dogura
Topura
Garuahi
Gadaisu
Naora
Alotau
NOO
Binibihali
1350
Nauabu
Milne Bay
Lelehudi
Orangerie Bay
Sariba I.
Basilaki I.
Sideia I.
Nuakata I.
Goschen Strait
Sehulea
Mataupa
Darubia
Esa'ala
Sanaroa I.
Mapamoiwa
Salamo
Fergusson I.
Kalo
1863
Wadalei
Kilia
Bolubolu
2535
Goodenough I.
Waibula
Ward Hunt Strait
d'Entrecasteaux Islands
Trobriand Islands
Kaibola
Lusancay Is.
Kaduaga I.
Losuia
Bwadela
Vakuta I.
Witu Islands
Ningau I.
Garove I.
Witu
Unea I.
Williamez Pen.
Woganakai
Bulumuri
L. Dakataua
Kimbe Bay
Talasea
Garu
Walindi Plantation Resort
Riebeck Bay
Hoskins
Tarobi
Kimbe
HKN
Galilo
Mosa
Silango
1920
Ubai
1950
Nakanai Mts.
Whiteman Range
Eseli
Kapiura R.
Sauren
Nukuhu
Karaiai
1406
Aria R.
Garimari
Goucester
Sagsag
Aumo
Arawe Is.
Wako
Kandrian
Akinum
Awio
Gasmata
Fulleborn
Uvol
242
830
1610
2165
7020
3292
1445
Coral Sea
227
2°
4°
6°
8°
10°
46
47
48
49
50
51

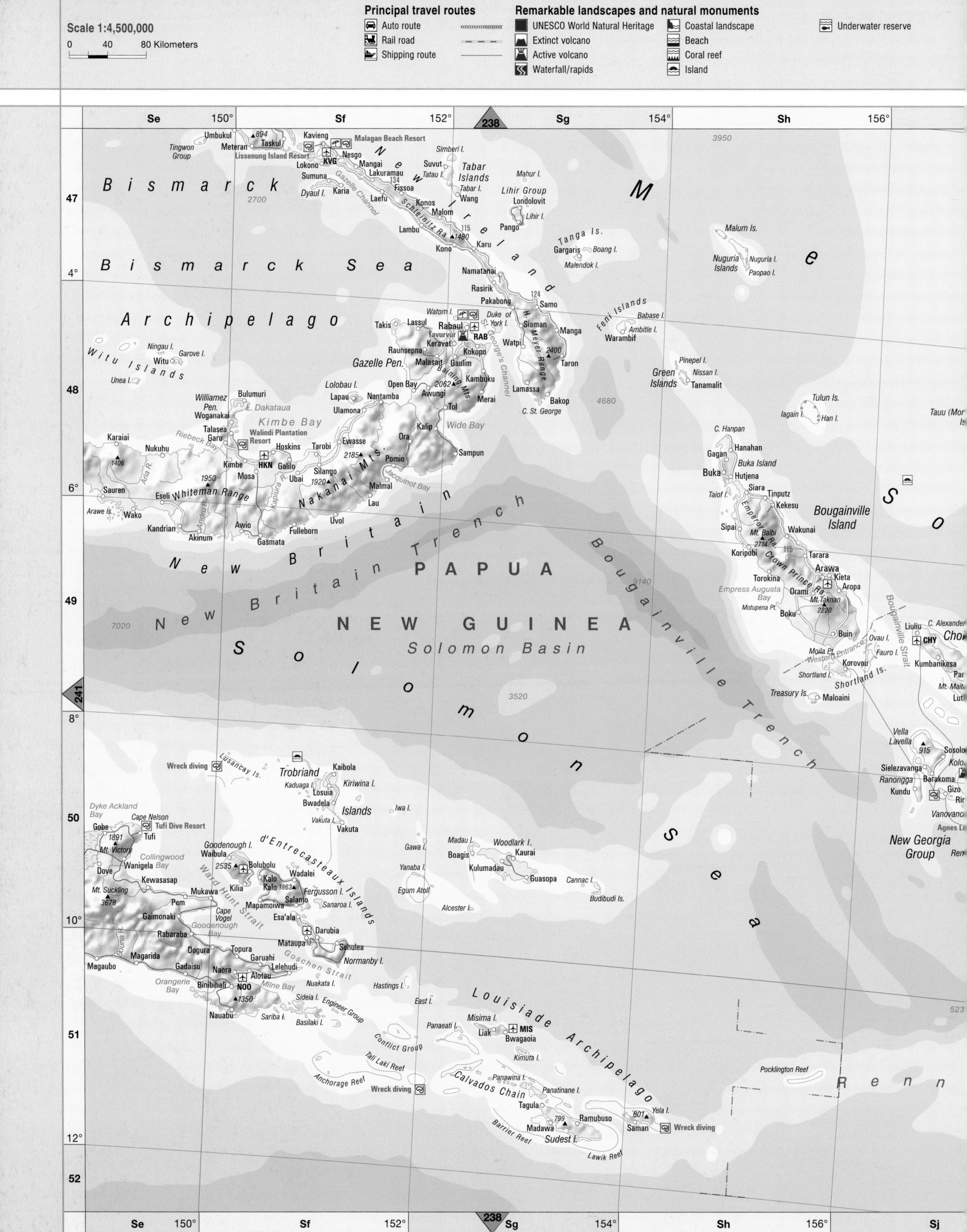
Scale 1:4,500,000
0 40 80 Kilometers
Principal travel routes
Auto route
Rail road
Shipping route
Remarkable landscapes and natural monuments
UNESCO World Natural Heritage
Extinct volcano
Active volcano
Waterfall/rapids
Coastal landscape
Beach
Coral reef
Island
Underwater reserve
Se
Sf
Sg
Sh
Sj
150°
152°
154°
156°
238
241
47
48
49
50
51
52
4°
6°
8°
10°
12°
Bismarck
Bismarck Sea
Archipelago
Witu Islands
New Ireland
New Britain
New Britain Trench
PAPUA
NEW GUINEA
Solomon Basin
Solomon Sea
Bougainville Trench
Louisiade Archipelago
Umbukul
Tingwon Group
Meteran
Taskul
894
Kavieng
Malagan Beach Resort
Lissenung Island Resort
KVG
Nesgo
Lokono
Mangai
Lakuramau
Sumuna
Fissoa
Dyaul I.
Karia
Gazelle Channel
Laefu
Konos
Malom
Schleinitz Ra.
Lambu
1480
Kono
Karu
Simberi I.
Suvut
Tatau I.
Tabar Islands
Tabar I.
Wang
Mahur I.
Lihir Group
Londolovit
Lihir I.
Pango
Tanga Is.
Gargaris
Boang I.
Malendok I.
Namatanai
Rasirik
Pakabong
124
Samo
Siaman
Manga
Watom I.
Duke of York I.
Takis
Lassul
Rabaul
Tavurvur
RAB
Keravat
Kokopo
Watpi
Raunsepna
Gazelle Pen.
Malasait
Gaulim
St. George's Channel
H. Meyer Range
2400
Taron
Baining Mts.
Kambuku
Lolobau I.
Open Bay
2062
Awungi
Lapau
Nantamba
Merai
Lamassa
Bakop
C. St. George
Ulamona
Tol
Wide Bay
Kalip
Ora
Williamez Pen.
Bulumuri
L. Dakataua
Woganakai
Kimbe Bay
Talasea
Walindi Plantation Resort
Garu
Riebeck Bay
Karaiai
Nukuhu
Hoskins
Tarobi
Ewasse
2185
Pomio
Sampun
1406
Aria R.
Kimbe
HKN
Galilo
Silango
Mosa
Ubai
1920
Nakanai Mts.
Malmal
Jacquinot Bay
1950
Sauren
Eseli
Whiteman Range
Lau
Arawe Is.
Wako
Kandrian
Akinum
Awio
Gasmata
Fulleborn
Uvol
Ningau I.
Garove I.
Witu
Unea I.
2700
3950
4680
9140
7020
3520
523
Feni Islands
Babase I.
Ambitle I.
Warambif
Pinepel I.
Nissan I.
Green Islands
Tanamalit
Malum Is.
Nuguria Islands
Nuguria I.
Paopao I.
Tulun Is.
Iagain I.
Han I.
Tauu (Mor
C. Hanpan
Hanahan
Gagan
Buka Island
Buka
Hutjena
Siara
Tinputz
Taiof I.
Kekesu
Bougainville Island
Emperor Ra.
Sipai
Mt. Balbi
2714
Wakunai
Koripobi
115
Tarara
Crown Prince Ra.
Arawa
Kieta
Torokina
Aropa
Orami
Empress Augusta Bay
Mt. Taknan
2220
Motupena Pt.
Boku
Buin
Bougainville Strait
Liuliu
C. Alexander
CHY
Ovau I.
Fauro I.
Moila Pt.
Western Entrance
Korovou
Kumbamkesa
Shortland I.
Shortland Is.
Treasury Is.
Maloaini
Vella Lavella
915
Sosolo
Sielezavanga
Ranongga
Barakoma
Kundu
Gizo
Vanovano
New Georgia Group
Wreck diving
Lusancay Is.
Trobriand Islands
Kaibola
Kaduaga I.
Kiriwina I.
Losuia
Bwadela
Vakuta I.
Vakuta
Iwa I.
Dyke Ackland Bay
Cape Nelson
Tufi Dive Resort
Gobe
1891
Tufi
Mt. Victory
Collingwood Bay
Wanigela
Dove
Kewasasap
Mt. Suckling
3678
Goodenough I.
Waibula
2535
Bolubolu
d'Entrecasteaux Islands
Ward Hunt Strait
Kilia
Kalo Kalo
1863
Wadalei
Mukawa
Fergusson I.
Salamo
Mapamoiwa
Sanaroa I.
Pem
Cape Vogel
Goodenough Bay
Gaimonaki
Esa'ala
Rabaraba
Darubia
Mataupa
Sehulea
Dogura
Topura
Normanby I.
Magarida
Garuahi
Gadaisu
Lelehudi
Goschen Strait
Magaubo
Naora
Alotau
Orangerie Bay
Binibihali
NOO
Milne Bay
Nuakata I.
1350
Sideia I.
Engineer Group
Nauabu
Sariba I.
Basilaki I.
Gawa I.
Madau I.
Woodlark I.
Boagis
Kaurai
Yanaba I.
Kulumadau
Guasopa
Cannac I.
Egum Atoll
Budibudi Is.
Alcester I.
Hastings I.
East I.
Misima I.
Panaeati I.
Liak
MIS
Bwagaoia
Conflict Group
Kimuta I.
Tali Laki Reef
Anchorage Reef
Panawina I.
Calvados Chain
Panatinane I.
Tagula
799
Ramubuso
801
Yela I.
Madawa
Saman
Sudest I.
Barrier Reef
Lawik Reef
Pocklington Reef
Renn

Remarkable Cities and Cultural monuments
UNESCO World Cultural Heritage
Remarkable Cities
Pl. of cult. interest to indig. peoples
Market
Sport and leisure destinations
Sailing
Diving
Wind surfing
Deep-sea fishing
Beach resort
158°
Sk
160°
Ta
239
162°
Tb
164°
Tc
46
2°
47
4°
48
6°
49
8°
50
10°
51
PACIFIC
OCEAN
1590
3020
Tasman Islands
(Nukumanu Atoll)
Frindsburg Reef
1745
Pelau I.
Ontong Java Atoll
Keila I.
Leuaniua I.
Roncador Reef
Bradley Reef
4610
4021
SOLOMON ISLANDS
Manning Strait
Ghaghe I.
Barora I.
Kia
Barora Ite I.
Baolo
Filuo
760
Santa Isabel
Ghoveo
Jejevo
Mt. Sasari
1220
Buala
Kaevanga
Tatamba
Vulavu
San Jorge I.
Vikenara Pt.
New
Georgia
Uepi Island Resort
Marvo Lagoon
Mt.
Vangunu
Mbatuna
Vangunu
1123
Ngatokae
1790
Dai I.
Maluu
Gounatolo
Dala
Auki
AKS
Atori
Malaita
Olomburi
Mt.
Kalourat
1436
Hauhui
Maru'ura
Maramasike
(Small Malaita)
Apio
515
Sa'a
Nialaha'u Pt.
Siodjuru
Ulawa I.
Stewart Is.
5705
Russell Is.
Pavuvu I.
XYA
Yandina
Yandina Plantation Resort
Mbanika I.
Buena Vista I.
Mbokonimbeti I.
Savo I.
Nggela
Sule
Chapuru
Siota
Tambea
Wreck diving
Nggela
Pile
Lambi
Honiara
Ndondo
HIR
Mataniko
Falls
Mt. Popomanaseu
Aola
4966
Mbambanakira
2449
AVU
Mt. Kaichui
1920
Guadalcanal
Avu Avu
Makina
Florida Islands
Indispensable Strait
Uki Ni
Masi I.
Three Sisters Is.
(Olu Malua)
Tadahadi
Tetere
Kirakira
Makira
IRA
1250
Arite
Wetee
Hauraha
Nasuraghena
Santa Ana I.
Bellona I.
Rennell I.
Manggautu
Taekau Reef
Great Reef
Lomlom
Reef Is.
Lipe
Nendo I.
Lata
Noka
Rise
South Solomon Trench
Sk
160°
Ta
162°
238
Tb
164°
Tc
166°
Td

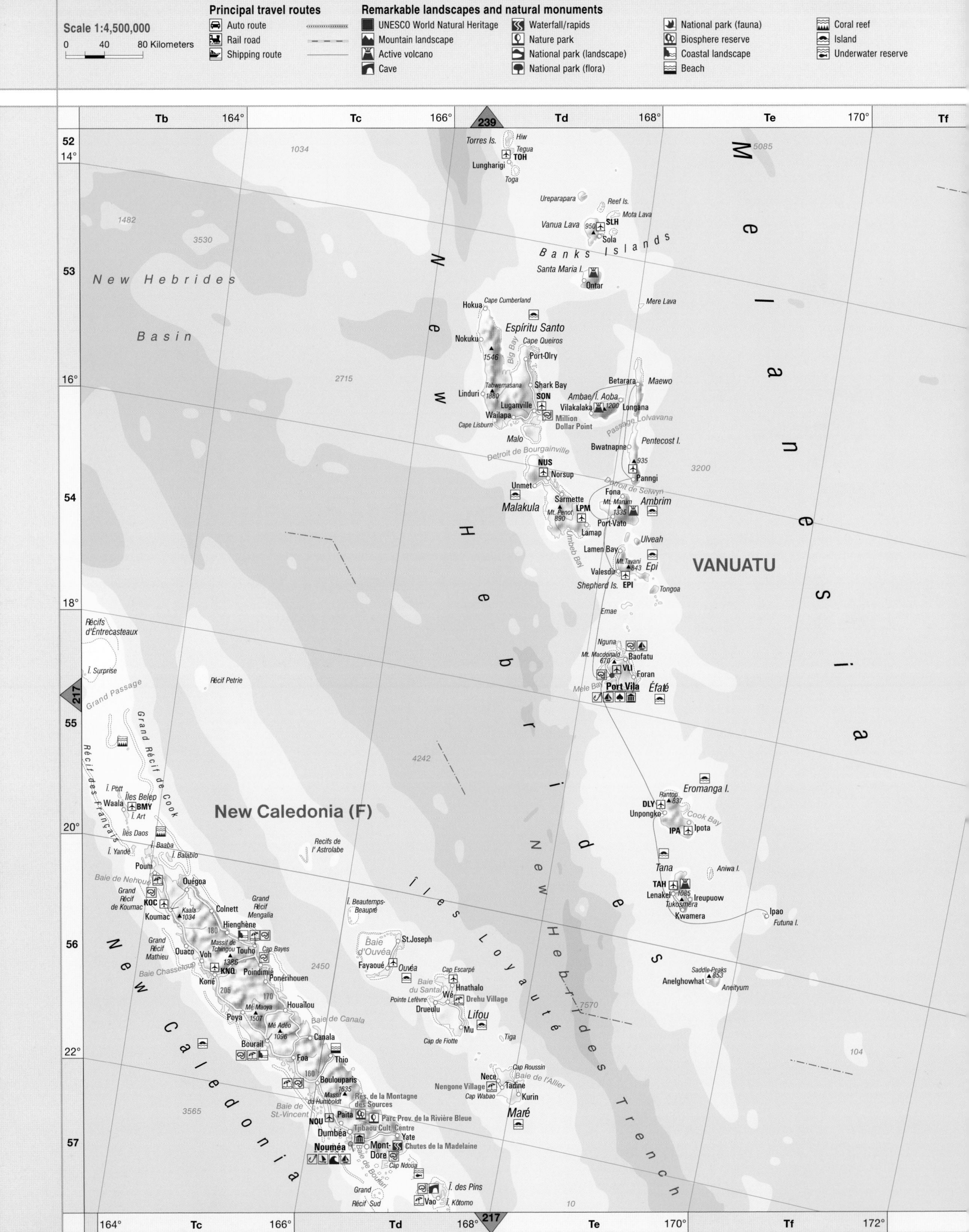

Scale 1:4,500,000
0 40 80 Kilometers
Principal travel routes
Auto route
Rail road
Shipping route
Remarkable landscapes and natural monuments
UNESCO World Natural Heritage
Mountain landscape
Active volcano
Cave
Waterfall/rapids
Nature park
National park (landscape)
National park (flora)
National park (fauna)
Biosphere reserve
Coastal landscape
Beach
Coral reef
Island
Underwater reserve
New Hebrides Basin
Melanesia
New Hebrides
VANUATU
New Caledonia (F)
Îles Loyauté
New Hebrides Trench
New Caledonia
Torres Is.
Banks Islands
Espíritu Santo
Malakula
Ambrim
Epi
Éfaté
Port Vila
Eromanga I.
Tana
Lifou
Maré
Nouméa

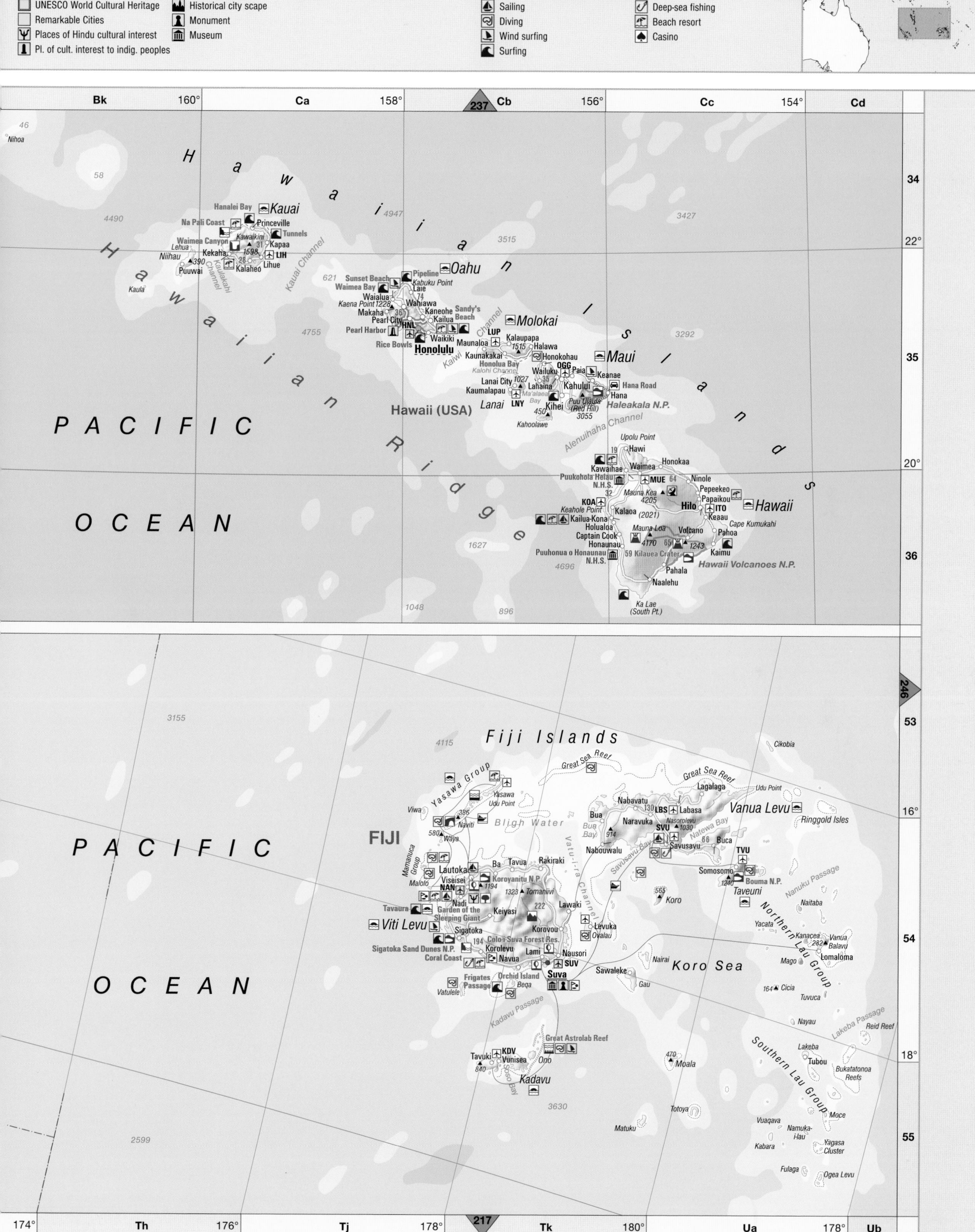

Remarkable Cities and Cultural monuments
UNESCO World Cultural Heritage
Remarkable Cities
Places of Hindu cultural interest
Pl. of cult. interest to indig. peoples
Historical city scape
Monument
Museum
Sport and leisure destinations
Sailing
Diving
Wind surfing
Surfing
Deep-sea fishing
Beach resort
Casino
Hawaiian Islands
Hawaiian Ridge
PACIFIC OCEAN
Hawaii (USA)
Nihoa
Kauai
Hanalei Bay
Na Pali Coast
Princeville
Tunnels
Waimea Canyon
Kawaikini
Kapaa
Lehua
Niihau
Kekaha
LIH
Lihue
Puuwai
Kalaheo
Kaula
Kaulakahi Channel
Kauai Channel
Oahu
Pipeline
Sunset Beach
Waimea Bay
Kahuku Point
Laie
Waialua
Kaena Point
Wahiawa
Makaha
Kaneohe
Sandy's Beach
Pearl City
Kailua
Pearl Harbor
HNL
Waikiki
Rice Bowls
Honolulu
Kaiwi Channel
Molokai
LUP
Kalaupapa
Maunaloa
Halawa
Kaunakakai
Honokohau
Honolua Bay
Kalohi Channel
Maui
OGG
Paia
Keanae
Wailuku
Lanai City
Lahaina
Kahului
Hana Road
Hana
Kaumalapau
Ma'alaea Bay
Lanai
LNY
Kihei
Puu Ulaula (Red Hill)
Haleakala N.P.
Kahoolawe
Alenuihaha Channel
Upolu Point
Hawi
Kawaihae
Waimea
Honokaa
Puukohola Heiau N.H.S.
MUE
Ninole
Pepeekeo
Papaikou
Mauna Kea
KOA
Keahole Point
Hilo
ITO
Hawaii
Kailua-Kona
Kalaoa
Keaau
Holualoa
Cape Kumukahi
Captain Cook
Mauna Loa
Volcano
Pahoa
Honaunau
Puuhonua o Honaunau N.H.S.
Kilauea Crater
Kaimu
Hawaii Volcanoes N.P.
Pahala
Naalehu
Ka Lae (South Pt.)
Fiji Islands
FIJI
PACIFIC OCEAN
Yasawa Group
Yasawa
Udu Point
Great Sea Reef
Cikobia
Viwa
Naviti
Waya
Bligh Water
Vatu-i-ra Channel
Nabavatu
LBS
Labasa
Vanua Levu
Ringgold Isles
Bua
Bua Bay
Naravuka
SVU
Nasorolevu
Natewa Bay
Savusavu
Buca
Nabouwalu
Savusavu Bay
TVU
Mamanuca Group
Lautoka
Ba
Tavua
Rakiraki
Koroyanitu N.P.
Viseisei
Malolo
NAN
Nadi
Tomanivi
Somosomo
Bouma N.P.
Taveuni
Nanuku Passage
Tavaura
Garden of the Sleeping Giant
Keiyasi
Lawaki
Koro
Naitaba
Viti Levu
Sigatoka
Korovou
Levuka
Ovalau
Yacata
Sigatoka Sand Dunes N.P.
Coral Coast
Colo-i-Suva Forest Res.
Korolevu
Navua
Lami
Nausori
SUV
Nairai
Koro Sea
Kanacea
Vanua Balavu
Lomaloma
Mago
Northern Lau Group
Frigates Passage
Vatulele
Orchid Island
Beqa
Suva
Sawaleke
Gau
Cicia
Tuvuca
Kadavu Passage
Nayau
Lakeba Passage
Reid Reef
Great Astrolab Reef
Southern Lau Group
Lakeba
Tubou
KDV
Tavuki
Vunisea
Ono
Moala
Bukatatonoa Reefs
Kadavu
Soso Bay
Totoya
Moce
Matuku
Vuaqava
Namuka-i-Lau
Kabara
Yagasa Cluster
Fulaga
Ogea Levu

Scale 1:4,500,000

0 40 80 Kilometers

Principal travel routes

- Auto route
- Rail road
- Shipping route

Remarkable landscapes and natural monuments

- UNESCO World Natural Heritage
- Active volcano
- Cave
- Waterfall/rapids
- Coastal landscape
- Beach
- Coral reef
- Island

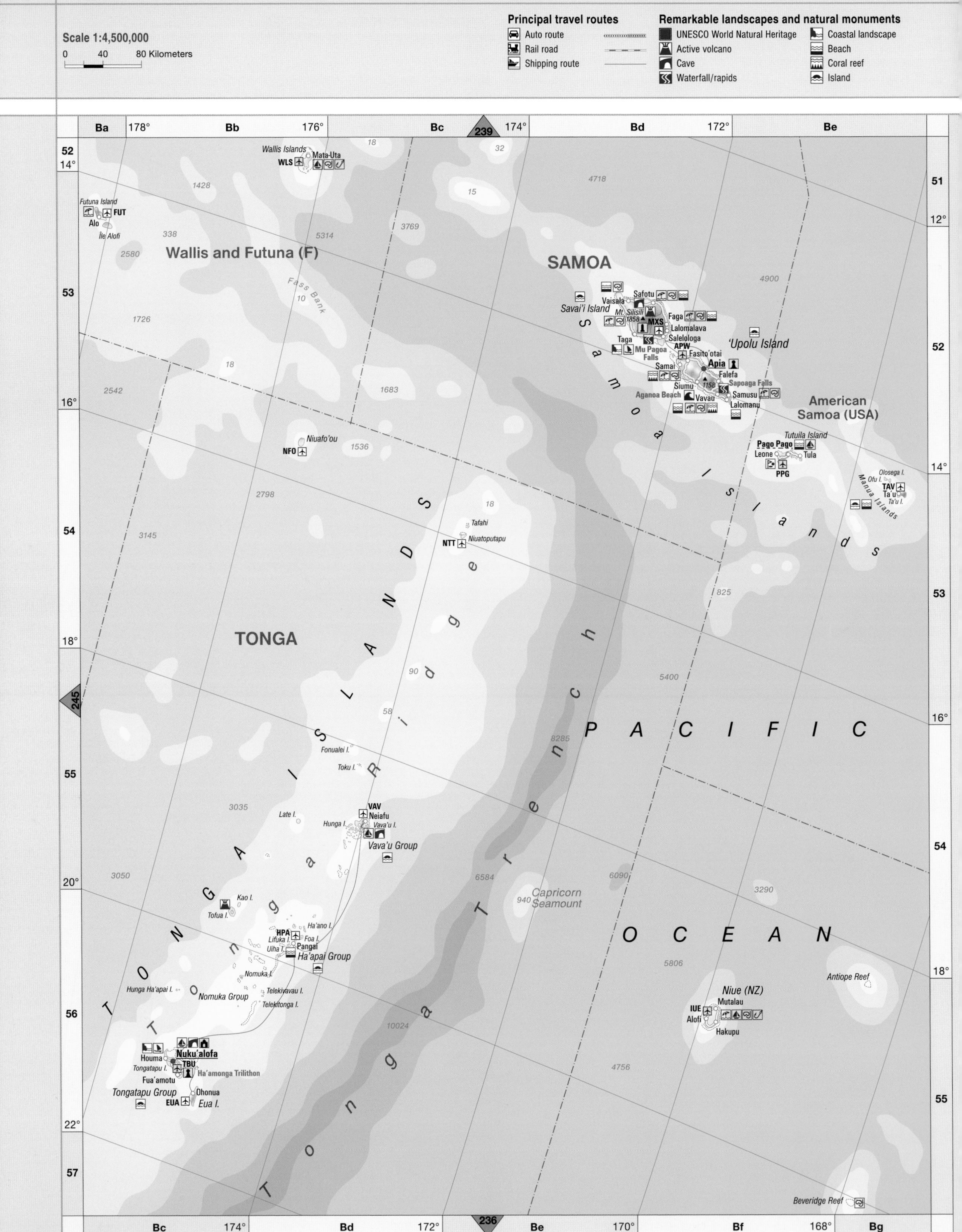

Remarkable Cities and Cultural monuments

- UNESCO World Cultural Heritage
- Remarkable Cities
- Places of Christian cultural interest
- Pl. of cult. interest to indig. peoples
- Castle/fortress/fort
- Palace
- Tomb/grave
- Monument
- Museum

Sport and leisure destinations

- Golf
- Sailing
- Diving
- Wind surfing
- Surfing
- Deep-sea fishing
- Beach resort

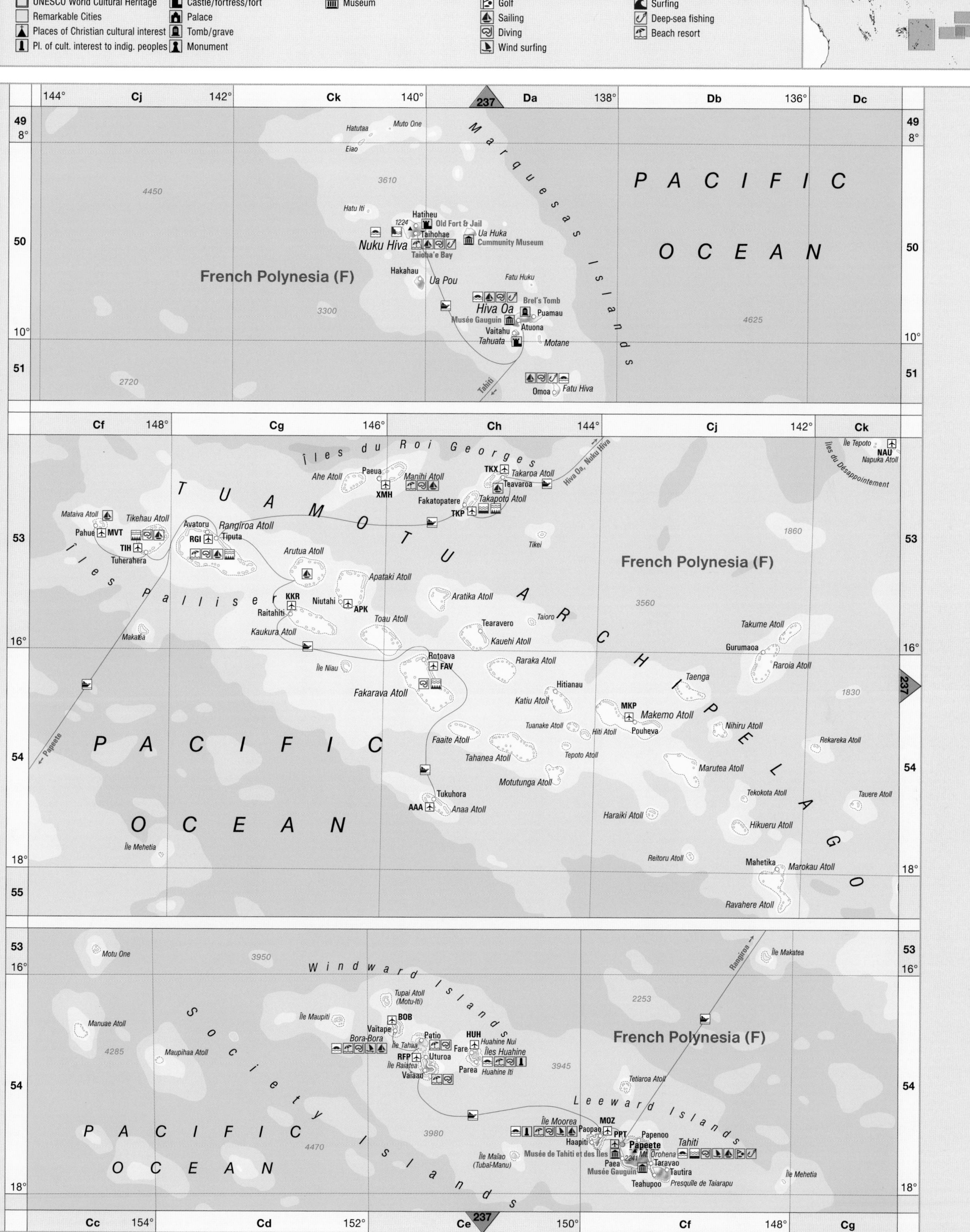

A

B

C

D

E

K

L

M

N

O

P

Q

R

S

T

Picture Credits

Abbreviations:

t = top
m = middle
b = bottom
le = left
ri = right
C = Column
CLK = clockwise

2/3: Premium; 4/5: Transglobe/Schmitz; 6/7: D. Fuchs; 8/9: Premium; 10/11: ifa/ J. Arnold Images; 12/13: D. Fuchs; 14/15 t: D. Fuchs; 14/15 b: Das Fotoarchiv/ Hympendahl; 16/17: Premium/Pan. Images/M. Segal; 20/21 t: D. Fuchs; 20 b: blickwinkel/ J. Hauke; 21 m: IPN/H. Brown; 21 b: laif/ Emmler; 22 R t: Corbis/Conway; 22 R b: ifa/Köpfle; 22.1: laif/Aurora; 22.2: D. Fuchs; 23.3+4: ifa/Siebig; 23 C t: laif/ Heeb; 23 C b: D. Fuchs; 24: Okapia; 25: Corbis/J. Sparks; 26/27: laif/Heeb; 28: Corbis/Allofs; 30 C: ifa/Gottschalk; 30.1: C. Emmler; 30.2: Schapowalow/Huber; 31.1: D. Fuchs; 31.2: Corbis/Y. Arthus-Bertrand; 31.3: D. Fuchs; 31.4 + 32/33: C. Emmler; 34 C + 1: laif/Emmler; 34.2: IPN/H. Brown; 35.3: visum/G. Wojciech; 35.4: IPN; 35.5+6: D. Fuchs; 36/37: Okapia; 38 C t: Okapia; 38 C b: Premium; 38.1: Look/H. Dressler; 38.2: Wildlife/ W. Fiedler; 39: Okapia; 40 C: ifa/Jakobs; 40.1: Look/H. Dressler; 40.2: C. Emmler; 41.3: Look/U. Seer; 41 C t+m+b: D. Fuchs; 42 t: laif/Heeb; 42 b: D. Fuchs; 44 Map le to ri, t to b: laif/ aurora, Corbis/Travel Ink/Enock, C. Emmler, D. Fuchs, IPN/H. Brown, C. Emmler, Corbis, ifa/Gottschalk, Corbis/Allofs; 45 Map CLK starting t le: IPN, visum/G. Wojciech, Okapia, ifa/ Jakobs, D. Fuchs, laif/Heeb, Premium, Mauritius/Nakamura, Corbis/Rotman. 46/47 t: C. Souders; 46 m: ifa/Panstock; 46 b: laif/Emmler; 47 m: Corbis/Fisher; 47 b: P/APL; 48 C: Okapia/Watts/Bios; 48.1: Corbis/Nowitz; 48.2: laif/Emmler; 49.3: Corbis/Souders; 49 C t+b: D. Fuchs; 50 t+b + 51 t+b + 52/53: D. Fuchs; 54: Corbis/ Nowitz; 55.1: C. Emmler; 55.2: ifa/ Gottschalk; 55 C: FAN/Heinrichson; 56/57 t+b: Premium; 58: ifa/Krämer; 59: laif/ Heeb; 60/61: Pix/APL/La Motta; 62.1: Premium; 62.2: Corbis/Allofs; 63.3: Premium/ Watts; 63.4: Corbis/Enock; 64/65: Y. Arthus-Bertrand; 66 C: Corbis/ T. Weedie; 66.1: Corbis/Souders; 66.2+3: ifa/Siebig; 67.4: Corbis/Royalty Free; 67 C t: Corbis/ Allofs; 67 C m: Corbis/ Conway; 67 C b: Corbis/Yamashita; 69 t+b: Huber; 70 Map CLK starting t le: Corbis/Nowitz, ifa/Gottschalk, Corbis/ Clarke, Corbis/Souders, Corbis, (Adelaide) laif/Emmler, (Coober Pedy) Corbis/Souders, (Traumpfade) Look/Dressler, (Uluru) ifa/ Picture Finders, Corbis/Mastrovillo; 71 Map le to ri, t to b: Corbis/Tweedie, Corbis/S. Kaufmann, ifa/Siebig, Corbis/ Allofs, ifa/Siebig, ifa/Index Stock, ifa/ Prenzel, Corbis/Clarke, Corbis/E. & D. Hosking, Corbis/Sparks, Corbis/Clarke, Corbis/M. & P. Fogden.
72/73 t: Premium; 72 b: Getty/Chesley; 73 m: Corbis/Lawrence; 73 b: Getty/ Chesley; 74 C t: Corbis/Johnson; 74 C b: Corbis/S. Widstrand; 74.1: ifa/J. Arnold Images; 75.2: Corbis/Orezzoli; 75 C: Premium; 76 t: laif/Heeb; 76 b: C. Heeb; 77: D. Fuchs; 78/79: D. Fuchs; 80 C: ifa/Osborne; 80.1: Das Fotoarchiv/ Matsumoto; 80.2: Corbis/Y. Arthus-Bertrand; 81.3: Corbis/P. Ward; 81 R: Premium/Hauke; 82 t+b + 85 t+b: D. Fuchs; 86/87: Premium; 88 small t: Premium/Minden; 88 small b: Premium; 88 large: D. Fuchs; 90/91: laif/Heeb; 92 C t+b + 1: Premium; 92.2: Das Fotoarchiv/ Cohen; 94/95: Premium/Pacific Stock/ D. Perrine; 96.1: Premium; 96.2: Corbis/ Y. Arthus-Bertrand; 97 Map le to ri, t to b, left-hand side: Corbis/T. Allofs, 2 x Premium, ifa/Held, ifa/Index Stock, Corbis/ D. Orezzoli, Corbis/M. Johnson, Corbis/ Casa Productions, right-hand side: Corbis/ P. Souders, Premium, ifa/Held, ifa/Siebig. 98/99 t: ifa/J. Arnold Images; 98 b: Corbis/ P. Souders; 99 m: ifa/AP&F; 99 b: Premium/Pacific Stock/J. Watt; 100 C: Premium/ APL; 100.1: Premium; 101.2: Corbis/P. Souders; 101 C: Reinhard; 102/ 103 t+b + 105 t: ifa/J. Arnold Images; 105 m: Premium/S. Bunka; 105 b: Premium/ APL; 106 + 108/109: C. Emmler; 110 C: Corbis/T. Allofs; 110.1: Premium/Pan. Images/Vladplans; 110.2: alamy/M. Rock; 111 C t: Corbis/B. Ross; 111 C b: Corbis/M. Harvey; 112/113: laif/Kreuels; 114.1: Corbis/M. Pole; 114.2: Premium/Voigt/ C. Voigt; 115 Map CLK starting t le: Corbis/ B. Ross, Corbis/M. Harvey, Premium/APL, Corbis/Y. Arthus-Bertrand, Corbis/Reuters, Premium/T. Brakefield, Corbis/B. Ross, Corbis/R. Holmes, Premium/APL, laif/ Emmler, Corbis/T. Allofs.
116/117 t: Premium; 116 M: Corbis/ R. Garvey; 116 b: Premium/Pacific Stock/ B. Schildge; 117 m: Corbis/P. Souders; 117 b: D. Fuchs; 118 C: Corbis/Osborne; 118.1: Premium/APL; 118.2: ifa/Siebig; 119.3: Corbis/R. Garwood & T. Ainslie; 119.4 + C: Premium; 120/121: ifa; 122 C t+b +1+2 + 123.3: Corbis/S. Houser/Post-Houserstock; 123.4: alamy/J. Drewitz; 123.5: Premium/ APL; 124 C: ifa/Hasenkopf; 124.1: ifa/ Panstock; 124.2: Premium; 124.3: Premium/Stock Image/K. Stimpson; 125.4: Premium/Image State; 125 C Corbis/ D. Houser/Post-Houserstock; 126/127: D. Fuchs; 129 t: Premium/Voigt/C. Voigt; 129 b + 130/131: D. Fuchs; 132 C: Corbis/ P. Johnson; 132.1: Corbis/M. Harvey; 132.2: Corbis/R. Glover; 133 Box: ifa/ Siebig; 134 C: Premium/APL; 134.1: Corbis/ P. Souders; 134.2: ifa/Gottschalk; 135.1+2: Corbis/P. Souders; 135 C t: Premium; 135 C b: Corbis/P. Souders; 136/ 137: Corbis/Y. Arthus-Bertrand; 138: Corbis/Strand; 139.1: Corbis/P. souders; 139.2: ifa/J. Arnold Images; 140/141 Map le to ri, t to b: Premium, ifa/ Gottschalk, Corbis, Corbis/D. Houser, 2 x Premium, Corbis/P. Souders, ifa/Gottschalk, Premium, (Kangaroo Island) Corbis/R. Clevenger, (Adelaide) Premium, (Melbourne) ifa/ Hunter, (Canberra) Premium/S. Bunka, (Otway National Park) Corbis/P. Souders, ifa/J. Arnold Images, 2 x Corbis/P. Souders, Corbis/H. Strand, Corbis/Y. Arthus-Bertrand, ifa/Gottschalk. 142/143 t: Premium/APSE; 142 m: Premium; 142 b: Bilderberg; 143 b: Corbis/ M. Everton; 144 C: ifa/J. Arnold Images; 144.1: ifa/Held; 144.2: ifa/J. Arnold Images; 145.3: ifa/Held; 145.4: Premium; 145 C: Getty; 146/147: laif/Le Figaro Magazine; 148: Premium/M. Allen/Image Stock; 149: Corbis/P. Thompson; 150/151: laif/ Hauser; 152 C t: ifa/Held; 152 C b: ifa/Pix; 152.1: Premium/S. Bunka; 152.2: Premium/G. Vickers; 153.3: Premium/ Schott; 154 R: Corbis/M. Pole; 154.1: ifa/ J. Arnold Images; 154.2: ifa/AP&F; 155 Map CLK starting t le: ifa/Direct Stock, 2 x Corbis/P. Souders, Corbis/A. Nachoum, Corbis/H. Stadler, 2 x ifa/J. Arnold Images, Corbis/J. Sparks, Corbis/P. Thompson, Premium, ifa/Pix, Premium/G. Vickers, ifa/Walsh.
156/157 t: Getty; 156 m: premium/Image State; 156 b: Premium/Minden/T. de Roy; 157 m: Premium/Image State; 157 b: ifa/J. Arnold Images; 158 C. Corbis/R. Holmes; 158.1: ifa/J. Arnold Images; 158.2: Premium/S. Bunka; 159.3: ifa/J. Arnold Images; 160 C t+b: Premium/Image State; 160.1: ifa/J. Arnold Images; 160.2: Premium/Image State/A. Apse; 161.3: Premium; 162/163 + 165 t+b: laif/Heeb; 166/167: laif/Kreusels; 168 C: Corbis/ R. Klune; 168.1: ifa/Panstock; 168.2: Premium/Image State; 168.3 + 169.1: Premium/Image State/A. Apse; 169.2: ifa/ J. Arnold Images; 169 R: ifa/AP&F; 170.1: ifa/Panstock; 170.2: ifa/J. Arnold Images; 171.3: Corbis/H. Stadler; 171 C: Premium/ Image State/M. Allen; 172 C: Corbis/ R. Holmes; 172.1+2: Premium/Image State/A. Apse; 173 Map CLK starting t le: Corbis/H. Roth, alamy/N. Cleave, 2 x ifa/ J. Arnold Images, Premium/A. Seiden, ifa/ J. Arnold Images, Premium/K. Wothe, ifa/ J. Arnold Images, Huber/Damm, Premium, Corbis/B.S.P.I., ifa/ J. Arnold Images. 174/175 t: Corbis/J. Flindt/NewSport; 174 b: Premium/Pacific Stock/K. Rothenborg; 175 m: Look/H. Leue; 175 b: Okapia; 176 R t: Corbis/B. Pelnar; 176 R b: Wildlife/ P. Oxford; 176.1+2: Look/H. Leue; 177.3: Corbis/M. Everton; 177.4: Okapia; 177.5: Corbis/G. Rowell; 177 C: Premium; 178 C: Corbis/M. Beebe; 178.1: Corbis/ N. Rabinowitz; 178.2: Corbis/O. van der Wal; 179.3: Corbis/B. Krist; 179.4: Look/ H. Leue; 180/181: Corbis/T. Bernhard/zefa; 182 C: Corbis/T. Nebbia; 182.1: Corbis/ B. Krist; 182.2: Look/H. Leue; 182.3: Premium/ Pacific Stock/K. Rothenborg; 183 Map le to ri, t to b: Corbis/M. Everton; 2 x Corbis/B. Krist, laif/Westrich; ifa/ J. Arnold Images; Corbis/N. Rabinowitz; laif/Heuer; laif/Westrich.
184/185 t: Premium/Pan. Images/ M. Segal; 184 b: Das Fotoarchiv/Wheeler; 185 m: Corbis/J. Raga; 185 b: Corbis/ F. G. Mayer; 186.1: Freelens/F. Stark; 186.2: Corbis/W. Kaehler; 187.3: Corbis/ D. Houser/ Post-Houserstock; 187.4: Corbis/N. Wheeler; 187 C: laif/Emmler; 188 C: Corbis/D. Peebles; 188.1: Y. Arthus-Bertrand; 188.2: Premium/Pacific Stock/ R. Dahlquist; 189.3: Corbis/Y. Arthus-Bertrand; 189.4: laif/Le Figaro Magazine; 189.5: laif/Emmler; 189 C t: laif/IML; 189 C b: Corbis/K. Su; 190 C t: laif/Kreuels; 190 C b: Premium/Pacific Stock/K. Rothenborg; 190.1: Premium/ Roda; 190.2: Corbis/ Y. Arthus-Bertrand; 191.3: laif/Emmler; 191 R: Corbis/A. Burkatovski; 192/193: Corbis/D. Gulin; 194 C t: laif/Le Figaro Magazine; 194 C b: Corbis/D. Gulin; 194.1: Look/H. Leue; 194.2: Corbis/C. Tuttle; 195 Map le to ri, t to b: FreeLens/F. Stark, Corbis/W. Kaehler, Corbis/O. van der Wal, Corbis/S. Frink/zefa, Premium/Pan. Images/ M. Segal, Corbis/Y. Arthus-Bertrand, Premium/Roda, Corbis/D. Peebles. 196/197 t: Getty/Pan. Images; 196 b: Premium/Pacific Stock; 197 m: laif/Heeb; 197 b: Pix/Pacific Stock; 198 C: laif/Heeb; 198.1: Premium/Pacific Stock/D. Cornwell; 198.2: laif/Heeb; 199: Premium/Pacific Stock/P. French; 200 C t+b: Premium/ Pacific Stock/E. Robinson; 200.1: laif/ Gollhard & Wieland; 200.2: Premium/ Pacific Stock/C. Shaneff; 200.3: Premium/Pacific Stock/D. Fleetham; 200 Box: Premium/Pacific Stock/G. Vaughn; 201.4: Premium/Pacific Stock; 201.5: Getty/Schafer/ Hill; 201 C: Premium/Pacific Stock; 202/203: laif/Gollhardt & Wieland; 204 C t: laif/Wieland; 204 C b: laif/ Gollhardt & Wieland; 204.1: Premium/ Pacific Stock/V. Cavataio; 204.2: Premium/ Pacific Stock/A. Seiden; 204.3: Premium/ Pacific Stock; 205.4: Premium/Pacific Stock/B. Black; 205 C t+b: Premium/Pacific Stock; 206/207 Corbis/Craig Tuttle; 208.1: Pix/ Pacific Stock; 208.2: laif/Heeb; 208.3: Premium/Pacific Stock/C. Shaneff; 209 Map le to ri, t to b: laif/Heeb, Premium/ Pacific Stock/A. Seiden, laif/Gollhardt & Wieland, ifa/Schüller, laif/Wieland, Premium/Pacific Stock/D. Cornwell, Corbis/ Houser, Premium/Image State/Lewis. 210/211: Premium/Stock Images; 212/213: ifa/J. Arnold Images.
Cover top large: Premium/Stock Image; t small:Premium/ImageState/M. Allen; b large + small: ifa/J. Arnold Images.

MONACO BOOKS is an imprint of Verlag Wolfgang Kunth

Translation: JMS Books LLP, UK

For distribution please contact:
Monaco Books
c/o Verlag Wolfgang Kunth, Königinstr.11
80539 München, Germany
Tel: +49 / 89/45 80 20 23
Fax: +49 / 89/ 45 80 20 21
info@kunth-verlag.de
www.monacobooks.com
www.kunth-verlag.de

ISBN 978-3-89944-534-3

Printed in Slovakia

All facts have been researched with the greatest possible care to the best of our knowledge and belief. However, the editors and publishers can accept no responsibility for any inaccuracies or incompleteness of the details provided. The publishers are pleased to receive any information or suggestions for improvement.